The Origins of the Criminal Justice System

The Origins of the Criminal Justice System

Historical Explorations by the Justice-Involved

Edited by
Omi Hodwitz

ROWMAN & LITTLEFIELD
Lanham • Boulder • New York • London

Published by Rowman & Littlefield
An imprint of The Rowman & Littlefield Publishing Group, Inc.
4501 Forbes Boulevard, Suite 200, Lanham, Maryland 20706
www.rowman.com

86-90 Paul Street, London EC2A 4NE

British Library Cataloguing in Publication Information available

Library of Congress Cataloging-in-Publication Data

Names: Hodwitz, Omi, 1977- editor.
Title: The origins of the criminal justice system : historical explorations by the justice-involved / edited by Omi Hodwitz.
Description: Lanham : Rowman & Littlefield Publishers, 2025. | Includes bibliographical references and index.
Identifiers: LCCN 2024040292 (print) | LCCN 2024040293 (ebook) | ISBN 9781538187074 (cloth) | ISBN 9781538187081 (paperback) | ISBN 9781538187098 (epub)
Subjects: LCSH: Criminal justice, Administration of–United States–History. | Criminal justice, Administration of–Political aspects–United States–History. | Criminal justice, Administration of–Social aspects–United States–History.
Classification: LCC KF9223 .O75 2025 (print) | LCC KF9223 (ebook) | DDC 364.0973–dc23/eng/20240830
LC record available at https://lccn.loc.gov/2024040292
LC ebook record available at https://lccn.loc.gov/2024040293

Dedicated to David M., a wonderful mentor and friend. You were a blessing to us all.

Contents

Foreword

A Project Crafted in an Idaho Prison

Brian Wolf

Emblematic of a nationwide crisis, the criminal justice system in Idaho is filled with paradoxes; with one of the lowest rates of crime in the country, the state also incarcerates substantially more people than any other, one of the highest per-capita rates outside the Deep South. However, tired old approaches, of warehousing correctional residents, privatizing prisons, and continued reliance on the criminal justice system to control almost every social problem, from mental health, to poverty, to a crisis in masculinity, were considered boilerplate go-to policies in the Idaho criminal justice system. Also in Idaho, as is the case in most other states, public and higher education suffer from neglect and disinvestment. Scholars have long noted the interrelationship between the two; the criminogenic effects of reduced spending on education and public programs are well documented. Colleges and universities, when funded, can also serve as incubators to rethink criminal justice, while giving a real-world perspective on pressing public issues. Criminal justice and public education are both critical public issues, yet personal stories of transformation, redemption, and self-development give salience to the impact of policy.

At first glance, this volume may seem like an ordinary academic engagement of various topics on the foundations and development of criminal justice. However, it is the result of several remarkable personal efforts from a few steadfast individuals . . . including correctional residents. This background is worth a brief explanation from a first-person perspective: in 2017 I had stepped into the role of department chair in a unit with a looming and substantial budget and enrollment crisis. I knew we needed a directional shift in the scope of what criminology was in Idaho, but budgets, established routines, administrative mandates, and competing interests made change glacial. Trapped in my own constraints and failure to imagine beyond the Ivory Tower, I certainly was not thinking of putting the college experience *inside* a state correctional institution. It was then that our new faculty member, Dr. Omi Hodwitz, the editor of this volume, first approached me about starting a prison education program.

Omi explained the "Inside Out" prison exchange program to me, as well as a far-reaching vision for a bold prison education initiative in Idaho. The program pairs campus-based college students in a course along with incarcerated adults inside a correctional setting to facilitate dialogue, mutual learning, and the understanding of difference. The Inside-Out Prison Exchange program was founded at Temple University in 1997. This century, many instructors and graduates have worked to spark what is now a global educational movement. It has since expanded to include fifteen countries, 1,500 instructors, and more than 65,000 alumni. However, no such program had been tried in the state of Idaho. Then, as is the case now, excessive approvals and paperwork made a simple field trip to a museum or routine public site visit tedious, if not fraught. Omi's idea to put University of Idaho students next to correctional resident learners was ambitious, unorthodox, and likely to receive some frowns or even formal disapproval from risk-averse administrators. Some might have called it reckless, but it was exactly the kind of initiative I'd dreamed of having for our students.

When I first agreed to pursue Inside Out with Omi, I thought we might offer the course for a semester or two. I had no idea that it would become a staple of our department, offered every term, through a pandemic, for seven years and counting. Inside Out at the U of I would open the door to expanded prison education opportunities and an initiative to offer degree-seeking, research, and publication opportunities to those incarcerated with the Idaho Department of Corrections. Even more astonishing is that this program would generate genuine scholarship from students of the Inside Out program, read by academics, criminal justice professionals, and the public around the whole country.

This volume represents the second iteration of this formal scholarship and epitomizes everything that has been delightfully remarkable about the University of Idaho's Inside Out program. The experience demonstrates how the problems facing higher education and criminal justice are entwined. There are several crises in higher education. These include a lack of state funding and public support, legitimate questions about the value of a college education, and a looming "enrollment cliff." Similarly, there are long-known and well-documented crises in the corrections system, including overcrowding, recidivism, and differential punishment based on race. Acknowledging the inextricable nature of these issues offers us the ability to see potential mutual solutions, and I think this is an important context for this unique volume featuring collaborative scholarship from our most promising "outside" scholars and the insight of convict criminologists . . . both brought together and cultivated through the Inside Out program.

CONVICT CRIMINOLOGY AND THE SOCIOLOGICAL IMAGINATION

Given the biographical background of the authors of each chapter, this book might be viewed, in part, as what is called "convict criminology." In 2001, Stephen Richards and Jeffrey Ian Ross engaged the concept as a remedy to criminological research that was stale, unimaginative, and primarily in service to the established notions of criminal justice. The result was policy reliant on a mix of both canonized expert and commonsensical ideas of "just deserts" and "law and order," repeated by politicians eager to score easy points among the public as being tough on crime. Richards and Ross's book was groundbreaking in that it combined the dual insight of convicts and their lived experience, with the academic expertise of criminology, while firmly creating the position of a "convict criminologist" as a potential lodestar in the broader understanding of crime and justice.

Prior to Richards and Ross's work, there had been examples of current and former correctional residents "doing" criminology before, especially in smaller critical and radical niches of criminological thought. For example, Shakur Sanyika's 1994 autobiography *Monster*, on his life as an LA gang member shook many assumptions at the core of criminal justice. Meanwhile, Mumia Abu-Jamal's *Live from Death Row* (1996) represents works that helped popularize the field of conflict criminology to a wider audience, albeit polarizing ones. However, the formal establishment of convict criminology in the past twenty years represents a "new criminology." This is a field that embraces the perspective of those who are or were incarcerated. This paradigmatic shift moves the lived experiences of current and formerly incarcerated individuals from the relatively obscure margins of criminological thought to a perspective in the field increasingly recognized as equally valid as those with biographies that do not include incarceration.

Besides the perception that criminology is strongly connected, and even captured by the criminal justice system, the field is rightly criticized for producing scholarship that is overly focused on reified dependent variables such as recidivism, indexed crimes, and latent reentry outcomes. Indeed, much of the scholarly research engaged in the field of criminology involves Ivory Tower experts with immense knowledge, but little personal connection to those most affected by the criminal justice system and incarceration. As a remedy to the abstracted empiricism found in much of the social sciences, this volume stokes a "sociological imagination" in ways that may be instrumental, but are at the foremost emancipatory to the subject, and reader of her contributions. In many ways, accomplishing this feat is the highest form of scholarship in the field of sociology.

In a similar vein to the challenge posed by convict criminology, the great mid-twentieth-century sociologist C. Wright Mills in his seminal work, *The Sociological Imagination* (1961), criticized much of the social sciences at the time as doing little more than producing deferential information in service of the administrative state. Mills was critical of social science that, far removed from the subject of inquiry, produced a type of knowledge that he deemed "abstract empiricism" devoid of any kind of theoretical orientation utilizing convoluted discourses, unintelligible to anyone except a small group of elites. He thought the social sciences needed to be historical, reflexive, and meaningful to those being studied. An advocate of public scholarship, Mills challenged the social scientist to produce work that was meaningful to those being researched using an approach that connects how personal troubles and public issues are interrelated. He argued that the highest feat in the social sciences was understanding how an individual's biography and history intersect, and how one's personal position is tied to and entwined with social forces larger than any one individual.

Mills championed a method in the social sciences as one that understands one's personal situation as being enmeshed in a larger historical epoch. While individual decisions certainly guide a person's life, those decisions take place within a larger social (i.e., structural) context. The work publicized here is an ideal expression of the promise that Mills proposed: understanding how personal troubles relate to public issues. Convict criminology deals with firsthand accounts of the effects and larger context of crime and punishment from those who have experienced incarceration, reflective of the true power of a sociological imagination. This "insider perspective" is perhaps the most interesting and authentic scholarship produced in the field of criminology today, and it masterfully answers the challenge posed by the central tenet of the sociological imagination. While some outside academics may exhibit deep empathy for victims and the incarcerated alike, their social position and inherent privilege constrain their thinking about the causes and consequences of crime. That is not to say a scholar who has never experienced incarceration is invalid. In fact, convict criminology can augment the academic field and reorient traditional scholarship with a fresh look at offenders, punishment, and corrections, as well as other issues related to crime and justice.

Perhaps most notable about this volume is that the biographies of each set of section authors intersect though an unlikely forum, the Inside Out Program. For the inside scholar, their path to authorship was channeled through individual choices and social circumstances well beyond their control that ultimately led them through the criminal justice system and incarceration. For the outside scholar, they followed an academic interest in criminal justice that led them to something unlike any other experience offered in college: the chance to learn alongside and from incarcerated individuals. Each student cohort came together to find mutual understanding and grow through the pursuit of education.

The chapters in this volume would be useful to anyone interested in tracing the historical origins of criminal justice and punishment. More notable are the many ways this book addresses the challenge posed by Mills more than sixty years ago and accomplishes this by combining the perspective and lived experiences of people who experienced incarceration with an analysis of punishment in a specific historical epoch. For an unknowing reader, this perspective may seem nonexistent; for one familiar with the backgrounds of some of the authors, the experience is reflected only subtly, as their position is not the point of each chapter and passage. What strikes me the most about the contributions to this volume is how a collaboration of authors triangulates the origins of punishment, putting a multifaceted perspective on a single issue. For example, on the surface chapter 1 is a linear tracing of the historical origins and philosophies of penology, yet nearly every passage contains a hint of insight from the inside, from retribution, to reform, to rehabilitation. In contrast, chapter 4 makes historical comparisons in a much different arch, from the ancient, to the present, yet clearly capturing a narrative that hints at an insider perspective. The dual perspectives in each engage a seemingly routine topic in the history of punishment, yet they derive multifaceted inferences.

In all, this volume of convict scholarship represents a revolutionary change to both criminology and education. The bringing of a very traditional residential college student experience, in line with an inclusion of those most familiar with the impact of criminal justice, has opened new avenues of research and important reappraisals of existing epistemologies. The Inside Out program has also seen many successes, including this work. Some incarcerated students have already reentered society; for others, this is a distant dream. Outside students have started their own careers or gone on to graduate school. The scholars featured here exhibit a talent and evaluation on the history of punishment that is worthy of someone holding a doctorate, but as they say, the "school of hard knocks" is the most salient.

REFERENCES

Abu-Jamal, Mumia. 1995. *Live from Death Row*. Boston: Addison-Wesley Publishing Company.

Mills, C. W. 1961. *The Sociological Imagination*. Oxford: Oxford University Press.

Richards, Stephen C., and Jeffrey Ian Ross. 2001. "Introducing the New School of Convict Criminology." *Social Justice* 28, no. 1 (Spring): 177–190. http://www.jstor.org/stable/29768063.

Shakur, Sanyika. 1994. *Monster: The Autobiography of an L.A. Gang Member*. New York: Grove Press.

Acknowledgments

We would like to thank the staff and faculty at the Idaho Correctional Institution–Orofino (ICI-O), particularly Terema Carlin, Kent Shriver, and Lisa Goodrich, for their unwavering support of our many academic adventures.

Introduction

What, Where, and When

Omi Hodwitz

As the title suggests, this is a book dedicated to exploring the historical roots of Western criminal justice systems. This may sound like a relatively simple task, but as is true with many things in this world (particularly in academia), very little is as simple as it seems. The first sentence in this chapter suggests that we (the writers) will provide you (the reader) with a simple introduction to the criminal justice system in various regions of the world over several historical eras. However, this is an unsatisfactory introduction, begging further elaboration on the *what*, the *where*, and the *when. What* is the criminal justice system? We all likely have some vague understanding of its facets and functions, but is the labyrinth-like set of institutions we know today representative of earlier times? *Where* is the Western world? Once again, common knowledge provides us with a ready answer, but is that answer informed by history? Lastly, *when* did the criminal justice system begin? Here, the reader may have a tentative answer or, more likely, a general uncertainty, unaided by a common narrative. This introduction aims to offer some guidance regarding these questions so that the reader may better enjoy the remaining pages of this book unencumbered by confusion or uncertainty.

For the sake of simplicity, we will begin with the first question: What is the criminal justice system? Consider your own response to this question. Are you now thinking of a judge presiding over court proceedings? Or perhaps you are imagining a carceral setting, complete with prison guards, bars, and metal bunks? Does a police officer in uniform come to mind? These are all accurate renditions of the criminal justice system today; each one of these images is a highly visible and fundamental part of modern justice systems. In fact, if you were to look up the definition of the criminal justice system, you would likely find a simple description of a network that consists of three parts: police, courts, and corrections. Although this is a palatable presentation of factors, it comes with flaws. The judge in the courtroom, the guard in the prison, and the officer in uniform are all relatively modern innovations, absent from the pages of more ancient narratives. If we were to abide by this definition, our historical investigations would be limited by the introduction of these contemporary roles. Therefore, we respectfully reject this definition of the criminal justice system and humbly ask the reader to adopt an alternative that is more forgiving and inclusive, a definition that acknowledges that history is a generous narrator that abhors definitional impositions.

Specifically, we suggest that the criminal justice system is an amalgam of individuals and institutions that seek to facilitate social control. This definition, if the reader chooses to accept it, offers a much broader scope and depth, allowing us to recognize and appreciate all manner of justice-related processes that, at one point or another, were integral to maintaining social control.

With the hope that the reader is willing to adopt a more generous understanding of criminal justice, we turn next to the question of the Western world. Once again, we ask you to consider your own interpretation of the meaning of this concept. Are you now thinking of North America and Europe? Perhaps you have thought to give a nod of acknowledgment to Australia? If so, you would be correct in this moment in time. However, similar to our discussion of the criminal justice system, this is a modern interpretation, informed by geopolitical boundaries that, due to such factors as colonization and war, have a historical tendency to rearrange themselves like a series of Rorschach inkblots. We turn to Australia to emphasize this point. Prior to the 1700s, when the British Empire arrived abruptly on its shores, Australia was primarily inhabited by indigenous communities. Should Australia be included in historical narratives addressing the Western world? As you may imagine, this is a question that could invoke much thought and debate. Therefore, we beg the reader once again for conceptual and definitional leniency. We have chosen to interpret the Western world as a cultural phenomenon, traced back to the Greco-Roman Empire, now presented in geopolitical form. At the risk of being reductive, we invite the reader to envision ancient Greece and Rome seated at the beginning of a three-dimensional temporal web. Within this web, these empires are viral-like cultural purveyors; over time, they spread from one region to the next, sometimes fading out and sometimes taking firm root, defining the region and the people within it. This allows more flexibility around the inclusion of specific regions at different points in time, even if they fall outside of modern interpretations of the boundaries of the Western world.

Having addressed the *what* and the *where*, we turn next to the *when*. When did the criminal justice system begin? This may seem like a relatively simple question to address; after all, assigning dates to historic events is a general practice used in all disciplines. But here again, we hit a roadblock, one that is informed in part by our first question regarding the meaning of the criminal justice system. If we were to adopt the more commonplace assumption that the criminal justice system is a network of law enforcement, courts, and corrections, we can then do what so many other authors have done before us by declaring that the criminal justice system began in the 1800s CE (policing), sometime around 600 BCE (the courts), or the 1700s CE (corrections). Our historical narrative, therefore, would suffer from temporal dysentery. If, however, we broaden our understanding of criminal justice to include recognized methods of social control, then the answer is simple: the criminal justice system began when we began. As societies formed, we developed systems of maintaining order and justice, thus our earliest histories of social growth, cultural development, and political cohesion are also our histories of evolving justice systems. Perhaps this seems too generous a timeline? This may be so, but we hope that as you peruse the pages of this book, you will find reason to grant us this leniency in temporal boundaries.

Although we have addressed the three questions presented at the beginning of this chapter, there is a fourth that hangs over our heads. *How* did the criminal justice system evolve over time? This is, of course, the impetus or driving force behind this book. We are a disparate group of authors, but we share a common interest in plumbing the depths of systems of control and justice, tracing them to their origins and observing them evolve and change in sometimes-macabre and unexpected ways. We are fascinated by the justice-themed viral tendrils that have originated in the Greco-Roman web, how they move through time and space, and the ways in which they impact the societies within which they take root. As is true with many avid enthusiasts, we adopt the oftentimes erroneous assumption that our interests, since they are paramount to us, are also paramount to everyone else. In the spirit of that assumption, we have created this book with the intention of sharing our collective fascinations regarding the evolution (and devolution) of the criminal justice system. Thus, the answer to the question of *how* is found in every page and chapter of this book.

FURTHER FINE-TUNING AND FOREWARNINGS

As alluded to earlier in this chapter, we aim to reduce any uncertainty and confusion that you, dear reader, may experience as you wend your way through our various narratives. In that spirit, we ask for your patience as we address a few remaining thoughts and considerations. First, we find value in acknowledging the diverging, yet intersecting nature of criminology and criminal justice. Second, as mentioned previously, we are a motley crew of writers, and as such, we feel it necessary to alert you to the oftentimes unique and occasionally overlapping narratives adopted throughout the book. Finally, we recognize the value of the bird's-eye view, thus we also present you with a summary of what to expect in the pages ahead.

Our first point of fine-tuning begins with criminology and criminal justice studies, scholarly sisters who share each other's company but still demand independence. Both focus on crime and deviance, but each claims jealous ownership over different fragments of this phenomenon. Criminology, the more elusive and abstract sister, is fascinated by the causes of crime and deviance, spending her life theorizing about social, political, and economic factors (to name but a few) that push, pull, or guide the individual toward antisocial behavior. Criminal justice studies, on the other hand, is the more practical and applied sister, wedded to the exploration of the consequences of crime, including institutional responses and legal measures. Despite this partitioning, each sister is inextricably linked to the other in a cyclical manner, as the causes inform the consequences, and the consequences inform the causes. Consider punishment in all its various forms. It is a consequence of crime, thus it firmly belongs in the realm of the criminal justice scholar. But does it? Punishment is designed to reduce crime, and thus it can be included in theoretical ponderings related to the causes of crime. Does not the absence of punishment potentially facilitate crime? This kind of question illustrates the deep ties that bind criminology and criminal justice studies. Bear that in mind as you explore this book; although the narratives are focused on criminal justice responses to crime, each one has tipped its hat to the criminological sister who adores causes, ensuring that her voice is present as well.

Having introduced the sisters, we turn next to authorship and content in the coming pages. Regarding authorship, most written works that fall within the criminological/

criminal justice discipline share a common theme: a degree-wielding intellectual drafts a narrative that replicates and ever-so-slightly expands upon what other degree-wielding intellectuals have drafted in the past. These narratives are informative, but they tend to lack luster, offering the singular perspective of the mid-career academic who is brilliant and book-smart, but also a little jaded and two-dimensional (no disrespect is meant by this comment; the author of this introduction is also a mid-career academic who is a little two-dimensional and lackluster). This book offers a different authorship entirely, one we hope you will appreciate and enjoy. Each chapter has been crafted by 1) one or more *convict criminologists*, incarcerated scholars whose expertise are both intellectual and experiential, and 2) one or more student criminologists, promising new scholars exploring the world of criminal justice from a fresh and (relatively?) untarnished perspective. These unlikely sets of co-authors have crafted narratives that depict the historical realities of the criminal justice system, but also reflect the sage wisdom of the incarcerated scholar and the passion of the student criminologist.

We have one final alert to offer the reader before we provide a road map to the pages ahead. Each chapter traces one part of the criminal justice system through the various eras that define human history. Although these individual parts are distinct in definition, they also overlap considerably in origin, purpose, and practice. For example, it is nearly impossible to discuss punishment in ancient antiquity (chapter 1) without also discussing the influence of class and privilege (chapter 8) on punitive measures. Thus, dear reader, you will likely find some degree of overlap between the chapters as each narrative is integrally intertwined with every other narrative. We invite you to consider the underlying significance of these intersections as you encounter them; they illustrate two key points. First, criminal justice is a *system*, or an interconnected network, and no single part stands alone. Second, criminal justice is a response to social and political narratives, shaped by the external might of privilege and status.

THE BIRD'S-EYE VIEW

As one final piece of business, we offer the reader an overview of the coming chapters. We invited the reader in the previous section to consider that 1) criminal justice is a system, and 2) it is informed by privilege and status. In recognition of this invitation, we have grouped the chapters along similar lines. Chapters 1 through 4 focus on the working parts of the criminal justice system, while chapters 5 through 10 explore the assumption that justice systems are the product of social and political forces, shaped by those in positions of power.

Where shall the chapter narratives begin? We posit there is value and significance in starting our journey with an intentional tribute to a relationship we described earlier: the reciprocal nature of the criminological and criminal justice siblings. Thus, our first narrative-driven chapter focuses on the history of penology (chapter 1), an exploration of punishment through the ages. In acknowledgment of the criminal justice perspective, the authors lead you through the dark and dismal practices of earlier times, into the softer reformative tones of yesteryear, before landing you in the mire of conflicting and competing measures of today. This account, however, also invites the reader to consider the underlying era-specific philosophies that guided these consequences of crime, including retribution, rehabilitation, incapacitation, and deterrence. The criminological sister is evident in these philosophies, as each is informed by assumptions regarding the causes of crime.

We follow penology with policing in chapter 2, a chapter that, perhaps more than any other, best encapsulates the broader definition of *criminal justice* that we offered the reader in previous pages. The authors present all manner of historical measures of maintaining order and control, from the security forces of warlords and the magistrates of ancient Greece, through to the uniformed police agencies that are in place today. Throughout the pages of this chapter, the reader will learn about the oscillating nature of public and private policing, the growing disconnect between public needs and state practices, and the few successes and many failures of the different models of policing that grace the historical palate.

We next turn our attention to the courts (chapter 3), one of the longest-standing organized elements of the criminal justice system. As legal statutes took form and became commonplace in ancient antiquity, so, too, did a system of courts and accompanying practices, including the magisterial role, the reliance on juries as outside arbiters, and the use of voting to determine justice-related outcomes. These practices, however, were (relatively) short-lived as the Middle Ages settled in and ecclesiastical and secular stakeholders constructed court-related institutions that often vied for control of the deviant faction, resulting in a rash of seemingly macabre and callous means of establishing guilt and penalty. These tumultuous times were eventually replaced, as the Age of Enlightenment, replete with her emphasis on rational, equal, and humane treatment, and the Scientific Revolution, the bearer of evidence-based outcomes, descended on the Western world, thus paving the path to the judicial proceedings of our modern time (which, despite the thousands of years of growth and development, once again bear a striking resemblance to the courts of ancient antiquity).

As mentioned previously, the three classic components of the criminal justice system include policing, courts, and corrections. Having addressed the first two in previous chapters, the last chapter of the criminal justice section tackles corrections (chapter 4). In this chapter, the authors invite you to expand your definition to include all manner of supervision and control, thus allowing them to begin their narrative long before the penitentiary and reformation eras of the 1700s and 1800s. Similar to previous chapters, these authors begin in ancient Greece and Rome, a period of temporary imprisonment and permanent hard labor. Over time, confinement became a profit-making venture, and medieval prisons filled with unfortunate souls, left to languish in filthy conditions, deprived of the necessities of survival. This shifted during the period of the somewhat rational and humane Enlightenment, leading to the introduction of penitentiaries and reformatories. Originally intended to correct behavior through solitude or labor, these institutions evolved into the model prominent in society today, one that emphasizes warehousing in a manner that echoes medieval times.

Having addressed the more recognizable components of the criminal justice system, we transition into the second part of the book, a collection of chapters that examine the impact of social and political factors, particularly measures of privilege and status, on criminal justice practices. We begin this exploration with an introduction to historical trends in crime, justice, and law (chapter 5) and we invite the reader to contemplate the cyclical or reciprocal action-reaction nature of these trends, as they both inform and are informed by social and political narratives. We see this in the relationship between social stratification and legal personhood in ancient antiquity, feudalism and punitiveness in the early Middle Ages, religious and royal power and the roots of deviance in the later Middle Ages and Renaissance, and urbanization and immigration and the criminalization of the socially undesirable during the Industrial Revolution. Examining these trends provides a necessary, albeit somber and perhaps a little depressing, context within which to better appreciate the remaining chapters of the book.

The next three chapters address the royal trifecta of social metrics that (unfortunately) inform status, power, and privilege in the Western world: race and ethnicity, gender, and class. We begin with race and ethnicity in chapter 6. Similar to previous chapters, the authors invite you to adopt a more generous definition, one that recognizes groupings based on unique physical or cultural traits. With this definition in hand, the authors then explore the lengthy and sobering history of oppressive criminal justice practices directed toward communities and peoples lacking the same physical and/or cultural practices of those in power. The authors unapologetically lead the reader through the granting of legal personhood in ancient antiquity, the persecution of religious minorities in the Middle Ages, the legally permissible enslavement and genocide of the colonial era, and finally the use of empirical evidence to inform perceptions of criminality and eugenic practices during the modern era.

The somber tones of the discussion continue in chapter 7, which explores the relationship between gender and the criminal justice system. These authors usher us through thousands of years of gender-based hierarchies that result in the criminalization and control of non-male persons. The Greco-Roman Era was a period of private control, with all power passed to the male head of household, while the Middle Ages was marked by religiously informed legal narratives that villainized large swathes of people, including the female-laden community of alleged witches. The Reformation and Enlightenment, for all their protestations of equality and rationality, were also excessively prudent, criminalizing the immodest and immoral. Finally, the Scientific Revolution and the modern era increased the stakes further by introducing the medicalization of female deviance.

The last of the royal trifecta, class, follows a theme similar to the one adopted by her gender- and race-based sisters. The authors of chapter 8 assume an investigative tone, plundering the pages of history and seeking evidence of class-based influences on criminal justice systems. Their quest does not disappoint. This chapter describes a class-based hierarchy that has stood the test of time, informing the laws and criminal justice practices of each era. The patricians in ancient antiquity; the feudal lords, the Church, and the Crown in the Middle Ages; and the capitalist giants during the Industrial Revolution, all have enjoyed the benefits of a malleable system of justice, one that can be wielded to criminalize the unsavory, to ensure a continued hierarchy, and to increase power and privilege. It is a sobering tale, but one that requires a place at the table of criminal justice narratives.

The last two topic-driven chapters acknowledge that, although race, gender, and class may be dominant forces in the creation and execution of justice, there are other seemingly less-visible factors that are also integral to Western systems of criminal justice. Age is one of these factors, often overlooked in the assessment of historical measures of justice, as is apparent in the notable lack of information pertaining to this topic prior to the 1800s. To address this deficit, chapter 9 explores the Western response to juvenile offending, straining to piece together a narrative for the first few thousand years of documented human history, then becoming hopelessly submerged in the onslaught of information that flooded more recent literature. The authors, who are brave souls to undertake such a daunting and piecemeal task, explore the invisibility of children, including deviant children, in the early ages of human history. Hidden from the public eye, disobedient youth were subjected to corporal punishment and oftentimes death for errant behaviors, and this continued unchecked until the end of the Middle Ages. Around this time, questions of culpability arose, and the Western world determined that youth should be subjected to the formal criminal justice system, without the benefit of additional protections. Before long, the public took notice that children were being warehoused with adult offenders, thus inspiring a rallying cry among reformers who demanded softer treatment. This ushered in the modern era of juvenile justice, replete with reformatories, juvenile courts, and legal protections.

The last topic-driven chapter does not match the somewhat-positive conclusion upon which the juvenile justice chapter ended. Instead, chapter 10, which explores the relationship between mental health and the criminal justice system, adopts the more dismal tones of the royal trifecta of race, class, and gender. The unfortunate souls afflicted with mental health differences have experienced a long and egregious history at the hands of the criminal justice system. Locked away in the darkest recesses of private homes in ancient antiquity, they were then subjected to exorcism, experimentation, incapacitation, and death during the Middle Ages. The Scientific Revolution ushered in the era of medicalization, and those deemed mentally unfit were institutionalized, sterilized, and overmedicated. Modern times continue to bode ill for this community, as they frequently rotate between institutionalization and incapacitation.

The last chapter of the book, chapter 11, summarizes the various threads and themes evident throughout each author's narrative and offers reflections on the presence and significance of these themes in modern times. The chapter extends no apologies; it is written out of respect for those who have suffered at the hands of the criminal justice system, both historically and in the present time. It is, quite simply, a solemn analysis, one that bears witness to the brutal nature of human history, resplendent in its macabre pursuit of justice.

With that road map in mind, we will leave you to roam the remaining pages of this text at your leisure. We are an unlikely group of ne'er-do-wells, but we have found a collective purpose and joy in creating and building this volume, and we hope you also find meaning and significance in our efforts.

Chapter 1

A History of Penology

Pony L. Jackson and Omi Hodwitz

INTRODUCTION

Crime and Punishment may bring to mind a famous novel by the Russian author Fyodor Dostoevsky, but these terms refer to a fundamental human struggle that predates any particular piece of classical literature. Crime and punishment are social constructs, linked together throughout the entirety of human history, as societies navigate the difficulties of defining deviance and crafting penalties in response. The result, a progression of castigatory sentiments and practices, is varied and oftentimes unexpected, beginning in a period with rudimentary laws and punitive approaches, then progressing to a time when the citizenry was granted the right to seek justice, guided by the accord that *might-is-right* or *revenge-is-mine*, before transitioning to more recent iterations that bestow the state with punitive power. Although this progression of penalization may be dark or unpalatable, it is never dull, nor predictable.

This chapter aims to introduce the reader to the history of punishment throughout the ages. It begins with an introduction to the philosophies of punishments, which alone or in partnership shape each era of punitive growth in the Western world. The chapter then bears witness to the often-bloody and barbaric palate of punishments evident throughout these eras, beginning with the fledgling legal codes of Mesopotamia through to the increasing popularity of restorative justice in modern times. We will review four thousand years of punitive development, pausing at different eras to peer over history's shoulder, catching a glimpse of the price demanded for deviance during that time. The reader is invited to join us as we traipse through the ancient civilizations of Mesopotamia, Greece, and Rome, before moving on to the Middle Ages of Europe, the Age of Enlightenment, and the Industrial Revolution, then ending our foray with a brief glimpse at the twentieth and twenty-first centuries.

PHILOSOPHIES OF PUNISHMENT

To help ease our travels along this twisting thoroughfare, we turn to the philosophies, or pillars, of punishment, which we can count as being the signposts pointing the way along our route. Each of these philosophies has been shaped by our understanding of deviance and crime and, thus, has shaped our responses to such acts, acting as a silent hand pulling our punitive strings. There are four (or five) of these philosophies, including retribution, deterrence, rehabilitation, and incapacitation (and, it could be argued, restoration) [Materni 2013, 263–304].

Crime typically involves a loss for some (the victim) and a gain for others (the offender). *Retribution*, or retributive justice, seeks to address this imbalance by introducing new loss directed at the offender (Alexander 1922, 239). In early times, retribution was often a personal affair, carried out between individuals or communities; however, in modern times, retributive agents typically represent the state, executing punishment in a businesslike manner, as a faceless, impersonal consequence to criminal conduct. A retributive presence can be traced through the ages in a variety of social control contexts, from the early Code of Ur-Nammu, King of Ur (c. 2050 BCE), which states, "If a man commits a homicide, they shall kill that man," through to contemporary legislation, such as life imprisonment in response to homicide (Roth 1995, 17). Thus, retribution has persisted, a measure of balancing the scales of justice between those who were harmed and those who harm.

Retributive justice complements the next pillar of punishment, *deterrence*. Proponents of deterrence posit that the threat of swift, certain, and severe punishment will discourage people from engaging in illicit activities; therefore, preventing crime requires the implementation and publicization of persuasively daunting punishments (Materni 2013, 290). Once sanctions are in place, deterrence can be achieved in two ways. First, punishment may deter deviance through modeling; potential offenders witness the punishment of others and are dissuaded from pursuing deviance themselves (general deterrence). Second, an individual may be deterred after receiving punishment for their own actions; the pain of the punishment dissuades them from engaging in further crime (specific deterrence). Conventional wisdom suggests that punishments inflicted or endured in the "public square" serve both a general and a specific function (Wenzel & Okimoto 2016, 241), allowing the average citizen to fully witness the outcomes of criminal activities while also inflicting pain and shame on the unfortunate offender (Alexander 1922, 238–39). Historically, examples of these types of punishments range from relegation to the stocks or pillory to the more sensational executions involving beheading, hanging, and burning. In modern times, the public square effect is achieved for lesser offenses through the use of some forms of community service or, for more severe offenses, by publicly broadcasting state executions.[1]

Another popular philosophy of punishment, particularly in the modern era, is *incapacitation*. As the name suggests, incapacitation involves sending an offender to prison or restricting their freedom in some manner (Materni 2013, 294–300). Incapacitation is a measure of social defense; transgressors are removed from the community as a means to protect society and reduce further offending. Terms of imprisonment vary greatly but are intended to reflect the specific level of egregiousness of the crime. A lesser form of incapacitation involves community supervision (e.g., temporary release during the Middle Ages, or probation or parole in contemporary terms); the deviant is monitored for a set period to ensure their compliance with law and societal norms as they reintegrate into society.

Institutional services and support play a large factor in our next philosophy of punishment, *rehabilitation*. The philosophy is premised on the assumption that offenders are not inherently deviant; instead, they possess the capacity to be good citizens, but they have suffered personal or social hurdles or disadvantages that have led them to crime. According to the rehabilitative ideal, their aberrant ways can be reformed through education, vocational training, and the use of interpersonal approaches, among other things (Alschuler 2003, 8). Rehabilitation guides the creation and implementation of a variety of historical and modern programs and policies, including required prayer in prison in the 1800s through to life-skills training in contemporary correctional settings.

Restorative justice, the last stop on this philosophical path, refers to an approach that recognizes that crime causes harm and attending to that harm requires the active participation of the offender, the victim, and the community (Braithwaite 1999, 6). Addressing deviance means acknowledging the harm caused and focusing on solutions that mitigate that harm for all affected parties (Zehr 2015, 33–36). This format gives the victim an opportunity to communicate directly with the wrongdoer while also creating a space for the offender to express remorse and share their own reasons for offending. Although the state may be involved in the process, the state is not central, as it is not typically directly affected by the offender's actions. Historically, restoration was central to indigenous communities; in contemporary times, however, restoration has begun to take prominence in several Western nations, although it would be a misnomer to suggest that it is widespread.

Armed with these pillars of punishment, we will begin our journey through the ages. As will become apparent, each era is marked by one or more philosophies that, although subtle and discreet, shape and craft responses to deviance. The early eras are retributive, only quietly hinting at other philosophies in passing, as though they were but a fantasy or a dark secret. It is only in the more recent eras that the remaining pillars gain prominence, as deterrence, incapacitation, and rehabilitation take center stage, to be eventually and tentatively joined by their restorative sister in the twenty-first century.

ANCIENT MESOPOTAMIA AND CODIFIED RETRIBUTION

Our story of crime and punishment begins in Mesopotamia, the earliest-recognized human civilization. Mesopotamian society was plagued with predatory deviance, resulting in the first known examples of codified punishment. A legal codex was a necessity of the era, a means to formalize social norms and punitive consequences while also giving the edicts authority in the eyes of citizenry. It would be a grave error to disparage the sophistication of these ancient societies; each Mesopotamian civilization, including Samaria, Assyria, and Babylonia, produced legal code that governed all manner of behavior, ranging from the minutia of daily life through to extreme acts of violence (Johns 1911, 1–59).

Social stratification bias was prevalent in these early laws. Individuals of higher status who harmed or violated those of reduced status faced lesser punishments than in instances of the reverse. In addition, the gender of the offender figured heavily into legal sanctions. Property owners were treated with the greatest deference, followed by freedmen, and finally slaves, and women ranked below men in every stratum (Urch 2022, 438).

Sanctions were rooted in a retributive philosophy, closely following the *eye-for-an-eye* precept. Punishments, in many cases, attempted to mirror the offenses in severity and consequence. One of the first recorded examples of a legal canon of this kind is the Code of Urukagina, named so after the twenty-fourth century BCE King Urukagina. Although no actual text has been discovered, a great deal can be construed from other available references (e.g., World History Project, n.d.). Urukagina's code established measures against theft, murder, and seizure of property and persons, and it set a precedence for later legal codes, such as the Code of Ur-Nammu c. 2100–2050 BCE and the Codex of Lipit-Ishtar c. 1870 BCE Unlike the Code of Urukagina, the content of these later canons was preserved, providing ready illustrations of the retributive nature of punishment in early Mesopotamia.

Translated laws from Ur-Nammu (Roth 1995, 17–18):

- *If a man commits a murder, that man must be killed.*
- *If a man detains(?) (another), that man shall be imprisoned and he shall weigh and deliver 15 shekels of silver.*

From the Codex of Lipit-Ishtar (Steele 1947, 163):

- *If a man went up(?) into the garden of (another) man and was seized for theft, he shall pay ten shekels of silver.*
- *If a man felled a tree in (another) man's garden, he shall pay one-half mina of silver.*

Possibly the most famously touted originator of early retributive justice is the Code of Hammurabi c. 1754 BCE, so named after the Babylonian king Hammurabi, who enacted it.[2] Once again, the *eye-for-an-eye* philosophy is evident in the explicit relationship between harm caused and harm received.

Laws of Hammurabi's Code (Hammurabi 2250 BC, 15):

If a son strikes his father, his hands shall be hewn off. If a man puts out the eye of another man, his eye shall be put out. If he breaks another man's bone, his bone shall be broken. If he puts out the eye of a freed man, or breaks the bone of a freed man, he shall pay one gold mina. If he put out the eye of a man's slave, or break the bone of a man's slave, he shall pay one-half of its value. If a man knocks out the teeth of his equal, his teeth shall be knocked out.

The early codification of these laws and punishments provided the foundation for the retributive generations that followed. Formalizing legal practices ensured that, when wrongdoing occurred, there was a swift and sure penalty. Although critics may question the ferocity of some punitive measures, the Mesopotamian systems of justice were an improvement on the unregulated punishments that predated the era. The codification of practices contributed to state and civil development, as well as the germination of justice-oriented ideas that would inspire other philosophies of punishment over time.

EQUITABLE RETRIBUTION IN ANCIENT GREECE

Greek civilization extended as far back as c. 3300 BCE and it lasted well into the first millennium CE. Modern historians separate Greek history into several eras, starting with the Bronze Age (c. 3300–1150 BCE) and continuing into the Hellenistic Period (323–146 BCE) [Williams 2016, 171]. Throughout these times, political, social, and economic practices were the purview of the *polis* (independent city-states); each of these walled cities was responsible for regulating the land and people within its borders. Therefore, as an independent entity, each polis adopted its own unique government, laws, military, religious beliefs, and culture.

Despite the independence of each polis, they shared underlying punitive themes, including both change and consistency. Regarding change, over the span of four millennium, Greek laws and punishments oscillated, reflecting a variety of influences. These ranged from the conviction that a pantheon of Greek gods meted out punishments, through to the Code of Draco, which liberally applied the death penalty in the name of equality (Freeman 2014, 240; Stearns 1936, 223). Regarding consistency, the Greeks shared a retributive sentiment while also being careful to avoid a vengeance-focused state response, in the name of creating a uniform and equitable system. The goal of punishment was to produce painful repercussions for crime while also avoiding the temptation of excess.

Key philosophers, such as Socrates, Plato, and later Aristotle, were also influential in developing conceptions of punishment in ancient Greece (Allen 2000, 36). As described in Plato's written dialogue, Socrates, when faced with execution as a punishment, opted to lay down his life rather than let Crito finance his escape, saying, "And so one should not repay an injustice with an injustice, as the many think, since one should never act unjustly" (Plato 399 BCE, 6). Socrates's fundamental premise was that the social contract between the citizen and the state should be infallible; the rules of conformity and punishment must exist outside the desires of the individual for the sake of all. Although aligned with the retributive sentiments of era, these scholars also provided the first early ponderings associated with deterrence and correction or rehabilitation. As noted by Julian Alexander (1922), "Even Plato justified punishment solely upon the grounds that the criminal was thereby through a severe chastening made better and the example of his extreme punishment acted as a deterrent to others" (238). These early references would remain aspirational during ancient antiquity, only taking hold in later eras.

Punishments imposed by the state ranged in severity, from fines, confiscation of property, and imprisonment, to the corporal and capital punishments of "stoning to death (lapidation); throwing the offender from a cliff (precipitation); binding him to a stake so that he suffered a slow death and public abuse while dying (apotympanismos, an early form of crucifixion); or the formal dedication of the offender to the gods, by a ritual cursing of him or forbidding all from any social communication with him" (Peters 1995, 5). In the case of incarceration, its popularity as a prescribed punishment grew in the latter part of Greek antiquity as prisons expanded, becoming sites for involuntary confinement as well as the execution and torture of prisoners.[3]

The Greeks were one of the earliest civilizations that recognized a need for justice and for the shifting of punitive powers from the populace to the government, but they still relied on retributive justice to punish offenders for wrongs committed. Philosophers like Plato introduced transformational ideas that, while not necessarily popular at the time, would be embraced in later years as a basis upon which to question the morality of excessive punishments.

LEX TALIONIS IN ANCIENT ROME

Ancient Roman civilization can be traced back to c. 753 BCE, enduring in the West until 476 CE and in the East until 1453 CE. Founded as a short-lived monarchy, it was ruled by kings until 510 BCE when it became a republic, before transitioning into an empire in 31 BCE when Octavian (renamed Augustus) became the first emperor (Williams 2016, 217). Unlike the Greeks, whose geopolitical structure revolved around *polis* communities, the Romans absorbed individuals, cities, and nations that demonstrated loyalty to the state. Roman society was divided into castes, including the *patricians*, which were descendants of the first one hundred senators appointed to the Senate by the king Romulus, and the *plebeians*, which referred to all citizens not included in the patrician caste. Foreigners were cast lower than the plebeians, outranking only the slaves who sat at the bottom-most station. Lastly, women were subject to male authority; in fact, the patriarch held the power of life or death for all members of his household.

Sometime around the second century BCE, the distinctions of *patricians* and *plebeians* gave way to two legal classes, referred to as the *honestiores*, or citizens of higher status, including senators, magistrates, army veterans, and equestrians, and the *humiliores*, or persons of the lower caste (Freeman 2014, 510). This legal distinction primarily benefited the honestiores, who could avoid imprisonment and torture. If convicted, the honestiores had the option of exile, and if sentenced to death, they could avoid the spectacle of a public execution. Meanwhile, the humiliores might be tortured, imprisoned, crucified, or sent to the public arena under a virtual death sentence. Regardless of social standing, however, the Roman system of jurisprudence followed a retributive path, seeking to inflict punishment commensurate with the harm incurred from the crime.

The prosecution of offenses perpetrated against private citizens fell to the aggrieved party, who would bring the case before the appropriate magistrate and an assembly of citizens (Peters 1995, 14–15; Freeman 2014, 373, 503). The magistrate and citizenry had a range of punishments from which to choose. The more fortunate offenders received fines or some other form of compensatory punishment, which could lead to forced servitude if the guilty party could not afford the cost of the prescribed penalties (Peters 1995, 15). Most punishments, however, resulted in death. Demonstrative of the *eye-for-an-eye* retributive sentiment, an arsonist may be burnt alive, while those found guilty of other offenses might be thrown from a cliff, beaten to death, hanged, or decapitated. Not all deaths were immediate, however; probably the most renowned form of execution was crucifixion, a painful and slow way to expire (Donnelly & Diehl 2011, 42–43).[4]

The Imperial period marked an overall increasing severity in punishment, reflecting the retributive nature of the era. Exile or banishment, for example, became an imposed penalty rather than a choice for the *honestiores*, while the torture of women, slaves, and foreigners increased, often resulting in death (Innes 2017, 17–21). Flogging, which involved being repeatedly struck with a whip made of leather thongs capped with lead balls, was a popular and feared punishment. Beyond retribution, these measures also took on a deterrent function (Peters 1995, 17). Emperors hosted extravagant executions, using the gladiatorial games as a means of carrying out death sentences. The guilty were forced to fight each other, professional gladiators, or, in a particularly gruesome show of punishment, savage animals.

Claiming that the retributive philosophy of an *eye-for-an-eye* (*lex talionis*) is the sum total of the Roman era of punishment, however, would be similar to claiming ice is the sole essence of Antarctica. Instead, punishment was a by-product of several factors, including the multifaceted caste system that permeated society. Retribution was central, but so, too, was status, gender, and citizenship. In addition, the Roman people were a tenacious lot, socialized to enjoy the entertainment of painful and gruesome sanctions. Out of this motley mix arose the Roman system of justice, structured to enforce disparities and suffering, but influential nonetheless, setting the stage for the Middle Ages.

FROM RETRIBUTION TO REFORMATION IN THE MIDDLE AGES

The period in Europe referred to as the Middle Ages, or the medieval era, extended from c. 500 CE through to the seventeenth century. After its fall in 476 CE, the Western Roman Empire was divided into several kingdoms, including the Vandals, Franks, Visigoths, and Ostrogoths (Reeves 2016, 266–70). Western Europe itself was in a constant state of upheaval as kingdoms rose and fell, some within decades of each other. Others, like the Eastern Roman Empire, persevered for another thousand years or more. During this time, Christianity spread throughout Europe, solidifying the Church's foothold and ensuring its growing influence over rulers, governments, legal codes, and punitive measures.

Unlike in earlier eras, punishment was less retributive during the Middle Ages, tempered by the belief that deviance was a sign of immorality and wickedness and punishment was a tool used to identify and respond to such evil (Donnelly & Diehl 2011, 47–48). This was due, in large part, to the shifting role of the Church. Although the medieval monarchy, which embraced retribution, wanted to retain power and authority, it was slowly supplanted by ecclesiastical institutions. As it gained power, the Church influenced the European citizenry and rulership, instilling a rigorous belief that sin, the work of Satan and his agents, was at the root of crime (Winther-Jensen 2019, 108–20). As such, no one was better equipped to respond to this scourge than the Church itself, countering the Crown's claim for ownership over the citizen body. The battle between the Church and State resulted in a motley array of punishments, increasingly harsh in practice, some designed to ferret out the sinful and others crafted to deliver harm commensurate with the crime (Brians 1998, 2). In addition, similar to divisions in Babylonia, Greece, and Rome, the divisions of class and gender played heavily into legal proceedings regardless of whether it was in the Crown's, the magistrate's, or the Church's court.

At the beginning of the medieval era, laws and punishments were primarily determined by local customs, reflecting the needs and values of each population (Peters 1995, 23). Egregious violations of local norms typically received the harshest punitive response. For example, on the isle of Gotland (present-day Sweden), men caught in the act of an adulterous relationship could reasonably expect to lose a hand or a foot. In Norway, those convicted of theft, adultery, or rape were oftentimes branded for the purposes of easy identification. If such an individual recidivated, the punishment was likely to be death. However, as the power of the Church and imperators grew and consolidated, local customs receded, slowly replaced by ecclesiastical and state law.

The Church's response to deviance was canon law. Bishops were charged with determining whether followers had violated religious directives, and when deemed guilty, selecting suitable punishments designed to discipline and correct (Peters 1995, 26–27). Deviants were sinners, and canon law sought to reform the offenders, returning them to the Church's good graces. It was through this process that prisons took on a new role as a penitential, or atoning, institution. For those who committed lesser sins or confessed privately, the Church would prescribe a penance or private form of contrition.[5] Sanctions became a public affair, however, when offenses were severe, in the public eye, or potentially scandalous. In these situations, the deviant might be prohibited from engaging with the body of the Church and sacraments or might face a measure of public humiliation. For particularly offensive acts, such as those involving magic, sorcery, or incest, the individual might be relegated to a monastic prison or the dreaded Inquisitor's prison; the latter was a site of particularly abhorrent and cruel conditions.

In the late 1100s, Roman jurisprudence was partially reinstated by secular rulers interested in legitimizing their control. Punishments more closely mirrored their predecessors' from ancient antiquity, focused on death, compensation, and exile (Peters 1995, 32–41). Mutilation also began to increase in frequency, evolving into a macabre art form by the end of the era. Suspected deviants were often disemboweled, attached to a rack, blinded, or subjected to other creative methods of inflicting pain. Lesser offenders might face the public stocks, dunking stools, or the pillory. More serious offenders were executed in any number of ways, including burning or live burial, hanging, decapitation, or drowning. Regardless of the offense, punishments were harsh and unforgiving.

Torture provides a ready example of the extreme nature of medieval measures. Broadly accepted as a form of punishment and aid in eliciting confessions from the "guilty," torture was used liberally and without restraint, particularly during the peak of the European witch trials. The prosecution of witchcraft was held in high regard by both the Church and rulers of the time, so it enjoyed an exuberant following. As noted by Innes (2017), "At Neisse in Silesia in the 1650s, the executioner built an oven in which, over nine years, he roasted to death more than a thousand people, including children as young as two years of age" (113).

In summary, the Middle Ages was a tumultuous period, prompted in part by a divide between the Church and State as both vied for control of the political body.

When it came to deviance, the Church focused on the soul of the citizenry, prioritizing the reformation of the sinful. Meanwhile, the Crown embraced retribution and, to a lesser extent, deterrence, crafting its punitive measures in a manner reminiscent of its Roman ancestors, resulting in increasingly grisly outcomes.

THE AGE OF ENLIGHTENMENT AND ENDING RETRIBUTIVE IDEALS

The era following the Middle Ages was a short but conspicuous epoch, spanning just two hundred years between 1600 CE and 1800 CE. This was a period of social and political advancement, as great minds tackled the mysteries of philosophy, science, and art, thus earning the title of the Age of Enlightenment, or the Age of Reason. Despite the advances occurring in other fields, the criminal justice system was particularly brutal during the first half of this period. Remnants of the Dark Ages remained, including a fear of sinful evil, the use of torture to elicit confessions, and harsh punishments designed to retribute and deter. Toward the second half of the Age of Reason, public sentiment played a critical role in forcing change in punitive measures as more retributive measures lost popularity, replaced by a desire to prioritize humane incapacitation and rational deterrence.

Although numerous examples would serve to demonstrate the nature of the punitive system at the beginning of the Age of Reason, the *boot* or *brodequin* and the *saw* provide particularly salient illustrations of the measures of the time, expectedly reminiscent of the Middle Ages. The boot involved placing an iron shell over the foot and lower leg of the accused. Wooden wedges were then driven between the boot and leg, crushing the limb to a pulp (Donnelly & Diehl 2011, 95, 131, 175). Used to elicit confessions, the boot produced "the most severe and cruel pain in the world"; in one account it was "so severe that the marrow of [the offender's] bones oozed out of his broken limbs" (Innes 2017, 131–32). The saw, on the other hand, was applied to heretics or those whose beliefs did not align with the Church (Donnelly & Diehl 2011, 189). These individuals were stripped naked, bound upside down in the spread-eagle position, before being sawed in half, beginning in the groin region. The slow loss of blood from this tactic ensured that the offender remained alive for a good portion of the punishment.

Sentiments and practices began to shift during the latter half of the Enlightenment period. Social conditions in Europe were improving, and the despotic actions of unelected officials were losing popularity (van Niekerk 2020, 1–10). Institutional reform was no longer a matter of regal decree but, instead, of legislative action. The physical, mental, and social welfare of the public became central for politicians, who were vying for the favor of the constituency (Spielvogel 2014, 489–90). The practices and punishments of the criminal justice system also came under scrutiny, and the public and those in positions of power alike began to question the morality and rationality of seemingly excessive and cruel acts of torture and execution (Foucault 1975, 7–16). Public critique of such practices, championed by several key reformers, would lead to the eventual decline of some of the more barbaric activities of the early Age of Reason.

Cesare Beccaria, Jeremy Bentham, and John Howard, all noted proponents of prison and punishment reform, were the primary instigators of punitive evolution in the latter half of the Enlightenment. Beccaria, a member of the intellectual and social elite, became one of the first outspoken advocates for the abolition of torture and capital punishment. In 1764, Beccaria published the treatise "On Crimes and Punishments," wherein he outlined his position, noting that prevention was a better method of reducing crime than retribution, torture was ineffectual, and state-sanctioned murder was counterintuitive. Beccaria's essay, originally written under a pseudonym for fear of state reprisal, gained popularity, inspiring others to publish similar written works.[6]

Bentham, also a vocal objector, offered similar arguments in his paper "The Rationale of Punishment." His rejection of physical punishments and executions is evident in how he chose to define such acts, as "an evil resulting to an individual from the direct intention of another, on account of some act that appears to have been done" (Bentham 1830, 2). Howard, on the other hand, offered a slightly different perspective, less concerned with torture and executions and more attentive to incarceration. As the sheriff of Bedfordshire, Howard had the opportunity to inspect prisons throughout Europe and was appalled by the conditions he encountered. Howard published his impressions in 1777 in "The State of the Prisons," providing in some detail such accounts of prisoner abuse, neglect, and corruption as to turn the stomach of even the highest authority. In Howard's own words, "In order to redress these various evils, the first thing to be taken into consideration is the Prison itself. Many County-Gaols and other Prisons are so decayed and ruinous, or, for other reasons, so totally unfit for the purpose, that new ones must be built in their stead" (Howard 1777, 40).

In addition to their prescriptions for criminal justice reform, Beccaria and Bentham were also early champions of modern deterrence theory (DiCristina, Gottschalk, & Mayzer 2014, 9–12). While others had alluded to the deterrent potential of punishment, these two served to formalize deterrence as a primary criminological philosophy. Their position regarding the causal connection between offending and punishment is captured in various well-read texts, providing a platform upon which to popularize the notion. Beccaria (1764), for example, posited: "the smaller the interval of time between the punishment and the crime, the stronger and more lasting will be the association of the two ideas of crime and punishment; so that they may be considered, one as the cause, and the other as the unavoidable and necessary effect" (12). In a similar vein, Bentham (1791) argued that the "expectation of the profit (pleasure)" served as "the impelling motive," while the "expectation of the punishment (pain)" served as "the restraining motive" (12). The collective intent and purpose behind these sentiments was the recognition that human nature was inherently hedonistic, driven to achieve pleasure and avoid pain. If applied strategically, the pain of punishment could outweigh the pleasure of deviance, thus serving to deter potential offenders.

The cumulative effects of the early reformers and deterrence enthusiasts were muted but persistent; justice practices that left prisoners suffering in county gaols and state prisons were suspect, subject to criticism and condemnation, and punishments without preventive and deterrent purposes lost popularity. Public officials had little choice but to consider shifts in punitive norms, leading to the introduction of new ideas.[7] According to Foucault (1975), "It was a new age for penal justice," a period during which using the body of an offender as the target for physical retribution was ended, replaced by the new practice of using the body as a medium through which the punishments, like the loss of liberty and suspension of rights, were conveyed (7). These ideas quickly gained traction as more and more public officials saw the benefits of such rhetoric in the political arena.

As punishments evolved over time, they also shifted over location. In the Americas, for example, most colonists hailed from England; however, due to the difficulties inherent in geopolitical separation, the colonists were "only required to 'establish laws not contrary to those in England'" (Blomberg & Lucken 2010, 11). This allowed a certain level of autonomy in the New World; undesirable or inappropriate laws were ignored, and punishments were selectively discarded based on their incompatibilities with the goals of the settlers. Instead, the colonies crafted a set of conditions and consequences that reflected their religious priorities and the unique environment within which they found themselves, where safety and order were of paramount concern.

Due to their circumstances, the colonists created a system of swift and severe reprimands. Fines, whipping, mutilation, banishment, and death were dominant, serving a retributive, deterrent, and defensive function. Rehabilitative sentiments were also present, but in a very limited capacity, specifically in the belief that deviants who sinned had the capacity for reformation and salvation. The fear of the unknown became prominent in punitive measures, as evident in the harsh treatment of outsiders and those accused of witchcraft. The latter was a carryover from the earlier witch craze in Europe, and it marked a particularly dark period in colonial history. Those suspected of engaging in witchcraft were placed in the pillory, flogged, branded, pricked, or hanged in a manner reminiscent of the Dark Ages (Donnelly & Diehl 2011, 95–123).[8]

Despite advancements in thought and reason during this era, the evolution of the criminal justice system was slow, clinging to retributive ideas even as those notions faded in popularity. However, outspoken reformers gradually moved the punitive pendulum away from a vengeance or a just deserts–based model. These same thinkers would lay the foundation that others would follow, eventually pushing the pendulum toward a path that would lead to incapacitation and rehabilitation.

THE 1800S AND A CENTURY OF REFORMS

As we near the end of our chronological journey, we shift to the nineteenth century, a brief period that held court to several significant eras, including the Scientific and Industrial Revolutions, the age of European imperialism and, in the United States, the Gilded Age. The world had developed a taste for modernization, not just in the sciences and technologies, but also in the theater of punishments. Following the sentiments of the Age of Reason, retribution began to lose its foothold, giving ground to the rehabilitative and incapacitative philosophies that had been but mere whispers in previous millennia. As societies grew aware of their status as communal amalgamations, they became more receptive to rational social health and well-being, sparking an active interest in using incapacitation as a reformative measure (Rafter 1997, 93–96; Spielvogel 2014, 506–7).

By the time the nineteenth century arrived, the horrific atrocities that had marked the previous era had faded, symbolically abolished throughout the Western world, at least as a spectacle to be celebrated in the public realm (Innes 2017, 157). Instead, the fields of psychology, psychiatry, sociology, and evolutionary science won the day, champions of the position that criminals suffered from a variety of ailments, advocating for a punitive model premised on reformation or treatment. Their efforts were rewarded with a new wave of institutions dedicated to the salvation of deviant bodies and minds. In the United States, for example, two unique methods of incapacitation began to take shape. The first was the Auburn System, originally introduced in 1823, so named in recognition of the Auburn Prison in New York. Prompted by the Puritan belief that criminals were intrinsically deficient in some respect, the Auburn System embraced the idea that reform was possible through unrelenting discipline, a vehicle by which to compel prisoners to obey social norms and mores (Roberts 1985, 106). Inmates were required to follow a regimented routine, including laboring in workshops and eating in communal dining halls, all the while keeping absolutely silent under the threat of flogging. This strict routine did have positive effects on inmate outcomes, although this was likely due more to the development of good work skills and habits and less to shifts in criminal thinking.

The second system of note was introduced in 1787, when liturgical and community leaders formed what has become known as the Pennsylvania System. This institutional system was premised on the Quaker belief that all humans held promise, bestowed with the "Inner Light of God's Grace" (Roberts 1985, 106). Solitary confinement was the lynchpin, removing the prisoner from temptation, allowing them the opportunity to contemplate their sins and repent, and alleviating further crime. By the mid-1800s, the Pennsylvania System had become standard practice, supported both socially and politically.

Other reformatories sprang up alongside the Auburn and Pennsylvania systems in the United States, driven by a similar conviction in the rehabilitative potential of structured incapacitation. The House of Refuge for juvenile delinquents opened in New York in 1824, followed shortly by a similar institution in Boston, both focused on providing trade skills and academic instruction (Rafter 1997, 96–97). Perhaps the most famous experiment, however, was the Elmira Reformatory, which opened in New York in 1876. Spearheaded by Superintendent Zebulon Brockway, Elmira relied on a regimented militaristic style of instruction and activity (Brockway 1870, 68–74). Prisoners were educated in tradecraft and scholastics, had access to various recreational and religious programs, but were also subjected to a merit-based system of advancement and regression that left many inmates stuck at the bottom of an institutional pecking order (Rafter 1997, 97–99). In addition, since Brockway was an advocate of indeterminate sentencing, the Elmira residents often languished behind prison walls much longer than they would have if given a set sentence.[9]

Brockway's use of the indeterminate sentence was in line with a larger trend that was sweeping the United States: the popularization of probation, which was billed as a form of community treatment. Parole boards became commonplace, serving as the final determinant of when an inmate was ready to reenter society. In keeping with the sentiments and practices of the time, the National Congress on Penitentiary and Reformatory Discipline declared that "the supreme aim of prison discipline is the reformation of criminals, concluding that "[s]entences limited only by satisfactory proof of reformation should be substituted for those measured by mere lapse of time" (Alschuler 2003, 3).

While the rehabilitative notions of the nineteenth century were taking root in the United States, another trend was unfurling overseas. The empirical aftermath of Darwin's theory of natural selection resounded across the criminological community in Western Europe, inspiring researchers to recast deviants as evolutionary throwbacks, physically and morally devolved. Led by Cesare Lombroso, this movement of criminal anthropologists paid credence to the rehabilitative potential of some offenders while also arguing that others were without hope of reformation, a group of unsalvageable ne'er-do-wells born into this world hardwired for deviance (Lombroso 1884, 161–66). For these unfortunate criminals, the only solution was incapacitation or execution.

Therefore, the age of reform was a motley array of institutional and punitive growth. The social and natural sciences invited an interest in the physical and mental morphology of the deviant human, adopting the position that deficits or defects could be addressed through structure and treatment. With the exception of Lombrosian speculation around criminal devolution, the theme of the century was a tribute to reformation leading to an array of fascinating and, at times, morally questionable practices. With some successes and some failures under its belt, the rehabilitative movement ushered in the twentieth century, ready to continue the reformative experiment.

MODERN-DAY RETRIBUTIVE REHABILITATION

The rehabilitative narrative and the reforms that accompanied it continued unchecked throughout the first half of the twentieth century. Meanwhile, incapacitation remained the punitive response of choice, a necessary measure for the isolation and treatment of offenders (Alschuler 2003, 6–9). As the century wore on, the punitive pendulum shifted a bit, weaving a familiar path back toward retribution, prompted in part by a loss of faith in the efficacy of the rehabilitation agenda (Martinson 1974, 22–23). Here it would waver indecisively before timidly backtracking toward rehabilitation. The close of the century would end in a muddle of conflicting punitive policies and practices, informed by both retributive and rehabilitative sentiments.

The twentieth century was a busy time for both criminologists and criminal justice practitioners. Regarding the former, Lombroso's criminal anthropology lost credibility, partly due to the harsh policy implications inherent in the "born criminal" narrative (DiChristina, Gottschalk, & Mayzer 2014, 14). He was quickly replaced by a new wave of research exploring the causes of criminality, spearheaded by the Gluecks, Sheldon, Eysenck, and others, focused in large part on the psychological and physical makeup of offenders and the continued rehabilitative potential of the criminal justice system (Walby & Carrier 2010, 273–75; DiChristina, Gottschalk, & Mayzer 2014, 14–16). Meanwhile, in the practitioner realm, Brockway fell from grace as his reformative agenda was revealed to be excessively harsh and unforgiving (State Board of Charities 1894, vi).[10] Despite this blow, reformation persisted until several factors took center stage, undermining the penal philosophy temporarily.

Rising crime rates in the latter half of the century prompted the scrutiny of punitive policies. Rehabilitation had claimed center stage for nearly a century, yet deviance continued unabated, seemingly impervious to state-sponsored interventions. This prompted a careful assessment of the efficacy of rehabilitative programming, one that resulted in the dismal claim that it was a lost cause, consuming state resources while failing to promote prosocial change (Martinson 1974, 48–50). Fear of crime, paired with a loss of faith in the rehabilitative ideal, paved the way for a retributive shift. States adopted policies and practices that were regimented, restrictive, and severe, informed by notions of social defence, deterence, and just deserts. The United States led the charge, where lengthy sentences, three-strike laws, and mandatory minimums drove the prison populations to new heights (Kleinfeld 2016, 938–39; Alschuler 1991, 929–31).

Rehabilitation experienced a resurgence in popularity in the wake of mass incarceration near the end of the century, particularly in European nations. Moving away from the warehousing model that had gained a notable foothold in the United States, European governments focused on reintegration instead. As such, offenders experienced a marked reduction in sentence length and severity, replaced with innovative policies and programs. Norway, for example, focused on professional development, teaching incarcerated populations various trades, such as plumbing and cooking (Materni 2013, 293). The maximum allotted sentence was set at twenty-one years, a stark contrast to the life imprisonment practiced by the United States. Germany provided another ready example of a shift from retribution; in 1977, the Federal Constitutional Court ruled that a sentence of life without parole violated the constitutionally protected principle of human dignity (Kleinfeld 2016, 951). Meanwhile, Australian criminologist John Braithwaite advocated for a shift to a restorative philosophy, a justice orientation rooted in the idea of offender responsibility, making amends, facilitating forgiveness, and the active involvement of all affected parties to achieve resolution (Braithwaite 1999, 5–6). Although still a fledgling addition to the punitive palate, the restorative philosophy has gained prominence in several Western nations, reshaping state responses to deviance.

We end the twentieth century and begin the twenty-first century in a state of eclectic punitive policy. Rehabilitation, retribution, deterrence, incapacitation, and restoration compete for center stage, each winning favor in one region or another. However, this will likely change as more empirical data become available, shaping public opinions and political practices. As we enter an evidence-based era of punishment, the costs and benefits of any given policy will be subject to scrutiny, determining the popularity and longevity of its existence, likely to send the pendulum in new (and old) directions.

CONCLUSION

As we find ourselves at the end of our narrative, we can look back on the previous pages and reflect on the punitive oscillations that we bear witness to through the lens of history. Both across and within each era, punishments were oftentimes unpredictable, irrational, and barbaric. However, they also held some element of consistency, aligning themselves with the philosophical orientation that was popular at the time.

While a retributive approach dominated in the early eras, this was eventually offset with an interest in deterrence, rehabilitation, incapacitation, and more recently, restoration. Sometimes working in concert, other times at odds, these philosophies served as a master to the punitive marionette. A brief summary of the pages of this chapter illustrates this point.

Our foray in history began in Mesopotamia, the birthplace of modern civilization. This region set the stage for subsequent eras, as rulers explored the codification of deviance and sanctification of punishment, proposing a retributive approach that would remain influential for subsequent generations. Greek antiquity would adopt this thread, weaving it through its city-states, allowing it to shape and inform each regional code of deviance. Although reprisal remained at the heart of the Greek approach, they would temper their practices, attempting to prioritize justice over personal vengeance. The Roman Empire would follow suit, employing a retributive stance on punishment, but formalizing it to reflect social and political stratification, levying punishments informed by citizenship, social status, and gender. Despite variations in approach and practice across Mesopotamian, Greek, and Roman empires, retributive justice remained central, often leading to harsh and violent outcomes.

The Middle Ages followed on the heels of the fall of the Roman Empire, denoting a remarkable shift in our understanding of deviance and punishment. The Church and Crown engaged in a fitful relationship, oftentimes at odds as each battled for supremacy over the social body and soul. The Church posited that deviance was an expression of sin, often the mark of supernatural influences, and thus that punishments should be used as a penance, cleansing the sinner of evil. The Crown, on the other hand, paid allegiance to the retributive stance of previous eras, although this was tempered with some suggestions of reform, perhaps as a means to distance itself from the cruelty of its Roman predecessors. Despite philosophical differences, the ecclesiastical and secular responses to deviance were comparably unpleasant, leading to injury, disfigurement, and death.

The Age of Enlightenment marked the end of a thousand years of medieval punishments. Although slow to adapt, the system of punishments eventually reflected the advancements seen in other areas of society. Public sentiment concerning the treatment of offenders held sway, influencing perceptions of punishment as oftentimes unnecessary or excessive. As a result, retribution shifted to deterrence, followed by rehabilitation, offering a diversity of approaches that had not been evident before this time. This softened approach carried into the nineteenth century, as rehabilitation took center stage, paired with an odd bedfellow, incapacitation. Deviance was recast as an ailment, eligible for treatment in the right conditions. Reformers argued that these conditions could be found in the prison system, giving rise to an era of incarceration and a variety of incapacitative systems, including the solitude-and-work approach of the Auburn and Pennsylvania systems, as well as merit-based reformatories, such as Elmira. Although these punitive systems experienced several failures, the allegiance to incapacitation and rehabilitation continued, although shifting public and political sentiment ensured that neither would take priority for any notable length of time.

As we enter a new century, we bear witness to the rise of another philosophy, one that has been present since the beginning of humankind but notably absent from the punitive palate until now: the philosophy of restoration. Although still new to Western civilization, the restorative approach offers tentative promise of yet another shift in our understanding of crime and punishment. Perhaps we will rid ourselves of the dark and macabre practices of the past, embracing an approach that prioritizes addressing and resolving harm. Or, if history is any metric, this may simply signal another brief moment of exploration, one that will eventually subside as the Western world falls back into the familiar world of cruel and unusual punishments.

NOTES

1. In the United States, for example, some offenders are required to dress in seemingly garish outfits while removing trash in public spaces. These outfits may include an explicit shaming aspect, such as clothing male offenders in gender-atypical colors (pink).

2. To ensure that everyone understood all 282 of his laws and their respective punishments, King Hammurabi had them carved into stone columns, which were then erected in major cities of his empire. Hammurabi's Code is notable for the protections granted to women, such as protection from rape and no-fault divorces. If a man was found to be guilty of sexual assault, the punishment was castration (Donnelly & Diehl 2011, 30–31).

3. One device of torture and death was the Brazen Bull, a hollow life-sized bronze bull into which an offender was forced via a trapdoor. Once the offender was securely inside, a large fire was lit under the belly of the bull, slowly roasting the trapped individual. The screams of the victim would be broadcast through a series of pipes, sounding much like the mournful lowing of a living bull (Innes 2017, 17).

4. One particularly interesting sentence was the *culleus*; offenders found guilty of killing a close relative were placed in a sack with an ape, a dog, and a serpent, before being thrown into the sea (Peters 1995, 15).

5. Church-prescribed penance and contrition soon led to the development of *indulgences*, in effect, a way to pay for one's sins without enduring punishment (Lindsay 1906, 236–39).

6. Within eighteen months of its original publication date, *On Crimes and Punishments* had been translated into twenty-two languages (Donnelly & Diehl 2011, 130).

7. One example of reform is found in Bentham's *Panopticon* or *inspection house*, a custodial building designed to increase surveillance of both residents and guards for the purposes of accountability (Bentham 1791, 4–14).

8. Suspected witches could be subjected to the *peine forte et dure*, or pressing to plead. The accused was laid on their back with arms and legs drawn tight with cords. Weights made of lead, iron, or stone were stacked upon their body, in effect "pressing" a confession from the subject. This tactic could also serve as a punishment as the recipient would literally be pressed to death by the weight of their deserts (Donnelly & Diehl 2011, 12, and 59–60).

9. The rehabilitative trend extended to other parts of the world, as well. At a British penal colony in Australia, for example, Alexander Maconochie implemented a point system designed to incentivize prisoners to reform; prisoners at Botany Bay who behaved themselves (and abstractly worked toward salvation) could earn their freedom if they acquired enough points (Stearns 1936, 227).

10. Zebulon Brockway's Elmira Reformatory opened with a much-lauded moral purpose: offender reform through a merit-based system. However, it soon devolved into a veritable torture chamber, as slight infractions were met with severe and injurious punishments. Prisoners were "manacled by the hand to a sliding ring on a bar on the wall, or to a ring in the floor, both day and night, so that they can not stand upright" or received beatings with a "heavy leather strap one foot ten inches long . . . affixed to a strong hickory handle" (The State Board of

Charities 1894, xi, & xiv). Over a five-year period, more than a thousand inmates were beaten in this manner at Elmira. In 1894, Brockway was found guilty of inhumane treatment, torture, and degradation; however, he remained the warden of Elmira until 1900.

REFERENCES

Alexander, Julian P. 1922. "Philosophy of Punishment." *Journal of Criminal Law and Criminology* 13, no. 2 (August): 235–50. https://doi.org/10.2307/1133492.

Allen, Danielle S. 2000. "What Is Punishment?" In *The World of Prometheus: The Politics of Punishing in Democratic Athens*, edited by Danielle Allen, 15–38. Princeton: Princeton University Press.

Alschuler, Alber W. 1991. "The Failure of Sentencing Guide Lines: A Plea for Less Aggregation." *Federal Sentencing Reporter* 4, no. 3 (November): 161–65. https://doi.org/10.2307/20639434.

Alschuler, Albert W. 2003. "The Changing Purpose of Criminal Punishment: A Retrospective on the Past Century and Some Thoughts about the Next." *University of Chicago Law Review* Volume 70, no. 1 (Winter): 1–22. https://doi.org/10.2307/1600541.

Beccaria, Cesare. 1764. *An Essay on Crime and Punishments*. Translated by Edward D. Ingraham. Albany: W.C. Little & Company.

Bentham, Jeremy. 1791. *Panopticon or the Inspection-House: Containing the Idea of a New Principle of Construction Applicable to Any Sort of Establishment in Which Persons of Any Description Are to Be Kept Under Inspection: And in Particular to Penitentiary-Houses Prisons Houses of Industry . . . and Schools: With a Plan of Management Adapted to the Principle: In a Series of Letters Written in the Year 1787*. London: T. Payne.

Bentham, Jeremy. 1830. *The Rational of Punishment*. London: Robert Heward.

Blomberg, Thomas, and Karol Lucken. 2010. *American Penology—A History of Control*. Piscataway: Transaction Publishers.

Braithwaite, John. 1999. "Restorative Justice: Assessing Optimistic and Pessimistic Accounts." *Crime and Justice* 25: 1–127. http://www.jstor.org/stable/1147608.

Brians, Paul. 1998. "The Enlightenment." The Website of Prof. Paul Brians. https://brians.wsu.edu/2016/10/12/the-enlightenment/.

Brockway, Zebulon R. 1870. "The Ideal of a True Prison System for a State." *Journal of Correctional Education* 46, no. 2 (June): 68–74. https://www.jstor.org/stable/23292027.

DiChristina, Bruce, Martin Gottschalk, and Roni Mayzer. 2014. "Four Currents of Criminological Thought." In *The Routledge Handbook of International Crime and Justice Studies*, edited by Bruce A. Arrigo and Heather Y. Bersot, 9–32. Oxford: Routledge.

Donnelly, Mark P., and Daniel Diehl. 2011. *The Big Book of Pain—Torture & Punishment Through History*. Cheltenham: The History Press.

Foucault, Michel. 1977. *Dicipline & Punish—The Birth of the Prison*. Translated by Alan Sheridan. New York: Pantheon Books.

Freeman, Charles. 2014. *Egypt, Greece, & Rome: Civilizations of the Ancient Mediterraneian*. Oxford: Oxford University Press.

Hammurabi. –2250. *The Code of Hammurabi*. Chicago: University of Chicago Press.

Howard, John. 1777. *The State of Prisons in England and Wales with Preliminary Observations, and an Account of Some Foriegn Prisons*. Warrington: Printed by William Eyres.

Innes, Brian. 2017. *The History of Torture*. London: Amber Books.

Johns, Claude H. W. 1911. *The Oldest Code of Laws in the World: The Code of Laws Promulgated by Hammurabi, King of Babylon, B.C. 2285–2242*. Translated by C. H. W. Johns. Edinburgh: T. & T. Clark.

Kleinfeld, Joshua. 2016. "Two Cultures of Punishment." *Stanford Law Review* 68, no. 5 (May): 933–1036. https://www.stanfordlawreview.org/wp-content/uploads/sites/3/2016/06/68_Kleinfeld_-_Stan._L._Rev._933.pdf.

Lindsay, Thomas M. 1906. *A History of the Reformation.* Edinburgh: T. & T. Clark.

Lombroso, Cesare. 1884. *Criminal Man.* Translated by Mary Gibson and Nicole Hahn Rafter. Durham: Duke University Press.

Martinson, Robert. 1974. "What Works?—Questions and Answers about Prison Reform." *Public Interest* 35 (Spring): 22–54.

Materni, Mike C. 2013. "Criminal Punishment and the Pursuit of Justice." *British Journal of American Legal Studies* 2, no. 1 (April): 263–304.

New York State Board of Social Welfare. 1894. "Report and Proceedings of the State Board of Charities Relative to the Management of the State Reformatory at Elmira, Transmitted to the Legislature, March 19, 1894." *State of New York* 89: i–xlii. Albany: James B. Lyon, State Printer. http://www.archive.org/details/cu31924024885067.

Peters, Edward M. 1995. "Prison Before the Prison—The Ancient and Medieval Worlds." In *The Oxford History of the Prison—The Practice and Punishment in Western Society*, edited by Norval Morris and David J. Rothman, 3–45. Oxford: Oxford University Press.

Plato. 399 BCE "Crito." Translated by Cathal Woods and Ryan Pack. Crito. Last modified January 26, 2022. https://papers.ssrn.com/sol3/papers.cfm?abstract_id=1023145.

Rafter, Nicole Hahn. 1997. *Creating Born Criminals.* Champaign: University of Illinois Press.

Reeves, Andrew. 2016. "Western Europe and Byzantium circa 500–1000 CE." In *World History: Cultures, States, and Societies to 1500*, edited by Eugene Berger, George L. Israel, Charlotte Miller, Brian Parkinson, Andrew Reeves, and Nadejda Williams, 266–95. Dahlonega: University of North Georgia Press.

Roberts, Leonard H. 1985. "The Historic Roots of American Prison Reform: A Story of Progess and Failure." *Journal of Correctional Education* 36, no. 3 (September): 106–09. https://www.jstor.org/stable/41970789.

Roth, Martha T. 1995. *Law Collections from Mesopotamia and Asia Minor*, edited by Piotr Michalowski. Atlanta: Scholars Press.

Spielvogel, Jackson. 2014. "The Eighteenth Century: An Age of Enlightenment." In Jackson Spielvogel, *Western Civilization: volume B: 1300–1815*, 486–515. Stamford: Cengage Learning.

Stearns, A. Warren. 1936. "Evolution of Punishment." *Journal of Criminal Law and Criminology* 27, no. 2 (January): 219–230. https://scholarlycommons.law.northwestern.edu/jclc/vol27/iss2/8.

Steele, Francis R. 1947. "The Lipit-Ishtar Law Code." *American Journal of Archaeology* 51, no. 2 (April): 158–64. https://doi.org/10.2307/500752.

Urch, Erwin J. 1929. "The Law Code of Hammurabi." *American Bar Association Journal* 15, no. 7 (July): 437–441. https://www.jstor.org/stable/25707711.

Van Niekerk, Frederik. 2020. "Reformation and Scientific Revolution: Historical Coincidence or Continual Renewal?" In die Skriflig /In Luce Verbi 54, no. 2 (March): 1–12. https://doi.org/10.4102/ids.v54i2.2538.

Walby, Kevin, and Nicolas Carrier. 2010. "The Rise of Biocriminology: Capturing Observable Bodily Economies of 'Criminal Man'." *Criminology & Criminal Justice*, 10, no. 3 (July): 261–85. https://doi.org/10.1177/1748895810370314.

Wenzel, Michael, and Tyler G. Okimoto. 2016. "Retributive Justice." In *Handbook of Social Justice Theory and Research*, edited by Clara Sabbagh and Manfred Schmitt, 237–56. New York: Springer Science+Business Media.

Williams, Nadejda. 2016. "The Greek World from the Bronze Age to the Roman Conquest." In *World History—Cultures, States, and Societies to 1500*, edited by Eugene Berger, George L.

Israel, Charlotte Miller, Brian Parkinson, Andrew Reeves, and Nadejda Williams, 171–216. Dahlonega: University of North Georgia Press.

Williams, Nadejda. 2016. "The Roman World from 753 BCE to 500 CE." *World History—Cultures, States, and Societies to 1500*, edited by Eugene Berger, George L. Israel, Charlotte Miller, Brian Parkinson, Andrew Reeves, and Nadejda Williams, 217–265. Dahlonega: University of North Georgia Press.

Winther-Jensen, Thyge. 2019. "The Reformation as a Religious, Political, and Educational Project." *Spanish Journal of Comparative Education* 33 (January): 106–21. https://doi.org /10.5944/reec.33.2019.22329.

World History Project. n.d. "The Reforms of Urukagina." Accessed April 26, 2022. https:// web.archive.org/web/20181117032017/http://history-world.org/reforms_of_urukagina.htm.

Zehr, Howard. 2015. "The Little Book of Restorative Justice." In *The Big Book of Restorative Justice*, edited by Lorraine Stutzman Amstutz, Allan MacRae, Kay Pranis, and Howard Zehr, 30–54. New York: Good Books.

Chapter 2

Policing through the Ages

Omi Hodwitz and William Jansen

INTRODUCTION

May 2020 was a social and political flashpoint in the history of the United States. George Floyd, an African American man, was immobilized by police officers on a public street in Minneapolis, and while laid out and begging for his life, he was killed by the weight of the officer kneeling on his neck. The backlash was immediate. Public ire ignited, leading to anti-police protests throughout the country and other Western nations. "Defund the Police" became a rallying cry, and law enforcement officers were targeted publicly and privately, reflecting an escalation in negative sentiment. Municipalities began to look critically at available resources, and some executed a redistribution of funds prioritizing social services over law enforcement. These changes were implemented alongside public protest and violence, making it difficult to assess the consequences of such modifications. The possible effects of curtailing law enforcement capabilities seemed to take second place to appeasing the public, a sign that the historical purposes and intentions of policing were temporarily forgotten or overshadowed.

This period of high emotionality was unsustainable, subsiding within the next year or two, leaving the political, professional, and intellectual communities with the task of disentangling the causes and consequences of the flashpoint. This is not an easy assignment, as understanding the present also requires an understanding of the past. To assess uncertainty around policing in modern times, we must look critically at how policing practices have formed and developed across the generations. The following pages attempt such a feat, providing an overview of the early roots of policing and tracing them throughout the eras to modern times.

Where do the early roots of policing begin? If we were to pick up a traditional textbook on policing, it would most likely focus on the nineteenth century, a time during which the policing systems that we know today were first introduced. However, this assumes a very narrow definition of policing, one that focuses on upholding the law. Instead, we invite the reader to broaden their understanding of this concept to one that includes the practice of preventing social harm, surveilling the population, and/or securing property and people. This allows us to reframe policing as the regulation of social norms, thus predating the protection of codified state laws and formal enforcement regiments.

With this new definition in hand, this chapter breaks rank with traditional textbooks, opting to pick up the policing thread several thousands of years ago, recognizing that the regulation of social harm existed long before the nineteenth century. We begin by exploring the rudimentary beginnings of policing in the pre-Grecian era, tracing it from its inception through to the complex mechanism of social control it is today (Pender 2016). Although not exhaustive in its descriptions, the chapter will offer a summary of key historical systems that illustrate the stepping stones leading to modern-day policing.

ANCIENT GREECE AND ROME

The world prior to the establishment of Greek law was savage in many ways. *Lex talionis*, or *an eye for an eye*, blood feuds, and vendettas were commonplace, and retaliation for a perceived wrong was more a matter of honor than of justice (Cantarella 2004). The ferocity of this era did not go unchecked, however, and herein we see evidence of the first measures of policing.

Reportedly, Egypt made the first attempt at organizing public security sometime around 3000 BCE, but the finer details of this entity are, like much of early human history, lost in the sands of time (Pender 2016). The role of policing was most likely considered part of the duties of the military and the personal protective forces of local warlords or rulers. Other forms of law, such as the Law of Moses, were transgressions against God's law (divine law), not state law, and thus, religious leaders policed their own congregations (Moses 600 BCE, as cited by Thomas Nelson Publishers 1990, 1–165).

Ancient Greece

Primitive approaches to policing were eventually supplanted as Greco-Roman civilization developed and expanded. Approximately 621–620 BCE, Greece's central city of Athens introduced the *Court of Areopagus* and *Draco's Code*, providing the first opportunity for official mechanisms of policing (Hunter 1994; Pender 2016).[1] These directives replaced the archaic oral laws and systems built on *lex talionis*, offering instead a codified systems of rules, regulations, and practices in its place. Part of these revisions included the designation of public officials to the position of *magistrates*.[2] These individuals served an array of functions, ranging from ensuring the cleanliness and upkeep of the city, through to overseeing public arbitration. Among their duties, however, were those linked to policing the public, including keeping order, security, and crime prevention.

The formalization of the role of the magistrate was but one aspect of the new codes. Under the Athenian system, it was no longer the sole responsibility of the affected party to seek remuneration for losses, though private initiative, also known as self-help, was still required for immediate action, such as when detaining a thief (Cantarella 2004). Instead, this responsibility was shared by the state, although enforcement was ill-defined. To address the issue, the city purchased three hundred *Scythian* slaves and deployed them in a manner reflective of crime prevention policing (Hunter 1994; Phillips 2013).[3] As slaves, they held very limited authority, acting only when ordered. Some of their tasks included standing guard in public meetings as a means of crowd control and order maintenance, pursuing escaped prisoners, or aiding in arrest procedures.

The Athenian public also shared policing responsibilities with the state and the victims. They were known to engage in spontaneous policing, organizing a group of acquaintances or passersby to conduct an arrest or bear witness to an event (Hunter 1994). When the public chose to make an arrest, they would transfer control of the accused to the magistrates, temporarily donning and then casting off the symbolic cloak of agent of the state.

Apart from the system of individual initiative, there was also the *ephegesis* method, which involved reporting an offense to the magistrates and appealing to them to make an arrest (Hunter 1994; Phillips 2013). The reporting citizen would lead the magistrates to the location of the purported offender, where, under the authority of the reporting citizen, the accused would be detained. This was the preferred method of arrest for those lacking a strong familial or social support system. Unfortunately, this method was ripe for abuse, and before long, it became a common practice among fraudsters, who would accuse others or threaten to report them, for the purposes of personal gain.

Although the system of legal enforcement was effective in many respects, it also had the potential for failure. A particularly intriguing case study illustrates the Athenian process of upholding the law while also highlighting the shortcomings of the system. Theophemus, a former *trierarch*, retained some of the State's property used in his duties after he was removed from the position (Christ 1998; Hunter 1994).[4] Theophemus was declared a debtor of the State, and the incoming trierarch was charged with recovering the State's assets. The court ordered that the equipment be returned, and though attempts were made to appeal to Theophemus for the property, he refused to comply. The new trierarch, accompanied by a public slave, went to Theophemus's house to confront him and demand the return of the state's property. An argument ensued, and the new trierarch attempted to physically force his way into Theophemus's house to seize Theophemus's personal property as security. Despite the subsequent physical altercation, he was rebuffed and left empty-handed. Because of the violence upon his person and household, Theophemus filed suit against the trierarch for damages and won. The new trierarch now owed Theophemus, and he still was unable to collect on equipment he initially sought to recover.

The Greek systems of law and policing were far from perfect: however, they were revolutionary for their time. By moving away from the oral laws and traditions and toward codification, those in positions of authority and governance were better able to manage the citizenry. In addition, the legal framework established by the Court of Areopagus and Draco's Code laid the foundation for subsequent systems, such as Rome's system of law, which closely emulated the Grecian system.

Ancient Rome

Unlike many other pre-industrial societies, the Romans limited the use of their standing army to maintain public order (Nippel 1984). It is unlikely the imperial authorities kept order in the empire at large using any formalized policing method, but within the city of Rome, several tactics were implemented to prevent crime and ensure the safety of the community (Kelly 2013). Like Greece, Rome utilized the office of magistrate, whose primary role was to oversee public order.[5] Three minor magistrates, the *tres-viri capitals*, took on a more traditional policing role, performing many duties, which included carrying out preliminary inquiries, investigating crimes, and overseeing the prison and executions.

As Rome grew and the need for order became more pressing, the office of *prefect* was created; this was the enforcement arm of the magistrates, and it performed various policing duties throughout the city (Reynolds 1928; Nippel 1984; Kelly 2013). The *urban prefect* was responsible for public order and could employ soldiers to perform basic policing duties, such as patrolling the city during public events to discourage muggers from preying on those attending. The *prefect of the vigiles* managed a paramilitary force aptly named the *vigiles*, whose responsibilities included conducting night patrols and extinguishing fires (Africa 1971). The vigiles held criminal jurisdiction over common crimes, such as burglary, theft, arson, and harboring those who committed these crimes. They could mete out minor corporal punishment for these offenses, unless the offense was particularly serious or the offender had a notorious reputation, in which case the *praetorian prefect* held jurisdiction and would take the offender into custody. The vigiles also had officials specifically tasked with arresting, interrogating, and incarcerating suspected criminals.

The magistrate/prefect system of order was not without flaws. There were periods during which conscriptions were low, and agents of the state were too few to effectively police the population of hundreds of thousands (Kelly 2013). In addition, virtually no mechanism for accountability existed for the forces policing the city, which led to corruption and abuse. There were incidents during which, instead of assisting the public, the praetorian and the vigiles would loot the city. There is also evidence some forces ran protection rackets, which targeted thieves and gamesters, as well as religious minorities such as early Christians and Jews.

Faced with corrupt or deficient state control, the public employed their own version of community policing, creating innovative methods of popular justice. A particularly unique example was *occentare*, or the act of singing a defamatory song or chanting in front of an offending person's home, thus drawing public attention to their misdeeds (Schisas 1926; Kelly 2013).[6] Another popular method of identifying offenders was *flagitatio*, or the practice of confronting a person in public, shouting at them, and demanding property.[7] *Flagitium*, a more violent form of community policing, involved dragging accused offenders from their homes and flogging them while their houses were set on fire and left to burn to the ground. A bizarre example of popular justice was the practice of *squalor*; a person who felt wronged would wander around in public dressed in rags looking generally disheveled, with the sole intent of casting odium on an offending person. The final example of popular justice, and in all probability the most used, was the practice of *implorare quiritum fidem*, which translates literally "to call upon the good faith of the citizens" (Kelly 2013, 417). This referred to the act of petitioning neighbors or passersby for aid during a robbery or attack.

Lacking contrary evidence, scholars suggest that crime rates were high and instances of violence were commonplace in Rome (Africa 1971; Kelly 2013). Safety and order were more the product of individuals' ability to provide protection for themselves and less an attribute of the strength of state policing agents or community policing efforts. By law, one could use lethal force to guard self and property, and those with resources would travel with slaves or hired hands charged with their safety. Those without means utilized more mundane measures, such as barricading doors and windows at night to prevent burglary and carrying weapons to defend themselves against assault. The evidence suggests that, despite Rome's grand splendor and lofty ideas, policing was sparse, and the citizens bore the consequences.

THE MIDDLE AGES

With the fall of the Western Roman Empire during the late fifth century CE, and the subsequent withdrawal of the occupying Roman military forces, Europe was in a state of flux, forming new countries and kingdoms and lacking centralized authority (Hanawalt & Wallace 1999). When it came to matters of crime prevention and community safety, family honor once again took center stage. In many ways, this could be viewed as social regression; fledgling state enforcement was replaced with archaic blood feuds and retributive factions. Before long, however, new systems of law, such as *early Germanic law*, were introduced and formalized, bringing much-needed order to the early Middle Ages. [8] [9]

Early Germanic law was just the beginning of medieval developments. Over the next thousand years, the role of policing shifted a great deal, reflecting social and political sentiments of the time and cultural and practical realities of various Western regions. For example, in the early Middle Ages, it was initially part of a ruling lord's responsibilities to police the lands under his charge (Summerson 1979). A lord would appoint one of his vassals, possibly a knight, to maintain peace and order on his private lands. As for public lands, the *tithingman, sheriff* (shire reeve), and *keeper of the peace* were created to enforce laws and punishments. These early agents were few in number, and their responsibilities were limited. They primarily focused on mediation and punishment rather than daily crime prevention, relying instead on the threat of hanging or beheading to deter those contemplating nefarious activities. If the need arose, however, agents had the authority to hunt down dangerous, threatening, or infamous offenders plaguing local communities (Harding 1960).

The Middle Dark Ages marked further shifts in social control and policing. The lords or barons and the sheriffs retained responsibility for maintaining the peace through to the end of the reign of King Stephen of Blois of England (1135–1154) [Backman 2003]. By 1170, however, due to misconduct and abuse of power, King Henry II sacked all the sheriffs in the realm and established a code of law, known as the *English Common Law*, which applied to all citizens not of noble birth.[10] He also introduced the *Assize of Clarendon* in 1166 CE, which made it possible for anyone who had knowledge of a crime to bring forth charges.[11] Prior to this, only the victim or the state could initiate charges. A further development was the creation of the English *constable*; these were unpaid individuals appointed locally to keep order. The French had a similar position known as *sergeants*, but in contrast to their English counterparts, they received pay for exercising their duties (Dean 2019).

During the thirteenth century, the Italians followed the French example, creating the position of the local *podestà*, who would utilize his personal entourage and hire local personnel to perform policing duties (Dean 2019).[12] These personnel, governed by a set of rules and requirements, ensured a more organized policing force. In the fourteenth and fifteenth centuries, the Italians expanded their policing mechanisms further by contracting foreign police forces, known as the *berroarrii*, or simply *birri* in modern terms. Over time, the birri became an organized uniformed force within many Italian cities. There were, however, difficulties with the foreign birri, including language barriers, cultural differences, and a general lack of local knowledge, and this hindered the integration of the birri and compromised their effectiveness.

While Italy was expanding its police force, England was formalizing local mechanisms of social control, including the creation of the *hundred court* (Brundage 1998; Morris 1910).[13] Presided over by the keepers of the peace or local officials, the court would meet regularly to hear grievances and serve as mediators (Summerson 1979). Community members were also required to report crimes and identify potential criminals to the court, with harsh punishments for failing to report offenses, especially if a community was harboring an alleged criminal. Since criminals moved frequently to avoid capture, these meetings also served as a forum to disseminate information about offenders, including physical descriptions and modes of operation, thus limiting the likelihood that rogue deviants could find refuge, support, resources, and potential targets.

The hundred court also maintained the *Frankpledge system*. Implemented in various regions across England, the Frankpledge system required men above the age of twelve to form groups known as tithings (Liddy 2016). Each tithing was responsible for policing the behavior of its own members, by detecting and reporting any deviance or nefarious behavior to the hundred court. This tactic forced the community to become "a neighborhood of voluntary spies" (Summerson 1979, 317). Although it had the potential for abuse, membership of a tithe was a badge of respect within the community, and typically, the members of a tithe were from the same family or social circle. Thus, when a person within a tithe committed a crime against others, it was akin to committing the crime against those they held dear, turning this form of self-policing into an effective deterrent.

The tithing system did have its flaws. If a member committed a crime and avoided capture, the rest of the group was held accountable and fined for the offender's behavior (Morris 1910; Summerson 1979). However, it was not unheard of to have members of the tithe collaborate with an offender to conceal a crime or allay suspicion, especially if the offense benefited the group or the offender held favor within the group (Taylor 2010). As a punishment for collaboration, tithe members faced fines, loss of property, or in extreme cases, banishment. Fines and loss of property were difficult for the poorer members of the community; however, banishment was particularly harsh, as the banished no longer benefited from the safety and security of the community, becoming pariahs condemned to wander alone.

Although tithings were popular, they were not absolute, and other forms of community policing supplemented or replaced tithings in some regions of England. An interesting example of medieval community policing is evident in local businesses.

Taverns or inns had the potential to experience high rates of crime, and the responsibility of maintaining order lay not with the state or the tithing, but instead, with the taverner or innkeeper. Maintaining control of their own clientele and keeping the peace within their place of business fell to these entrepreneurs (Liddy 2016). They were also responsible for informing their patrons of the laws of the area and providing protection to the patrons who were frequenting their business (Hanawalt & Wallace 1999).

The hundred court, tithings, and community policing were a direct tribute to the compartmentalized nature of medieval communities. Villages in the Middle Ages were very insular, harboring deep suspicions about strangers and their intentions (Gorski 2009). Every village employed watchmen who held the specific task of detecting threatening or untrustworthy outsiders and taking them into custody (Summerson 1979). This practice was especially critical during the summer months, when the dispossessed wandered from community to community seeking employment. It was against the law for a stranger to stay for more than one night in a village unless the host was willing to take responsibility for the stranger, including seeking pledges or references attesting to the stranger's good behavior. Over time, this decree loosened to allow for the employ of strangers during harvesttime; however, access to the community was restricted to daylight hours, and strangers were forced to leave before nightfall. If a member of the community observed a stranger violating these parameters, they could raise the hue, calling out to the members of the community for assistance during a time of crisis.

Once a person was accused of a crime, whether it was through tithing or other forms of community policing, that person was required to prove themself innocent (Summerson 1979). Sometimes the accusation was simple hearsay, lacking evidence and corroboration, but despite the potential veracity of the accusation, the responsibility still fell on the accused to provide evidence of their innocence. If agents of the courts were unable to take a person into custody, the accused was required to appear and stand trial at the hundred court gathering. The suspect was deemed guilty and declared an outlaw if they failed to report for four consecutive gatherings, and their name, physical description, and a list of their alleged offenses were circulated to other communities. They were considered "wolves heads," meaning it was legal to kill them on sight if an arrest was not possible (Coyle 2005).

The heavily romanticized medieval outlaw lifestyle promised implicit freedom from repressive societal rules, with idealized tributes found in poems, ballads, songs, and fictional writings (Harding 1960).[14] This nostalgic view carried over into modern popular culture, as tales of Robin Hood recast the villain as the hero. The concept of a noble-born outlaw stealing from the rich and giving to the poor combined just the right amount of compassion for the peasantry with a flagrant disregard for an authoritarian ruling class (Bellamy 1964). Unfortunately, these stories were based on the deeds of real outlaws, such as the Coterels, who plagued the English countryside in the fourteenth century, engaging in murder, extortion, kidnapping, and protection rackets (Coyle 2005; Gregory-Abbot 2009). In contrast to the empathetic outlaw from popular fiction, these criminal groups were a legitimate problem for the population and for law enforcement, forcing them to expend considerable time, money, and effort in the attempt to apprehend these glorified folk heroes.

The pursuit and capture of outlaws became a point of contention between the secular state and ecclesiastical powers (Coyle 2005). It was not unheard of for an outlaw to seek refuge, sanctuary, protection, and provisions within a church (Gregory-Abbot 2009). This created a means of escape as agents of the state were not permitted to pursue a suspect onto church property once sanctuary had been granted. Instead of continuing the chase, pursuers stood watch outside the church until the accused surrendered, slipped away from the area, or chose to abjure.[15] There are records indicating that, in some instances, agents of the state had no choice but to keep watch for weeks and, in one such case, agents of the Crown maintained a post outside the Berkshire Church for fourteen weeks before the thief absconded (Summerson 1979).

Despite the conflicting interests of granting sanctuary, the actions of the secular state often supported ecclesiastical mandates (Backman 2003). This concept was ratified at *The Concordat of Worms* in 1122, and is often referred to as the *Two Swords* theory.[16] The theory asserts that God created both the secular and ecclesiastical governing bodies with the intention of harmonious cooperation. The collaborative expectations of the Two Swords theory are not without merit; they can be found in number of medieval policing endeavors, including the Inquisitions. During the dark days of witch hunts and heresy, papal edict charged Catholic sects with the pursuit and punishment of those believed to have broken God's law. The alleged heretical targets included Christians who belonged to non-Catholic sects, Jews, pagans, and those accused of witchcraft (Pavlac 2009). As a measure of reciprocity, the Church garnered the favor and support of several kingdoms and their secular heads, including the king of France and the king of Spain, who benefited politically from their involvement.

The practice of identifying and punishing heretics and witches illustrates not only the Two Swords theory, but also that social control was a matter for both the Crown and the Church. While the State implemented its own systems of control, including tithings, the hundred court, and other forms of systematic surveillance and enforcement, the Church relied on the Inquisition to police the population. Over time, these ecclesiastical measures of control became quite formalized and far-spread. Bernard Gui, arguably the most famous medieval Inquisitor, provides a ready example of formalized Church control. He authored the *Practica Inquisitionis Heretice Pravitatis* (The Practice of the Inquisition of Heretical Depravity), which outlined the major forms of heresy, for the purposes of identification and prosecution (Bailey 2006). His work also briefly covered the topics of sorcery, divination, and demonic invocation. This tome became the central source for the detection of violations of Church mandates and led to the capture and interrogation of accused heretics and witches. Though initially not sanctioned by the Church, confessions (many of which were likely false) were obtained through torture, coercion, and threat, resulting in summary executions of the guilty using methods such as hanging, boiling in water, impaling, breaking on the wheel, and burning at the stake (Kelly 1991; Pavlac 2009).

The Inquisition's use of hostile interrogation methods and aggressive means of information-gathering did not serve to instill trust and faith in the ecclesiastical authorities. As for secular enforcement, state efforts to police their populations were also repressive, often leaving the citizens feeling harassed and incensed (Dean 2019). Public resentment oscillated, but at times, it reached a fever pitch that demanded violence, often directed toward state or Church authorities.[17] Thus, although social control and legal enforcement were varied and adaptive during the Middle Ages, they were not without conflict.

Despite the oftentimes cruel and unusual methods of medieval investigation and detainment, the Middle Ages was a meritorious step in the evolution of law enforcement and social protection. This era ushered in necessary change, modifying the Greco-Roman model to emphasize organized law enforcement, thus meeting the social and political needs of the time. However, as is often true of new innovations, the flawed first iteration illustrated a stark need for improvement, a task for the next era.

IN SEARCH OF ENLIGHTENMENT (RENAISSANCE AND SCIENTIFIC REVOLUTION)

The Renaissance served as a transitional period between the Middle Ages and the Scientific Revolution, memorable in part due to its innovative contributions, particularly in the arts, architecture, and philosophy (Monfasani 2016; Brotton 2006; Sider 2005). In addition, the study of science and technology became more prevalent, leading to pioneering breakthroughs that changed the trajectory of the Western world. Despite this notable era-specific footprint, not all aspects of the Renaissance experienced exponential growth, including in the realm of social control. Many *proto-forms* of policing, such as watchmen, constables, and *thief-takers*, were still commonplace (Mulone 2018).[18] [19] [20] Secular and religious governing bodies, resistant to change despite having succeeded in becoming all-encompassing empires, remained stagnant and locked in the past, often punishing those who defied the status quo (Soyer 2015). The inquisitorial model, under the control of the Catholic Church, retained power and authority during the Renaissance, while independent kingdoms enforced local laws.

While the manifestation of social control resembled earlier eras, methods of monitoring the citizenry did evolve, focusing more on the systematic collection and study of information than previous periods (Liddy 2016). King Francis I of France, for example, created the *maréchaussée*, an early policing system that combined the constabulary with the marshalcy of France (Pender 2016). One of the primary functions of the maréchaussée was to gather data on the population for the purposes of investigation and control. This approach was also prevalent in the Inquisition (Keitt 2004; Soyer 2015; Green 2012). Using a variety of techniques, inquisitors would gather information on subjects and doggedly investigate any mention, no matter how small, of heresy or impropriety.

Although the Inquisition's investigative practices were improving, its primary goals remained the same. In addition to the more traditional act of pursuing accused heretics, inquisitors were also tasked with verifying rumors of divine exploits, which became more commonplace during the Renaissance (Keitt 2004; Soyer 2015; Green 2012). The Catholic Church suggested that most reported miracles could be due to natural or supernatural causes. Regarding the latter, the Church asserted that instances of divine revelation, raptures, and prophetic visions might be holy, the result of demonic possession, or the by-product of practicing witchcraft. As for the former, many cases were disproven as medical malady or the product of an elaborate fraud.

Eugenia de la Torre of Madrid presents an interesting case illustrating supernatural investigations (Keitt 2004). Eugenia claimed to experience visions, revelations, and raptures, and witnesses reported Eugenia would go through fits, during which time she was posessed by a "beneficent angel" speaking in tongues. Eugenia herself asserted she was often tormented by demons, who would carry her from her bed and pitch her in with the pigs. There, the demons would taunt her and routinely beat her, leaving her bruised and bleeding. Many witnesses were convinced Eugenia was the embodiment of the struggle between good and evil. During her trial, Spanish inquisitors ruled out natural causes, such as hallucinatory drugs or psychological ailments. Reluctant to accept Eugenia's claims of demonic intervention, the inquisitorial tribunal eventually concluded that Eugenia was a *sacrilegious imposter*, guilty of crafting a fraud that not only consisted of demonic undertones, but divine ones as well (242). The tribunal (comprised exclusively of men) cited her gender and questionable moral character as contributing factors, concluding that Eugenia was guilty of subterfuge designed to financially defraud her community. One of the inquisitors in Eugenia's case stated:

> I judge it imperative to impose a drastic remedy for the abundance of feigned revelations and miracles. Since miracles are one of the arguments for and proof of our faith, if the miracles which these self-proclaimed holy people claim as true turn out to be false, as happens every day, it will give the heretics great force to say that miracles done in conformity with the faith have been, and are, false as well. (as quoted by Keitt 2004, 244)

As this statement suggests, the aggressive prosecution may have been well-intentioned, at least in some respects. However, the power and authority of inquisitors could easily be, and often was, abused. Many who were likely innocent of any real malfeasance where persecuted, imprisoned, and put to death during this era.

Thus, in many respects, the Renaissance mirrored its predecessor in goals and practices of social control, particularly in the ecclesiastical context. The one notable advancement, data-collection, provided foreshadowing of the next era, the Scientific Revolution, a period of impressive scientific advancements (Mulone 2018). This era sought to separate scientific endeavors from the constraints of philosophy and religion, emphasizing the value of empirical observations and quantifiable evidence. This shift in epistemology translated into changes in law enforcement and control. Perhaps one of the more prominent changes was in relation to the agents of control. As science and reason began to replace religion and faith as the purveyors of fact, it became necessary to establish secular enforcement bodies with more depth and breadth. In addition, the Scientific Revolution ushered in a period of industrialization and urbanization, thus reinforcing the need for a professional force. As a consequence, European nations sought to modify their means of social control in a manner more fitting for the demands of the time.

France provides a ready case study, albeit a potentially unpopular example, of modification in policing during the Scientific Revolution (Mulone 2018). In 1667, King Louis XIV created the position of Lieutenance Générale de Paris (Lieutenant of Police). Gabriel Nicolas de la Reynie, the first to hold this role, set out with a weighty agenda: to establish the centralized *haute* police, also known as the Paris Model. This model was innovative, particularly given that the previous era had relied primarily on proto-policing (militia-style policing) and the Inquisition.[21] Unlike modern law enforcement, members of this body did not wear uniforms, nor did they conduct patrols. Instead, they were primarily practitioners of *high policing*, officially created to maintain order and enforce the law, but largely serving as a tool of the monarchy to conduct surveillance on citizens, particularly those who questioned the governing power (Brodeur 1983; Brodeur & Leman-Langlois 2005; Deflem 2018; Lévy 2012).[22] [23] They were a top-down authority, seeking to control the population and ferret out threats to the hierarchy.

In sum, at the close of the Scientific Revolution, social control had advanced in many respects. No longer driven by superstition, policing turned toward science as a means of collecting information. In addition, as society became more industrialized and urbanized, professional law enforcement became more prominent. However, in many respects, policing continued to be a tool to bludgeon the population, and thus, it remained a work in progress.

THE BIRTH OF MODERN POLICING (VICTORIAN ERA)

The Industrial Revolution facilitated the urbanization of many Western countries, leading to a shift in the political and social views of the citizenry and an influx of new residents to urban centers. A new model of social control was needed to maintain peace among the ever-changing population of strangers in these burgeoning cities, and thus, it was within this context that the modern police force was born.

Modern policing began in London, England, in 1829, with Sir Robert Peel's *Metropolitan Police Act*, and the Metropolitan Police Service (Pender 2016; Mulone 2018; Rawlings 2012; Brodeur 1983; Thackrah 1986).[24] The officers of the Metropolitan Police Service, commonly referred to as "Bobbies," were a salaried and uniformed force that would routinely patrol the streets of London, actively attempting to identify crime.[25] Their model of policing became known as *low policing*, a notable shift to a preventive criminal-centric approach that aimed to halt crime before it occurred.

Both the Paris and London models (high and low policing, respectively) were comprised of government agencies working toward preserving order. However, in contrast to its Parisian predecessor, the London model did not embrace a political agenda, seeking instead to enforce the law and protect the citizenry (Brodeur 1983; Mulone 2018; Rawlings 2012). The Paris model brought forth images of covert agents working behind the scenes, gathering information on individuals deemed to be a threat to high authority. The London model, on the other hand, depicted readily identifiable uniformed officers, public representatives of authority, security, and public safety.[26] In addition, the latter model embraced the idea of *policing by consent*, which placed a priority on the active participation of the public in establishing and maintaining social control, a key part of Peel's agenda.

Word of the London model spread far, and many British colonies and Western countries adopted it as a blueprint for their own policing needs (Mulone 2018; Pender 2016). In the 1830s, Australia and Canada established their own police forces modeled in a similar manner. The United States experimented with day watches in Philadelphia before introducing its first official London-style police force in 1838 in Boston, and within a few decades, all major US cities followed suit (Potter 2013). The public response was positive; the citizenry supported the new model of modern policing with its full-time professional forces, its standard set of procedures, and its commitment to transparency and accountability. As the use of this system expanded and citizen support continued, the scope and specialization of duties also grew, leading to the creation of specialized departments and skill sets, ensuring further efficient and effective methods of social control (Mulone 2018).

The influence and expansion of modern policing was not exclusively reserved for the government domain; in many nations, an industry of private security developed, paralleling official police in function, use, and popularity (Mulone 2018). Allan Pinkerton provides a ready example of this growing enterprise. In 1850, in response to a public desire for additional security in the United States, Pinkerton created the Pinkerton National Detective Agency (Johnston 1992; Mulone 2018; Pender 2016).[27] The Pinkertons, as they were known, were an independent force who were available for hire by public or private interests alike. Although its methods were often questionable and even violent, Pinkerton's agency gained popularity, especially among business owners seeking to supress labor disputes. The federal government also contracted Pinkerton's agency on various occasions, such as when it served as the initial internal investigating unit of the original Department of Justice in 1871. The Anti-Pinkerton Act of 1893 ended this, however, by prohibiting federal contracts with private security interests.

In summary, during the Victorian Era, society experienced a shift toward modernity. Due in large part to the urbanization of the population, an influx of new citizens, and the socioeconomic and political context, a change in methods of social control was necessary. This need was met with the introduction of the London model of policing, consisting of professional police forces designed not only to enforce the law, but also to protect the citizenry (Mulone 2018). Thus, innovations throughout the nineteenth century changed the definition and dynamic of law enforcement in a manner that was necessary and welcomed. The London style of policing, however, was not impervious to misapplication, and it would take a turn for the worse in the coming years.

CONTEMPORARY POLICING (TWENTIETH CENTURY)

The Western world was in a state of flux at the beginning of the twentieth century. Advancements in technology, coupled with shifts in social and economic wealth and influence, brought new opportunities to many in urban environments. The role and reputation of the police was also changing, taking a downturn from previous years. The professionalism of the Victorian era had been drawn into question, as the police began accommodating political interests, oftentimes at the expense of the citizenry. Despite notable attempts on behalf of police officials to reform policing practices, public opinion continued to sour and, by the twenty-first century, this rocky relationship was earmarked with violence.

In the early part of the 1900s, the reputation of the police was suffering due to questionable entanglements and various scandals (Potter 2013).[28] Elements of both high and low policing were evident in policing practices, muddying the waters of transparency and accountablity, and the police were vulnerable to corruption, a potential tool for use by the crafty politician or crooked businessperson. The United States provides a ready example of the controversy surrounding policing at this time. Public scandals erupted, unveiling unsavory involvements between the police, organized crime syndicates, and politicians (Worrall 2014). Evidence suggested a *quid pro quo* that threatened public opinion. Corrupt police officers were accused of developing partnerships with organized crime, turning a blind eye to criminal activities in exchange for a range of benefits. In addition, shady politicians offered political favors in exchange for election intereference, which manifested in police favoritism in specific voting blocs, particularly those in the more-affluent neighborhoods.

In addition to prioritizing the needs of criminal syndicates and political ne'er-do-wells, police in the early twentieth century also favored wealthy business owners, often at the expense of the working class, particularly those who threatened commercial interests (Worrall 2014). In Britain, the working class refered to the bobbies as "a plague of blue locusts," due to their tendency to swarm labor protests (Reiner 1992, 762). In the United States, the use of "Public Order" arrests and "Tramp Acts" were weaponized against striking workers, unions, and unemployed citizens (Potter 2013). Locked alarm or call boxes were strategically placed around cities, thus allowing respectable citizens (businesspeople), who were issued keys, to call for police at any given time of day. Incidents of heavy use of force were common, with young men, immigrants, and minorities bearing the brunt of the violence.[29]

Given the incidents of corruption, abuse of power, and questionable use of force, public perception of the police was understandably poor (Potter 2013). Recognizing the need for change, key police officials sought to remedy the problems inherent in contemporary police practices and rebuild a reputation of professionalism. August Vollmer, the police chief in Berkeley, California, spearheaded efforts to cleanse police of political influence, to implement stronger standards for the selection and training of new recruits, and to advance the use of technology in policing, thus ensuring that evidence, rather than discretion, guided police investigative practices (Vollmer 1933; Wilson 1953). Ushering in a new era of policing, Vollmer worked with the University of California, Berkeley, to establish the first criminal justice degree program in 1916 and was the first to introduce the use of the crime laboratory, which led to the creation of the first national crime database (Pender 2016; Potter 2013).[30] [31]

Vollmer's innovations were adopted by other regions and nations, and for a time, public attitude toward the police shifted in a positive direction (Potter 2013). In Britain, the bobbies updated their own policing practices, and as a consequence, their reputation as "blue locusts" was suspended, replaced with warmer sentiments (Reiner 1992). Throughout the 1950s and '60s, the majority of the English population expressed trust and confidence in their police forces. In the United States, Orlando W. Wilson, Vollmer's protégé, carried on with Vollmer's vision, focusing on police reform through professionalism (Uchida 1993). Wilson became the go-to for other modern police organizations, with his emphasis on militaristic discipline, efficiency, crime control, and a centralized police command structure.

Unfortunately, despite the positive advances in the areas of professionalism, training, oversight, and nonpartisanship of the police in the Western world, things soured again in the latter half of the twentieth century.[32] More incidents of violence and scandal erupted in the 1960s through the 1990s. The attempts to separate politics from policing were only partially successful, and corruption continued in select deparments across Western nations. Despite Vollmer and Wilson's efforts to ensure discipline, police continued to employ aggressive tactics, such as stop and frisk, which instilled feelings of resentment among members of the community subject to such practices (Simmons 2014).[33] In addition, this period was home to several key political moments, such the Vietnam War, civil rights unrest, and the Watergate scandal, and the use of police to supress public responses to these issues, often with excessive force, served only to damage their reputation further. Lastly, the world could not ignore the overtly biased nature of police attention, directly predominantly toward communities of color (Cunningham & Gillezeau 2014; Soss & Weaver 2017).

Thus, the twentieth century ended on a low note. Police practices were called into question, seen as excessively biased, forceful, and subject to corruption. The public had lost faith and confidence in law enforcement, wearied from a century of instability and abuse. Meanwhile, many officers embraced a culture that favored self-preservation over public relations. Thus, in some regions, the police and the public found themselves on two opposing sides in the quest for social control.

CONCLUSION

Before closing out this chapter, there is one last installment in the historical trajctory of policing that allows us to depart on a more positive note. Western nations, recognizing the need to improve police-public relations, ushered in the twenty-first century with a new model of policing: community-oriented policing. As the name suggests, this method of policing relies heavily on strong relationships between the police and the communities they serve (Goldstein 1987; Oliver 2004). Police officers aim to have a visible and accessible presence, facilitating positive dynamics with residents, and ensuring open communication. Citizens play a more active role in policing agendas, serving as advisors and consultants, and although crime prevention remains a primary goal, this has been joined by the twin priorities of reducing citizen fear and increasing citizen satisfaction. Although this is not the only change evident in twenty-first-century policing, nor is it the most recent, it is perhaps the one that best illustrates the era we find ourselves in now.[34] Is this model effective? It depends on the metric of success. Citizen-police relations have improved while crime rates seem impervious (Gill et al. 2014). That said, the twenty-first century ushered in something else, a more informed view of crime, specifically the recognition that crime is determined by a number of factors that have little to do with policing, such as the social and political ills of poverty, discrimination, and lack of opportunity. Thus, an improvement in public relations is a notable victory, one that should not be overshadowed by a less-promising crime rate.

This ends our exploration of the history of policing. From Greek and Roman antiquity through to the present century, the Western world has borne witness to diverse and ever-changing approaches to social control, sometimes relegated to the private world, other times to the public sphere, sometimes in oppositition to the citizenry, and other times in cooperation with the people. In other words, the broad definition of *policing* as "a complex mechanism of societal control" is just as relevant today as it was thousands of years ago, and the methods and means of policing require continued scrutiny, with the unending goal of improving upon the past.

NOTES

1. The Court of Areopagus refers to the Grecian high court in Athens, where Draco, one of the first legislators in ancient Greece, introduced written law.

2. The *magistrate* was one of the highest offices in ancient Greece and Rome. Magistrates held both judicial and executive power.

3. Scythian refers to nomadic people living in proximity to the Pontic steppe between the seventh and third centuries BCE.

4. A *trierarch* is an officer responsible for a *trireme*, a type of warship.

5. This could include a wide range of duties, such as supervising the markets and the public baths, as well as collecting fines.

6. Picketing in protest is a modern equivalent of this early form of justice.

7. An incident from the second century BCE provides a somewhat-comedic example of this form of policing. A woman who had loaned money to her estranged husband ordered one of her slaves to follow him around the city shouting and demanding repayment.

8. Germanic Law was a European code of law developed by the Germanic people between the fifth and ninth centuries, largely influenced by Roman law, canon law, and tribal customs.

9. Ironically, Justitia, the Roman goddess of justice, from whom our modern Lady Justice is derived, was adopted as the representation of justice in the Middle Ages (Harding 1960). With her scales weighing truth in one hand, and a sword ready to mete out swift justice in the other (the blindfold was a later addition), Justitia is the judicial system personified. Jurisprudence was a masculine act during this period; however, Justitia's female form conveyed a sense of mercy within an otherwise-harsh system. Unfortunately, mercy was not necessarily central to the Middle Ages; the era was rife with incidents of false imprisonment and corruption. In addition, the criminal justice system tended to favor the affluent and oppress those of humble means, though some scholars suggest this institutional bias may have been less pronounced than historians first believed (Ormrod & Musson 1998).

10. English Common Law refers to judge-made law, which serves as the historical origin of the modern English legal system.

11. Assize of Clarendon is an act or amendment to the English Law, which led to trial by jury.

12. The *Podestà* was the chief magistrate and the highest civil office common within central and northern Italian city governments during the late Middle Ages.

13. The hundred court maintained the frankpledge system through the administration of the law and keeping the peace.

14. Ballads such as "The Nut Brown Maid" (as cited in Coyle 2005, 57) glorify the outlaw lifestyle. A number of medieval songs also take liberties in their representation of the outlaw experience, as illustrated by this translation of Middle English lyrics: "I will keep within the woods, in the beautiful shade there is no deceit there, not any bad law, in the forest of Belregard, where the jay flies and the nightingale always sings without ceasing" (as cited in Summerson 1979, 327). Along similar lines, the popular fictional writing of Sir Walter Scott, John Keats, and Pierce Egan also romanticize the outlaw moniker.

15. To *abjure* is to formally renounce something; in this context, it refers to forsaking bonds and leaving the realm.

16. Two Swords theory was first envisioned by Pope Gelasius I in approximately 492 AD

17. Government engaged in overreach with restrictive edicts prohibiting actions considered a natural right of the peasantry, such as hunting or simply gathering wood; regulating them only seemed to benefit the ruling class (Hanawalt & Wallace 1998).

18. The term *proto-form* refers to earlier forms of policing, such as thief-takers and tithingman.

19. Some historians have attempted to make direct associations between the proto-form police, suggesting the first archetypes of the patrol officer were the watchmen; the first enforcers were constables; and the first investigators were thief-takers. Mulone (2018), however, disagrees with this assessment, stating that the term *policing* is misunderstood and oversimplified, and more modern forms did not necessarily supplant the proto-forms.

20. Thief-takers were paid individuals or groups hired by victims to retrieve their stolen property and assist in the catching and prosecution of criminals. They were still very common in London through the end of the seventeenth century, but they fell out of vogue due to scandals and the implementation of defense lawyers (Mulone 2018).

21. *Haute* is French for "high" or "grand," so in this context it is the "high police," or the predominant method of policing (Collins 1991).

22. High policing is intelligence-led policing created with the purpose of domestic intelligence-gathering, typically used to enforce a political agenda.

23. Members of the early Parisian haute police force maintained large networks of informants to assist them in their duties of monitoring the population, stamping out sedition, protecting the king, and enforcing his agenda.

24. Sir Robert Peel, who served as the home secretary (a senior minister of the Crown and a senior member of the British cabinet), introduced the Metropolitan Police Act to Parliament, and he is often considered the father of modern policing in recognition of his efforts to reform England's defunct law enforcement system.

25. The nickname "Bobby" for English police officers referred to the custodian helmet they traditionally wore while on duty.

26. The officers of the Metropolitan Police Service wore blue uniforms, which visually separated them from the red uniforms worn by the army. Although this made them recognizable, it also served as a reminder they were a professional force who, unlike the military, would respond more fairly and less violently to issues of crime and disorder (Mulone 2018).

27. The Pinkerton Detective Agency was the world's largest private law enforcement organization during its heyday. From its founding, Pinkerton made the innovative choice to hire women and minorities, despite the fact that doing so was an uncommon practice (Johnston 1992; Mulone 2018; Pender 2016).

28. In the United States, several investigatory commissions were appointed to combat corruption, including the Curren Committee (1913), which investigated police collusion with gambling and prostitution in New York City, and the Wickersham Commission (1929), which was appointed by President Hoover to examine rising crime rates and police ineffectiveness (Potter 2013).

29. Patrol wagons, or paddy wagons, were used to expedite the arrest and transport of large groups of people. Horseback patrols were also used to break up gatherings of strikers and demonstrators. Police were issued longer nightsticks to aid them in dispensing their duties.

30. Vollmer embraced the idea of incorporating technology into policing. For example, Vollmer created the first motorized force, using cars equipped with radios and motorcycles to conduct patrols. He also supported the use of early polygraphs, developed at the University of California.

31. Vollmer was a progressive in his time, breaking both the racial and gender barriers by promoting the hiring and training of African Americans and women as police officers.

32. The reader may notice that the role of technology in contemporary policing is absent from this chapter. Although this is a subject of particular interest to diverse audiences, it requires an entire volume of its own. Therefore, we thought it best to direct the reader's attention to existing books that cover the topic well, rather than attempting to summarize it in a scant paragraph or two. McGuire and Holt (2017) and Weisburd and Braga (2019) provide two such texts.

33. A *frisk* is a quick search, consisting of a physical pat-down and checking the contents of pockets.

34. Evidence-based policing, for example, is a key addition to the twenty-first century, as is problem-oriented policing.

REFERENCES

Africa, Thomas W. 1971. "Urban Violence in Imperial Rome." *Journal of Interdisciplinary History* 2, no. 1 (Summer): 3–21. https://doi.org/10.2307/202441.

Backman, Clifford R. 2003. *The Worlds of Medieval Europe.* New York: Oxford University Press.

Bailey, Michael. 2006. "Bernard Gui." In *Encyclopedia of Witchcraft: The Western Tradition, Vol. 2,* edited by Richard M. Golden, 465. London: Bloomsbury Publishing.

Bellamy, John G. 1964. "The Coterel Gang: An Anatomy of a Band of Fourteenth-Century Criminals." *English Historical Review* 79, no. 313 (October): 698–717. http://www.jstor.org/stable/560525.

Brodeur, Jean-Paul. 1983. "High Policing and Low Policing: Remarks about the Policing of Political Activities." *Social Problems* 30, no. 5 (June): 507–520. https://doi.org/10.2307/800268.

Brodeur, Jean-Paul, and Stephane Leman-Langlois. 2005. "Surveillance Fiction or Higher Policing?" In *The New Politics of Surveillance and Visibility*, edited by Kevin Haggerty and Richard Ericson, 171–98. Toronto: University of Toronto Press.

Brotton, Jerry. 2006. *The Renaissance: A Very Short Introduction.* Oxford: Oxford University Press.

Brundage, James A. 1998. Review of *The Formation of the English Common Law: Law and Society in England from the Norman Conquest to Magna Carta*, by John Hudson. *Law and History Review*, October 28, 2011.

Cantarella, Eva. 2004. "Controlling Passions or Establishing the Rule of Law? The Functions of Punishment in Ancient Greece." *Punishment & Society* 6, no. 4 (October): 429–436. https://doi.org/10.1177/1462474504046122.

Christ, M. R. 1998. "Legal Self–Help on Private Property in Classical Athens." *American Journal of Philology* 119 no. 4 (Winter): 521–45. http://www.jstor.org/stable/1561916.

Coyle, Danielle. 2005. "The Outlaws of Medieval England." *Hohunu: A Journal of Academic Writing* 3: 57–59. https://hilo.hawaii.edu/campuscenter/hohonu/volumes/documents/Vol03x13TheOutlawsofMedievalEngland.pdf.

Cunningham, Jamein P., and Rob Gillezeau. 2018. "Racial Differences in Police Use of Force: Evidence from the 1960s Civil Disturbances." *American Economic Association Papers and Proceedings* 108 (May): 217–21. https://doi.org/10.1257/pandp.20181110.

Dean, Trevor. 2019. "Police Forces in Late Medieval Italy: Bologna, 1340–1480." *Social History* 44, no. 2 (May): 151–172. https://doi.org/10.1080/03071022.2019.1579974.

Deflem, Mathieu. 2018. "Introduction: Social Control Today." In *The Handbook of Social Control*, edited by Mathieu Deflem, 1–6. Hoboken: Wiley-Blackwell Publishing.

Gill, Charlotte, David Weisburd, Cody W. Telep, Zoe Vitter, and Trevor Bennett. 2014. "Community-oriented Policing to Reduce Crime, Disorder, and Fear and Increase Satisfaction and Legitimacy Among Citizens: A Systematic Review." *Journal of Experimental Criminology* 10 (August): 399–428. https://doi.org/10.1007/s11292-014-9210-y.

Goldstein, Herman. 1987. "Toward Community-Oriented Policing: Potential, Basic Requirements, and Threshold Questions." *Crime & Delinquency* 33, no. 1 (January): 6–30. https://doi.org/10.1177/0011128787033001002.

Gorski, Richard. 2009. "Justices and Injustice? England's Local Officials in the Later Middle Ages." In *Outlaws in Medieval and Early Modern England Crime, Government, and Society, c. 1066–c.1600*, edited by John C. Appleby and Paul Dalton, 57–74. Farnham: Ashgate Publishing.

Green, Toby. 2012 "Policing the Empires: A Comparative Perspective on the Institutional Trajectory of the Inquisition in the Portuguese and Spanish Overseas Territories (Sixteenth and Seventeenth Centuries)." *Hispanic Research Journal* 13, no. 1 (July): 7–25. https://doi.org/10.1179/174582011X13183287338013.

Gregory-Abbot, Candace. 2009. "Scared Outlaws: Outlawry and the Medieval Church." In *Outlaws in Medieval and Early Modern England Crime, Government, and Society, c. 1066–c.1600*, edited by John C. Appleby and Paul Dalton, 75–89. Farnham: Ashgate Publishing.

Hanawalt, Barbara A., and Davvid Wallace. 1999. *Medieval Crime and Social Control*. Minneapolis: University of Minnesota Press.

Harding, Alan. 1960. "The Origins and Early History of the Keeper of the Peace: The Alexander Prize Essay." *Transactions of the Royal Historical Society* 10 (February): 85–109. https://doi.org/10.2307/3678775.

Hunter, Virginia J. 1994. *Policing Athens: Social Control in the Attic Lawsuits, 420–320 B.C.* Princeton: Princeton University Press.

Johnston, Les. 1992. *The Rebirth of Private Policing*. Oxford: Taylor & Francis.

Keitt, Andrew. 2004. "Religious Enthusiasm, the Spanish Inquisition, and the Disenchantment of the World." *Journal of the History of Ideas* 65, no. 2 (April): 231–50. http://www.jstor.org/stable/3654208.

Kelly, Benjamin. 2013. "Policing and Security." In *The Cambridge Companion to Ancient Rome*, edited by Paul Erdkamp. Cambridge: Cambridge University Press.

Kelly, F. P. 1991. "The Inquisitor's Procedure in the Name of the Rose." *Adelaide Law Review* 13, no. 2 (January): 289–99. https://classic.austlii.edu.au/au/journals/AdelLawRw/1991/12.pdf.

Lévy René. 2012. "About the Proper Use of Policing 'Models.' What Sociology and History Have to Say on Jean-Paul Brodeur's 'The Policing Web,'" translated by Helen Arnold. *Champ Pénal/Penal Field* 9 (October). https://doi.org/10.4000/champpenal.8276.

Liddy, Christian D. 2016. "Cultures of Surveillance in Late Medieval English Towns: The Monitoring of Speech and the Fear of Revolt." In *The Routledge History Handbook of Medieval Revolt*, edited by Justine Firnhaber-Baker and Dirk Schoenaers, 311–29. Oxford: Routledge.

McGuire, Michael, and Thomas J. Holt. 2017. *The Routledge Handbook of Technology, Crime and Justice*. Oxford: Routledge.

Monfasani, John. 2016. *Humanism, from the Middle Ages to Modern Times*. Oxford: Taylor & Francis.

Morris, William A. 1910. *The Frankpledge System*. New York: Longmans, Green, & Company.

Mulone, Massimiliano. 2018. "History of Policing." In *The Handbook of Social Control*, edited by Mathieu Deflem, 209–20. Hoboken: Wiley-Blackwell Publishing.

Nippel, Wilfried. 1984. "Policing Rome." *Journal of Roman Studies* 74 (November): 20–29. https://doi.org/10.2307/299004.

Oliver, Willard M. 2004. *Community-oriented policing: A systemic approach to policing.* Hoboken: Prentice Hall.

Ormrod, Mark W., and Anthony Musson. 1998. *The Evolution of English Justice: Law, Politics and Society in the Fourteenth Century.* London: Macmillan Education.

Pavlac, Brian A. 2009. *Witch Hunts in the Western World: Persecution and Punishment from the Inquisition Through the Salem Trials.* Santa Barbara: American Bibliographical Center-Clio.

Pender, Lionel. 2016. *To Serve and Protect: The History of Policing.* New York: Rosen Publishing Group.

Phillips, D. 2013. *The Law of Ancient Athens.* Ann Arbor: University of Michigan Press.

Potter, Gary. 2013. "The history of policing in the United States." *Eastern Kentucky University School of Justice Studies* 1, no. 16 (June). https://ekuonline.eku.edu/blog/police-studies/the-history-of-policing-in-the-united-states-part-1/.

Rawlings, Philip. 2012. *Policing: A Short History.* London: Willan.

Reiner, Robert. 1992. "Policing a Postmodern Society." *Modern Law Review* 55, no. 6 (November): 761–81. http://www.jstor.org/stable/1096856.

Reynolds, Paul K. B. 1928. "The Police in Ancient Rome." *Police Journal: Theory, Practice and Principles* 1, no. 3 (July): 432–42. https://doi.org/10.1177/0032258X2800100308.

Schisas, Pandias M. 1926. *Offences Against the State in Roman Law and the Courts Which Were Competent to Take Cognisance of Them.* London: University of London Press.

Sider, Sandra. 2005. *Handbook to Life in Renaissance Europe.* New York: Facts On File, Incorporated.

Simmons, Kami Chavis. 2014. "The Legacy of Stop and Frisk: Addressing the Vestiges of a Violent Police Culture." *Wake Forest Law Review* 49 (January): 849–71. https://ssrn.com/abstract=2873807.

Soyer, François. 2015. "Enforcing Religious Repression in an Age of World Empires: Assessing the Global Reach of the Spanish and Portuguese Inquisitions." *Journal of the Historical Association* 100, no. 341 (June): 331–53. https://doi.org/10.1111/1468-229X.12109.

Summerson, Henry R. T. 1979. "The Structure of Law Enforcement in Thirteenth-Century England." *American Journal of Legal History* 23, no. 4 (October): 313–27. https://doi.org/10.2307/844686.

Taylor, Jamie. 2010. "Witnesses and Outlaws in the Later Middle Ages." *English Language Notes* 48, no. 2 (September): 85–97. https://doi.org/10.1215/00138282-48.2.85.

Uchida, Craig D. 1993. "The Development of the American Police: An Historical Overview." In *Critical Issues in Policing: Contemporary Readings*, edited by Roger G. Dunham and Geoffrey P. Alpert, 19–35. Long Grove: Waveland Press.

Vollmer, August. 1933. "Police Progress in the Past Twenty-Five Years." *Journal of Criminal Law & Criminology* 24, no. 1 (May): 161-175. https://doi.org/10.2307/1135158.

Weisburd, David, and Anthony A. Braga. 2019. *Police Innovation: Contrasting Perspectives.* Cambridge: Cambridge University Press.

Wilson, Orlando W. 1953. "August Vollmer." *Journal of Criminal Law, Criminology, and Police Science* 44, no. 1 (May): 91–103. https://doi.org/10.2307/1139476.

Worrall, John L. 2014. "The Politics of Policing." In *The Oxford Handbook of Police and Policing*, edited by Michael D. Reisig and Robert J. Kane, 49–67. Oxford: Oxford University Press.

Chapter 3

The Development of the Court System

Silas B. Parks, Rachel Galli, and Omi Hodwitz

INTRODUCTION

Imagine a courtroom with a great deal of hustle and bustle and endless piles of paperwork. The recent call for documents from public records, due to a question of citizenship, just came back. Someone is filing claims of forgery, accompanied by a request for a handwriting expert. Of course, this could just be a play for time, but it is all well within normal practices, so the court allows it. This may seem dull for a modern courtroom TV drama, but it is actually typical events from court proceedings in ancient Rome, circa 230 CE.[1]

This chapter seeks to present the court and sentencing procedures of Western history, from Greco-Roman antiquity through the Middle Ages and into modern times. This includes a number of processes, from the levying of an accusation of wrongdoing to the determination of punishment. Different regions and eras had various ways of detaining suspected offenders, establishing guilt, and assigning punishments, and each of these variations is a fascinating development when cast upon the footprint of their juridical ancestors. For example, juries became commonplace in ancient Greece, but they were massive affairs, often involving hundreds of people (Von Dornum 1997). They fell out of favor during Roman rule, remaining dormant for a thousand years before being revived at the end of the Middle Ages (Harries 1999; Pollock 1899). In contrast, paid advocates (a historical precursor to modern-day lawyers) were illegal in ancient Greece, common in Rome, then severely curtailed during the period of Enlightenment (Horovitz 2007; Phillips 2013). Meanwhile, torture remained popular from ancient Greece until the end of the Scientific Revolution (Cameron 1898). Each of these trends illustrates both cyclical consistency and generational diversity and offers an invitation to the reader to explore further. This chapter aims to guide the reader on this historical journey, providing a chronological overview of these processes while also reflecting on the social, juridical, and legislative evolutions that were influential at the time.

ANTIQUITY: ANCIENT GREECE

The social and legal structures of ancient Greece were based around the idea of citizenship.[2] While the women and children of Greek descent were called citizens, they lacked the civic responsibilities, protections, and rights of Greek men (Phillips 2013). Men defined law and deviance, "distinguished by superiority from the rest of the population, [but] equal among themselves" (Sealey 1994, 24). There were many free foreigners, called *metics*, and slaves within Greece; however, there was no path to citizenship available to them. Early in the classical period, around 451 BCE, citizenship became even more restrictive, only extended to children born of two citizen parents.

When a crime was committed, it was the duty and right of every adult male citizen to point it out and to prosecute it, and doing the former often meant doing the latter (Von Dornum 1997). Depending on the crime, there were often multiple options for a victim or a prosecutor to pursue justice (Phillips 2013). One of the largest distinctions was between public or private lawsuits. A public lawsuit was similar to a modern criminal trial, while a private lawsuit was more often a matter of arbitration.

While any adult male citizen could bring forth a public lawsuit, only the victim could bring forth a private lawsuit. There were several reasons for a victim to choose either route, depending on their situation, such as risk to themselves or their desired outcome (Harris & Rubinstein 2004). Risk was a key factor in pursuing a public lawsuit, as the prosecutor who failed to obtain votes from at least one-fifth of the jury, presumably due to having a weak case, was subject to a heavy fine. Also, a public lawsuit often had proscribed punishments for the offender, while private cases had more flexibility. A victim could seek financial compensation for their woes with a private suit or try to inflict maximum punishment through a public one.

If a public trial was chosen, a jury would be randomly selected from a pool of six thousand jurors empaneled each year.[3] The jury for a trial could easily range from 201 to 501 jurors, while trials involving issues of heightened public interest might involve more than a thousand jurors (Phillips 2013). These jurors were tasked with listening to the prosecution and defense, then deciding between them without discussion or further debate. The trial itself would last no more than a day, starting with a brief statement of facts that had been gathered from both sides (Kapparis 2019). The prosecution would then make its case, followed by the defense.[4] Each side received equal time, as measured by a water clock. All facets of the case, from witness statements to relevant laws to character assessments, would need to be presented within those sessions.

After the prosecution and defense finished speaking, the jurors would immediately vote on the party they felt had made the stronger case. This was done anonymously by dropping ballot stones into urns (Phillips 2013). The stones were then counted, with a simple majority determining guilt or innocence. If the offender was found guilty of a specific offense that did not have a statutorily demanded punishment, the process would start again, with each side arguing for a preferred punishment. The jury would vote again, this time between the two presented punishments. The prosecutor and defendant also had the option to confer and agree on a punishment, thus eliminating the need for this step in the process (Kapparis 2019).

Among the most famous of Greek trials is that of Socrates, the founder of Western philosophy. The seventy-year-old intellectual was accused of morally corrupting the youth, as well as impiety, or refusing to recognize the gods (D'Amato 1976). Socrates repeatedly characterized the charges against him as being the result of enmity and the embarrassment of influential people, due to his philosophical challenges:

> I am still even now going about and searching and investigating at the god's behest anyone, whether citizen or foreigner, who I think is wise; and when he does not seem so to me, I give aid to the god and show that he is not wise. . . . And in addition to these things, the young men . . . often imitate me themselves, and then they undertake to examine others; and then, I fancy, they find a great plenty of people who think they know something, but know little or nothing. As a result, therefore, those who are examined by them are angry with me, instead of being angry with themselves, and say that 'Socrates is a most abominable person and is corrupting the youth.' (Plato et al. 1964, 9–10)

The 501-member jury convicted Socrates with a margin of approximately thirty votes (D'Amato 1976). This verdict could be blamed on political maneuvering, religious zeal, or possibly as a reaction to Socrates's own unwillingness to compromise; "I say to you, men of Athens . . . either acquit me, or not, knowing that I shall not change my conduct even if I am to die many times over" (Plato et al. 1964, 18). As for Socrates's punishment, his accuser, Meletus, proposed death. Socrates countered by proposing that he deserved to instead be given his meals in the Prytaneum.[5] In the end, Socrates was sentenced to death and chose to drink a poisonous concoction of hemlock rather than seek escape and exile, thus portraying himself as a martyr for law, justice, and honor. "In battles it is often plain that a man might avoid death by throwing down his arms and begging mercy of his pursuers; and there are many other means of escaping death if one is willing to do and say anything. But, gentlemen, it is not hard to escape death; it is much harder to escape wickedness, for that runs faster than death" (Plato et al. 1964, 26).

As evident in Socrates's trial, once a jury had made its decision, there was no opportunity for appeal (Phillips 2013). The only decision that could be appealed was that of a magistrate, such as would more often occur in a private lawsuit. Instead of appeal, however, the losing party had other options. These included a countersuit, such as against an opposing witness for false testimony. This would be particularly appropriate if the defendant had been fined, as they could try to recoup their losses from the dishonest witness. For more serious punishments, there was a possibility to overturn the verdict, as the victim had the right to pardon their offender (Kapparis 2019).

In ancient Greece, special legal and religious considerations were given to the crime of murder, no matter how lowly the status of the victim. Murder caused *miasma*, or blood pollution, to cling to the perpetrator (Calhoun 1927). A person accused of murder was required to stay away from public places, for fear of spreading this miasma to others.[6] Breaking this rule and potentially spreading miasma was a high crime in and of itself. In incidents of homicide, it was expected that the victim's family would prosecute. If they first refused to do so, other citizens were then permitted to press the case (Kapparis 2019). Interestingly enough, a murderer was allowed to flee into exile to escape prosecution or punishment, as this also succeeded in removing the miasma from the community. Unlike other criminal cases, a victim's family had to agree unanimously to pardon a killer from death or exile and dispel the miasma (Blecker 2006).

From murder to mayhem and other crimes, the Western history of courts and sentencing begins in ancient Greece with its liberal use of magistrates, jury systems, and the democratic process of voting. The Grecian system of courts is often described as an amateur system, as participation in all parts of the legal system was expected of, and handled by, ordinary citizens (Phillips 2013). Citizens were required to bring attention to and prosecute crimes and determine guilt and punishment. In addition, citizenship was limited by both heredity and gender, thus restricting the role of a good portion of the population. Despite these characteristics, ancient Greece set the stage for further advancement and refinement that would dictate the court proceedings of the modern day.

ANTIQUITY: ANCIENT ROME

In contrast to the Greek orators, from whom we have a clear picture of court proceedings, the ancient authors of Rome were less descriptive. As Harries (1999) put it, they took knowledge of the common procedures of the time for granted. Instead, the Romans were more attentive to individual roles, describing the duties of judges, *praetors*, jurists, and advocates. The accounts of these key players give a sufficient, if often debated, foundation upon which to extrapolate the workings of ancient Roman courts.

In the era of the Roman Republic, one of the major actors in the legal system was the annually elected praetor. Praetors were not directly involved in cases, but instead they appointed judges who were given the authority to obtain evidence and oversee cases (Wieacker 1981). Praetors would also hand down an edict or instructions for how cases should be handled during their short term. When praetors retained instructions from their predecessor (*ius honorarium*), this effectively created statutes that became entrenched in Roman jurisprudence.

Praetors were more politically than legally aligned, and the judges they appointed also tended to have limited legal expertise (Urch 1929). Instead, judges were advised by jurists (*iurist consultus*), or professional legal experts. Jurists had no official role in the workings of the court; instead, they were typically wealthy men who could afford to advise pro bono, seeking political and social advancement through their specialty. Their place should not be minimized, however, as their advice (*respondere*) was often recorded, analyzed, and used to create precedent for future counsel (Wieacker 1981). This created a system similar to English common law, where new cases were influenced or decided by prior rulings.[7]

Judges appointed by a praetor would preside over a trial, but guilt or innocence was typically determined by juries (*iudices*) [Stachan-Davidson 1901]. This was, of course, unless the defendants actually confessed or were caught red-handed, in which case the judge immediately determined punishment (Bauman 1996).[8] Once the Republic was replaced by the Empire, jury trials became less common, eventually replaced with hearings that took place in front of a judge (*iudex*).

For a trial or hearing to begin, a private individual had to come forward and levy an accusation against a person or persons (Bauman 1996). The state, as a general rule, did not start criminal proceedings, but left it up to the public to instigate the process with an accusation of wrongdoing. Unlike Greece, which put the trial firmly in the hands of the accuser and the accused, professional advocates acting on behalf of each party were common in all Roman court proceedings. The advocates had to be well versed in the practices and tactics of the day, as litigation was a chaotic melee, with records that "show judge, advocates, witnesses, and litigants boisterously engaged in verbal disputes" (Harries 1999, 99).[9]

During a trial, the reliability of witnesses was often based on status; higher status and financial stability suggested a more trustworthy witness (Harries 1999). Without a high-standing witness, multiple witnesses were often required if an evidentiary point was to hold weight. Much like in Greece, a slave's testimony could only be accepted if it was extracted through torture. In the later Roman Empire, higher-class citizens (*honestiores*) were not subject to torture except in cases of treason (Lamoreaux 1995). Low-class citizens (*humiliores*) who were witnesses or defendants, however, were potentially subject to torture, even for cases that did not directly involve them.

If the trial went poorly for a defendant, appeals were possible, although less so for more serious offenses, such as capital crimes (Harries 1999). An appeal was often a highly regulated affair, with strict time limits and rules, and appellants were restricted from introducing new evidence. The rules of appeal were enforced with a system of hefty fines. This, combined with the standard court fees and increased fees for higher courts, made appeals prohibitively expensive for most individuals.

In 318 CE, Constantine added another dimension to the Roman legal system by creating the episcopal courts (Lamoreaux 1995). In these courts, Christian bishops presided as judges, deciding cases and their outcomes as they saw fit. Of particular note is that, at any time throughout traditional secular proceedings, either party could demand that the case be transferred to the ecclesiastical courts, and the request would be fulfilled. In addition, the decision of the presiding bishop was definitive and, therefore, not subject to appeal. After the death of Constantine, the powers of these courts were greatly lessened. A number of criminal matters were removed from the court's jurisdiction, and both parties had to agree before a criminal case could be transferred. Over time, ecclesiastical proceedings were curtailed to the point that clergy would be punished if they insisted on being tried by the Church for criminal matters (Humfress 2011).

From the constant complaints found in the writings of the early church bishops, it is clear that the episcopal courts were extremely busy (Lamoreaux 1995). There are several possible reasons for this, including the lack of fees which were such a prohibitive part of the secular courts. In addition, there appeared to be less use of torture in the proceedings, as well as less severe punitive consequences. This is possibly because the bishops tended to run their courts in the style of arbitration, seeking to restore harmony in the community.

In contrast to the early experimental legal proceedings of ancient Greece, the Romans developed a system of codified professionals and precedence-driven processes. The Roman jurists' emphasis on legal expertise facilitated the academic study of law, and their practice of advising created an enduring legacy of jurisprudence. Many ideas that shape our legal proceedings today were drafted and discussed in this era. Ideas that we consider fundamental, such as "it is better to leave crime unpunished than to punish the innocent,"[10] and "the justice which is truly preventative is more desirable than the justice which is strictly punishing"[11] were originally conceived in Roman antiquity (Garishvili 2012, 20).

MIDDLE AGES

The court and legal systems of the Middle Ages can be separated into three periods.[12] After the withdrawal and fall of the Western Roman Empire, the lack of overarching government brought much of Europe back into the realm of community and family justice. This period is characterized by simple legal systems for the most extreme of crimes, such as blood feuds and blood money (*wergild*). Then came feudalism, which was typified by various religious ordeals, as well as judicial combat and compurgation.[13] Finally, in the late Middle Ages, the legal system came under centralized state control and moved toward either jury trial in England or a restored Romanized legal system on the continent and within the Church.

The fall of Roman civilization caused a shift in Western systems of justice, more specifically a return to practices that predated classical Greece. Communities, for the most part, regulated themselves, and most offenses were dealt with on a case-by-case basis. As mentioned previously, blood feuds became commonplace for more severe crimes such as murder (Pollock 1899). Blood feuds were vengeance-based, premised on the idea that only the victim's family had the right to seek retribution from the offender or the offender's family. The blood feud decreased the likelihood that whole communities would go to battle over the misbegotten actions of a few (Jenks 1898).

As an alternative to violence, communities developed the practice of blood price, or *wergild* (Pollock 1899). In these cases, as long as both parties agreed to it, blood feuds could be settled for a price. As this process became formalized, it created the opportunity for greater state involvement (Jenks 1898). This was due to a number of factors, including the consideration that the peace afforded by the *wergild* required an outside party with the strength to enforce it, which would reasonably fall within the purview of the ruling monarch. In addition, the king would be able to tax the *wergild*, giving him a personal stake in the process. Thereby, refusal to pay for one's crime became an offense not only against private parties, but also against the state.[14]

The rise of feudalism, along with further stability and growth, created the need for a more formal and comprehensive means of dispensing justice. The resulting systems, split between ecclesiastical and secular interests, were fueled by a unique combination of superstition and necessity. Secular practices included trial by combat and the wager of law, otherwise called compurgation. Religious practices included the ordeals of cold water, hot water, and hot iron. Each of these practices, although differing in content, shared the common characteristic of being a negative system of proof (Cameron 1898). Rather than requiring physical evidence for a conviction, the accused was instead expected to prove their innocence.

Trial by combat was among one of the more romanticized and preferred medieval trials. Designed to determine guilt and dispense justice, the brutalities of combat, hidden behind a veneer of chivalry, was well-suited for the culture of warfare popular at the time.[15] As the name suggests, trial by combat required that the accused and accuser engage in a duel as a means of settling legal and criminal disputes. The winner of the duel was credited with currying God's favor and, as such, was judged to be in the right. In practice, professional fighters were often paid to champion whichever side could afford it, or during the height of chivalry, knights would step in as a champion for a worthy cause. Regardless of who dueled, the fight was often fierce:

> In a twelfth-century combat between two noble knights over complicity in Charles the Good's assassination, one knight was able to throw the other to the ground and beat him nearly senseless with his gauntlets, but the other managed to slip his hand under his opponent's coat of mail and rip off his testicles, thereby demonstrating the justness of his cause. (Rubin 2003, 264)

Compurgation offered a less-violent and less-popular form of defense, at least in secular courts (Cameron 1898). In this form of trial, the accused were sworn against the charges brought against them. They would then have to find enough people (*compurgators*) of equivalent rank and good standing who would swear, not to the facts of the case, but to their belief in the word of the defendant (Leeson 2012). This practice fell out of use in feudal courts due in part to the popularity of trial by combat, but it was later revived with the rise of state and ecclesiastical courts (Helmholz 1983).

There were a wide variety of religious ordeals designed to show whether the accused had curried God's favor, meaning they were innocent or, at the very least, forgiven (Cameron 1898, 438–49). The most popular and well-recorded of these are the trials of hot water, hot iron, and cold water. Each of these ordeals were presided over by a priest and were often preceded by ritual fasting and prayer. In the case of hot water, often a ring or stone was thrown into a pot of boiling water (Leeson 2012). The accused would have to plunge their hand into the water and fish out the object.[16] On the third day following submersion, their hand was inspected, and if it showed no sign of infection, they were deemed innocent (or forgiven). In the ordeal of the hot iron, the accused was made to hold a piece of iron, freshly pulled from a fire, and to walk a number of paces while holding it (Kerr, Forsyth, & Plyley 1992).[17] Their hand was then bound and, similar to the trial by hot water, was checked on the third day for infection. In the ordeal of cold water, the accused was bound and tied to a rope, then submerged in water. If they were innocent, the water would embrace them, and they would sink. If guilty, the water would reject them, and they would float.

These trials officially fell out of use after 1215 CE, when Pope Innocent III abolished them (Horovitz 2007). At this time, many states were trying to wrest power back from the feudal nobility, and gaining control of the court systems was one popular means of accomplishing this goal (Cameron 1898). In addition, the Church was expanding its own ecclesiastical system of justice. This facilitated a state-led desire to revise or build upon the court system. The response came in the form of jury trials, which became especially popular in England, and in a revival of Roman legal practices, which were used more across continental Europe and in the ecclesiastical courts.

In England, an early form of jury trial was the self-informed jury (Rubin 2003). In small and stable communities, a person's reputation preceded them, and if there was trouble, most of the community knew about it long before a royal officer came to convene the court. Under these circumstances, there was little need for debate, witnesses, or the presentation of evidence; the jury members had already heard it and could make a ruling after a simple presentation of the facts. As such, an English royal officer would make circuits of the country, convening such a court in each region a few times a year (Pollock 1899). In this style, the court could easily run through a dozen cases in a morning.

As for continental Europe, the popularization of Roman legal practices resulted in the recognition and implementation of select rights that had been previously absent from jurisprudence (Cameron 1898). Courts now required positive evidence to convict a person, the accused had the right to hear the charges laid against them, the examination of witnesses was now permitted, and the defense was now granted time to gather evidence and prepare their case. Of course, these prima facie rights were often effectively overridden through the common use of torture to gather evidence. There were few rules limiting the timing or the severity of torture, particularly when used to force a confession.

In summary, the Middle Ages was a period of long struggle, beginning with stories of brutality and torture, but eventually transitioning to formalized methods and practices. The Europeans sought to recover from the fall of the Roman Empire by returning to their old ways, including blood feuds and _wergild_. This was eventually supplemented by the ordeals, then a centralized court system, as Europe embraced the idealized legal systems of ancient Rome. While continental Europeans sought a revival of Roman legal theory, England experimented with jury trials.

THE RENAISSANCE AND THE SCIENTIFIC REVOLUTION

The Renaissance and the Scientific Revolution had several notable characteristics, and one that stands out for justice scholars is the liberal use of the inquisitorial model.[18] This model was exemplified by the Roman Catholic Inquisition, although the secular courts of the day also fervently embraced it. Even England, which emphasized its systems of common law jury trials, developed specialized courts called prerogative courts, which acted in an inquisitorial manner within their limited jurisdictions. Another characteristic of the era was the disconnect between ritual and purpose. Following on the heels of the Middle Ages, the Renaissance and the Scientific Revolution were replete with judicial practices that, in hindsight, were illogical or indefensible. In addition, this was an era of change and growth, and legal practices could be exceptionally harsh in response to these new realities.[19]

Let us begin in England, where the core of the legal system was the common law jury trial. As noted by Shaffern (2009), "The essential feature of the common law were courts beholden to the king, such that whatever rulings were handed down by these courts were 'common' to the whole realm" (155). This meant the court's decision could result in the formation of a new law, particularly for novel cases and unique circumstances. Originally still reliant on the self-informed jury, this quickly became impractical as English populations became more densely urbanized. As a consequence, the justice of the peace, who oversaw jury trials, adopted an inquisitorial role, investigating crimes and examining witnesses and suspects, then presenting the evidence to juries, who were becoming increasingly impartial to the proceedings (Langbein 1974).[20] In non-capital cases, the process became even more curtailed; in these instances, the entirety of the process could be determined by magistrates, who were responsible for investigating the crime, deciding guilt, and assigning punishment.

The prerogative courts, each with its own specialized jurisdiction, were created by the Tudor monarchs in sixteenth-century England (Berman 2006). One such court was the Privy Council, which oversaw crimes of cunning, including fraud, forgery, and extortion. There was also the Court of High Commission, which dealt with heresy and nonconformity to social norms, and the High Court of Admiralty, which handled crimes committed at sea. These courts cast aside the jury model and, much like the rest of Europe, embraced instead a fully inquisitorial model, one that relied on the use of torture to gather evidence and prove guilt. Despite these changes, the common law courts retained some authority, particularly in capital cases, and they eventually became the dominant model when prerogative courts were abolished with the English Revolution.[21][22]

As for the rest of Europe, the most popular European legal system between the fifteenth and seventeenth centuries was the Inquisition. An ecclesiastical system tasked with ferreting out heretics, the Inquisition followed a scripted process of prosecution (Pavlac 2009). First, a panel of inquisitors would be sent to a specific district to ask for reports of heresy, after which they would issue summons to alleged witnesses and suspects. This was followed by an inquisitorial examination (often including confinement and torture) of the summoned individuals, with the goal of eliciting a confession. The next stage involved a trial, which was typically a quick, ritualistic affair, as a confession had ideally already been acquired. Finally, the inquisitors determined the verdict and punishment, of which the latter could vary dramatically, ranging between simple penance to being burnt alive. This variance was due, in part, to the fact that the Inquisition frequently embraced a two-strike system (Wickersham 2012). With the first conviction, the inquisitors might seek restoration and mercy. A relapse into a second offense of heresy, however, warranted the death penalty, often by fire.[23] To further complicate things, although the Church granted some rights to the accused, the inquisitors were the arbiters of disputes of procedure and were rarely limited or censured for their actions. Thus, the style of justice could vary greatly depending on the disposition of the inquisitor.[24]

Among the famous trials of the Roman Inquisition is that of Galileo Galilei. In the year 1616, heliocentrism, the theory that the earth orbits the sun, was declared heretical, and Galileo was commanded to abandon the theory (Kelly 2016). In 1632, Galileo published his *Dialogue*, written as a debate between three characters on the Copernican (heliocentric) and Ptolemaic (roughly geocentric) systems.[25] While the book's preface declared that heliocentrism could never be proven true, the text offered support for the proofs of the Copernican system. Galileo was eventually summoned to Rome to be formally questioned, where he dismissed any accusations of heliocentric advocacy.[26] At a later date, Galileo was again questioned, this time under threat of torture, and he continued to deny advocacy, although apparently unconvincingly. He was finally sentenced, receiving "imprisonment at the discretion of the Holy Office, commuted after one day to villa arrest, along with three years of weekly penitential prayer" (Kelly 2016, 725). This was typical of sentences handed out by the Inquisition, at least for a first offense.

While Galileo's trial may seem an oddity to the modern-day reader, it was, in actuality, relatively routine for the period, easily overshadowed by even more seemingly bizarre cases, particularly those of non-human animals. While there have been hundreds of recorded instances of animals on trial throughout human history, the lion's share arose from this period (Girgen 2003). Of particular note, non-human animals on trial during this period were treated virtually the same as their human counterparts. They were assigned advocates, summoned to court, and subject to an evidentiary burden and sentencing. Both ecclesiastical and secular courts had their own versions of animal trials. The ecclesiastical courts dealt with groups of vermin, such as rats, locusts, or termites, and the destruction of crops or other property. Perhaps unsurprisingly, when summoned to court, the pests usually failed to appear, leaving their advocates to present impressive and creative excuses for their absence.[27] Secular proceedings typically focused on domestic animals that were accused of causing physical harm to humans. Pigs, in particular, were frequently charged with maiming or killing young children and, thus, were often present as defendants in court. Unlike the punishments of ecclesiastical courts, which were typically spiritual (such as being declared *anathema*), the secular courts used arbitrary forms of corporeal punishment, often simulating the harms the animal had caused before putting them to death.[28]

Non-human animals aside, most convicted offenders, such as Galileo, received only light punishments and fines during this period; however, a fair number continued to be legally brutalized and put to death. Although the Renaissance and the Scientific Revolution witnessed impressive advances in human achievement, accountability or oversight and the investigative abilities necessary for the modern sensibilities of justice were still woefully lacking. This led to shortcuts in legal proceedings, including summary decisions by magistrates and the practice of using torture as a preferred means of gathering information. The potential for abuse was tangible, which likely provided some degree of inspiration for the Enlightenment philosophers.

THE ENLIGHTENMENT

The eighteenth-century period of Enlightenment is renowned for its philosophical giants, including Cesare Beccaria, who advocated for equality, transparency, proportionality, and humanity in criminal justice outcomes (Bessler 2016). This period is also commemorated as the birthplace of the social sciences, including such disciplines as penology, criminology, and criminal justice (Sherman 2005). However, these academic and philosophical endeavors were slow to take shape, often whispered about behind closed doors, due at least in part to the brutal response to dissension evident during this time. The ruling class managed the criminal justice system with an iron first, adept at using it whenever the slightest hint of protest was detected. In addition, the punitive system was riddled with excessively harsh punishments, as minor offenses often warranted the death penalty. Despite these conditions, the inequities and inhumanities evident in the courts of the era became a point of contention, spurring on advocates who demanded change.

In the century leading up to the Enlightenment, England disbanded its prerogative courts in favor of common law courts. As a consequence, the common law courts expanded their jurisdiction, now hearing cases that had been beyond their historical purview, such as poaching or adultery.[29] As the common law courts were traditionally able to inflict capital punishment, this expansion allowed for a more liberal application of capital punishment for a greater number of crimes (Berman 2006). Increasing severity in the criminal justice system was also amplified by social shifts in the population. Specifically, the ruling class, which had traditionally been rooted in the monarchy, was expanding to include wealthy merchants and landowners, leading to legal changes designed to protect their property and their interests (Rousseaux & Dwyer 1997). Crimes that were previously considered merely misdemeanor trespassing, such as taking fruits and vegetables from a landed estate or hunting without a license, became capital offenses.

While there was an inflation of death penalty cases, in many places the number of executions actually decreased (Horovitz 2007). This is due, in part, to the sensibilities of juries. They had the option of convicting offenders for lesser offenses, particularly ones that did not result in capital punishment, such as replacing an alleged burglary with a charge of theft (Langbein 1987). This phenomenon was called undervaluing, partial verdict, or pious perjury, and English juries engaged in it with some frequency, even when it was not technically permitted.[30] This practice was also commonly followed in France, not because of an overabundance of capital sentences, per se, but due instead to the rigid fixed sentences written into the French code (Delivré & Berger 2014).

While juries were finding ways to circumvent a harsh system of justice, Enlightenment thinkers were also regularly calling for a rational system of justice, one that did not rely on barbaric punishments, capital sentences, and torture. For example, Beccaria advocated for a separation between legislators and judges, arguing that the latter should not have the right to construct laws. He also vehemently rejected torture, noting that it countered the expectation that the accused was innocent until proven guilty, since torture was, in essence, a punishment in and of itself (Bessler 2016). Along similar lines, Beccaria advocated for lighter sentences, positing that overly harsh punishments compromised the integrity of the criminal justice system. Ironically, Beccaria's suggestions were published anonymously as he feared he would face severe legal repercussions for his opinions. Despite potential repercussions for the dissenters, the calls for reform voiced by Beccaria and other Enlightenment thinkers spread throughout Europe, and from the 1740s onward, various Western countries began to adjust their punitive approaches to crime (Jenkins 1984). Capital punishment, for example, became largely obsolete in Russia and Austria. In addition, Prussia took great steps to eliminate torture, the death penalty, and corruption among judges, while also attempting to streamline the legal process (Shaffern 2009).

As capital punishment lost popularity in some nations, other measures were implemented that altered court systems further. In England, for example, the use of counsel for both prosecution and defense gained favor, leading to a host of developments, including the growth of the modern adversarial system (Horovitz 2007). Methods of cross-examination were refined, as were the rules of evidence, particularly pertaining to hearsay. In addition, as torture became less desirable, the legal system responded by requiring new laws of proof (Langbein 1987). These changes, although occurring in fits and starts, served to protect the rights of the accused and preserve the integrity of the courts.

In summary, the court systems changed throughout the period of Enlightenment, inspired in part by the reformist narratives and in part by necessity. Some modifications were readily adopted, such as the alleviation of excessively cruel punishments, while others were slow in implementation, such as the separation between legislators and the judiciary or the elimination of absolutist justice (Simon 2009).[31] Regardless, change was afoot, and the success of the English, French, and American political revolutions, as well as the Industrial Revolution, gave credence to and helped spread many of these burgeoning ideals throughout the Western world.

LATE MODERN PERIOD

The modern era can be characterized in a number of ways, but when addressing the courts, this period provided an intersection between the ideas and practices of the past and the discoveries of the present. The modern era embraced the philosophical principles of the Enlightenment, as well as the Scientific Revolution's commitment to empiricism, but it did so against a backdrop of rapid change, as intellectual giants, such as Charles Darwin and Cesare Lombroso, reshaped social and political perceptions of the relationship between evolution, biology, psychology, and deviance. These advancements had a particularly striking and long-term effect on the criminal justice system.

The empirical focus of the Scientific Revolution was particularly apparent in the early modern era. Criminologists were especially motived to apply the laws of science in a manner that would allow them to observe and identify deviant traits. If such traits were catalogued, then perhaps they could be used to predict who would commit crime and how to best punish them. One popular biological theory, phrenology, proposed that the brain was comprised of different faculties, each having its own function, and the under- or overdevelopment of these faculties could affect both the personality and the shape of the skull (Rafter 2005). A professional phrenologist could then purportedly examine a person's skull and identify various character traits, such as a propensity for violence. These ideas were the birthplace of modern criminology, advancing the discipline beyond using religious methods (such as the ordeals) to identify criminality. Spurzheim, a proponent of phrenology, proposed that people could develop and train the various faculties of the brain, thus setting the stage for the rehabilitative movement in sentencing decisions.

Phrenology, although popular for a time, was most influential in that it created a foundation for another theory of crime: criminal anthropology. Criminal anthropology was introduced by Cesare Lombroso, whom many consider to be the father of criminology. Inspired by Darwin's idea of natural selection and by the physiological implications of phrenology, Lombroso made a key connection between specific physical traits and criminal behavior, one that would shape criminal justice practices dramatically. Specifically, Lombroso posited that criminals were evolutionary throwbacks to a morally underdeveloped stage of human development and "could be identified on the basis of '*atavistic* stigmata'—physical characteristics from more primitive stages of human evolution, such as a large jaw, a sloping forehead, and a single palmar crease" (Raine 2014, 12). According to Lombroso, these evolutionary throwbacks, called atavists, were born criminals, hardwired to engage in immoral behaviors that reflected their naturally regressive state of being. For a time, sentencing hearings revolved around atavistic traits; having a large jaw or jug ears, for example, could earn a person a longer prison sentence, as these indicated the accused was a born criminal and thus a natural danger to society. This practice lost favor over time, however, as criminal anthropology was challenged for being unscientific, incorrect, and largely drawn along ethnic lines.[32]

While evolution and physiology were dominant forces in early modern criminal justice practices, so, too, were issues related to the relationship between mental health and criminal responsibility. The first written law addressing compromised mental competency was drafted in 1581, stating that people who had no knowledge of good and evil could not commit a felony (Torry & Billick 2010). By the turn of the nineteenth century, the relationship between psychology and accountability had evolved to include a phenomenon known as moral insanity. This affliction, a precursor to modern-day psychopathy, referred to individuals who had full intellectual capacity but little to no appreciation of morality, thus affecting their understanding of right and wrong (Rafter 2006). The proposition that someone could experience emotional madness without intellectual disturbances was controversial and eventually lost out to a more traditional understanding of insanity. However, these ideas served as a platform upon which to facilitate change in the courts, particularly around issues of mental competency, guilt, and accountability.

The contemporary version of the insanity defense was developed in the nineteenth century with the M'Naughten rule. This was named after Daniel M'Naughten, a Scottish citizen who harbored delusions that he was being persecuted by the British prime minister. As a result of his psychological instabilities, M'Naughten ended up killing the prime minister's secretary, Edward Drummond. M'Naughten was found not guilty by reason of insanity, creating a judicial precedence that persists to this day. The M'Naughten rule includes two criteria, each of which will excuse criminal conduct. A person's guilt is mitigated if they are either operating under such a mental deficit that they do not know what they are doing or that they do not know what they are doing is wrong.[33] Although still informative in Western courts, the use of this rule, and the idea of being not guilty by reason of insanity, has been and continues to be contentious (Hanganu-Bresch 2019).[34]

Between attempts to understand insanity and fledgling biological theories, the nineteenth century could literally and figuratively be dubbed the era of mad science. Many researchers and practitioners of the time believed they were on the cusp of understanding and thus eradicating all forms of criminality, and this unchecked expectation further fueled their radical ideas and activities. Unfortunately, inherent biases were often the inspiration of these theories, especially the biological ones, turning mad science into bad science.

CONCLUSION

History is often interpreted as an inevitable march forward, denoting evolving progress. However, reality is far messier than depicted by simple timelines. Ideas wax and wane, falling in and out of favor, and the criminal justice system is not immune to these oscillations. Jury trials illustrate this point; their use has fluctuated dramatically as a result of the struggle between ritual, idealism, and more recently, efficiency. Jury trials have long been seen as a way to guarantee the rights of an individual, "as a bulwark, standing between the criminal defendant and the powerful state" (Sarat, Ewick, & Marder 2015, 134). However, in modern adversarial systems of justice, jury trials are in steep decline. Instead, plea bargaining is greatly encouraged and occurs in the vast majority of cases, due primarily to concerns centered around the cost and time commitment required for jury proceedings. This is not without controversy, particularly given the coercive nature of plea bargaining (Langbein 1978).[35] Despite criticisms, the expansive rules of evidence and complexity of jury trials, designed to protect the rights of the accused, have tempered the appeal of such practices.

This raises the question of the future of courts and sentencing. Similar to jury trials, other methods of assigning guilt and punishment have shifted over time, including the use of torture, rules of evidence, the right to counsel, and the resulting adversarial system. In addition, the role of the magistrate and judge has shifted, reflecting the political culture of the era. This suggests that courts and sentencing are in flux, and their future is uncertain. History has taught us that these shifts are often implemented in a manner designed to protect the integrity of the court and to instill great rights on behalf of the accused. However, if the current state of jury trials (and plea bargaining) is any indication, those goals may be taking a back seat to expediency and efficiency. This is an ominous foreshadowing of what may be in store for the next era of criminal justice practices.

While the future of courts and sentencing is potentially murky, the past is definitive and greatly influential. The Western world's contemporary courts still use structures developed and implemented thousands of years ago.[36] Throughout continental Europe, for example, the Roman-inspired inquisitorial systems are still the norm (Wieacker 1981). In addition, becoming a legal practitioner and scholar requires the careful study of ancient Roman law since it is fundamental to contemporary codes and statutes. Along the same lines, the jury system, or being tried by one's peers, may look nothing like the massive affairs that took place in ancient Greece, but the general underpinnings of the jury process remain the same in the twenty-first century. These are but two periods that continue to shape Western systems of today, but they illustrate a point that can be extended to all eras of human history: specifically, although the future of courts and sentencing is unclear, once it arrives, it will be better understood through the lens of the past.

NOTES

1. For further details, see Harries (1999).
2. So important was the concept of citizenship that there was a specific and severe punishment, called *atimia*, which was the removal of citizenship status (Sealey 1996).
3. Juries could be convened for private lawsuits as well, although usually with smaller numbers. See Kapparis (2019) for more details.
4. Sometimes a second round of speaking would be included, allowing further rebuttals of the first round.
5. The *Prytaneum* was a term used for the seat of governance. To be fed or maintained in the Prytaneum was to be considered an honored guest of the people and was used to court foreign dignitaries or have feasts for Olympic champions.

6. There were cases where the accused would have to stand in a boat just offshore in order to participate in their trial.

7. This also effectively created new laws.

8. At the time, if punishment was not determined statutorily, then it was often given to the victim to decide what would be appropriate.

9. The case of Maesia of Sentinum was notable because of the lack of an advocate. In the face of criminal charges, Maesia chose to represent herself and won with a near-unanimous vote from her jury (Marshall 1990). A woman representing herself, or anyone, while not against the law, was certainly taboo. It was rare for women to even be publicly charged with a crime (Strachan-Davidson 1901). Lesser crimes, at least, would typically be taken care of by family tribunal or private arbitration. Maesia's acts were so remarkable that history does not even record the crime of which she was accused. While Maesia's case was recorded as a censure for her abandonment of womanly decorum, she can now be celebrated for her courage during an era that did not accept women as full citizens (Garishvili 2012).

10. *Satius esse impunitum reliqui facinus nicentis quam innocentem damnari.*

11. *Mellior est iustitia vere praeviniens quam severe puniens.*

12. This assumes, of course, that a great deal of overlap existed, and it varied in time from place to place.

13. Also called the Wager of Law, Canonical Purgation, or Canonical Compurgation.

14. Jenks notes that another reason for the state to become involved in such crimes is that the loss of each man is the loss of a warrior to defend the state (Jenks 1898).

15. As Cameron put it, "The judicial duel acquired in the early part of the eleventh century an almost universal dominion, so that even the most notorious criminal might escape from justice by an appeal to the edge of the sword" (Cameron 1898, 444).

16. How deep they had to immerse their hand, be it a pot or cauldron, often varied due to the severity of the crime.

17. The severity of the crime often influenced the weight of the iron, or the number of paces required.

18. In the inquisitorial model, the court, magistrate, or judge(s) have investigative powers, regularly questioning suspects and witnesses and examining evidence. This is often contrasted with the adversarial system, which is characterized by an impartial third party, such as judge and jury, deciding a case between two other parties who present arguments and evidence. A judge who has investigative powers, such as in an inquisitorial system, is not considered an impartial third party.

19. One example of this is with the treatment of mass vagrancy that occurred in the wake of war. Jobless workers and displaced, penniless people were often labeled "vagrant" and given the harshest treatment. Not only was vagrancy considered a crime, but it was also often punished with branding, torture, or death, often without any sort of trial (Rousseaux & Dwyer 1997).

20. While this started as common practice, the Marian Statutes of 1554 then required justices of the peace to conduct investigations in felony cases.

21. One exception to this is the Act of Attainder, whereby a legislative act of parliament would declare a person a traitor, circumventing the courts to sentence a person to death (Darsie 2019). This was used in cases of high treason, which was loosely defined, as poisoning someone was considered high treason. Throughout the sixteenth century, this was a tool of literal political assassination.

22. The prerogative courts were, in essence, legal courts in direct control of the Crown (Berman 2006). When the Long Parliament revolted against the Crown in 1640, the prerogative courts also naturally fell.

23. The Church forbade its representatives from shedding blood and, therefore, executions were facilitated by the local government.

24. The famous inquisitor Bernard Gui "reported he had burned 548 people and had ordered eighty-eight dead bodies dug up so he could properly punish the corpses of heretics" (Pavlac 2009, 42).

25. Prior to the work of Galileo and his contemporary, Kepler, the Ptolemaic and Copernican systems both had mathematical flaws (Ecklund & Ecklund 2014). However, accepting the Copernican system required accepting that the earth was not the center of the universe, which went against the religious sensibilities of the day, and also that the earth was in constant motion, which went against the supposed common sense and experience of that time.

26. This put Galileo in the category of having committed a crime, *appearing* to support heresy, but without heretical intent. Technically, the procedures of the time required that the suspect be tortured at this point, to be sure of the truth. Galileo avoided torture, likely because of his advanced age and infirmity.

27. In the 1522 proceedings against the rats of Autun, counsel first argued that the rats, spread over such a large swath of countryside, had not been given due notice, and so the summons should be declared in multiple areas (Slabbert 2004). In the next hearing, he asked for a delay so that the rats might have time to migrate to the court. Finally, at the last session, he argued that the rats could not lawfully obey the summons, as they were in danger because of how unpopular they were with the local populace, the plaintiffs in this case, and especially so with their cats. The court was then unable to determine an appropriate time for the rats to appear, and so court was adjourned with the complaint against the rats being thrown out by default. Far from being a jest, this lawyer and Romano-canonical jurist, Chassenée, then published a treatise on the excommunication of insects, which was reprinted multiple times, and later served in the parliaments of Dijon and Aix in France.

28. To be anathemized was similar to being excommunicated, except animals were not technically participants in religious communion, and so could not be excommunicated.

29. Such activities had not been crimes under the common law system and were criminalized with the vast legislation put into the prerogative courts.

30. Pious perjury, meaning that the jury knowingly gave a false verdict in the interest of justice.

31. Under absolutist justice, the monarch was able to repeal or rearrange any part of the legal process or individual case as they saw fit. Such systems also often emphasized crimes against the state that also had to be reported to the sovereign, such as scandalous libel, treason, or treasonous words (Stolleis & Halpérin 2011).

32. Lombroso's work included a clear chart of evolutionary hierarchy, with Jews and Northern Italians at the top as the most evolved. Southern Italians were placed at the bottom of the chart, along with Bolivians and Peruvians (Raine 2014, 12).

33. It should be noted that this does not cover the instance whereby a person feels morally justified in their criminal behavior, but only when there was a lack of understanding. This also contrasts with moral insanity, where a person would understand that their behavior was considered wrong but could not or would not control themselves.

34. Through the twentieth century, in the United States, the standards for the insanity defense were slowly lowered until their final form was determined by the apparent irresistibility of a young actor. This was the Hinckley incident. John Hinckley Jr. shot United States president Ronald Reagan as an offering of love to an actor he had been stalking (Tory & Billick 2010). A jury found him not guilty by reason of insanity. The public outcry from this event pushed legislation forward, reverting the insanity defense to a version almost identical to the M'Naughten rule, but also requiring proof of a severe mental disease or defect.

35. In comparing plea bargaining to torture, Langbein argues that the difference between them is merely a matter of degree (1978). Both use coercion, be it physical pain or a

combination of promises and threats, to resolve a case without needing, or regardless of, facts and truth. His worry coincides with a commonly understood truth, that "even without [physical] torture, normal people suddenly thrust into the criminal machinery, variously restrained, confined, isolated, intimidated, and surrounded, can break down and confess to things they did not do, in an attempt to restore normality" (Pavlac 2009, 38–39).

36. Many of the same debates are also occurring today as they did thousands of years ago. In ancient Rome, the validity of the death penalty was often a hotly debated topic, much as it is today (Bauman 1996). There is also the question of who is better qualified to make laws, the ruling body of a nation through the act of legislation versus judges and juries in the systems of common law. Moreover, there is the debate over discretion in sentencing, whether there should be more stringent guidelines or if the courts should have full case-by-case purview (Hofer et al. 2005). These questions do not have easy answers, and the various cultures today and throughout history have come down on all different sides.

REFERENCES

Bauman, Richard A. 1996. "Trial by Magistrate and People." In *Crime and Punishment in Ancient Rome*, edited by Richard Bauman, 7–15. Oxford: Routledge.

Berman, Harold J. 2006. "The Transformation of English Criminal Law." In *Law and Revolution, II: The Impact of the Protestant Reformations on the Western Legal Tradition*, edited by Harold J. Berman, 306–29. Cambridge: Harvard University Press.

Bessler, John D. 2016. "The Economist and the Enlightenment: How Cesare Beccaria Changed Western Civilization." *European Journal of Law and Economics* 46, no. 3 (September): 275–302. https://doi.org/10.1007/s10657-016-9546-z.

Blecker, Robert. 2006. "Ancient Greece's Death Penalty Dilemma and Its Influence on Modern Society." *USA Today*, (July): 60–65. https://digitalcommons.nyls.edu/cgi/viewcontent.cgi?article=1579&context=fac_other_pubs.

Calhoun, George M. 1927. "The Homeric Age." In *The Growth of Criminal Law in Ancient Greece*, edited by George M. Calhoun, 15–24. Oakland: University of California Press.

Cameron, J. S. Taylor. 1898. "Roman Law in the Early Middle Ages III," *Juridical Review* 10 (3): 438–449.

D'Amato, Anthony. 1976. "Obligation to Obey the Law: A Study of the Death of Socrates." *Southern California Law Review* 49: 1079–1108.

Darsie, Heather R. 2019. "Thomas Cromwell's Influence on the Laws of England: A Basic Review of the English Legal System and Reforms in the Early 16th Century and the Rise of the Act of Attainder," *Northern Illinois University Law Review* 39, no. 2 (Spring): 273–87.

Delivré, Émilie, and Emmanuel Berger. 2014. In *Popular Justice in Europe (18th–19th Centuries)*, edited by Émilie Delivré and Emmanuel Berger, 71–88. Bologna: Società editrice il Mulino.

Ecklund, John E., and Constance Cryer Ecklund. 2014. "The Seventeenth Century and the Scientific Revolution." In *The Origins of Western Law: From Athens to the Code Napoleon*, edited by Constance Cryer Ecklund, 620–38. Austin: Talbot Publishing.

Garishvili, Marina. 2013. "Characteristics of Ancient Rome Criminal Law Process." In *Journal of Law*, edited by Besarion Zoidze, 5–22. Tbilisi: Tbilisi University Press.

Girgen, Jen. 2003. "The Historical and Contemporary Prosecution and Punishment of Animals." *Animal Law* 9: 97–133. https://www.animallaw.info/article/historical-and-contemporary-prosecution-and-punishment-animals.

Halperin, Michael and Jean-Louis. 2011. "Judicial Interpretation in Transition from the Ancient Regime to Constitutionalism." In *Interpretation of Law in the Age of Enlightenment from the Rule of the King to the Rule of Law*, edited by Yasutomo Morigiwa, 3–17. Dordrecht: Springer Netherlands.

Hanganu-Bresch, Cristina. 2019. "Public Perceptions of Moral Insanity in the 19th Century." *Journal of Nervous and Mental Disease* 207, no. 9 (September): 805–814. https://doi.org/10.1097/nmd.0000000000001035.

Harries, Jill. 1999. "In Court." In *Law and Empire in Late Antiquity*, edited by Jill Harries, 99–117. Cambridge: Cambridge University Press.

Harris, Edward, and Lene Rubinstein. 2004. *The Law and the Courts in Ancient Greece*. London: Bristol Classical Press.

Helmholz, R. H. 1983. "Crime, Compurgation and the Courts of the Medieval Church." *Law and History Review* 1, no. 1 (Spring): 1–26. https://doi.org/10.2307/744000.

Hofer, Paul J., Charles Loeffler, Kevin Blackwell, and Patricia Valentino. 2005. "Fifteen Years of Guidelines Sentencing: An Assessment of How Well the Federal Criminal Justice System Is Achieving the Goals of Sentencing Reform." *Federal Sentencing Reporter* 17, no. 4 (April): 269–76. https://doi.org/10.1525/fsr.2005.17.4.269.

Horovitz, Anat. 2007. "The Emergence of Sentencing Hearings." *Punishment & Society* 9, no. 3 (July): 271–99. https://doi.org/10.1177/1462474507077495.

Humfress, Caroline. 2011. "Bishops and Law Courts in Late Antiquity: How (Not) to Make Sense of the Legal Evidence." *Journal of Early Christian Studies* 19, no. 3 (Fall): 375-400. https://doi.org/10.1353/earl.2011.0033.

Jenkins, Phillip. 1984. "Varieties of Enlightenment Criminology." *British Journal of Criminology* 24, no. 2 (April): 112–130. https://www.jstor.org/stable/23637024.

Jenks, Edward. 1898. "The Administration of Justice." In *Law and Politics in the Middle Ages: With a Synoptic Table of Sources*, edited by Edward Jenks, 100–47. London: J. Murray.

Kapparis, Konstantinos A. 2019. "The Administration of Justice in the Polis." In *Athenian Law and Society*, edited by Konstantinos Kapparis, 18–69. Oxford: Routledge.

Kelly, Henry Ansgar. 2016."Galileo's Non-Trial (1616), Pre-Trial (1632–1633), and Trial (May 10, 1633): A Review of Procedure, Featuring Routine Violations of the Forum of Conscience." *Church History* 85, no. 4 (December): 724–61. https://doi.org/10.1017/S0009640716001190.

Kerr, Margaret H., Richard D. Forsyth, and Michael J. Plyley. 1992. "Cold Water and Hot Iron: Trial by Ordeal in England." *Journal of Interdisciplinary History* 22, no. 4 (Spring): 573–95. https://doi.org/10.2307/205237.

Lamoreaux, John C. 1995. "Episcopal Courts in Late Antiquity." *Journal of Early Christian Studies* 3, no. 2 (Summer): 143–67. https://doi.org/10.1353/earl.0.0052.

Langbein, John H. 1974. "The Origins of Examination by the Magistrates in England." In *Prosecuting Crime in the Renaissance: England, Germany, France*, edited by John H. Langbein, 63–97. Cambridge: Harvard University Press.

Langbein, John H. 1978. "Torture and Plea Bargaining." *University of Chicago Law Review* 46, no. 1 (Autumn): 3–22. https://doi.org/10.2307/1599287.

Langbein, John H. 1987. "The English Criminal Jury on the Eve of the French Revolution." In *The Trial Jury in England, France, Germany, 1700-1900*, edited by Antonio Padoa Schioppa, 13–39. Berlin: Duncker & Humblot.

Leeson, Peter T. 2012. "Ordeals." *Journal of Law and Economics* 55, no. 3 (August): 691–714. https://doi.org/10.1086/664010.

Marshall, Anthony J. 1990. "Roman Ladies on Trial: The Case of Maesia of Sentinum." *Phoenix* 44, no. 1 (Spring): 46–59. https://doi.org/10.2307/1088565.

Pavlac, Brian Alexander. 2009. "Medieval Origins of Witch Hunts." In *Witch Hunts in the Western World: Persecution and Punishment from the Inquisition through the Salem Trials*, edited by Brian A. Pavlac, 25–50. Lincoln: University of Nebraska Press.

Phillips, David D. 2013. "Archaic and Classical Athens: A Short History." In *The Law of Ancient Athens*, edited by David Phillips, 1–43. Ann Arbor: University of Michigan Press.

Plato. 1964. *Plato, with an English Translation*. Translated by Harold North Flower, Walter R. M. Lamb, Robert Gregg Bury, and Paul Shorey. Cambridge: Harvard University Press.

Pollock, Frederick. 1899. "The King's Peace in the Middle Ages." *Harvard Law Review* 13, no. 3 (November): 177–89. https://doi.org/10.2307/1322581.

Rafter, Nicole. 2005. "The Murderous Dutch Fiddler." *Theoretical Criminology* 9, no. 1 (February): 65–96. https://doi.org/10.1177/1362480605048943.

Rafter, Nicole. 2006. "The Unrepentant Horse-Slasher: Moral Insanity and the Origins of Criminological Thought*." *Criminology* 42, no. 4 (March): 979–1008. https://doi.org/10.1111/j.1745-9125.2004.tb00542.x.

Raine, Adrian. 2014. "Basic Instincts." In *The Anatomy of Violence: The Biological Roots of Crime*, edited by Adrian Raine, 11–36. London: Penguin Books.

Rousseaux, Xavier, and Kevin Dwyer. 1997. "Crime, Justice and Society in Medieval and Early Modern Times: Thirty Years of Crime and Criminal Justice History." *Crime, Histoire & Sociétés* 1 (1): 87–118. https://doi.org/10.4000/chs.1034.

Rubin, Edward L. 2003. "Trial by Battle, Trial by Argument." *Arkansas Law Review* 56, no. 2 (May): 261–94.

Sarat, Austin, Patricia Ewick, and Nancy Marder. 2015. "Jurors and Juries." In *The Handbook of Law and Society*, edited by Austin Sarat and Patricia Ewick, 134–39. Hoboken: Wiley-Blackwell Publishing.

Sealey, Raphael. 1996. "Scope of the Inquiry." In *The Justice of the Greeks*, edited by Raphael Sealey, 1–24. Ann Arbor: University of Michigan Press.

Shaffern, Robert W. 2009. "The Enlightenment." In *Law and Justice from Antiquity to Enlightenment*, edited by Robert W. Shaffern, 201–9. Lanham: Rowman & Littlefield Publishers.

Shaffern, Robert W.2009. "The Jurisprudence of St. Thomas Aquinas." In *Law and Justice from Antiquity to Enlightenment*, edited by Robert W. Shaffern, 148–54. Lanham: Rowman & Littlefield Publishers.

Sherman, Lawrence W. 2005. "The Use and Usefulness of Criminology, 1751–2005: Enlightened Justice and Its Failures." *Annals of the American Academy of Political and Social Science* 600, no. 1 (July): 115–35. https://doi.org/10.1177/0002716205278103.

Simon, Fabrizio. 2009. "Criminology and Economic Ideas in the Age of Enlightenment." *History of Economic Ideas* 17 (3): 11–39. https://www.jstor.org/stable/23723447.

Slabbert, Melodie. 2004. "Prosecuting Animals in Medieval Europe: Possible Explanations." *Fundamina: A Journal of Legal History* 10: 159–79.

Strachan-Davidson, J. L. 1901. "Mommsen's Roman Criminal Law." *English Historical Review* 16, no. 62 (April): 219–91. http://www.jstor.org/stable/548653.

Torry, Zachary D. and Stephen B. Billick. 2010. "Overlapping Universe: Understanding Legal Insanity and Psychosis." *Psychiatric Quarterly* 81, no. 3 (April): 253–62. https://doi.org/10.1007/s11126-010-9134-2.

Urch, Erwin J. 1929. "Modern English and Ancient Roman Criminal Procedure." *United States Law Review* 63, no. 5 (September): 451–60. https://heinonline.org/HOL/LandingPage?handle=hein.journals/amlr63&div=48&id=&page=.

Von Dornum, Deirdre Dionysia. 1997."The Straight and the Crooked: Legal Accountability in Ancient Greece." *Columbia Law Review* 97, no. 5 (June): 1483–1518. https://doi.org/10.2307/1123441.

Wickersham, Jane K. 2012. "The Mercy of the Court." In *Rituals of Prosecution: The Roman Inquisition and the Prosecution of Philo-Protestants in Sixteenth-Century Italy*, edited by Jane K. Wickersham, 121–54. Toronto: University of Toronto Press.

Wieacker, Franz. 1981."The Importance of Roman Law for Western Civilization and Western Legal Thought." *Boston College International and Comparative Law Review* 4, no. 2 (Fall): 257–82. https://scholarship.law.cornell.edu/cgi/viewcontent.cgi?httpsredir=1&article=1570 &context=clr#:~:text=In%20conclusion%2C%20it%20may%20be,element%20in%20the %20individual%20legal.

Chapter 4

Tracing Corrections through Time

Stace L. Grove, Grace Meyer, and Omi Hodwitz

The vilest deeds like poison weeds
Bloom well in prison-air:
It is only what is good in Man
That wastes and withers there:
Pale Anguish keeps the heavy gate,
And the Warden in Despair.

(Wilde 1928, 103)

INTRODUCTION

Join us on a journey while we investigate the historical roots of the correctional system within Western civilization.[1] In the simplest terms, the term *corrections* refers to the supervision and control of those believed to have committed deviant acts, usually through a process of incarceration.[2] Despite this seemingly parsimonious definition, the purpose, meaning, and practice of corrections has varied wildly throughout history. In some eras, prisons were merely holding stations between a crime and punishment. In others, corrections reformed or changed, punished and tortured, generated labor, or simply eradicated undesirable riffraff from the streets. In this chapter, we seek to unlock the rusted gates of history's past and expose these multilayered and diverse façades of correctional practices.

This chapter begins at the beginning, traveling as far back as historical records allow. This places us in ancient antiquity, where we examine the earliest methods of imprisonment and confinement employed in Greece and Rome. Next, we move into the Middle Ages, a period that fittingly earned the epithet "Dark Ages," informed in part by inhumane and barbaric conditions, systematic extortion, and a deadly plague. Next, we visit an era of progress, including the Renaissance and the Age of Enlightenment. Despite advancements in the arts and sciences, this period embraced corrections in a ruthless manner, mirroring previous eras.

Shifting our geopolitical focus, we travel across the Pacific Ocean to an emergent nation, the United States, which offered its own dramatic contributions to the world of corrections. Consequently, the prison industry grew, testing ethical and moral boundaries. In response, the eighteenth and nineteenth centuries became a period of reform, as society and authorities attempted to refine and improve corrections. We end the chapter with an examination of modern times and the prison boom of the twentieth century, a touch of old wine in a new bottle.

ANCIENT ANTIQUITY: CONFINEMENT, EXILE, AND DEATH

During the age of antiquity, the Greco-Roman civilization laid the paving stones that would eventually become the foundation for much of modern Western corrections. The Greek and Roman empires were limited in patience and clemency, demanding loyalty through compliance, eager to deploy captivity, exile, or death when these expectations were not met. When these civilizations faded, so, too, did many of their punitive records, leaving historians with the task of piecing together what they could from what remained. We, too, will engage in this task, focusing first on ancient Greece, mythology, and detainment, before shifting to ancient Rome, prisons, and punishments.

In ancient Greece, mythology was central to social identity, serving to entertain but also to instruct, offering guidance on human relations and behaviors. If myth offered a prescription, it was likely to be embraced and incorporated into daily life, and carceral captivity was no exception to this trend. *Prometheus Bound*, a Greek tragedy composed sometime between 479 and 424 BCE, for example, is one of the earliest and more primitive expressions of detainment from this period (Flintoff 1986). In this narrative, Prometheus stole fire from the gods and gave it to humankind; in response, Zeus bound him to a rock. In agony, Prometheus exclaimed: "See in what tortures I must struggle . . . this shame, these bonds, are put upon me by the new ruler of the gods" (Aeschylus and Euripides 1937, 100). Although the tale is fictitious, the practice of being bound was eventually accepted as a means of punishment, to be used as needed, in unique and unsettling ways.[3]

Once detainment was introduced through mythology, it was applied to all members of Greek society. This was unique, given that most punishments were determined by class or status. Slaves lived under a separate system of laws than did freemen, and as a result, punishments varied between the two groups (Johnston 2009). Penalties for slaves were often corporal, whereas punishments for the free involved fines, banishment, or death (Barkan 1936). Captivity, however, was available for all, regardless of whether the detained was enslaved or a freeperson, which undoubtedly made it an undesirable outcome for anyone contemplating deviance.

The Greeks implemented various spaces as a means of imprisonment, including buildings, ditches, quarries, and pits, each acting as a prison, despite the variance in form. A group known as the Eleven would oversee the day-to-day operations of these spaces, forcing the detained to carry out whatever commands were given to them (Hunter 1997). The Eleven did not act alone but were instead assisted by the *hyperetai*, or public slaves. The hyperetai helped the Eleven fulfill certain duties, including acting as the turnkey who placed the incarcerated in bonds and stocks, or guardians on the grounds at night (Folch 2021). The hyperetai were also often responsible for mixing and administering hemlock poison for executions.

Records suggest that Greek versions of prisons were, to put it kindly, undesirable places. Socrates (470 BCE – 399 BCE), the renowned Greek theorist and founder of Western philosophy, was found guilty of corrupting the youth and defying the gods. When given the choice of fines, exile, or suicide, Socrates selected the latter (Johnston 2009). "When Socrates was asked [at his trial] to propose a counter penalty he said: 'What penalty shall I propose? Imprisonment? And why should I live in prison, a slave to those who may be in authority?'" (Barkan 1936, 341). This statement confirms both the presence of long-term imprisonment and the undesirable nature of such an outcome. In the end, Socrates's choice was honored, and he died by ingesting a cup of hemlock brew while under the watchful eye of the Eleven. This was perhaps one the most famous deaths in Greek antiquity, in part because of Socrates's reputation and in part because of the choice of death over incarceration.

The Greek and Roman empires overlapped in time, and as such, the Romans borrowed heavily from the Greeks, replicating institutions and practices. This included punitive policies, such as the use of detainment and captivity. Although present, these measures were limited in scope and use. According to the Twelve Tables, the first set of Roman laws, delinquency of debt was the only crime that would result in long-term incarceration (Deac 2021).[4] As for short-term detainment, this was reserved almost exclusively for those awaiting trial or execution.

The Romans utilized unpleasant sites for the purposes of detainment, including the infamous Carcer Tullianum. Built in the seventh century BCE, the Carcer Tullianum was Rome's earliest and most secure prison.[5] Mazzoni (2017) described the Carcer Tullianum in the following way: "It was the top-security prison for the Roman state, consisting then, like today, of two rooms: a top one (the Carcer) made of travertine and tufa stone, and another below it (the Tullianum), a round structure, also made of stone and originally built around a natural spring of water" (246).[6] The prison was infamous for its blinding darkness, overwhelming stench, unfettered temperatures, and noisome conditions, due in part to its mass overcrowding. Confinement for any length of stay would have likely invoked extreme suffering and despair.

Beyond incarceration, ancient Roman punishment came in other interesting and diverse forms. *Ergastalums* were labor sites, either exposed to the sun or buried underground, where the enslaved worked in chains (Francese 2007).[7] The male head of the Roman household also employed ergastulum as a domestic cell for disorderly members of the family who challenged house rules. Somewhat compatible with ergastulum, offenders could also receive a life sentence of hard labor. Such sentences were essentially a form of institutional slavery that placed the prisoner at the will of the republic to labor anywhere its representatives saw fit (Johnston 2009). Exile, the antithesis of detainment, was yet another punishment. If one was so unlucky as to face this fate, there were two different variations from which they might have suffered. There was *relegatio*, which was exile from Rome, or *desportatio*, banishment to a particular place, often remote and harsh (Morris & Rothman 1995).[8] Exile could be just as catastrophic as any other punishment, including incarceration or life in chains.

In the Roman era, it was just as intolerable, if not more so, to be socially ostracized as it was to lose life, limb, or freedom.

Thus, the age of antiquity, whether in reference to ancient Greece or ancient Rome, was marked by punitive creativity and cruelty. The Greco-Roman Empire embraced a zero-tolerance approach to crime and had a palette of punishments to draw upon. Confinement could involve putrid, dark, and damp pits, places filled with famishment, fear, and suffering.[9] For those unfortunate souls who received a sentence other than incarceration, their remaining days consisted of a life at hard labor in chains, exile into the unknown, or death. Given this era's seemingly stark approach to corrections, it begs the question of the fundamental objective behind such measures. Virginia Hunter (1997) best answers this inquiry, at least regarding ancient Greece, when she states:

> Did the Athenians envision any larger purpose for the prison in addition to custody? In answer to this question, we can reject one possible answer, reform. In popular discourse on punishment, there is no talk of penitence or reformation as an aim of the prison. Indeed, only in the vaguest way were the laws themselves and the penalties they imposed thought to "make people better." (317)

THE MIDDLE AGES: DARKNESS TO DARK-LESS

The Middle Ages arose on the heels of the Roman Empire, and similar to its predecessor, it left an indelible footprint on the criminal justice system.[10] The era, which spanned a thousand years, was subdivided into three sections that varied in social, political, and spiritual characteristics: the early, high, and late Middle Ages.[11] The earliest stage, also known as the Dark Ages, was a particularly troublesome time, filled with conflict and feverish fervor, while the mid-to-later stages hinted at progression, growth, and tolerance. During all three periods, prisons served primarily as holding places for the accused before they faced trial or for the condemned awaiting execution, rather than places of long-term punishment or reformation (Tsougarakis 2014).

Given that medieval prisons were primarily used for temporary holding, they rarely took the form of the traditional fortified structure that modern scholars envision when discussing corrections. Instead, sites of incarceration were diverse, including makeshift holding cells in castles and towers, or more permanent cells in dungeons. In addition, depending on the offense and the governing rule (ecclesiastical or secular), the laity might be confined to monasteries or nunneries (Gloria 1974, as cited in Geltner 2013, 32). As the Middle Ages progressed, however, permanent fortified prisons became more commonplace.

There were several prisons that garnered notoriety during medieval times, including Le Chatelet de Paris, the Tower of London, the Fleet, and Newgate. The deepest and darkest underground dungeon at Le Chatelet de Paris imprisoned offenders in a room built in the shape of an upturned cone. Known as the dreaded Fosse, its dimensions were too small for one to stand up or lie down (Bassett 1944). The Tower of London, founded around 1066 CE, was used to incarcerate anyone who dared cross or defy the Crown. Historical tales recount how prisoners in the Tower were chained by the neck, left to wallow in their own filth, and only offered food forbidden by their religion; the extreme measures were purportedly designed to break their will (Ahnert 2009). These conditions, however, were not unique to Le Chatelet de Paris and the Tower of London. Other less-notorious prisons shared similar characteristics; they were overcrowded and filled with the sickly and malnourished, many of which were chained to decomposing dungeon walls or other poorly ventilated quarters (Babington 1972).[12] Medieval prisons were home to random acts of violence, administrative misconduct, and unsanitary conditions. In addition, they were ground zero for the deadly gaol (jail) fever, a sickness that crept through carceral settings, ending many lives in suffering.[13]

As the Middle Ages progressed, the correctional profile and subsequent use of prisons developed into more of a businesslike entity. The Fleet, which operated between 1197 CE and 1846 CE, was one of the largest prisons in England. For hundreds of years, the role of warden of the Fleet was occupied by members of the same family, passed down through the generations (Bassett 1944). Over time, this desirable role, which could garner quite a profit, was sold off to the highest bidder, regardless of background or experience. The Fleet was, to put it simply, a moneymaker; the detained were forced to pay rent and purchase food and drink from a kitchen operated at the discretion of the warden or the sheriff.

Newgate prison, which operated between 1188 CE and 1902 CE, had similar practices and harsh repercussions for those who did not or could not pay. For example, Hugh de Croydon, a jailer at Newgate prison, found it amusing to lock low-risk criminals into the dungeon with dangerous felons and torture them until they paid his fees (Bassett 1943).[14] Although this act was motivated by profit, it also illustrated the overall condition and practices of the prison; "it was squalid, dirty, and disease-ridden, reviled as 'a "tomb for the living,"' the mansion of misery and even 'Hell itself'" (Sheehan 1977, as cited in Hunter 1977, 229).[15]

In addition to over-the-counter profit, a dishonorable pay-to-play system was common within many of these prisons. If the detained had personal finances, they could live in some degree of comfort while incarcerated (Morris & Rothman 1995). However, if a prisoner had no family or friends or was without financial support, they were likely to live in squalor, deprived of food and in jeopardy of catching the gaol fever, which would have certainly put an end to their life. This unfortunate contrast between the haves and have-nots is illustrated in the case study of the Marquis de Sade, who was confined inside the Bastille prison.[16] While incarcerated, the Marquis de Sade was given access to furnishings from his home, as well as his paintings and personal library, which he used to adorn his prison living quarters. He also brought in a live-in valet and pets, along with gourmet meals prepared for him by his spouse. In sharp contrast, the rest of the population served out their sentences in the rancid lower levels of the prison (Johnston 2009).

Although medieval prisons were, for the most part, fetid and inhumane, they did improve during the late Middle Ages. Separate living quarters were introduced, dividing up the incarcerated population based on the nature of the offense, gender, and socioeconomic status (Bassett 1944). Over time, separate living quarters evolved into separate prisons, further improving the outcome for those found guilty of committing lesser crimes.[17] In addition, it became commonplace to inspect correctional facilities, thus increasing safety and improving supervision. For example, in 1643, the Alderman issued a directive; Newgate and Ludgate were to be subject to four annual inspections with the goal of inserting oversight and accountability (Babington 1972). Lastly, modernized conveniences were slowly introduced to select prisons. Newgate received several notable upgrades, including the addition of chimneys to each room, a recreation area, pleasant chambers placed in the turrets of the gate, a properly lit and spacious chapel, and even the installation of a drinking fountain (Bassett 1943).

Thus, although carceral practices during the Middle Ages were terrible, they did improve over time. The early years were brutal and barbaric, managed by self-interested administrators who treated the detained as sources of profit rather than humans deserving of dignity and respect. As a consequence, prisons were dark and deadly places (Ahnert 2009). Over time this shifted, as prisons became specialized and, in some cases, modernized. These changes took time, appearing in fits and starts and restricted to select prisons; therefore, they were not overtly overwhelming. They were, however, a far cry from the days of grasping for life in a stifling ergastulum or withering away in a sun-soaked quarry pit while awaiting death. In addition, these subtle shifts were a harbinger of what was to come next, a period of positive change.

RENAISSANCE AND THE AGE OF ENLIGHTENMENT: ORDER FROM CHAOS

The Renaissance and the Age of Enlightenment were consecutive periods in European history that bridged the gap between the Middle Ages and modernism.[18] This era was marked by pronounced social change, including in the area of corrections, although punitive practices evolved at a slower pace than other institutional changes during this time. As noted by Wolfgang (1990), torture and executions continued, but imprisonment took on a new meaning, used as a punishment in and of itself, not simply as a means of detainment while awaiting trial or execution. In addition, prison governance softened with an eye toward creating humane conditions, informed in part by social narratives surrounding the historical cruelty of such places. In other words, although this era still bore witness to harsh correctional conditions, it also invited progress and reform.

Le Carceri delle Stinche, commonly called Le Stinche (1300 CE–1833 CE), was the central debtor's prison in Florence during the Renaissance period (Geltner 2013). Unlike many of its predecessors, Le Stinche included an infirmary and a space for the mentally ill, as well as separate wards for males and females. Le Stinche was generally overseen by four to six wardens, a handful of guards, and other facility personnel, including a priest, a custodian, and a practitioner, many of whom lived at the prison. Despite these progressive characteristics, Le Stinche was not without problems, including a lack of organized labor, behavioral management systems, and constructive programming. However, there are several metrics that lead historians to believe that Le Carceri delle Stinche was, perhaps, a bearable place to be imprisoned, including reduced deaths due to violence and disease, limited escape attempts, and limited altercations between inmates and staff (Klapisch-Zuber 2008, as cited in Geltner 2013, 41).[19]

Bologna also oversaw its own system of corrections during the late Middle Ages and throughout the Renaissance. Elected guardians, known as custodes, oversaw the communal prisons, while the jails of the podesta and capitano operated independently. These prisons housed mainly debtors, but records also indicate the incarceration of foreigners and others with which officials found fault.[20] Corporal and capital punishment, although rare, did occur in these facilities, and the average length of stay ranged from hours to days, but typically not more than a month. The prison populations were customarily low, although written accounts do indicate that these numbers were considerably higher in the earlier years as opposed to further into the late fourteenth century, presumably in direct correlation to the black plague. Soon thereafter, the circumstances shifted from greater turnover with lesser fees to lesser turnover with greater fees (Dean 2017).

The House of Correction, or Bridewell, was another type of correctional establishment; it was created with the intention of keeping minor offenders and the impoverished out of the gaols, which were used primarily to detain common criminals and debtors. The Bridewell Palace, given to London by Edward III, was the first institution to open its doors that dealt primarily with such low-risk individuals.[21] In 1576, under the order of Elizabeth I, justices set up similar institutions in every county (Johnston 2009). These Houses of Correction, although seemingly beneficial, were less than ideal; they became oppressive warehouses for the elderly, sick, and underprivileged (categorized most respectfully as "the deserving poor"), reflecting a legal system that punished those of lower social and economic standing (Babington 1972, 11).[22] As time went by, the distinction between the Bridewells and the gaols got lost in translation, and before long, the two became one; the House of Correction was just as much a gaol as the gaol was a House of Correction.

Gallery slavery was one final method of justice dispensed during this era. Born out of Athens, this penalty eventually spread across Europe, becoming particularly commonplace in England and France (Johnston 2009).[23] Put forth as an alternative to imprisonment during times of war, the convicted served this sentence in the holds of ships, as slaves to the oar.[24][25] Although not intended as a death sentence, it often was, particularly in countries with limited natural ports, such as France. Many of the galley slaves never made it onboard to begin serving their sentences; they would succumb to the elements during the excruciating chain gang–style death marches from the prison to the ships (Bamford 1973).

Similar to the Middle Ages, the Age of Enlightenment and the Renaissance were marred by problems, but also indications of progress. As the purpose of imprisonment advanced beyond a simple means of temporary detainment, correctional institutions became more commonplace, reflecting the progressive tone of the era. However, as these facilities grew, so, too, did their scope, expanding to include control of the socially undesirable, particularly the impoverished and the homeless. Despite the unethical widening of the correctional net, some facilities, such as Le Stinche, served as a beacon of hope, demonstrating that correctional practices could be both dignified and successful. It was also becoming apparent that society was growing weary of inhumanity in the name of punishment, and thus, they were ready to listen should a strong voice arise that promoted change.

COLONIAL ERA: BIRTH OF CORRECTIONS REFORMATION

As the eighteenth century progressed, so, too, did corrections, pulled in various ways by people, events, and places. On both sides of the Atlantic Ocean, reformers took an active interest in prison conditions, adopting a narrative of change. Meanwhile, the United States and Britain warred, leaving Britain without a North American port to which to send its criminals, leaving them in floating prisons or hulks off the English coastline. At the same time, the United States adopted the traditional European almshouse, reshaping it to meet correctional needs.[26] Lastly, prison architecture came under scrutiny, reflecting a shift in perspective about the purposes of such facilities. It was a demanding era, full of change and development.

Moreso than previous eras, prison reform claimed a place of prominence at the end of the eighteenth century, championed by several notable proponents. John Howard (1726–1790) was one of the more vocal reformers of this time, drawing attention to the plight of the incarcerated and advocating for improvement. Howard, appointed high sheriff of Bedfordshire in 1773, visited local prisons and prison hulks to examine the wellbeing of those inside (Simon 2013). Howard's 1777 piece, *The State of the Prisons*, focused predominantly on the disease-stricken atmosphere of these sites, noting the lack of food and fresh water, the limited bedding and clothing, and the intolerable poor ventilation, all of which facilitated sickness and death. Howard (1780) spoke about his own reticence to enter the prisons for routine welfare checks, fearing that he, too, would be vulnerable to the deathly sickness rampant within: "These effects are now so notorious, that what terrifies most of us from looking into prisons, is the gaol-distemper that frequents in them" (3). Howard's influence spread throughout Europe and the United States, inspiring others to focus on prison reform and disease awareness.

Elizabeth Fry (1780–1845) was an English prison reformer, social crusader, Quaker, and philanthropist who, much like Howard, critically examined the safety of prisons.[27] Fry believed that God had called upon her to become a reformer, particularly for women, and thus she focused her attention on female facilities.[28] Fry's campaign began with the women of Newgate Prison. After visiting the facility for the first time, Fry described the prisoners as malnourished, loosely dressed, and drunk (Cooper 1979). Fry demanded that prisoner oversight remain under the strict authority of officers of the same gender, believing that male officers were taking advantage of female prisoners at Newgate. Fry's proposal, and many others like it, became the foundation of modern female corrections (Freedman 1981).

While the English people, such as Howard and Fry, were leading the charge to improve prison conditions, the British state was making them worse. Britain expanded its prison palette beyond land-based sites, looking to the sea as a potential place to house prisoners. In 1775, the British introduced prison ships, confining prisoners to sea vessels off the coastline. This addition was due to two factors: English facilities were overcrowded, and the state could no longer transport convicts to the United States due to the ongoing American Revolutionary War (Jarvis 2021). Unfortunately, these ships would eventually break down, becoming floating hulks that ensured miserable confinement for those relegated to their tight quarters. Prison ships, hulks, and

various other floating jails became a mainstay of the times, and this manner of detention is still in use today.

The English seas were not the only place that witnessed correctional hardship
during the colonial period. In the American colonies, corrections were a chaotic
affair, informed in part by growing economic disadvantage. During the colonial
era, the Western world was rapidly evolving, creating aggravated hardships for
those with limited means. As such, institutions known as almshouses became commonplace in Europe; these were charitable houses designed to lodge the poor and
elderly. The United States adopted the almshouse model, introducing the first one
in Boston. Over time, the almshouse was expanded to include a prison, then later
a neighboring workhouse (Herndon 2012). Thus, although almshouses originated
with the intention of assisting the poor and elderly, in time the congregate of local
officials and authorities transformed this source of assistance into a correctional
entity.[29]

Later into the eighteenth century, the use of imprisonment as a long-term punishment became particularly popular, overshadowing any remaining allegiances to the
medieval use of corporal punishments. These changes were particularly prominent in
the United States beginning in the 1770s (Barnes 1921). During the colonial period,
jails and workhouses were the central means of detainment; however, these eventually
merged into one, creating the foundation of the modern prison. Once merged, *penitentiaries* became commonplace. In this context, *penitentiary* bears some resemblance
to our modern-day understanding of the term, but it also refers to places of penance.
Penitentiaries at this time were designed with the goal of facilitating the salvation of
the incarcerated, through silence, solitude, and work.

The first penitentiary was Philadelphia's Walnut Street Jail. This institution was
constructed in 1776 and functioned as both Philadelphia's city jail and Pennsylvania's state prison (Miller 2012). Its construction helped to ease the overcrowding
at the burdensome High Street Jail, a local facility. The structural design of Walnut Street Jail set a precedent in prison architecture, not only in Pennsylvania, but
across the Western world.[30] In addition, the Pennsylvania Commonwealth eventually claimed control of the site, relieving the local sheriff of the responsibility, thus
creating the first state prison and penitentiary (DePuy 1951). The institution and
reform system were a success for a period of about fifteen years, but overcrowding
eventually proved too much, and the prison regressed back into its original form
as a county jail. Despite this, the goal of penance and salvation continued into the
next century.

Thus, the colonial era marked a period of institutional change and revision. Proponents of reform championed a new vision, one rooted in humane practices and
policies. Meanwhile, the English, ever so creative when it comes to the criminal
justice system, introduced floating prisons, relegating deviants to hulks moored in the
Thames. Across the Atlantic Ocean, the United States was throwing its own creative
hand into the mix, repurposing almshouses and inventing the penitentiary. All these
various measures and movements would prove unshakable, retaining their hold into
contemporary times, but the penitentiary, in particular, would become a prominent
feature on the correctional landscape.

THE NINETEENTH CENTURY: PENITENTIARIES AND REFORMATORIES

The nineteenth century was marked by two competing correctional philosophies: first, penitentiaries and subsequent salvation, and second, reformatories and subsequent rehabilitation. The early half of the century was focused on continuing the legacy of the Walnut Street Jail; thus, penitentiaries dominated the incarceration landscape. However, unforeseen problems began to emerge, causing a push for reformation. Reformers sought to use correctional facilities as a source of rehabilitation, believing that key changes in these sites would incentivize positive change. This section explores the fundamental shift from penitentiary to reformatory during this period, beginning first with institutional structural changes, then philosophical changes in purpose.

The penitentiary started as a prototype, but over time, it became a goliath in the correctional world. Finding inspiration in the architectural design of the Walnut Street Jail, English philosopher and social theorist Jeremy Bentham (1748–1832) designed a new type of correctional warehouse known as the *panopticon* (Knapton 2017).[31] The central feature of the panopticon was a single tower, surrounded on all sides by tiers of holding cells, each facing inward toward the tower in a somewhat circular fashion. A single sentinel stationed in the tower would thus have the ability to monitor all inmates without being detected. As described by Pratt (1993):

> At the periphery, an annular building; at the center, a tower; this tower is pierced with wide windows that open onto the inner side of the ring; the peripheric building is divided into cells, each of which extends the whole width of the building; they have two windows, one on the inside corresponding to the windows of the tower; the other, on the outside, allows the light to cross the cell from one end to the other. All that is needed, then, is to place a supervisor, in a central tower and to shut up in each cell a madman, a patient, a condemned man, a worker or a schoolboy. (374)

Critics stated that Bentham's all-seeing penitentiary was simply a far-fetched fantasy, but eventually these large and invasive buildings would become commonplace.[32] In time, their unmitigated reputation would earn them the nickname "Big House" (Cox 2009).

While Bentham was reshaping the design of correctional warehouses in Europe, officials in the United States were continuing to modify their use of penitentiaries. Eastern State Penitentiary, which opened in 1829 in Cherry Hill, Pennsylvania, introduced a new aspect of confinement: forced and constant silent solitude (Ward & Werlich 2003). Inmates ate, toiled, prayed, and slept in isolation, a practice that became known as the Pennsylvania, or *aggregate*, system. The only interaction the prisoners were permitted was with their guards, chaplains, and a few other authorized individuals. Eastern State Penitentiary came under harsh scrutiny for facilitating physical and mental illness, due in part to the strict parameters of silence and solitude.[33] Although the Pennsylvania system would find a home in most countries in Europe and South America, it soon fell out of favor in the United States (Teeters & Shearer 1957).

After the fall of the Eastern State Penitentiary, Auburn Prison (1818–present) in New York took center stage. The Auburn or, *congregate*, system was informed by the Puritan belief that criminals were corrupt; the only means of breaking offenders of their resolve and, thus, offering them a path to salvation was to expose them to relentless discipline and punishment (Roberts 1985). Auburn incorporated elements of the Walnut Street Jail and the Pennsylvania system, relying on unconditional silence at night and military-style activity by day. Inmates were required to move in lock-step, to eat at attention, and to work long hours, with an expectation that this would facilitate complete obedience. The congregate system became popular in the United States, especially in the nineteenth century, due primarily to a labor shortage. Inmates incarcerated under these conditions worked efficiently and at a fraction of the cost of liberated workers, thus increasing the commercial appeal of the system (Johnson, Rocheleau, and Martin 2016).

Sing Sing, another influential facility in the United States, was created while the aggregate and congregate systems rivaled each other for dominance. Originally named Mount Pleasant, Sing Sing opened in 1826 (Cox 2009). Elam Lynds (1784–1855), who played a central role in the creation of the congregate system, served as the warden of Sing Sing for the first five years it was in operation. The Auburn influence was clear in the expectations around work and social exchanges. The walls were built by the prisoners themselves, who worked long hours while all the while remaining silent under threat of corporal punishment.

Sing Sing was not restricted exclusively to male prisoners. In 1844, Eliza Farnham (1815–1864) became matron of the women's ward at the facility, replacing a previous matron who retired following a riot in response to the inhumane conditions at the prison. With education as her top priority, the new matron offered something that was virtually unheard at the time: non-religious literature (Floyd 2006).[34] Farnham was also central to abolishing the silent rule, and by 1846, female prisoners were permitted to speak with each other. Sadly, this improvement was short-lived; by 1847, due to work-related transgressions, silence reigned once again over the women of Sing Sing. Not long after, Farnham left her position as matron, mired in administrative conflicts, heated inspections, and bad publicity. Despite her departure, Farnham's influence would continue, as evident, for example, in prison libraries today.

Across the Atlantic, penitentiaries were also becoming popular, and in 1842, another controversial institution took center stage. Pentonville Penitentiary, stationed in Northern London, became well known for its divisive measures. It was as strict and as silent as a monastery, a place where a simple gesture, sign, smile, or whisper could land one down into the dark cells of the basement for an unforeseeable amount of time. Pentonville prioritized the rigorous supervision of prisoner movements and activities, believing that seclusion and silence, intermixed with industrial training, moral education, and religion, would serve to correct the errant offender (Ignatieff 1978). Over time, Pentonville's staff began leaking concerning reports. They wrote bizarre letters home, sharing unsettling stories of delusional prisoners who believed they were visited by apparitions of dead relatives, objects moving unassisted, and "things" crawling out of the ventilation systems. They also expressed the belief that they were poisoned and slowly dying. Equally disturbing was Pentonville's extensive suicide history, an outlier among other penitentiaries (Cox & Marland 2013).

Although Pentonville was modified over time for the betterment of the prisoners, it remained a dark and ominous institution.

Thus, the penitentiary enjoyed an era of popularity; however, the numerous problems inherent in its very design, including issues with mental and physical health, and human rights abuses and indignities, led to its eventual fall from grace (Johnson, Rocheleau, & Martin 2016). Incarceration for the purposes of atonement, warehousing, and punishment was replaced by the novel idea of rehabilitation. Proponents of this perspective believed that juveniles and many adults had the ability to change for the better if offered the right setting, programming, and incentives. As the penitentiary faded, the reformatory gained prominence.

Reformatories became popular on both sides of the Atlantic, beginning first in Europe and quickly spreading to North America. The first reformatory in the United States was the New York House of Refuge, which opened in 1824, inspired in part by a juvenile facility located in London (Lewis 1922).[35] The primary purpose of the House of Refuge was to save new and young offenders from being channeled into a regular prison, where they would most certainly become more hardened in their criminal resolve.

The House of Refuge was overshadowed by the introduction of another New York correctional juggernaut a half century later. In 1876, the Elmira Reformatory, also known as the Hill, was beginning operation, ready to receive its first set of young offenders.[36] The state had constructed the facility in anticipation of the return of Civil War soldiers, but it lacked both a philosophy and a leader. Zebulon Brockway (1827–1920), celebrated by many as the father of prison reform and parole, would provide both (Pisciotta 1994). Brockway was a proponent of education, training, and incentivization as grounds for rehabilitation. Therefore, the Elmira system relied heavily on educational programming, trade schooling, physical activity, and a classification, or *mark*, system, which allowed inmates to gain incentives, including release, through good behavior (Maconochie 1857).[37] Brockway also believed in the gradual state of rehabilitation, thereby insisting on indeterminate sentencing and parole, thus allowing rehabilitation to occur at its own pace (Pisciotta 1994).

By the end of the nineteenth century, the Elmira Reformatory had taken center stage and become the standard in correctional practices. Brockway was lauded across the Western world for his innovative and forward-thinking approach; however, this period of popular esteem was short-lived. Before long, reports of extreme corporal punishment and institutional misconduct inside Elmira began to surface. The mark system had failed; prisoners languished at the lowest level, unable to advance, thus living in terrible conditions. In addition, there were reports of beatings, some executed by Brockway himself, and the indeterminate sentencing structure led to prison overcrowding (Keve 1999). By July 1900, Brockway reluctantly submitted his resignation due to the damning allegations.

Although Elmira was surrounded in controversy, the reformatory continued as the preferred approach to corrections in the United States and abroad, at least for a short time (Pisciotta 1994). Eventually, the reformatory would fade in popularity, primarily due to the expensive nature of the programming and the infrastructure required to support such an institution. As the Great Depression settled over the Western world, the reformatory became obsolete. Instead, the old idea of warehousing resurfaced, as its proponents overlooked the pains of the past and delivered reformation a shot to the heart.

THE TWENTIETH CENTURY: SUPER LOCKDOWNS

The twentieth century would prove to be a test of moral ethics for those overseeing the world of corrections. Although this period was a time of political and social growth, several factors, including voracity, overcrowding, and extreme violence rooted in mental health and gang activity, provided the catalyst for a return to an institutional philosophy thought dead and gone: warehousing. Leaving the ideas of rehabilitation and reform behind, the correctional world turned its eye toward incapacitation for the sake of social defense. In this context, prisons were simply places to store criminals, without an agenda of promoting change. Much of this shift took place in the United States, setting it apart from its Western neighbors and creating a divide in correctional philosophy that persists to this day.

Although there are many examples of a change in correctional philosophy, perhaps the most notable is found in San Francisco near the beginning of the century. In 1933, the Federal Bureau of Prisons turned its attention toward Alcatraz Island in San Francisco Bay, selecting it as an ideal site upon which to enact a *concentration* model, consisting of units designed to address specific issues (King 1999). In addition to unit specialization, the site was intended for high-risk offenders, or "a 'super prison for the super criminals caught by the super cops'" (Powers 1983, as cited in Ward & Werlich 2003, 44).[38] Contact with the outside world was restricted, limiting island access to media, news, and all other channels (Ward & Kassebaum 2009).[39] Although Alcatraz, also called the Rock, was a correctional figurehead, it soon became too costly to operate, situated on an island where all materials, including water, needed to be transported by boat, and where the salt winds of the San Francisco Bay deteriorated its allegedly invulnerable walls (Cox 2009). In 1963, Alcatraz closed, signifying for many the end of the Big House era.

Alcatraz was shortly followed by a new phenomenon, informed in part by a massive upsurge in prison populations and newly passed legislation that restricted correctional staff from adopting a hands-on approach inside prisons (Pizzaro & Steinus 2004). In an attempt to control mayhem inside troubled facilities, the United States introduced super-maximum-security (supermax) prisons (Ward & Werlich 2003). Supermax prisons are control-unit institutions that provide long-term and isolated lockdown for those deemed to be of the greatest threat to themselves, each other, and society (Mears 2012). Although supermax prisons are relatively new, they incorporate practices that are reminiscent of primitive confinement, demanding isolation and solitude.

In 1963, the United States opened USP Marion (1963–present), a federal prison intended as a replacement for the costly Alcatraz site.[40] On October 23, 1983, the violent assassination of two correctional officers at separate locations in the facility prompted an unprecedented three-year lockdown. Over time, the administration opted to impose a full-time lockdown of the prison, thus converting FCI-Marion into the country's first supermax.[41] Before long, supermax institutions began surfacing across the country, a phenomenon later characterized as "Marionization." By 1994, the

Administrative Maximum Penitentiary in Florence, Colorado, also known as "Alcatraz of the Rockies", became the newest supermax (Johnson, Rocheleau, & Martin 2016). Some claim that ADX Florence is the most impenetrable prison in the United States.[42] The supermax is controversial, fueling debates among critics and advocates, but it remains a prominent feature of correctional practices, at least within the United States.

Thus, the twentieth century is marked by antiquated notions of confinement, as apparent in United States supermax prisons. Warehousing has become a common practice again. However, this is not the only theme of contemporary correctional philosophy; instead, there are also elements of rehabilitation evident here and there in the Western world. Educational courses, programming, and trade schooling have crept into correctional institutions, refining and improving upon the practices of the historical reformatory. These measures have better equipped the incarcerated population with skills that have proven beneficial in reducing recidivism rates (Lopes 2002). Although history dictates that more change is on the horizon, this approach seems to have temporarily stemmed the tide of the revolving-door policies of the past.

CONCLUSION

Although a conclusion usually demands a neat and perfunctory summary of the contents of the chapter, this conclusion is, instead, going to adopt a lyrical tone. Throughout this chapter, we have aimed to present information in a way that is more palatable to an academic audience. The first author of this chapter is, however, a poetic speaker, and now, in this section, he has chosen to adopt a tone that comes more naturally to him. We invite you to cast aside the temptation to skip over the conclusion, believing it to be redundant as conclusions tend to be, and instead, enjoy the lyrical nature of an incarcerated poet. In summary . . .

. . . Western corrections has overseen the malefactors of society longer than one dare imagine. Throughout its eclectic history, corrections and its all-encompassing systems have come to symbolize both the whisper of the seraph and the hiss of the serpent. As the sands of time filtered down through the hourglass, evolution became the lifeblood of its everlasting salvation. Confinement has come before us by way of a God thrusting man in bonds, a quarry pit, and an exiled citizen. The omnipotent castle, its formidable towers, and its doom-laden dungeons, all have acted as accomplices inside the convoluted world of incarceration. Narcissistic exploitation beckoned captivity to strew throughout the nunnery, sea vessel, and the unkempt almshouse for the vagabond maliciously plucked from civilization. Corrections has served as a punisher and a teacher, an executioner and a saint, all the while making a dark mind see light, and a warm heart turn cold. Like the scaly epidermis of the ever-changing chameleon, it has been who it has needed to be, where it was needed, when it was needed.

When reflecting back upon the decadent history of Western corrections, a wide range of unencumbered emotions may attack the psyche, and in this you are not alone. Truth be told, it is almost impossible to distinguish between inhumane behavior and societal justice when the crux of the case may simply lie within the order of the times. Each period throughout the course of history has had its own unique formula for handing down the consequences called upon to control the masses and ultimately settle the score; determining right or wrong is purely speculation. We must never ignore the lessons from history, and when these lessons center upon corrections, there is absolutely no exception to the rule. While advancements in corrections have far exceeded most expectations, the foundation of the modern prison undeniably traces back all the way to the very beginning, back to the ones who initially laid the foundation and back when the world was young and at the precipice of an unforgiving cage.

NOTES

1. Oscar Wilde wrote this poem in mid-1897 while in exile in Berneval-le-Grand. Before his exile, he served time in the Reading Gaol in Reading, England. "The poem narrates the execution of [Charles Thomas] Wooldridge; it moves from an objective story-telling to symbolic identification with the prisoners as a whole" (Sandulescu 1994, 308).

2. The Bureau of Justice Statistics (2021) refers to *corrections* as the "supervision of persons arrested for, convicted of, or sentenced for criminal offences."

3. In one example, Alcidamas, a prominent sophist and rhetorician, describes how the once-incarcerated were disfigured and unable to move upright due in part to being held in bonds during confinement (Allen 1997).

4. The Twelve Tables were founded around 450 BCE They were later engraved in bronze and publicly displayed so all Romans would recognize and abide by the decrees (Deac 2021).

5. During medieval times, its name was changed to Mamertine (Morris & Rothman 1995).

6. The natural water spring at the bottom of the Carcer Tullianum was used by the first pope Saint Peter, to baptize his fellow prisoners. Some believe this spring was a miracle that enabled Saint Peter to continue his holy work in a very unholy setting (Mazzoni 2017).

7. Ergastalum and its translation are one of the first references to chain-gang labor (Johnston 2009). This form of punishment was eventually deemed to be unlawful during the reign of Hadrian (117 CE–138 CE); this was part of a series of revisions designed to improve conditions for slaves (Smith 1878).

8. The Roman emperor Domitian exiled John the Apostle to the island of Patmos during the late first century. It was on this island that he reportedly wrote the book of Revelation (Hill 2013).

9. "The fourth century comedian Alexis *(fr. 220–221.10)* refers to a daily prison diet as consisting of one clean wheat cake and one cup of water" (Allen 1997, 129).

10. Although records are limited, graffiti tagged on walls and floors of the prison house allow historians to piece together life inside the world of the incarcerated (Ahnert 2009).

11. The Middle Ages were a period in the history of Europe that lasted from the fifth to the late-fifteenth century.

12. "A wide variety of contraptions was used, including manacles for the wrist, fetters and shackles for the ankles, and iron collars for the neck—any of these could, if necessary, be chained to a ring in the floor or to a staple on the wall" (Babington 1972, 5).

13. The gaol fever's widespread panic began in the earliest times and saw an end around the latter part of the eighteenth century. "Gaol fever is now believed to be a form of typhus, resulting from poverty, overcrowding, dirt, and lack of sanitation" (Babington 1972, 8).

14. "Mediaeval records are unanimous in their description of the vileness of Newgate. A 'fetid and corrupt' atmosphere hung about the prison and penetrated every nook and cranny" (Bassett 1943, 244).

15. Under the rule of King Henry III, Newgate suffered such extreme famines that those inside turned to cannibalism. Those involved reported seeing a ghostly black hound following them throughout the prison (Hutton 1596). According to legend, the Blacke Dogge of Newgate haunted and consumed the responsible parties, even following some after their escape from the prison.

16. The Bastille prison was operational from 1370 CE–1790 CE (Morris & Rothman 1995).

17. "Freemen of the city committed to ward for 'all kinds of debt, trespass, account, contempt, and such like' were spared the horrors of the criminal prison, and went instead to the free prison of Ludgate. Only those charged with felony or maiming were still sent to Newgate" (Bassett 1943, 238).

18. "Crane Brinton has graphically pointed out; the Early Renaissance and the Late Middle Ages are fused like a trainwreck in time. The Renaissance was less a time period than a mode of life and thought" (Wolfgang 1990, 574).

19. Records indicate that the Italian Renaissance diplomat, philosopher, and writer Niccolò di Bernardo dei Machiavelli (1469–1527) was briefly detained at Le Stinche in 1513 while being interrogated vis-à-vis his role in a local conspiracy (Wolfgang 1990).

20. Documentation shows that women belonging to the outlawed Lambertazzi faction in late-thirteenth-century Bologna were booked into custody and ushered away into urban nunneries (Geltner 2013).

21. It reopened as a prison in 1556 (Johnston 2000, as cited by Johnston 2009, 33).

22. Documents record the cruel punishments levied against idlers and vagabonds by the justices of peace starting in the late 1300s. These punishments came in the form of gaol, whippings, brandings, and confinement to the stocks (Babington 1972).

23. "Those condemned to the galleys for life in Louis XIV's reign were branded with the letters GAL. That brand denoted condemnation to the oar for a capital crime" (Bamford 1973, 173). Gallery slavery was eventually extended in 1540 to include the homeless and impoverished.

24. The prison reformer, John Howard, described slave galleys maintained by Pope Pius VI (1775–1799). Sentences were typically three years to life. The prisoners received three pounds of bread a day and on holy days beef and wine (Howard 1792/1973, as cited by Johnston 2009, 12S).

25. Not all galley slaves existed during times of war. This punishment also extended to discovery expeditions as galley slaves took the oars for such explorers as Columbus, Vasco de Gama, and others (Ives 1914).

26. An almshouse is a charitable house for destitute and elderly individuals.

27. Quakers were particularly influential in criminal justice and corrections reform. The founder of the sect, George Fox (1624–1691), was imprisoned in the Derby gaol in 1651 (Cooper 1979). During his time, he was exposed to appalling conditions and egregious acts, such as the execution of children under the charge of theft.

28. In 2001, Fry's work with prison reformation was commemorated by placing her on the English five-pound note (Craig 2006). She was replaced by Winston Churchill in 2016 (Allen 2013).

29. In an early-nineteenth-century letter, Dr. John Gorman chronicled his treatment of mania at the Boston almshouse (Quen 1968). He reported administering opium to almshouse residents whom he deemed to be insane.

30. The Walnut Street Jail incorporated individual cells in a manner aligned with the modern-day prison tier; these cells were to be used for the purposes of solitary confinement and for salvation. It also sought to warehouse large numbers of individuals in common rooms.

31. Jeremy Bentham's preserved head is occasionally on display in London. At one time, the severed head was a party favor for his friends to display at get-togethers (Knapton 2017).

32. In 1925, Crest Hill, Illinois, unveiled Stateville Prison to the world. Stateville is the only version of Jeremy Bentham's panopticon found in the United States (Cox 2009).

33. "John Haviland, a recently arrived British architect, used a radial layout similar on a large scale to the many lunatic asylums and little county prisons being erected in both Ireland and England at the time. The prison was known generally as Cherry Hill well into the 20th century, after a nearby burial ground" (Johnston 2009, 20S).

34. Farnham was fascinated with phrenology as a means of analyzing and treating female prisoners. This contentious new science was based on the premise that character traits could be read by studying the outer shape and protuberance of the head (Floyd 2006).

35. The European reformatory, or asylum, typically held the children of convicts and those deemed "trained to evil courses" (Lewis 1922).

36. Elmira served individuals between the ages of sixteen and thirty years.

37. The mark system was a penal system that permitted prisoners to receive honors and early release by accruing marks by way of moral performance, goal-oriented accomplishments, and frugality (Maconochie 1857).

38. "[Alcatraz] called for confining a group of highly publicized gangsters, including John Dillinger, 'Machine Gun' Kelly, 'Pretty Boy' Floyd, the Barker-Karpis mob, and especially, Al Capone, in a new, small 'maximum custody-minimum privilege' penitentiary" (Ward & Werlich 2003, 55).

39. "During World War II news about the war in Europe and against Japan was posted on a blackboard in the yard or the dining hall; these bulletins prompted speculation about Japanese air attacks in the San Francisco Bay Area given that antiaircraft guns had been mounted on the roof of the cell house" (Ward & Kassebaum 2009, 109–10).

40. "In 1973, other federal penitentiaries and 36 of the 50 states began sending their most violent prisoners and gang leaders to a 'Control Unit' established at Marion. The purpose of the Control Unit was 'to separate those offenders whose behavior seriously disrupted the orderly operation of an institution from the vast majority of offenders who wish to participate in regular institutional programs'" (US Department of Justice 1973, as cited by Ward & Werlich 2003, 57).

41. By the 1970s, gangs such as the Mexican Mafia, Nuestra Familia, Black Guerrilla Family, and the Aryan Brotherhood were all battling each other and the staff for control inside the FCI-Marion (Ward & Werlich 2003).

42. "Contemporary Florence residents [of 'Bombers Row'] have included Theodore Kaczynski (the so-called Unabomber), Timothy McVeigh (until his transfer for execution) and Terry Nichols (convicted in the Oklahoma City bombing), Ramsey Yousef and other 'terrorists' found guilty in the first World Trade Center bombing and in the plot to destroy the United Nations Building and other New York City landmarks, and members of Al Qaeda convicted in the bombing of two US embassies in Africa" (Ward & Werlich 2003, 60).

REFERENCES

Aeschylus and Euripides. 1937. *Three Greek Plays: Prometheus Bound, Agamemnon, the Trojan Women.* Translated by Edith Hamilton. New York: W. W. Norton & Company.

Ahnert, Ruth. 2009. "Writing in the Tower of London During the Reformation, ca. 1530—1558: Prison Writings in Early Modern England." *Huntington Library Quarterly* 72, no. 2 (June): 168–92. https://doi.org/10.1525/hlq.2009.72.2.168.

Allen, Danielle. 1997. "Imprisonment in Classical Athens." *Classical Quarterly* 47, no. 1 (May): 121–35. https://doi.org/10.1093/cq/47.1.121.

Allen, Katie. 2013. "New £5 Note Replaces Elizabeth Fry with Sir Winston Churchill." *Guardian*, April 26, 2013. https://www.theguardian.com/business/2013/apr/26/winston-churchill-new-five-pound-note.

Babington, Anthony. 1972. *The English Bastille: A History of Newgate Gaol and Prison Conditions in Britain, 1188–1902.* New York: St. Martin's Press.

Bamford, Paul W. 1973. *Fighting Ships and Prisons: The Mediterranean Galleys of France in the Age of Louis XIV.* Minneapolis: University of Minnesota Press.

Barkan, Irving. 1936. "Imprisonment as a Penalty in Ancient Athens." *Classical Philology* 31, no. 4 (October): 338–41. https://doi.org/10.1086/361963.

Barnes, Harry E. 1921. "Historical Origin of the Prison System in America." *Journal of the American Institute of Criminal Law and Criminology* 12, no. 1 (May): 35–60. https://doi.org/10.2307/1133652.

Bassett, Margery. 1943. "Newgate Prison in the Middle Ages." *Speculum* 18, no. 2 (April): 233–46. https://doi.org/10.2307/2850646.

Bassett, Margery. 1944. "The Fleet Prison in the Middle Ages." *University of Toronto Law Journal* 5, no. 2 (January): 383–402. https://doi.org/10.2307/824490.

Bureau of Justice Statistics. 2021. "Corrections." Accessed June 5, 2023. https://bjs.ojp.gov/topics/corrections.

Cooper, Robert A. 1979. "The English Quakers and Prison Reform, 1809–23." *Quaker History* 68, no. 1 (Spring): 3–19. https://doi.org/10.1353/qkh.1979.0030.

Cox, Catherine, and Hilary Marland. 2018. "'He Must Die or Go Mad in This Place': Prisoners, Insanity, and the Pentonville Model Prison Experiment, 1842–52." *Bulletin of the History of Medicine* 92, no. 1 (Spring): 78–109. https://doi.org/10.1353/bhm.2018.0004.

Cox, Stephen. 2009. *The Big House: Image and Reality of the American Prison.* New Haven: Yale University Press.

Deac, Adriana. 2021. "The Twelve Tables Law, the Most Important One from the Roman Law." *Perspectives of Law and Public Administration* 10, no. 1 (March): 5–11.

Dean, Trevor. 2017. "Getting Out of Jail: Suicide, Escape, and Release in Medieval and Renaissance Bologna." *Historical Research: The Bulletin of the Institute of Historical Research* 90, no. 249 (August) 449–64. https://doi.org/10.1111/1468-2281.12190.

DePuy, LeRoy B. 1951. "The Walnut Street Prison: Pennsylvania's First Penitentiary." *Pennsylvania History: A Journal of Mid-Atlantic Studies* 18, no. 2 (April): 130–44.

Flintoff, Everard. 1986. "The Date of the Prometheus Bound." *Mnemosyne* 39, no. 1 (January): 82–91. https://doi.org/10.1163/156852586X00040.

Floyd, Janet. 2006. "Dislocations of the Self: Eliza Farnham at Sing Sing Prison." *Journal of American Studies* 40, no. 2 (July): 311–25. https://doi.org/10.1017/S002187580600139.

Folch, Marcus. 2021. "Political Prisoners in Democratic Athens, 490–318 BCE, Part 1: The Athenian Inmate Population." *Classical Philology* 116, no. 3 (July): 336–68. https://doi.org/10.1086/714591.

Francese, Christopher. 2007. *Ancient Rome in So Many Words.* New York: Hippocrene Books.

Freedman, Estelle B. 1981. *Their Sisters' Keepers: Women's Prison Reform in America, 1830–1930.* Ann Arbor: University of Michigan Press.

Geltner, Guy. 2013. "A Cell of Their Own: The Incarceration of Women in Late Medieval Italy." *Signs: Journal of Women in Culture and Society* 39, no. 1 (Fall): 27–51. https://doi.org/10.1086/670768.

Herndon, Ruth W. 2012. "Poor Women and the Boston Almshouse in the Early Republic." *Journal of the Early Republic* 32, no. 3 (Fall): 349–81. https://doi.org/10.1353/jer.2012.0064.

Hill, Marc L. 2013. "A World Without Prisons: Teaching Confinement Literature and the Promise of Prison Abolition." *English Journal* 102, no. 4 (March): 19–23.

Howard, John. 1780. *The State of Prisons in England and Wales, with Preliminary Observations and an Account of Some Foreign Prisons and Hospitals.* London: William Eyres.

Hunter, Virginia. 1997. "The Prison of Athens: A Comparative Perspective." *Phoenix* 51, no. 3–4 (October): 296–326. https://doi.org/10.2307/1192540.

Hutton, Luke. 1596. *The Discovery of a London Monster, Called, the Blacke Dogg of Newgate; Profitable for All Readers to Take Heed By.* London: M.P. for Robert Wilson.

Ignatieff, Michael. 1978. *A Just Measure of Pain: The Penitentiary in the Industrial Revolution, 1750–1850.* New York: Pantheon Books.

Ives, George. 1914. *A History of Penal Methods: Criminals, Witches, Lunatics.* London: S. Paul & Company.

Jarvis, Robert M. 2021. "Prison Ships." *British Journal of American Legal Studies* 10, no. 2 (August): 281–334. https://doi.org/10.2478/bjals-2021-0002.

Johnson, Robert, Ann Marie Rocheleau, and Alison B. Martin. 1987. *Hard Time: A Fresh Look at Understanding and Reforming the Prison.* Hoboken: Wiley-Blackwell Publishing.

Johnston, Norman. 2009. "Evolving Function: Early Use of Imprisonment as Punishment." *Prison Journal* 89, no. 1 (January): 10S–34S. https://doi.org/10.1177/0032885508329761.

Keve, Paul W. 1999. "Building a better prison: The first three decades of the Detroit House of Correction." *Michigan Historical Review* 25, no. 2 (Fall): 1–28. https://doi.org/10.2307/20173826.

King, Roy D. 1999. "The Rise of the Supermax: An American Solution in Search of a Problem?" *Punishment & Society* 1, no. 2 (October): 163–86. https://doi.org/10.1177/14624749922227766.

Knapton, Sarah. 2017. "Severed head of eccentric Jeremy Bentham to go on display as scientists test DNA to see if he was autistic." *Telegraph*, October 2, 2017. https://www.telegraph.co.uk/science/2017/10/02/severed-head-eccentric-jeremy-bentham-go-display-scientists/.

Lewis, Orlando. 1922. *The Development of American Prisons and Prison Customs, 1776–1845: With Special Reference to Early Institutions in the State of New York.* New York: Prison Association of New York.

Lopes, Jenna. 2002. "There's Got to Be a Better Way: Retribution vs. Restoration." *Osprey Journal of Ideas and Inquiry* 116: 52–66. https://digitalcommons.unf.edu/ojii_volumes/116

Maconochie, Alexander. 2017. *The Mark System of Prison Discipline.* London: Mitchell & Son.

Mazzoni, Cristina. 2017. "Locked Up and Locked In: Of Roman Imprisonments and Lilberations. *Spiritus* 17, no. 2 (September): 246–51. https://doi.org/10.1353/scs.2017.0030.

Mears, Daniel. 2013. "Supermax Prisons: The Policy and the Evidence." *Criminology &Public Policy* 12, no. 4 (November): 681–720. https://doi.org/10.1111/1745-9133.12031.

Miller, Wilbur, editor. 2012. *The Social History of Crime and Punishment in America: An Encyclopedia.* Thousand Oaks: Sage Publications, Incorporated.

Morris, Norval, and David Rothman. 1995. *The Oxford History of the Prison: The Practice of Punishment in Western Society.* Oxford: Oxford University Press.

Pisciotta, Alexander W. 1994. *Benevolent Repression: Social Control and the American Reformatory Prison Movement.* New York: New York University Press.

Pizzaro, Jesenia, and Vanja M. K. Stenius. 2004. "Supermax Prisons: Their Rise, Current Practices, and Effect on Inmates." *Prison Journal* 84, no. 2 (June): 248–64. https://doi.org/10.1177%2F0032885504265080.

Pratt, John. 1993. "'This Is Not a Prison': Foucault, the Panopticon and Pentonville." *Social and Legal Studies* 2, no. 4 (December): 373–95. https://doi.org/10.1177/096466399300200402.

Quen, Jacques M. 1968. "Early Nineteenth-Century Observations on the Insane in the Boston Almshouse." *Journal of the History of Medicine and Allied Sciences* 23, no. 1 (January): 80–85. https://doi.org/10.1093/jhmas/XXIII.1.80.

Roberts, Leonard H. 1985. "The Historic Roots of American Prison Reform: A Story of Progress and Failure." *Journal of Correctional Education* 36, no. 3 (September): 106–109.

Sandulescu, George C. 1995. *Rediscovering Oscar Wilde*. Lanham: Rowman & Littlefield Publishers.

Simon, Johnathan. 2013. "The Return of the Medical Model: Disease and the Meaning of Imprisonment from John Howard to Brown v. Plata." *Harvard Civil Rights—Civil Liberties Law Review* 48, no. 1 (Winter): 217–56. https://journals.law.harvard.edu/crcl/wp-content/uploads/sites/80/2013/04/Simon_217-256.pdf.

Smith, William. 1878. *A Dictionary of Greek and Roman Antiquities*. London: John Murray.

Teeters, Negley K., and John D. Shearer. 1957. *The Prison at Philadelphia Cherry Hill: The Separate System of Penal Discipline: 1829–1913*. New York: Columbia University Press.

Tsougarakis, Nickiphoros I. 2014. "Prisons and Incarceration in Fourteenth Century Venetian Crete." *Mediterranean Historical Review* 29, no. 1 (January): 29–55. https://doi.org/10.1080/09518967.2014.897052.

Ward, David A., and Gene Kassebaum. 2009. *Alcatraz: The Gangster Years*. Oakland: University of California Press.

Ward, David A., and Thomas G. Werlich. 2003. "Alcatraz and Marion: Evaluating Super-Maximum Custody." *Punishment and Society* 5, no. 1 (January): 53-75. https://doi.org/10.1177/1462474503005001295.

Wilde, Oscar. 1928. *The Ballad of Reading Gaol*. New York: E.P. Dutton & Co., Inc.

Wolfgang, Marvin E. 1990. "Crime and Punishment in Renaissance Florence." *Journal of Criminal Law & Criminology* 81, no. 3 (October): 567–84. https://doi.org/10.2307/1143848.

Chapter 5

Trends in Crime, Justice, and Law

Trip Finity Taylor, Amara Bailey, and Omi Hodwitz

INTRODUCTION

Hence the uncertainty of our notions of honour and virtue; an uncertainty which will ever remain, because they change with the revolutions of time, and names survive the things they originally signified; they change with the boundaries of states, which are often the same both in physical and moral geography. (Beccaria 1764, as quoted in Blom 2010, 218)

Crime is a social construction, referencing actions that deviate from cultural norms and are punishable in society, shifting from generation to generation and region by region. Criminal justice is the system or institution that determines crimes and punishments and, historically, has been driven by a diverse array of goals, including simple retribution, deterrence, incapacitation, and rehabilitation. Thus, there is one constant with crime and justice; it is expectedly fluid, ever-changing, and subject to the unique influences and regions within which it exists. At different points in time, criminal justice has been a private matter, removed from the scrutiny of the state, while at other times, those in positions of power have been responsible for its administration. Along the same lines, while some crimes, such as rape and murder, have warranted summary justice, others, such as theft and forgery, have been subject to a wide swath of potential punishments, dictated by the cultural beliefs and practices of the era. Many a time, these determinations reflect a social hierarchy, as those in positions of power vilify and oppress behaviors traditional to those on the fringes of society. The result is a swinging pendulum in time and space as power shifts and acceptable behavior are redefined.

This chapter examines historical trends in crime and justice in the Western world. It begins in ancient Greece and Rome, two cultures that embraced private justice before eventually transitioning to a public forum. Citizenship was a key determinant of privilege and power, and threats to the citizenry were met with retribution, including slavery and fines, and the repercussions for non-citizen offenders were particularly harsh. Law and justice lay firmly in the hands of the political and social elite, informed by polytheistic narratives, and punishments were public spectacles, designed to entertain, inform, and deter. The reign of these monolithic empires was unstable, however, and they eventually collapsed into a period of darkness that lasted hundreds of years.

During Europe's Dark and Middle Ages, crime and justice became a local matter, overseen by community councils and landholders. This period was defined by a rigid class structure, determined in part by financial worth, and thus punishments for deviance were also informed by monetary considerations. Social norms were set by the economic elite, and violations of social norms were often met with fines or indentured servitude. In addition, this era experienced an increase in religiosity, particularly a devotion to monotheism, or a single God. Thus, deviance and punishment tended to target the impoverished, minority cultures, and heretics (particularly women). In the later years, this was set on the backdrop of a growing pestilence that decimated the population, forcing European society to adapt and rebuild, leading to social and institutional rebirth.

Following the Middle Ages, the chapter next explores the Renaissance and Enlightenment periods. As kingdoms grew, power and control were centralized in the hands of a select few, and Christianity became entangled with the state, thus redefining sin as crime. Justice was swift and oftentimes brutal; death became commonplace as a penalty for repetitive and seemingly minor crimes, and public beatings were used as a deterrent. European societies valued purity in action, and those who did not fit this ideal were castigated and punished. Philosophers and reformers took issue with this practice, and with the advent of the printing press, they voiced their objections to a growing audience. Corporal and capital punishment were recast as inhumane and arbitrary, offensive to the enlightened. By the close of the eighteenth century, significant portions of European society were dissatisfied with institutional responses to crime, justice, and inequality.

Various revolutions led to drastic changes, including industrial development and growth, and crime and justice shifted accordingly. The working class expanded, as did their appetites for unseemly leisurely activities, conflicting with the sentiments of the Victorian elite. Vice was viewed as morally repugnant, a source of further deviance and crime, motivating reformers to lobby for stricter regulations of gambling and drinking, as well as to advocate for increased education and the conformity of youths. As economies improved and more behaviors were maligned, crime rates rose. Official police units were introduced, becoming commonplace by the end of the nineteenth century, and the corporal practices of the previous eras were replaced by incarceration. As technology improved, facilitating greater collaboration between nations, crime and justice evolved, entering the age of globalization.

The chapter closes with a brief examination of crime and justice in the modern Western world, with a focus on the United States. Various issues informed twentieth-century narratives, including transnational crime, illustrating oscillations in both crime and justice. This glance into contemporary times is brief, but it aids in closing out the discussion of the ever-changing, yet often contiguous, trends of crime and justice prevalent throughout human history.

ANCIENT GREECE AND THE ROMAN EMPIRE
(800 BCE TO 476 CE)

During their different periods of rule, ancient Greece and the Roman Republic and Empire changed justice practices, shifting from private to state control and back again.

Vengeance and arbitration were commonplace, applied liberally by victims and the state alike. Judges, whether private or public, listened to accusers, witnesses, the gods, or none of the above, while determining guilt and selecting from a popular array of penalties, ranging from simple fines to execution. Class conflicts shaped the law, and reflexively, changes in the law shaped class conflicts. By the fall of the Roman Empire in 476 CE, the Western world was defined by chaos and social stratification. This section relays this story in greater detail, offering a simple introduction to the trends of crime and justice during this period.

Ancient Greece began as a collection of small towns and villages until the establishment of the formal polis, or city-state, of Athens in the seventh century BCE (D'Amico 2010). Order was maintained through a social contract, or a collective understanding of right and wrong and an implicit agreement to protect collective well-being (Cherry 1890). The social contract established rules and expectations regarding private property and personal boundaries, thus creating a rudimentary version of criminal law. Being a member of the community and enjoying the benefits of membership meant abiding by, maintaining, and enforcing these norms, thus circumventing the need for public courts or police. Thus, at this time, crime and justice was a private affair, defined and negotiated by the victim, the perpetrator, and the community. Informal and communal rule persisted until the establishment of Athens and the rule of the Archons (D'Amico 2010). The Archons introduced the first formalized legislation regarding crime and justice, ushering in an era of codified laws, crimes, and punishments.

Draco was the first Greek leader credited with codifying formal laws (Hyde 1918; Smith 1922). He was particularly well-known for his punitive measures; in 621 BCE he decreed that most offenses were punishable by death, without the benefit of mercy or clemency (D'Amico 2010).[1] Draco's statutes lasted for scant decades before being overturned, but their brief existence left an indelible mark on public perceptions of crime and deviance. After Draco, Solon's reign was perhaps one of the more transformative periods for Athenian justice. Solon sought to further formalize state control of crime and justice, expanding the reach of the government, and casting customary justice, such as private incarceration or indentured servitude, as improper and undesirable (Hyde 1918; Smith 1922). Predictably, public jails became a necessity, a commonplace feature of this period.[2] Solon also determined that criminal fines would be given to the state rather than the plaintiff, thus contributing to a decline in citizen engagement in justice proceedings.

During the Solonian era, the state took over absolute control of criminal law and punishment. Athenians, particularly the poor and undereducated, were impacted by these changes, souring public opinion for Solon (Hyde 1918). State reliance on fines had severe consequences for the lower classes, and this penalty was eventually abandoned given the sheer number of people affected by it. Time-based sentences were then instituted, but these measures did little to improve the lot of the poor, as most of the incarcerated were impoverished (D'Amico 2010). Income equality became a hallmark of Athens due in part to the shifts in political and penal policy that followed in Solon's wake, and the Athenians' tolerance for state-based differential treatment of the wealthy and the poor grew thin, leading to the overthrow of the Archons (Hyde 1918). Subsequently, Athens bore witness to a number of temporary leaders who gained power through flattery and bribery, until violence took the forefront as a means to combat perpetual discord (Wood 1981). Eventually, crime and justice became a matter for the gods.

Since the birth of the polis, the gods held an influential role in the daily lives of early Grecians. During the Hellenistic period (between the fourth and first centuries BCE), divine authority became a keystone in Greek culture, including regarding conformity and deviance. Socrates's infamous trial demonstrates this assumption of absolute rule (Vaughan 1976). The philosopher was charged and convicted of corrupting the youth; this corruption stemmed from his debates regarding the existence of the gods (D'Amico 2010). In addition to shaping social perspectives of crime, the gods were also the authority on punishments. Records recount trials during which women were accused and convicted of various offenses, including casting spells or poisoning others. Each defendant was turned over to the gods (through the religious courts) for sentencing, typically resulting in death or banishment (Eidinow 2010). Thus, as social structure and political leadership fluctuated, the Grecian people turned to the gods for guidance.

By the end of the first century BCE, ancient Greece had been overshadowed by the commanding Roman Republic. The Republic took root around the fifth century BCE, formalizing Roman law through a series of legislative mandates publicly displayed on large tablets known as the XII (Twelve) Tables (Cherry 1890). Originally compiled by Decemvirs, the XII Tables were, in some respects, reminiscent of pre-Solonic Greece. Vengeance was the sole object of punishment, crimes were offenses against the individual and not the state, and the injured party was able to recover the penalty directly from the perpetrator (Cherry 1890; Radin 1925). The XII Tables outlined just four classes of crime: theft, robbery, injury to property, and injury to person. The XII Tables remained the ultimate authority on crime and justice until the introduction of the Lex Calpurnia de Repetundis in 149 BCE and Leges Corneliae in 79 BCE (Cherry 1890), which shifted control from the public to the state.

In early Rome, social stratification was as prominent a feature as it had been in ancient Greece. Some of the earliest social uprisings were prompted by the differential treatment of the plebeians (common class), particularly between 499 to 287 BCE (Bradley 2017). The lower-class plebs were dissatisfied with the distribution of labor and benefits in Roman society; while they contributed to the survival and success of Roman society, they were denied equal law and justice. The first plebeian secession was paired with the demand for elected tribunes that would protect their interests; otherwise, they threatened to leave Rome and create their own city elsewhere (Cole & Symes 2016). The patricians (upper class) eventually agreed to this demand, avoiding a plebeian exodus. Despite this concession, secessions continued throughout the years, as the common class fought for additional rights and democratic processes (Bradley 2017).

Plebeian demands led to institutional revisions. The criminal justice system fell under state control, leading to the implementation of the first criminal court under Lex Calpurnia de Repetundis in 149 BCE (Epke 2021). Prior to this set of legislative measures, political influence and partiality permeated systems of justice, and penalties were neither consistent nor proportional. Oftentimes, a criminal's social status was a more reliable indicator of their sentence than their guilt or inflicted injury

(Cherry 1890). The Lex Calpurnia, however, instituted judicial independence under the auspices of fairness and equality before the law. Unfortunately, the new judicial system became rife with bribery and impropriety as Rome sank into civil war in the first century BCE (Hoeflich 1984).[3] Before long, social stratification increased once again, until the military took control of the government and the Republic faltered. In 79 BCE, the Leges Corneliae (law) sought to revise Roman courts, thus making prosecution more efficient, as well as imposing harsher penalties for select offenses, such as murder, bribery, fraud, and heresy (Cherry 1890). Soon thereafter, the Republic crumbled, and the militaristic Roman Empire arose in its place.

As the new Roman Empire replaced the fallen Roman Republic, urbanization and expansion, both of which were made possible by slave and criminal labor, became fundamental to its development and growth (Radin 1925). The practice of social "othering" pervaded the Empire, and the citizenry adopted terms, such as *noxii* (those who caused harm to society) and *infames* (those "without reputation"), to brand barbarians, rebels, deserters, fugitive slaves, forgers, and murderers (Carucci 2017, 221–27). The social and political elite turned justice into a public spectacle, celebrated with macabre and deadly displays. *Summa supplicia*, the execution of wrong-doers, became regular public events; spectators were treated to the sight of beheadings, crucifixions, burnings, gladiator fights, and *damnatio ad bestias* (death by wild animal) (Carucci 2017, 215–18). The Empire's interpretation of justice proceedings was a sadistic and theatrical affair.

The Roman penal system under the Empire was unabashedly biased in nature; free citizens of higher rank were all but immune to serious punishments (Carucci 2017). Everyone else was untrustworthy, othered, and subject to inhumane justice. Romans were not particularly religious people, and faith did little to protect the socially suspect. However, similar to the Republic, the empire's reign was not indefinite. Beginning with the Edict of Milan in 312 CE, the spread of Christianity catalyzed the collapse of the Roman Empire, and by 476 CE, the entire empire had crumbled.

Although ancient Greek and Roman civilizations eventually perished, each had lasting effects on future criminal justice systems. Vengeance and retribution, in both the private and public spheres, were fundamental pillars. In addition, justice was inequitable, with common or lower classes bearing the brunt of punitive consequences. Court and judicial proceedings were influenced by bias and personal gain. Lastly, punishment was sensationalized for public consumption. These ancient criminal justice systems and the crime trends of the era were, in sum, significantly influenced by social status, religion, and revenge, sentiments that are similar to those found in modern times.

THE DARK AND MIDDLE AGES
(476 CE TO THE FIFTEENTH CENTURY)

Following the collapse of the Roman Empire and its system of centralized authority, many European communities returned to localized protection and control. Land ownership and trade increased, accompanied by a rise in property crime and robbery. Some people relied on the family for sanctuary while others offered labor and taxes to wealthy landowners in exchange for security. Economic value eventually became the metric of the era, defining status, employment, crime, and death. Religion gathered a large and ardent following with promises of comfort and hope. Actions considered unholy or impure were criminalized, and new forms of establishing guilt, such as the trials by ordeal, became commonplace. Community health was threatened by external forces, including natural (raiders) and supernatural (demonic) threats, but it was brought to its knees by a force more powerful than previously known, the Black Death. These were the aptly named Dark and Middle Ages.

At the inception of the Dark Ages, Germanic social and cultural structures revolved around the importance of kinship (Drew 1987). The family was integral to keeping peace and maintaining prosperity. In the vacuum created by the fall of the empire's centralized system, the kinship system of control spread throughout Europe. Germanic practices combined with elements of Roman rule, and by the sixth century, they had created a new justice system known as *wergeld* (Briggs et al. 1996; Wileman 2015, 67). Within this system, each family or kin group was assigned a value informed by their status and prestige, and should a perpetrator cause harm to a member of that kin group, their punishment was decided according to the wergeld.[4] If the offender was unable to make recompense, they might have become an indentured servant until the debt was settled (Drew 1987).

The kin system was effective in rural and disparate communities, but it was less fitting for newly developing population centers or migrant communities. As such, a new system of justice and control was necessary, which took the form of feudalism (Briggs et al. 1996). Feudalism relied on wealthy landowners who owned large lots of land; they leased these lands to vassals, who then paid the owners for protection and order (Drew 1987). The less fortunate would receive protection from roaming bands of thieves or raiding outsiders, while the wealthy lords received income and had the ability to recruit a militia if necessary (Briggs et al. 1996). The reciprocity underlying feudalism ensured its longevity well into the Middle Ages.

Both the kin and feudal systems developed methods of bringing criminals to justice. Given the difficulty of medieval travel, crime was often committed by someone already known to a specific community and region, thus simplifying identification and resolution (Briggs et al. 1996). Some communities created *moots*, or assemblies comprised of free citizens, that would oversee the judgment of the perpetrator. It was in everyone's interest to see justice done, so attendance at these assemblies was consistently high (Wileman 2015). In feudal areas, specific individuals were given the task of identifying and catching offenders, who would then be brought to trial at the lord's estate.[5] Ensuring just outcomes, however, was more complicated if the perpetrator was not local or difficult to identify.

The seventh, eighth, and ninth centuries bore witness to the renewed growth of kingdoms throughout the European continent. This development was driven, in part, by the pressing need to protect communities from Viking invaders and looters (Briggs et al. 1996). Kinship and lordship systems had not provided sufficient protection from Northman attacks, and the perpetrators frequently escaped justice. The Carolingian Empire was the largest to arise during this period, located in what would later become known as France. Under the militaristic rule of Charlemagne, the empire effectively defended itself from Viking raiders while also facilitating urbanization and commerce throughout the Western world. Charlemagne became even more influential when he established close ties with both the Byzantine Empire and the Christian Church (Mäkinen & Pihlajamäki 2004). The latter, in particular, held power and prestige, quickly becoming one of the most important institutions of the Middle Ages.

As early as the fourth century CE, Christianity had spread throughout Europe, shaping social and political beliefs and practices. Theologians and scholars, such as (future Saint) Augustine, wrote of the sins of heresy and sorcery, equating them to criminal behavior (Mäkinen & Pihlajamäki 2004; Wileman 2015). The influence of the Church and the weight of these scholarly arguments associating sin with deviance impacted perceptions of crime and justice, leading to large-scale punitive measures directed toward perceived religious nonconformity (Mäkinen & Pihlajamäki 2004). The Great Schism, for example, occurred in 1054 CE, causing the Roman Catholic Church to separate from the Eastern Orthodox Church, facilitating an increase in religious intolerance and persecution (Cox 2018). The Crusades provide another example; between the eleventh and thirteenth centuries, the Crusades aimed to quell heretical beliefs that challenged Church authority and to reclaim holy land from non-believers (Theron & Oliver 2018). In addition, the Church developed its own system of justice to identify, try, and punish religious deviants. By the fourteenth century CE, the Church had remade crime and justice into its own image, although the state (the Crown) retained partial control of formal justice systems.

Kingdoms grew stronger alongside the Holy Empire of the Church, claiming rulership of crime and justice that equaled Christian dictates. Kings could not ignore the benefits of social control, including reaping profits from financial criminal penalties and stomping out political treason or rebellion in the name of justice (Briggs et al. 1996). Although royal control differed in some respects from religious control, the Church canon and the Royal Court were inextricably bound during this period, sharing the common and frequently oppressive goals of compliance and conformity. Abusive power facilitated frequent social revolutions, and by the time the Black Death wiped out more than half of the European population in the mid-fourteenth century, social unrest and poverty were commonplace, facilitating new crime trends (Hatcher 1994). The plague, however, upended much of the fervor that had defined the Middle Ages, and a period of reformation was inevitable.

In summary, the pendulum swung heavily after the collapse of the Roman Empire, and much of the Western world fell into darker times. People relied on those closest to them for safety and security, and justice systems were contingent on these close ties. Wergeld remained prominent during the early Middle Ages, replacing vengeance with compensation. Over time, however, urbanization and migration increased the need for formal organization, and familial and community control was replaced by feudal lordships and centralized kingdoms. Christianity gained favor during these troubled times, and deviance and sin became synonymous. Outsiders and non-believers were criminalized, spurring the Crusades and heretical trials. Then came the bubonic plague, which decimated European society, and once again, the Western world found itself on the cusp of a new era.

THE RENAISSANCE
(FOURTEENTH TO SEVENTEENTH CENTURIES)

Beginning in the late fourteenth century, a cultural and philosophical renaissance took root in select locations, and by the seventeenth century, it had spread through much of the Western world. Post-plague society found renewed hope and wonder in advancements in science and explorations in art. The Roman Catholic Church retained its position of influence, shaping social perceptions of morality, sin, and crime. While some citizens pushed back on ecclesiastical depictions of right and wrong, others embraced the narrative, resulting in moral panics and witch hunts across Europe and North America. On the secular front, court and justice systems were marred with inconsistent protocols and unfair outcomes. Petty crimes increased, judges turned to summary judgments and personal discretion to ease the case-load, and prisons and houses of correction became commonplace and overloaded. The Renaissance was, thus, both a period of emergence and a point of divergence for the criminal justice system.

During the early Renaissance, England was confronted with a spate of petty crimes, including increased incidents of drunkenness, scolding, slandering, and theft (Shoemaker 1991). The creation of professional police forces was still several hundred years in the future, so communities relied on volunteer parish constables or other local officials to bring offenders to justice tribunals (Sharpe 1982). Overwhelmed by the sheer volume of petty cases, judges passed swift judgment, with little consideration for the individual circumstances of each one. Summary judgments replaced lengthy trial proceedings, which further bolstered conviction rates (Shoemaker 1991). The English court, although subject to criticism for its lack of individualized and equitable justice, was notably efficient when compared to its predecessors. England was not alone in experiencing judicial change; other countries were also going through justice-related transitions, although the nature and degree of this change differed between nations (Langbein 1974). Italy provides a ready example of changes occurring in other parts of Europe.

Florence and Venice were both growing city-states during the late Middle Ages and the early Renaissance. Florence adopted the *ius commune* system, a combination of Roman Empire law and Roman Catholic canon, as the foundation of its justice system (Stern 2004). Venice, on the other hand, relied on executive councils controlled by the elite families of the city. Despite these differences, each city shared the principle of *arbitrium*, or judicial discretion. Judges were given the freedom to rely solely on their conscience when interpreting laws and determining case outcomes (Ruggiero 1978). Similar to what was occurring in England, discretion increased efficiency through summary proceedings, but it also led to trials in absentia, partial proofs, a reliance on secret accusers, and methods of torture (Ruggiero 1978; Wolfgang 1990). During this period, the goal of the justice system was simple: punish all crimes, without due consideration of the potential for wrongful convictions.[6] Punishments were harsh for the common classes, including prison time, mutilation, and even death. Thus, as the English and Italian justice systems illustrate, during the early Renaissance, crime rates were high, judicial discretion was paramount, and systems of justice were efficient, but biased and harsh (Wolfgang 1954; Wolfgang 1956).

Similar to previous eras, differential treatment was also commonplace in many Renaissance courts. Political vendettas received a slap on the wrist, while members of the common class were branded as *malfamati* (disreputable), particularly if they engaged in repetitive criminal behavior (Stern 2004). Those without wealth were imprisoned in terrible conditions while nobles received short periods of house arrest. Thus, secular systems were defined not only by efficiency and biased punitiveness, but also by inequitable treatment of the socially and economically disadvantaged (Wolfgang 1956).

Ecclesiastical justice also suffered from unfair procedures and punishments during the Renaissance. Despite the disastrous results of the medieval Crusades, the Church continued to criminalize immoralities and heresies well into the seventeenth century (Theron & Oliver 2018). Charges of blasphemy (challenging the supremacy of God or the sacrosanctity of the Church) were liberally levied for a variety of behaviors, ranging from speaking out against the Church to vague moral transgressions that were found to be in violation of social expectations (Nash 2007). The Inquisition, a harsh and unforgiving institution, was charged with rooting out and punishing incidents of blasphemy, with some receiving penance while others received death. These practices, although accepted by many, were condemned by others. After Jan Hus was burned at the stake for heresy in the fifteenth century, Bohemia witnessed a series of protests and rebellions (Pelz 2016). Soon thereafter, Martin Luther challenged the teachings of the Church, prompting the Protestant Reformation. Anti-Church sentiments were further facilitated by the invention of the printing press (Nash 2007). Thus, throughout the Renaissance, the Church was subject to internal and external conflict; this was particularly prominent after it took umbrage at women.

The period between 1560 and 1660 was particularly prosecutorial, as the remnants of feudalism disappeared, firmly replaced by centralized authority. Regarding the state, indictments increased as criminal definitions expanded to include further sinful and ill-mannered behaviors (Sharpe 1982). As for the Church, errant and nonconforming women became a central focus, as did accusations of sorcery and witchcraft. For more than a century, authorities fervently pursued and prosecuted the accused, facilitating what some would later call "gender-cleansing" witch hunts (Pelz 2016, 27). While men were also accused of witchcraft and sorcery during this era, evidence suggests that more than three in every four executions were of female offenders (Currie 1968). Healing, midwifery, and other practices that were traditionally carried out by women were criminalized, as was insubordinate or atypical behavior. The aftermath of this period added to the growing discontent around ecclesiastical practices, and by the end of the Renaissance, the Church had lost further favor.

In summary, crime and justice took a turn during the period of the Renaissance. In the aftermath of the plague, petty crimes and legal statutes increased, reflecting the criminalization of perceived immoralities and wickedness. Judicial discretion permeated Western courts, increasing efficiency but amplifying bias and severity. In addition, justice systems replicated disparities and stratification, subjecting the poor to harsh measures while the nobility enjoyed leniency. These characteristics, although deeply troubling, paled in comparison to the events that occurred near the end of the era, namely the criminalization of nonconformity (particularly among women) and subsequent witch trials. Thus, the Renaissance, named such in recognition of a period of rebirth, was also a period of harsh and disparate treatment, informed in part by gender, status, and wealth.

THE ENLIGHTENMENT
(SEVENTEENTH TO LATE-EIGHTEENTH CENTURIES)

The seventeenth century experienced a rise in scientific investigation, world exploration, and profound philosophical writings, shaping the way that society viewed crime and responded to it. At the beginning of the Enlightenment, powerful Western nations sought to extend the reach of their empires, prompting further exploration and colonization. Social and cultural differences were exaggerated, bringing the practice of othering to new heights. Poverty was commonplace, and those without status faced oppressive circumstances. The justice system was punitive, relying heavily on capital punishment and expulsion, and it grew increasingly public, as hangings, pillories, and gibbets were placed in town squares. Although grim, the mire of the Enlightenment was also galvanizing; it roused revolutions in North America and Europe, and influential reformers took center stage, calling for institutional change in justice practices.

The Enlightenment was a short-lived era in time, beginning in the late 1600s and ending in the early 1800s. It was, however, an important period for trends in crime and justice. European crime rates were high, informed in part by rampant poverty and the lack of opportunity (Hay 1980). The lower classes were struck hard by hunger, homelessness, and joblessness, and they had few opportunities to address these issues through legitimate means (Cribelar 2001). While the previous era viewed poverty as sin, Enlightenment society saw it as an expression of laziness, thus curtailing charitable efforts and social support, further exacerbating the situation. The justice system also lacked sympathy for those who turned to crime, preferring to rely on harsh and dehumanizing forms of punishment as a method of deterrence (Stern 2004).

The punitive practices of Enlightenment justice systems, although evident across European and North American nations, are perhaps best exemplified by English practices. England relied on physical punishment and executions as its primary form of justice, and criminals convicted of treason, murder, breaches of trust, sexual offenses, and other habitual crimes were often publicly punished in a deliberately dehumanizing way (Hay 1980).[7] Convicted criminals were frequently stripped bare and scourged through the streets until blood dripped from their backsides, or locked in a public pillory or gibbet (a metal cage suspended above the ground), laughed and scoffed at for days or weeks on end. Worst of all, however, were the frequent hangings, occurring at a rate of approximately seven hundred per year (Cockburn 1994). In these instances, perpetrators were paraded through town to the public square, then hanged by the neck and left to die by way of strangulation. In 1718, an alternative punishment was offered to some English felons in lieu of execution; they were granted pardon conditional on their transportation to the American colonies.

Trends in crime and justice did not shift dramatically throughout the era of Enlightenment, but they did serve to inspire social upheaval and subsequent critical thought, which would influence trends substantially in the next era. These points of inspiration often came from written works, the primary form of communication throughout the

Western world at this time, beginning with the popular press (Cockburn 1994; Hay 1980). The popular press sensationalized public punishments, providing detailed descriptions of gallows executions and other gruesome measures of justice (Cockburn 1994). Media accounts caught the attention of the public, contributing to large throngs of often-intoxicated spectators at and along the path to the gallows. These massive processions, however, often turned violent, resulting in mobs, riots, and general social unrest (Hay 1980).[8]

High crime rates, macabre punitive measures, and social violence and unrest facilitated an increasing interest in justice-related philosophies and practices. Arguably one of the most important justice-related set of writings of this era was drafted in 1764 by Cesare Beccaria. In *On Crimes and Punishments*, Beccaria criticized the traditional corporal and capital punishment system for its moral and social failures. Informed in part by the musings of Voltaire, Rousseau, and Locke, Beccaria presented a detailed critique of court proceedings, judicial practices, sentencing disparities, and measures of punishment (Jenkins 1984). He argued against physical punishment, expulsion, or execution, positing that incarceration was a more humane and just alternative, and championed proportionality in sentencing (Blom 2010).[9] Beccaria was joined eventually by Jeremy Bentham, who argued that humankind was hedonistic, driven by the pursuit of pleasure and the avoidance of pain (Bentham 1843). As such, the effectiveness of the criminal justice system depended on providing punitive measures that were costly enough to outweigh the benefits of crime. He also argued for proportionality, noting that punishments that were too severe would likely defeat any hedonistic calculation of costs and benefits (Jenkins 1984).

The consequences of Enlightenment crime, justice, and reformist ideas were felt as the era came to a close. Poverty and increasing crime rates hindered community health and safety. Public executions and transport to New World colonies had lasting effects on social cohesion. Riots in England in the late eighteenth century destroyed parts of the Old Bailey and Newgate prisons, further igniting social unrest. France faced similar societal inequalities and social rebellions, sparked by the writings of the Enlightenment reformers. The storming of the Bastille became a pivotal moment in the popular battle against royal authority, and the North American colonies proclaimed freedom from the overreach of the British monarchy. As the nineteenth century approached, significant change was all but certain.

REVOLUTION AND THE VICTORIAN ERA
(LATE-EIGHTEENTH AND NINETEENTH CENTURIES)

The Industrial Revolution brought about a period of dramatic change for the Western world. Economic development exacerbated inequality as wages stagnated and working conditions worsened, leading to an increase in juvenile delinquency, property crime, and other offenses. Governments responded with professional police forces and increased incarceration. Meanwhile, Victorian society turned to sensationalist media to inform their understanding of crime, further inciting public fears. As the twentieth century loomed, crime rates oscillated, formal policing was prevalent, jails and prisons were over capacity, and the public was misinformed and fearful.

Prior to the Industrial Revolution, many rural English communities managed justice-related issues locally, relying on regional justices of the peace and constables, as well as informal retributive justice (Philips & Storch 2000). Only crimes against the government, such as treason or coin forgery, were addressed through more formal means. Beginning around 1750, private associations of neighbors formed to combat local crime (Koyama 2014). These groups eventually grew to include formal membership dues and written constitutions. By the early nineteenth century, these associations were the primary deterrence for property and petty crime throughout England, a precursor to the professional police forces that would come to populate Western nations, appearing first in France in response to the Revolution of 1789 and later in England, following an increase in vice and the subsequent Peterloo Massacre and riots of 1819 (Koyama 2014).[10]

The changes in policing reflected, in part, changes in crime trends. Industrialization and improved transportation of goods and people throughout the world led to an expansion of new and popular forms of socializing. Public houses (pubs) became centers for companionship, entertainment, and other social functions, all fueled by alcohol consumption (Thompson 1981). Victorian elites saw these locations as dens of indecency and depravity, sites for unadulterated sex, gambling, and criminal activity (Philips 2003). Many also blamed the corruption of Victorian ideals on an influx of Irish-born migrants (Swift 1997). This was paired with the assumption that many young migrants were not as keen to assimilate to the new industrial lifestyle and instead turned to carousing and petty crime (Bindler & Hjalmarsson 2017). The newly founded police forces spent much of their time patrolling pubs or the outdoor fairs that would spring up throughout the year. Incarceration for short periods of time, sometimes just long enough to "dry up" or become sober, became the preferred response, thus skirting the complexities of some of the more severe available punishments (Thompson 1981).

While pubs and drinking were an annoyance, they were not the only form of deviance that troubled Victorian society. Another notable crime trend developed during the Industrial Revolution, one rooted in poverty and desperation. As industry developed, the working class was expected to labor throughout the day, leaving youth to roam the streets in search of food or companionship (Lane 1974). Lack of supervision and prosocial opportunities led to an increase in juvenile delinquency as youth learned to steal, fight, and survive on their own. Victorian reformers posited that religious instruction in piety and virtue might save this seemingly lost generation of children (Thompson 1981). At the time, education for all children was not yet required in many places, but the reformers succeeded in their agenda to educate the errant youth; education became mandatory in Britain and much of the Western world by the dawn of the twentieth century (Philips 2003).

Public concern about youth and vice were inflamed by media accounts. Print media became a primary method of communicating during the Industrial Revolution. Daily or weekly "penny dreadful" periodicals were full of amusing and graphic tales of deviance, sparking anxiety in late-Victorian society (Springhall 1994). Social unease was further inflamed by major newspapers of the day, such as the *Northern Star* and the *London Times*, which were guilty of overpublicizing sensational crimes, such as murder, suicide, rape, and infanticide, while ignoring the relatively benign petty crimes

(Rodrick 1996). The consensus of society, caused in some part by the news media of the period, was that violent crime was on the rise.

By the end of the nineteenth century, justice had become an entirely state-controlled institution. The circumstances of the era demanded it. As the economy changed, vice and juvenile delinquency became commonplace. In response, nations introduced professional police forces, increased incarceration levels, and bowed to reformers' demands for mandatory childhood education. As crime trends fluctuated in response to these changes, the media recast crime as a voracious plague, further exacerbating social anxieties. Fear of violent crime led to the reintroduction of the death penalty in England in 1863, a somber end to the era (Casey 2011).

THE MODERN AND POSTMODERN ERAS
(TWENTIETH CENTURY TO THE PRESENT)

The rise of urbanization, industrialization, and globalization during the twentieth century affected crime and justice trends throughout the Western world. Maintaining order and controlling crime was placed solely in the hands of local, regional, and national police organizations. Crime syndicates formed and began expanding their networks to other countries, leading to new and complex jurisdictional issues. An increase in transportation capabilities and advancements in communication technology further complicated matters relating to authority, responsibility, and accountability. In the aftermath of two world wars, united and interconnected judicial bodies were established to address these issues. Meanwhile, the United States embarked on a War on Drugs, positioning it as the world leader in incarceration, a role it continues to hold today. While the United States cracked down on crime, other Western countries tempered their justice systems with rehabilitation and reformation. It was, in sum, an era of blurring borders, international crime, and diverging responses to crime.

In the early twentieth century, police assumed a number of roles that extended beyond simply responding to crime. Officer duties included a variety of tasks, such as regulating public markets, street-cleaning, light maintenance, and licensing newspapers (Sheptycki 1995). Over time, these services were delegated to other government departments, and the police became what is now prominent in Western nations: the sole gatekeepers of crime and social order, expected to display civility, but also permitted to apply force in the execution of their duties (Bitner 1974).[11] The policing system, although imperfect, met the needs of the time, balancing crime and order locally. Jurisdictional issues did arise occasionally, however, when different agencies found themselves overlapping on cases, which led to competition for recognition and results (Johnston 1992). Over time, as technology increased travel and communication capabilities, criminal enterprise began expanding beyond traditional borders, introducing further jurisdictional issues. International trafficking rings, multinational fraud schemes, and transnational theft presented new problems for police agencies that demanded a solution: an international police force (Sheptycki 1995).

Following the First World War, Western nations recognized that collaboration was key to avoiding or responding to conflict. Interpol, or the International Criminal Police Commission, was formally constituted in 1923 as a means for police forces from different nations to interact more efficiently and effectively (Sheptycki 1995). No single nation oversaw Interpol; instead, it was created through the efforts of several European police associations. Their efforts were successful as the new organization improved police abilities to catch criminals outside of their immediate jurisdiction, as well as to locate and impede transnational criminal syndicates (Johnston 1992). Interpol served as a model that shaped additional international organizations, including Europol and the United Nations (Anderson 1989). Thus, by the end of the twentieth century, policing had transformed considerably, as crime and order became its sole responsibility, both nationally and internationally.

Policing was not the only significant change during this era. Laws and crime rates were also shifting considerably, particularly in the United States. Following World War II, crime rates escalated quickly, mostly in regard to violent crimes (Cook & Winfield 2013; LaFree 1990).[12] This was likely due in part to several social changes, including an increase in gang membership, social strife about government actions and policies, poverty, access to guns, and drug use. In 1971, President Nixon launched a War on Drugs, a campaign that linked Black communities, illicit drug abuse, and crime (Ahrens 2020).[13] The results were drastic: drug-related convictions and incarceration skyrocketed, predominantly among minority and marginalized groups, and the United States became the world leader in mass incarceration.

In the 1990s, crime rates began declining the United States. Although some may attribute it to the War on Drugs or increased incarceration, most experts suggest it is due to other factors, such as an aging population (baby boomers), an increase in average incomes, advancements in security technology, and prevention programs (Blumstein & Wallman 2020).[14] Despite the shift in crime trends, the United States continued to embrace a philosophy of incapacitation, in contrast to its Western counterparts, who approached crime control in a somewhat different manner (Ahrens 2020; Blumstein 1983).

While other nations also experienced increases in crime rates in the latter half of the twentieth century, these tended to be lower than the United States, most notably in relation to violent crime (Kalish 1988). Nations differed in how they responded to this issue, but overall, the European response was softer than that employed by the United States. England abolished the death penalty in 1965, prioritizing incarceration over other measures of justice (Sharpe 1990). The nation also embraced a rehabilitative approach, introducing open prisons that provided training and programming, allowed residents to leave during the day to work, and helped ease a rehabilitated prisoner's transition back into the community (Mjaland et al. 2023). Other European nations, such as Wales and Denmark, adopted a similar reformative approach, prioritizing open prisons that provided increased programming, freedoms, and transitional support (Sheptycki 1995). Similar to the United States, European crimes rates began to decline in the 1990s, suggesting that similar forces were driving Western crime rates, independent of punitive measures (Kalish 1988).

As the twentieth century concluded, crime and justice bore little resemblance to their former selves. Geopolitical borders blurred, and international crime increased. Policing organizations adapted, creating international associations. Crime rates escalated across Western nations, causing the United States to embrace mass incarceration, while its European counterparts balanced incarceration with rehabilitative practices.

Thus, the twenty-first century was greeted in a manner not seen in previous eras, tasked with tackling crime and justice in an era of globalization, criminal innovation, organizational cooperation, and punitive divergence.

CONCLUSION

> There is not a single act that, by its very content, would be a criminal offense; and acts of murder and salvation, truth and lies, theft and giving, enmity and love, sexual licentiousness and abstinence, etc.—all these acts could and were both a crime and not a crime in various codes, depending on who they are committed, against whom they were committed, under what conditions they occurred. Therefore, to classify certain acts by their very content as criminal offenses . . . is a hopeless task. (Sorokin 1992, as quoted in Gilinsky 2022, 77)

Crime occurs in every community, culture, and country. The causes of crime range considerably, carried out for the sake of survival, in rebellion, or as an act of selfishness. Society responds by attempting to curtail its instigation or its impact. In these efforts, communities have relied on enslaving, beating, incarcerating, or executing those accused of criminal behavior. On some occasions, the meaning of and responses to criminal behavior have been decided by those in positions of power while, on other occasions, it has been determined by the public, who pressure the government for change or take matters into their own hands. Measures of punishment have oscillated over time, shifting back and forth from private retribution, public deterrence, and incapacitation, with a suggestion of rehabilitation in more modern times. While some measures endured, others enjoyed but a moment in time. One thing can be said for certain; crime and justice are fluid. Crime changes. Justice changes. Society changes.

NOTES

1. The term *draconian* originates with Draco and his punitive measures.
2. The rule of Seisachtheia, the relief of burdens, changed the definition of citizenship so that no Athenian could subject bodily force upon another, nor could they incarcerate a citizen because it made them slave rather than a citizen (D'Amico 2010).
3. In the first century BCE, Cicero described three causes of judicial impropriety—gratia (exchange), potentia (coercion), and pecunia (bribery) (Hoeflich 1984). Unfair judgments also were caused by ignoratia (ignorance).
4. The complex *wergeld* system was intended to reduce the likelihood of revenge because by accepting compensation, the victim was avoiding any loss of honor (Wileman 2015). However, that did not stop the rise of blood feuds when kin were unwilling to let the death go unavenged (Drew 1987).
5. In later years, this person became known as the shire-reeve, similar in nature to today's sheriff (Wileman 2015).
6. The conviction rate for theft in Venice was 99 percent between 1270 and 1403, with some receiving the death penalty (Stern 2004, 230–33).
7. The Waltham Black Act of 1723 increased the number of offenses subject to the death penalty to all incidents during which the accused was armed or disguised (Hay 1980).

8. "The majority non-wealthy population of eighteenth-century England was known as the 'labouring poor' when quiet, and as the 'mob' when otherwise disruptive" (Hay 1980, 46).

9. Sweden abolished the death penalty in 1772, and Grand Duchy of Tuscany followed suit in 1786, inspired in part by Beccaria's writings (Blom 2010). Earlier, Elizabeth of Russia and Frederick of Prussia banned torture and limited capital punishment (Jenkins 1984).

10. Patrick Colquhoun, a contemporary of the English philosopher Jeremy Bentham, published a plea for an organized, paid police force in his 1795 Treatise on the Police of the Metropolis (Philips 2003).

11. Egon Bitner quipped, "The policeman and the policeman alone, is equipped, entitled and required to deal with every exigency in which force may have to be used" (Bitner 1974).

12. Property crime doubled during this period, while violent crime quadrupled (LaFree 1999).

13. Race has historically played a key role in United States drug legislation. Before 1914, many US states only regulated alcohol and other substances with laws against importation or sales (Ahrens 2020). Drugs like opium became illegal due to their connection to the unwanted immigrant populations from China. Some states similarly criminalized marijuana in the 1920s and '30s, due to the plant's ties to immigrants from Mexico and Central America.

14. Donahue and Levitt argue that legalized abortion led to a decrease in the crime rates decades later due to the decrease in number of children living through poverty or being unwanted. Other researchers refute this claim (Donahue & Levitt 2001; Lott & Whitley 2006).

REFERENCES

Ahrens, Deborah M. 2020. "Retroactive Legality: Marijuana Convictions and Restorative Justice in an Era of Criminal Justice Reform." *Journal of Criminal Law and Criminology* 110, no. 3 (Summer).

Anderson, Malcolm. 1989. *Policing the World.* Oxford: Oxford University Press.

Bentham, Jeremy. 1843. *The Works of Jeremy Bentham, vol. 7 (Rationale of Judicial Evidence Part 2).* Edinburgh: William Tait.

Bindler, Anna, and Randi Hjalmarsson. 2017. "Prisons, Recidivism, and the Age-Crime Profile." *Economic Letters* 152 (March): 46–49. https://doi.org/10.1016/j.econlet.2017.01.002.

Blom, Philipp. 2010. "Crime and Punishment." In *A Wicked Company: The Forgotten Radicalism of the European Enlightenment*, edited by Philipp Blom, 217–29. New York: Basic Books.

Blumstein, Alfred. 1983. "Selective Incapacitation as a Means of Crime Control." *American Behavioral Scientist* 27(1): 87–108. https://doi.org/10.1177/000276483027001006.

Blumstein, Alfred, and Joel Wallman. 2020. "The Recent Rise and Fall of American Violence." In *Crime, Inequality and the State*, edited by Mary Vogel, 103–24. Oxford: Routledge.

Bradley, Guy. 2017. "Mobility and Secession in the Early Roman Republic." *Antichthon* 51: 149–71. https://doi.org/10.1017/ann.2017.10.

Briggs, John, Christopher Harrison, Angus McInnes, and David Vincent. 1996. "The medieval origins of the English criminal justice system." In *Crime and Punishment in England, 1100–1990: An Introductory History*, edited by John Briggs, Christopher Harrison, Angus Mcinnes, and David Vincent, 1–13. London: Palgrave Macmillan.

Carucci, M. 2017. "The Spectacle of Justice in the Roman Empire." In *The Impact of Justice on the Roman Empire*, edited by Olivier Hekster and Koenraad Verboven, 212–34. Leiden: Brill Publishers.

Casey, Christopher A. 2011."Common Misperceptions: The Press and Victorian Views of Crime." *Journal of Interdisciplinary History* 41, no. 3 (Winter): 367–91. http://www.jstor .org/stable/40985739.

Cherry, Richard R. 1890. *Lectures on the Growth of Criminal Law in Ancient Communities.* New York: Macmillan Publishers.

Cockburn, James S. 1994. "Punishment and Brutalization in the English Enlightenment." *Law and History Review* 12, no. 1 (Spring): 155–79. http://www.jstor.org/stable/30042825.

Cole, Joshua, and Carol Symes. 2016. "The Civilization of Ancient Rome." In *Western Civilizations: Their History & Their Culture*, edited by Joshua Cole and Carol Symes. New York: W. W. Norton & Company, Incorporated.

Cook, Steve, and Tom Winfield. 2013. "Crime across the States: Are US crime rates converging?" *Urban Studies* 50, no. 9 (July): 1724–1741. https://doi.org/10.1177/0042098012466602.

Cribelar, Teresa. 2001. "From sin to laziness: early modern views of the poor and poor relief." https://www.eiu.edu/historia/cribelar.pdf.

Currie, Elliott P. 1968. "Crimes without Criminals: Witchcraft and Its Control in Renaissance Europe." *Law & Society Review* 3, no. 1 (August): 7–32. https://doi.org/10.2307/3052793.

D'Amico, Daniel J. 2010. "The Prison in Economics: Private and Public Incarceration in Ancient Greece." *Public Choice* 145, no. 3/4 (December): 461–82. http://www.jstor.org/ stable/40927129.

Drew, Katherine F. 1987. "Another Look at the Origins of the Middle Ages: A Reassessment of the Role of the Germanic Kingdoms." *Speculum* 62, no. 4 (October): 803–12. https://doi .org/10.2307/2851780.

Eidinow, Esther. 2010. "Patterns of Persecution: 'Witchcraft' Trials in Classical Athens." *Past & Present* 208 (August): 9–35. https://www.jstor.org/stable/40783312.

Epke, Sierra, 2021. "Criminal Law and Parricide in a Reflection of Social Parameters from the Roman Monarchy into the Early Empire." Honors Theses, University of Nebraska-Lincoln.

Gilinsky, Yakov I. 2022. "Postmodern Criminology: About Crime and Punishment. Sociology of Law." *Sociological Research* 4: 76–84.

Hatcher, John. 1994. England in the Aftermath of the Black Death. *Past & Present* 144 (August): 3–35. http://www.jstor.org/stable/651142.

Hay, Douglas. 1980. "Crime and Justice in Eighteenth- and Nineteenth-Century England." *Crime and Justice* 2: 45–84. https://www.jstor.org/stable/1147412.

Hoeflich, Michael H. 1984. "Regulation of Judicial Misconduct from Late Antiquity to the Early Middle Ages." *Law and History Review* 2, no. 1 (Spring): 79–104. https://doi.org/10 .2307/743911.

Hyde, Walter W. 1918. "The Homicide Courts of Ancient Athens." *University of Pennsylvania Law Review*: 319–62.

Jenkins, Philip. 1984. "Varieties of Enlightenment Criminology: Beccaria, Godwin, de Sade." *British Journal of Criminology* 24, no. 2 (April): 112–30. http://www.jstor.org/stable /23637024.

Johnston, Les. 1992. *The Rebirth of Private Policing.* Oxford: Routledge

Kalish, Carol B. 1988. *International Crime Rates Bureau of Justice Statistics Special Report.* US Department of Justice, Bureau of Justice Statistics.

Koyama, Mark. "The Law & Economics of Private Prosecutions in Industrial Revolution England." *Public Choice* 159, no. 1/2 (April): 277–98. http://www.jstor.org/stable/24507672.

LaFree, Gary. 1999. "Declining Violent Crime Rates in the 1990s: Predicting Crime Booms and Busts." *Annual Review of Sociology* 25 (1): 145–68. https://www.jstor.org/stable/223501.

Lane, Roger. 1974. "Crime and the Industrial Revolution: British and American Views." *Journal of Social History* 7, no. 3 (Spring): 287–303. http://www.jstor.org/stable/3786308.

Langbein, John H. 1974. "Prosecuting Crime in the Renaissance: England, Germany, France." *University of Chicago Law Review* 42: 224–33.

Mäkinen, Virpi, and Heikki Pihlajamäki. 2004. "The Individualization of Crime in Medieval Canon Law." *Journal of the History of Ideas* 65, no. 4 (October): 525–42. http://www.jstor.org/stable/3654267.

Mjåland, Kristian, Julie Laursen, Anna Schliehe, and Simon Larmour. 2023. "Contrasts in Freedom: Comparing the Experiences of Imprisonment in Open and Closed Prisons in England and Wales and Norway." *European Journal of Criminology* 20 (5): 1641–62. https://doi.org/10.1177/14773708211065905. https://www.jstor.org/stable/223501.

Nash, David. 2007. "Analyzing the History of Religious Crime. Models of 'Passive' and 'Active' Blasphemy since the Medieval Period." *Journal of Social History* 41, no. 1 (Fall): 5-29. https://www.jstor.org/stable/25096438.

Pelz, William A. 2016. "'The Other Reformation': Martin Luther, Religious Dogma and the Common People." In *A People's History of Modern Europe*, edited by William Pelz, 18–29. London: Pluto Press.

Philips, David. 2003. "Three Moral Entrepreneurs and the Creation of a Criminal Class in England, c. 1790s–1840s." *Crime, Histoire & Sociétés* 7 (1): 79–107. http://www.jstor.org/stable/42708518.

Philips, David, and Robert D. Storch. 2000 "Policing Provincial England, 1829–1856. The Politics of Reform." *Crime, Histoire & Sociétés* 4 (2): 122–24.

Radin, Max. 1925. "Fundamental Concepts of the Roman Law." *California Law Review* 13, no. 3 (March): 207–28. https://doi.org/10.2307/3475643.

Rodrick, Anne B. "'Only a Newspaper Metaphor': Crime Reports, Class Conflict, and Social Criticism in Two Victorian Newspapers." *Victorian Periodicals Review* 29, no. 1 (Spring): 1–18. http://www.jstor.org/stable/20082893.

Ruggiero, Guido. 1978. "Law and Punishment in Early Renaissance Venice." *Journal of Criminal Law and Criminology* 69, no. 2 (Summer): 243–56.

Sharpe, James A. 1982. "The History of Crime in Late Medieval and Early Modern England: A Review of the Field." *Social History* 7, no. 2 (May): 187–203. https://www.jstor.org/stable/4285163.

Sharpe, James A. 1990. *Judicial Punishment in England*. London: Faber and Faber Limited.

Sheptycki, James W.E. 1995. "Transnational Policing and the Makings of a Postmodern State." *The British Journal of Criminology* 35, no. 4: 613–35.

Shoemaker, Robert B. 1991. *Prosecution and Punishment: Petty Crime and the Law in London and Rural Middlesex, c. 1660-1725*. Cambridge: Cambridge University Press.

Smith, Gertrude. "Early Greek Codes." *Classical Philology* 17, no. 3 (July): 187–201. http://www.jstor.org/stable/263596.

Springhall, J. 1994. "'Pernicious Reading'? 'The Penny Dreadful' as Scapegoat for Late-Victorian Juvenile Crime." *Victorian Periodicals Review* 27, no. 4 (Winter): 326–49. https://www.jstor.org/stable/20082795.

Stern, Laura I. "Politics and Law in Renaissance Florence and Venice." *American Journal of Legal History* 46, no. 2 (April): 209–34. https://doi.org/10.2307/3692441.

Swift, Roger. 1997. "Heroes or Villains?: The Irish, Crime, and Disorder in Victorian England." *Albion: A Quarterly Journal Concerned with British Studies* 29, no. 3 (Autumn): 399–421. https://doi.org/10.2307/4051670.

Theron, Jacques, and Erna Oliver. 2018. "Changing Perspectives on the Crusades." *HTS Teologiese Studies* 74, no. 1 (March). http://dx.doi.org/10.4102/hts.v74i1.4691.

Thompson, F.M.L. 1981. "Social Control in Victorian Britain." *Economic History Review* 34, no. 2 (May): 189–208. https://doi.org/10.2307/2595241.

Vaughan, Frederick. 1976. "The Trial of Socrates: Recent Reflections." *Osgoode Hall Law Journal* 14, no. 2 (October): 407–13. https://doi.org/10.60082/2817-5069.2166.

Wileman, Julie R. 2015. "Dark Age Crimes." In *Past Crimes: Archaeological & Historical Evidence for Ancient Misdeeds*, edited by Julie Wileman, 66–75. Barnsley: Pen and Sword Books.

Wolfgang, Marvin E. 1954. "Political Crimes and Punishments in Renaissance Florence." *Journal of Criminal Law, Criminology, and Police Science* 44, no. 5 (January): 555–81. https://doi.org/10.2307/1139605.

Wolfgang, Marvin E. 1956. "Socio-Economic Factors Related to Crime and Punishment in Renaissance Florence." *Journal of Criminal Law, Criminology, and Police Science* 47, no. 3 (September): 311–30. https://doi.org/10.2307/1140321.

Wolfgang, Marvin E. 1990. "Crime and Punishment in Renaissance Florence." *Journal of Criminal Law and Criminology* 81, no. 3 (Fall): 567–84.

Wood, Ellen. 1981. "Marxism and Ancient Greece." *History Workshop*, no. 11 (Spring): 3–22. http://www.jstor.org/stable/4288345.

Chapter 6

Crime, Race, and Ethnicity across the Generations

Silas B. Parks, Jazlin Branting, and Omi Hodwitz

INTRODUCTION

Identity informs inequality. Whether identity is shaped by skin color, religion, gender, sexuality, or affluence, to name but a few, there have been notable disparities throughout history. These disparities are inherently social in nature, expressed as tensions between individuals, but they are also institutional, permeating politics, education, health, and other fundamental structures, including the legal and criminal justice systems. Given that justice systems can be an influential part of organized societies, inequitable treatment from such institutions can have a substantial impact on the health of a community, necessitating careful exploration and understanding of such inequalities. This chapter provides such an exploration, highlighting how the justice systems of the past were influenced by perceptions of identities, specifically those rooted in race and ethnicity.

The very act of categorizing people is a cultural process informed by the timing and position of those making such decisions (Heng 2011). Humans have a natural tendency to label and evaluate characteristics in others, thus providing the foundation for biases, allowing us to establish who we like or dislike, view as good or bad, and label as part of the "us" or the "them." This proclivity has led to the acceptance and ostracization of different groups of people, informed by a variety of factors, key among them physical and cultural characteristics. Over time, the us/them divide determined by physical and cultural traits has shifted between groups, sometimes disadvantaging one, other times another. Thus, throughout this chapter the term *race* will be used to refer to a group that has unique physical or cultural traits that distinctly sets it apart from other groups in a specific period or era. *Ethnicity* bears a close resemblance to race, although historically it has included more emphasis on culture.

With those definitions in mind, this chapter will explore the response of legal and criminal justice systems to different races and ethnicities throughout history. This will include an examination of ancient Greece and Rome and the empires' treatment of outsiders, followed by an assessment of medieval Christendom and its response to Jews and Muslims. The chapter will then explore the European reaction to indigenous people and African slaves during the Colonial Period, as well as the post-Enlightenment development of biological theories of crime. While the appearance and expression of legal inequities varied greatly across different eras and groups of people, an overarching theme will become clear, one of enhanced prosecution and diminished protection of minority racial and ethnic groups.

ANTIQUITY

Ancient Greece is often referred to as the birthplace of Western civilization. Home to the great philosophers Socrates, Plato, and Aristotle, and the lauded source of modern democracy, Greek antiquity is often cast in an idyllic light and held in high regard. The histories, myths, and innovations of ancient Greece are a mainstay in both popular culture and academic settings. While this era has earned justifiable praise, it is not without its indignities, as well. The ancient Greeks may have blazed a trail in progressive thought and action, but they were also cruel and tyrannous toward others, particularly those whom they deemed as outsiders.

Despite its many accomplishments, ancient Greece was a highly ethnocentric community. For Athenians, there were two primary groups of people: the Greeks and the barbarians (Tuplin 1999).[1] Barbarians, or non-Greeks, were believed to be lesser peoples who lacked the intelligence, temperament, and skills to be members of the superior Greek class. This perspective was embraced by all, becoming a deeply ingrained part of Greek identity. Even Aristotle, whose works have been read, referenced, and revered throughout the Western world, adopted this perspective, believing not only that barbarians were inferior, but that they were also best fit to serve as slaves. In Aristotle's (1999) view, "barbarians and slaves are by nature identical," determining that "for these it is both right and expedient that they should serve as slaves" (27 and 34). Moreover, the Greeks went to great lengths to ensure that no barbarians would have the opportunity to overcome the divide in citizenship; after 451 BCE it was proclaimed that only the children of two citizens were themselves citizens (Philips 2013).[2] Forced to lived on the edge of Grecian territory, non-Greeks tried to overcome ostracization by claiming Trojan ancestry, thereby granting themselves a place in the Greek world (Hunt 2017). This was an effective tactic at times, as Troy had been destroyed and its citizens scattered, thus making these claims difficult to disprove.

The Grecian criminal justice system was a public affair within which citizens had a duty and a right to participate (Allen 2002).[3] The process was simple; private citizens would accuse another of wrongdoing, thus instigating a court trial for the purposes of prosecution.[4] The public courts of ancient Greece were large-scale jury trials, consisting of anywhere from two hundred to one thousand or more jurors (Von Dornum 1997). Each trial was expected to last a single day, with equal time allotted to both the prosecution and the defense to state their arguments (Kapparis 2019). Guilt was determined by a majority vote, and if the defendant was found guilty, each side would propose a punishment and the jury would vote on the two options available, unless a set punishment was mandated by statute.

Non-Greeks did have some standing in the courts of Greece. *Metics*, who were free foreigners, could both bring lawsuits and be called as witnesses (Phillips 2013). This was an important privilege, as it gave metics the ability to respond to crimes perpe-trated against them. However, it was not necessarily easy for outsiders to acquire the status of a free-standing foreigner. To become a metic, non-Greeks had to locate and produce a Greek patron and then register as a foreigner in their place of residence. Despite this difficulty, the metic status remained an option, as the Greeks could not ignore the fact that foreigners who were particularly skilled, wealthy, or influential had utility for the community, as long as they followed the prescribed rules.

Slavery was a prominent part of Greek culture and a factor that further facilitated the divide between Greeks and barbarians. For a time, it was legal to have Greek slaves, particularly when a debt was owed, but this was outlawed under the rule of Solon in the sixth century BCE (Forsdyke 2005).[5] Generally speaking, the Grecian world held an aversion to the enslavement of its own people, preferring instead to relegate non-Greeks to lives of servitude (Roger 2000). Thus, the slave class in ancient Greece consisted primarily of non-Greeks, many of whom were entangled in debt-bondage, had been taken captive, or were born into it (Hunt 2017). In addition, accusations of criminal activities could also lead to slavery, even in the absence of evidence.[6]

When slaves were accused of committing crimes, they were traditionally addressed as part of the *oikos* (family) system of justice. It was within the rights of the patriarch to oversee all aspects of slave lives, thus crimes that were localized to the household or were petty in nature were often settled privately by the head of the house (Kapparis 2019). In addition, slaves were believed to be untrustworthy, making them unsound witnesses in a court of law. If they were required to testify, the courts required that they received some degree of torture first, as a measure of assurance that their words held truth (Phillips 2013). As a consequence, slave owners were reluctant to involve their slaves in legitimate court proceedings, sometimes out of concern for their well-being, but also often simply because they wanted to avoid permanently crippling their property.

Greek ideals regarding philosophy and law, culture, and the superiority of their own people spread across the empire during the Hellenistic Period. Price (1986) notes that this early Greek influence was "seen as the innocent gift of civilization to the benighted barbarians" (321).[7] Alexander the Great and his many conquests spearheaded this dispersion, as he built new cities beyond the walls of Athens and appointed kings to regions that had otherwise remained relatively untouched, such as modern-day Afghanistan. These new sovereigns then pressed Greek culture on to the native population, thus ensuring that the barbarian/citizen narrative flourished. In addition, they created cultural city centers, including gymnasiums, which served as sites for physical and intellectual instruction. If native people wanted to claim Greek heritage, participate in Greek life, and be granted the benefits of the legal system, they were required to reject their native culture and beliefs and embrace the offerings of these city centers. This could be an offensive requirement, as they had to engage in activities that were otherwise foreign to them, such as "exercis(ing) in the *gymnasium* naked—an abomination to non-Greeks" (Price 1986, 322).

Within a couple of centuries, the rising Roman Republic had claimed much of the land acquired by Alexander the Great. Rome and Greece shared many of the same perspectives and ideals, particularly regarding non-citizens: barbarians were lesser people, in need of instruction and enlightenment. However, Rome did differ in the absolute nature of citizenship; blood was not a prerequisite, and citizenship could be attained if barbarians would give up their unsavory ways and embrace Roman culture (Rawson 1986).[8] If citizenship was not desirable, non-Romans could still participate in society if they contributed taxes, and the military received soldiers from the local community. Within this framework, native officials were often permitted to continue in their role, with a Roman magistrate assigned to oversee their duties. Thus, citizenship only required a relatively mild imposition of culture, and "Roman identity was often constructed through appeals to blood and descent" (Townsend 2009, 236).[9]

If the term *race* had been used in the Roman Empire, it would have referred to differences in culture and practice. To be a Roman, you must act Roman.[10] The Greeks, on the other hand, were more reserved in their interpretation of otherness. Greek identity was a familial right, not granted outside of birth. Despite these different perspectives, both Greeks and Romans shared the common belief that they were superior to their neighbors in all ways and the world benefited from their example and their rule. Various writings from ancient antiquity illustrate that these early empires held little concern, if not outright hostility, for the rights and needs of those whom they deemed to be outsiders.

MIDDLE AGES

> The king met with four Saracens, who were black and blue as lead . . . Never before that hour did anyone see so horribly shaped a creature. Their black hue was marvelous, and their mouths were in their breasts . . . Their mouths were so broad, their eyes so large, that it made their faces repulsive . . . David held (the rods) out to them to kiss; they kneeled and kissed them. Immediately their skin became as white as milk, and they took on the hue of high blood, and all their appearance was made new. (Cursor Mundi 1875, as quoted by Hahn 2001, 14)

During the Middle Ages, color began to gain prominence as a means of creating group membership. White was believed to represent purity and nobility, while black was associated with demons and evil (Heng 2011). Moreover, skin color became intertwined with religious affiliation, leading to the belief that differences in religion facilitated differences in skin color. Medieval literature often contained fanciful tales of conversions from Islam to Christianity that were accompanied by a change in skin color.[11] Thus, color and religion determined identity during the Middle Ages, with the latter taking priority, creating fierce lines of division between groups. Given that the Middle Ages was a period of Christendom, this ensured that other religious groups, particularly those faiths that were practiced by individuals with darker skin color, were viewed as outsiders socially, politically, and legally. Rarely, for example, was a Jew or a Muslim considered a full citizen with legal protections in any medieval Christian European country.[12] However, in the highly segregated, kinship-based social strata, outsiders of any type were typically treated harshly.

In the early Middle Ages, feudalism and superstition informed justice systems. Feudalism was a strata-defined system, consisting of lords who oversaw large areas of land and the people who lived and worked on those lands, also known as serfs. The serfs were beholden to the lords, who held relatively unchecked power.[13] In some criminal matters, the local lord might simply opt to pass judgment while, in others, guilt or innocence was established through a series of ordeals. These ordeals were designed to demonstrate divine providence or godly determination of purity or sin. If, for example, an ordeal resulted in a burn or a wound, the healing of the affliction was a sign from God indicating the person's innocence. The same applied to a person's buoyancy in a pool of blessed water or the success of a champion in combat.[14]

As power slowly transferred from feudal lords to larger states, the legal systems also evolved. In England, common law trials overseen by juries became commonplace (Berman 2006). These juries consisted of local representatives who, according to the logic of the time, did not require evidence, since they were presumed to already be aware of the goings-on in their communities. Meanwhile, the rest of continental Europe turned toward a formal Romanized system of justice. Legal representatives were responsible for presenting the positions of the defense and the prosecution according to set guidelines (Pavlac 2009). Unfortunately, lacking modern forms of evidence, guilt was often established through torturous methods, casting medieval legal proceedings in an unsavory light. Thus, throughout the Middle Ages, the finding of proof and guilt was an unpleasant affair, transitioning from superstitious ordeals to confession through torture. These systems of justice were notably harsh for outsiders, particularly for those with different religious or ethnic identities.

The Jewish community was a prominent group of outsiders during the Middle Ages. European laws ensured their segregation, as did Jewish custom, and they were regularly treated as scapegoats for a variety of social ills, such as plague or famine (Worsham 2014). Occasionally they were allowed to remain in a community as they provided valuable benefits, such as financial services, but when their assistance was not needed or their presence was deemed inconvenient, they were often driven out of an area.[15] The dislike and distrust of Jewish people was deeply rooted in European perceptions of outsiders; even those who converted to Christianity were treated with contempt and hostility (Muldoon 2000).

During the era of feudalism, local lords would oftentimes find it convenient to allow a community of Jews to live within their domain, primarily so they could take advantage of Jewish banking and courier services. These groups could remain and govern themselves if they kept to their own community and did not cause any trouble (Muldoon 2000). However, the lords often overextended themselves with loans from the Jewish community, resulting in a large debt they were reluctant to pay. In these situations, the lords were likely to contrive an offense, assign guilt to the Jews, then expel them from the area while also declaring that the outstanding debts were null and void (Worsham 2014). At one particularly dark point, the Jewish people were nearly entirely driven out of England, due in part to the fact that the royal treasuries were strained by efforts to repay the debts owed to Jewish financiers.

Over time, feudalism waned, and the Church and state became more influential across Europe. As a consequence, legal statutes and practices were standardized, including those governing the Jewish communities (Worsham 2014). Informed in part by Ancient Roman codes, Jews were required to wear visible markings, such as badges on clothing; they were prohibited from marrying Christian partners; and they were forbidden from bearing witness against Christians in court (Heng 2011; Worsham 2014).[16] In addition, the Inquisition, which was intended for the identification and punishment of heretics and apostates, shifted attention to non-Christian groups, including the Jews and Muslims (Schoeneman 1975). The law determined that inquisitors were only permitted to prosecute non-Christians who had converted to Christianity and then committed heresy, but the inquisitors often employed their own discretion in these matters.

Whether by ecclesiastical or secular decree, there are numerous records denoting the official and legal slaughter of the Jewish people throughout the Middle Ages. Several crusades, such as the Popular Crusade, the First Crusade, the Second Crusade, the Shepherds' Crusade, and the Third Crusade targeted Jewish citizens, executing them in large numbers (Heng 2011). In addition, social ills were commonplace and often led to the wholesale genocide of Jews. The era of the Black Death, from 1348 to 1351, provides a ready example. Blaming the plague on the Jewish community, the citizenry turned on them, decimated their population, and nearly annihilated them from specific regions, such as the Rhineland (Cohn 2007). In one particularly unsavory move, Emperor Charles IV of Bohemia granted immunity to the local elites if they chose to engage in the killing of Jews and the disposal of their property. He also cancelled many of the debts the same elites owed to the local Jews.[17]

Muslims in Europe were treated in a manner similar to the Jews. Many of the same restrictive laws that applied to Jews also applied to Muslims (Muldoon 2000). However, Muslims were less prevalent in Europe, and therefore, if they kept to themselves, they were usually permitted to govern themselves. This did not, however, change the animus directed toward the Muslim community. Medieval literature would often display images or descriptions of demon-like or overly large Saracen enemies, or they were filled with stories of Muslim conversions to Christianity, accompanied with a lightening of the skin (Hahn 2001; Heng 2011). Interactions between Christian Europeans and Muslims occurred most often within the context of war or a crusade, as the former sought to expel the latter from an area.[18]

One by-product of the regular wars and crusades during the Middle Ages, not to mention famine and plagues, was large groups of landless, dispossessed people (Rousseaux 1997). These refugees and transients, whose primary focus became the search for food, work, or a place to shelter, were labeled as vagrants or vagabonds. They were outsiders to the communities in which they traveled and tried to settle. In the best-case scenario, they could expect to be jailed, unless they had some sort of surety or property to show their value (Langbein 1974). Under less favorable conditions, "provosts and marshals pursued them relentlessly, arresting them, judging them and executing them, sometimes without any form of trial" (Rousseaux 1997, 104).

To be an outsider or an "other" in the Middle Ages meant to live with disparities and differential treatment. In this era, legal rules and proceedings were oftentimes capricious and arbitrary for everyone, but this was particularly applicable to religious and ethnic minorities. If these groups kept to their own devices, being careful to display markings and to avoid intermingling with the majority, they might be allowed to live in peace and govern themselves. However, when it was convenient for those in power, the displacement and execution of minority groups was easily made legal.

THE COLONIAL ERA

The era of colonialism began at the end of the Middle Ages as European countries sought to expand their empires beyond traditional borders. The Western colonial powers, namely the English, French, Spanish, and Portuguese, began establishing settlements in different regions of the world, thus prompting encounters with the people indigenous to these areas (Parker 2010). These encounters presented the colonizers with a new quandary: how best to proceed with these strange communities. Solutions varied considerably, with some focusing on exploitation and extermination, while others prioritized a "civilization" process, one that forced Western culture and traditions on the original inhabitants. Each solution was rooted in the assumption that the local communities existed in a "savage" state, stemming from differences in religion, social practices, or a nomadic lifestyle, and thus required modification, as defined by the industrious Christian morality of the colonizing countries (McVeigh & Rolston 2009). This required the attention of all Western institutions, including justice systems. As such, laws and proceedings were altered considerably to address the recently colonized, differing in both content and execution from those used in the empires' homelands (Johnson, Salvatore & Spierenburg 2012). The colonized were often deemed too "uncivilized" for modern law, and therefore, they were lesser people, subject to different standards and rules; "these constructions of civilization and barbarism were at the heart of colonial domination, justifying expansion and control" (McVeigh & Rolston 2009, 3). All manner of ignoble deeds, including slavery for the purposes of religious salvation, were justified with the supposition that the savages required a strong arm or intensive socialization (Treitler 2016). The resulting systems of justice that arose from this mire varied between the empires and resulting colonies, although, as summarized below, they shared some common themes. This section will explore three regions, including Ireland, North America, and India; each of these provide an illustration of the relationship between race, culture, and legal and criminal justice systems during the colonial era.[19]

The Colonial Era: Ireland

While Ireland is part of Europe, and technical rulership had been held by England for hundreds of years, effective control was lost until Elizabeth I attempted to reconquer and colonize the island in the sixteenth century (Canny 1973). This occurred alongside early attempts to colonize North America, and the English experiences in Ireland served to inform the future expansion of the British Empire. In fact, records indicate that some leaders of colonization efforts in Ireland were then deployed in North America.[20] Thus, the practices in this region of the world demonstrate justice responses to the "other," particularly those who differ in culture, and set the stage for further expansion into other diverse regions.

At the time that England attempted to reclaim Ireland, there were already laws in place regarding interactions between the English and the Irish. In 1376, the Statutes of Kilkenny "made it punishable for English persons to trade with the Irish, intermarry with them, wear Irish dress, or hairstyles, speak the Irish language, and they even outlawed Irish games, poetry, and music" (Treitler 2016, 217). Two centuries later, however, the mission had changed; no longer was the priority to protect the English from the blight of Irish culture but, instead, to ameliorate Irish culture and instill English traditions and practices in its place. This could be accomplished through whatever means necessary, including violence and forced servitude (Canny 1973). The plantation system was particularly popular at this time, as it ensured English rule of large tracts of land and oversight of the Irish communities that were required to work said lands.

From the Protestant English perspective, Irish barbarity and savagery was rooted in their nomadic lifestyle and their Catholic beliefs (McVeigh & Rolston 2009). Forcing them to settle on and develop plantation lands was informed, in part, by a desire to instill obedience into their otherwise-uncivilized lives.[21] This desire was paired with the priority of profiting off Irish labor, a particularly appealing incentive for the English overseers (Treitler 2016). In light of this mission, the English seized large tracts of land, crafted rules outlawing nomadic temporary dwellings, and forced local families and communities to build permanent housing. The policy became one of "extermination or enslavement" (Treitler 2016, 218).[22]

The Colonial Era: North America

The colonization of North America had notable consequences for two groups of people: the indigenous communities inhabiting these regions and the slaves who were brought along to help establish and run the colonies, most often of African origin.[23] Each group had its own set of legal challenges and disadvantages. The indigenous people were treated in a manner similar to other colonized groups. They were viewed as a lesser race, and as such, laws were crafted that were designed to push them out of the region, assimilate them into the dominant Eurocentric culture, or eradicate them (Lujan & Adams 2004). The situation was also grim for the African slaves, although legal rule of them differed from that of the indigenous communities.

Throughout most of the era of colonization in North America, Black slaves legally lacked personhood and were instead considered property (Finkelman 1998). Even the US Constitution did not recognize slaves as full citizens (Pate & Plouffe 2009). It was repeatedly upheld, such as in the Supreme Court's *Dred Scott* decision of 1856, that abusive actions taken against slaves were not a crime, as they were property and not persons.[24] As such, their owners were permitted to treat them in any manner they saw fit; however, if someone else caused harm to them in a manner that threatened their value for their owner, that person could be held criminally responsible. This latter stipulation was integral to the prosperity of the colonies, as unmarred slaves were an essential component of agricultural and financial success.

The colonization efforts in North America were dependent upon cash crops and the slave labor required to maintain them, thus it was advantageous for the colonists and their benefactors to develop principles that justified human enslavement. One such belief embraced by the colonizers was the theory of *polygenesis* (Knepper 1996). In contrast to *monogenesis*, which suggested that humankind descended from a single source, such as Adam and Eve, polygenesis proposed that people originated from two distinct lines. It was often argued on both scientific and religious grounds that the "Negro is not a human being" (Carroll 1900, 162). This period of slavery, and the justifications that accompanied its continuance, were the foundation of the modern system of racial segregation (Knepper 1996).

Using race to justify and maintain slavery created a new problem, namely the need to keep racial lineage distinct. The criminal law provided a ready solution, allowing European colonizers to ban *miscegenation*, or interracial reproduction (Treitler 2016). The details of the laws varied depending on the nature of the offense. In some colonies, for example, white women who bore non-white children would receive a fine, while interracial married couples would face banishment (Knepper 1996; Treitler 2016).[25] Despite some variance in law and punishment, the sentiment was the same: whiteness must be protected both in law and in practice from the sullying effects of interracial relations. In cases where mixed children were produced, early US legislators created the "One Drop Rule," whereby a person with any amount of Black heritage was legally considered racially Black (Knepper 1996).[26]

Simply discussing the legal response to Black enslavement does little to capture the extent of the suffering bestowed on African captives.[27] The criminalization of Black people in North America is accompanied by a longer narrative, one that begins in Africa. Seeking human labor, European empires descended on Africa, sweeping up large numbers of the original inhabitants. These captives were forced to march to the ocean, where they remained imprisoned until it was time to board a slave vessel bound for North America (Warren 2007). Upward of 20 percent of the captives died before even boarding the ship, due in part to exhaustion from marching, starvation, dehydration, and sickness. Once aboard a ship, African slaves endured months at sea, chained and shackled in tight and unrelenting quarters, surrounded by blood, vomit, and diarrhea. If they survived the journey, which many did not, their captors were likely to hide their illness rather than treating it, such as forcing caulking into their anuses to mask diarrhea, with the intention of facilitating an immediate sale. Once sold, African slaves were legally passed off as property, subject to the whims of their masters.[28] Even after emancipation, many former slaves continued to face bonded and forced labor as their only means of livelihood (Scanlan 2016).[29] The laws changed, but sociocultural expectations were slower to evolve. This is the legacy of the African slave trade, all done by legal means according to the colonial powers, a by-product of the slowly transforming ethnic and racial hierarchy in the Western world.

In contrast to Africans, the communities indigenous to North America faced issues more typical of people in a colonized region. They encountered assault and death when the colonizers engaged in warfare against them, they were sold into slavery, they were confined to settlements wherein they were forced to adopt Western culture and religious beliefs, or they were simply displaced from their ancestral lands (Lujan & Adams 2004). Over time, these practices shifted, reflecting a transition from external to internal colonization as the British Empire was replaced by the newly founded United States government.[30]

The United States formalized the otherness of indigenous peoples in Paragraph 29 of the Declaration of Independence, with the description of "the merciless Indian Savages, whose known rule of warfare, is an undistinguished destruction of all ages, sexes and conditions." Despite this clear condemnation of native heritage, policy oscillated from that point forward, sometimes reviling, other times denouncing, and more recently, paternalizing indigenous peoples (Canby 2014). Accompanying this shift in perspective, the justice system transitioned from presenting indigenous communities as separate from non-indigenous ones, to making both subject to the same stipulations. For example, the 1785 Treaty of Wyandot "agreed that U.S. law would punish Indians committing crimes on U.S. land, and Indians would punish settlers committing crimes on Indian land as each government saw fit" (Lujan & Adams 2004, 12).[31] By 1817, however, the United States determined that it held jurisdiction over all interracial federal crimes, regardless of territory. By 1885, the federal government also claimed the right to prosecute federal crimes committed between Native Americans (Canby 2014). Thus, as perspectives shifted, so, too, did the legal system.

The Colonial Era: India

In 1858, the British government took over the colony of India from the East India Company (Brown 2005). The stated intent of the Indian colony at this point was one of improvement; the British Empire could gift the Indian people with English civility and culture while shaping them into a more lucrative trading partner. The 1861 Indian Councils Act, although it did not permit self-governance, did allow for the inclusion of native elites in local governmental processes. Under the East India Company, a hybrid system of laws had formed, combining British law with local customs (Subramanian 2019). This continued under British rule, "with the British colonial state positioning itself as a neutral arbiter standing above religious communities" (Subramanian 2019, 844). Among the most notable pieces of criminal legislation used in India at this time were the Track Laws and the Criminal Tribes Act.

The Track Laws authorized group accountability for criminal actions. These statutes determined "that if an offender could be tracked to a village, but not located within it, then the responsibility for the crime would be borne by the village as a whole" (Brown 2005, 78). This was informed, in part, by a sentiment that was in vogue at the time: inherited criminality or the belief that behavior was passed down through the generations. As such, it was rational to assume that communities were interlaced with inherited deviance; thus, group punishment was justified (Brown 2005). The subsequent legal enforcement of this logic placed communities in a difficult position; they must either shoulder the punishment for criminal acts or root out the accused, who might very well be a community or family member.

The Track Laws, in combination with the long-held belief that a forced agrarian lifestyle was the best way to civilize a group, led to the Criminal Tribes Act. Under this act, a provincial government could apply to have a tribe declared criminal if they showed a great propensity for antisocial behavior (Brown 2005). The exact requirements for this designation were quite vague.[32] Once declared a criminal tribe, members were forced to register and partake in regular roll calls, forbidden to leave their village without a passport and acceptable justification, and required to work in an agricultural or industrial profession (Brown 2005). The tribe could also be subject to relocation and resettlement.[33]

These many forays into colonization were a confirmation, for Europeans, of a belief that was held long before any modern conception of race; they were a superior people with a superior civilization (Levine 2012). Colonialism, in addition to being the means to acquire additional land, power, and resources, was also a way by which to spread

European practices, beliefs, and institutions among the uncivilized. While the period of colonization cemented lines of difference or otherness in the collective European consciousness, there remained uncertainty around the source of these differences and the inexplicable reticence of the savage communities to adopt Euro-centric lifestyles. One solution to these queries, which was uncovered during the Enlightenment, would prove to be as dangerous as the perspectives that had informed the colonial era.

THE ENLIGHTENMENT AND BIOCRIMINOLOGY

The Enlightenment ushered in a period of scientific growth and progression, driven by a collective desire to pursue knowledge and understand the empirical world.[34] Scientific advancement ran parallel to a growing narrative of human equality, thus prompting new questions regarding individual and collective capacities for survival and success. The inability of select groups to conform to social norms and cultures, suggesting an inherent antisocial orientation, led to the "Southern Question" in Italy (Caglioti 2017), the "Jewish Question" throughout Europe (Fine & Spencer 2017), and the "Negro Problem" in the United States (Du Bois 1898). These quandaries intrigued Enlightenment thinkers, and they turned to popular scientific processes as a means of providing answers. Their research led them down a biological path, one that was inspired by Darwin and his ideas regarding natural selection and heredity.

The study of the relationship between biology and human behavior can be dated back to ancient antiquity; however, these early forays were limited and sporadic. It was not until the late eighteenth and early nineteenth centuries that a concerted and collective interest formed, resulting in studies in physiognomy and phrenology. Physiognomy came first, a pseudoscientific belief that personality and character traits could be determined though the comparison of outward appearances, especially in the structures of the face (Rafter 2009). A physically attractive person, for example, had more positive qualities than someone who was less attractive. In addition, comparisons could be made with other species. A resemblance to a mule, for example, indicated a stubborn or lazy personality, while lion-like features suggested a brave and fierce personality (Lavater 1817).

Physiognomy passed out of favor, eventually replaced by phrenology. Phrenologists proposed that the shape and contours of the skull could be used to identify personality traits, such as combativeness, conscientiousness, and inhibition, all factors believed to be related to deviance. According to phrenologists, areas of the brain controlled these various traits and the over- or under-development of these areas influenced their size, thus impacting the cranium (André 2018, 277). Phrenologists would measure the lumps and divots in a skull, and based on their findings, they would proclaim certainty about the character of that individual.[35] Notably, both phrenology and physiognomy played on the prejudices of the day, often using Asian and African physical traits as a baseline for negative social qualities. If these scientific endeavors had simply been passing fancies, short-lived and historically irrelevant, the use of racial identifiers to determine character during this period would likely be no more than a footnote in this chapter. However, these early ideas provided inspiration for future thinkers, particularly when paired with Darwinian logic.

Early biocriminological pursuits gained favor for a number of reasons; they were easy to understand, they were supported by empirical evidence (comparative images for physiognomy and measurements for phrenology), and they were accessible to the general public. Of equal importance, they aligned with Darwinian logic, which had become a popular point of view during this period. In the 1850s, Darwin published *On the Origin of the Species*, which made the bold claim that humankind was simply a species, like all other species, subject to the same evolutionary advantages and disadvantages that marked other non-human animals (Paul & Moore 2012). This logic offered a new perspective that had been previously absent from criminological conversations: the supposition that criminality might be a sign of evolutionary inferiority. Darwin's ideas inspired many, not the least of whom was Cesare Lombroso, the father of modern criminology and the founder of the increasingly influential area of study, criminal anthropology. Lombroso borrowed the phrenological and physiognomic focus on physical features and paired them with Darwin's proposition of human evolution, applying them to the "Southern Question" or the observation that southern Italians seemed more crime-prolific and impoverished than their northern counterparts. In doing so, "he investigated the hereditary transmission of physical and psychological traits and linked them to criminal behavior" (Caglioti 2017, 463). His conclusions were game-changing; according to Lombroso, criminals were *atavists*, or evolutionary throwbacks, morally inferior and primitive in character (Ferrero & Lombroso 1911). In addition, this evolutionary inferiority manifested physically, suggesting that criminals could be identified by their behaviors and by their appearance. Crime was not a choice or a product of socialization; it was a birthright. In simple terms, criminals were born, not made.

Criminal anthropology was informed, in part, by preconceived notions about race and ethnicity. Lombroso determined that southern Italians were more criminally predisposed due to intermixing with Asians and Africans (Bolognani 2009). He also noted that the skulls of criminals were shaped much like the skulls of Africans, suggesting that Africans were inherently criminal (Rafter 2008). Lombroso's work was repeatedly used to demonstrate that people of color were naturally born criminals (Gabbidon 2020).[36]

A major consequence of criminal anthropology was a greater propensity to punish the criminal rather than the crime. In other words, the degree of punishment required for a given crime had more to do with whether the perpetrator displayed the physical attributes of a born criminal, thus indicating there was no chance of rehabilitation or reformation of said individual. Of course, due to historically entrenched prejudices, social, ethnic, and racial outsiders traditionally received harsher punishments. However, Lombroso's theories granted these practices a greater degree of legitimacy; it became a scientific imperative to punish "inferior races," and the recommendation to punish deviants based on race was normalized in various countries and colonies (Gabbidon 2020). These ideas were particularly influential in the younger and more flexible justice systems of the United States, resulting in an avid interest in incorporating eugenics into legal realms (Simon 2020).

Eugenics had been bandied about for hundreds of years, but Darwinian and Lombrosian ideas regarding evolution and human behavior pushed it to the forefront of criminological discussions and practices. Eugenics refers to the selective breeding of a species with the intention of fostering desirable traits (positive eugenics) or eliminating undesirable traits (negative eugenics) [Levine & Bashford 2012]. Pairing Darwin's perspective with Lombroso's theory resulted in a simple and undeniable conclusion: to eliminate criminality, it is necessary to engage in negative eugenics, or the assurance that criminals cannot reproduce. In addition, since biocriminology was informed in part by a racial narrative, this ensured that any attempts to curb criminal reproduction, such as forced sterilization, would also target minority groups (Jenkins 1984; Levine & Bashford 2012; Simon 2020). These were policies that Western governments could and did embrace.

The passage of eugenic laws had wide-ranging social and legal implications. From 1900 to 1914, a variety of acts were passed in England to relocate dysgenic people (such as repeat criminals and those with mental defects) to colonies and homes where they were kept indefinitely, thus thwarting their reproductive capacities (Jenkins 1984). In addition, several Western countries passed immigration laws limiting the number of people coming in from dysgenic populations, such as southern Italians, Jews, and Eastern Europeans (Caglioti 2017). The United States, in particular, embraced eugenic practices, sterilizing more than sixty thousand people in only two decades (Knepper 1996). In the controversial case of *Buck v. Bell*, U.S. Supreme Court justice Oliver Wendell Holmes made a particularly notable statement that illustrated the sentiments of criminal justice practitioners at the time:

> It is better for all the world, if instead of waiting to execute degenerate offspring for crime, or to let them starve for their imbecility, society can prevent those who are manifestly unfit from continuing their kind. The principle that sustains compulsory vaccination is broad enough to cover cutting the Fallopian tubes. Three generations of imbeciles are enough. (1927, 207)

Historical analyses of eugenics in the 1900s tend to focus on Nazi Germany; however, Germany's leadership took their cue from the United States, praising and replicating US practices and science. Hitler even drafted a thank-you letter to a US eugenicist, complimenting a book the eugenicist had written (Treitler 2016). It was, however, Nazi Germany's use of eugenics that finally soured public opinion. Unlike other Western nations that pointed to criminality as justification for their practices, Germany made no such justification, targeting groups that were simply deemed undesirable, including "Jews, Gypsies, the handicapped, homosexuals, the poor and other 'asocials'" (Rafter 2008, 299). The wholesale slaughter of millions of innocent people forced the Western world to recognize the inherent inhumanity in eugenic practices.

CONCLUSION

The racial system is a compilation, then, of superstitions and folk beliefs. (Treitler 2016, 214)

The modern meaning of race is a simply a social construction, but the principles and prejudices it engenders have had very real and serious consequences throughout human history. To illustrate this point, we invite you to reflect on the United States for a moment. Its founding constitution declared that all persons (men) were equal, but it did not extend this right to persons of color. The author of the Declaration of Independence, Thomas Jefferson, owned hundreds of Black slaves, refusing to free any of them until his death (Finkelman 1998).[37] The United States is not alone in this checkered history; most Western nations harbor similar hypocrisies in their historical pledges to equality. This is not only a problem of the past; racial and cultural strife continues today in the Western world, particularly in legal and criminal justice systems. While racial and ethnic groups are no longer overtly criminalized as they were during, for example, the colonial era, they are subject to oversurveillance and mass incarceration, due to such agendas as the war on drugs, the war on terror, and the war on gangs, to name but a few. As McVeigh and Rolston (2009) put it, "Contemporary western civilization undoubtedly regards itself and presents itself as 'peaceful' and 'understanding of diversity' and 'tolerance' but this is closer to imperial psychosis than 'reality' in many parts of the world" (6). Given the historical focus of this book, it is fitting that we end our narrative in the late 1900s, but we encourage the reader to further explore the contemporary relationship between race, ethnicity, and the criminal justice system. Although less overt, the reader will likely find that the relationship has changed little over time.

NOTES

1. The origin of the term *barbarian* comes from the Greek word *barbaroi*, which refers to foreigners whose languages sounded, to the Greek ear, like they were saying "bar-bar" (Rhodes 2010).

2. This could be compared to the One Drop laws that developed in the United States, whereby if a person had any amount of Black ancestry, they were considered Black.

3. It should be noted that only adult male citizens could prosecute crimes in court. Women and slaves were not granted this right.

4. There were notable exceptions to this, including the ability for people to bring the accused before a private court, much like the contemporary notion of arbitration or civil court (Carey 2004).

5. Spartans would still take Greek slaves, but from other ethnic tribes within the Greek world (Wrenhaven 2013).

6. This applied to both barbarians and free foreigners. The latter might have escaped slavery if they could locate a reputable Greek friend to speak to their innocence.

7. The dispersion of Greek values and practices was a precursor and a template for the later spread of the Roman Empire and the colonization of the world by European settlers.

8. Rawson notes some of the barbarian ways that had to be given up included "the habit of some Spanish tribes of washing their teeth in urine" (1986, 436).

9. Blood, and its symbolic form in sacrifice, were important parts of Greek and Roman citizenship (Townsend 2009). The Greeks held a ritual sacrifice for the transition from boyhood to manhood and full citizenship. For the Roman Empire, in 250 CE, a sacrifice to the gods was a basic requirement for citizenship.

10. This same difficulty of requiring people to give up their unique culture for citizenship appears throughout history, such as with the "Jewish Question" of the Enlightenment period. This was where the olive branch of citizenship was offered to Jews throughout Europe, if they would only conform to the laws and standards, or culture, of the nation they were in.

11. An example from *The King of Tars*, as a sultan sees his son after the child had a Christian baptism, reads: "His skin, that had been black and loathsome, became all white, through God's grace, and was spotless without blemish. And when the sultan saw that sight, well he believed on almighty God . . . (He returns to his chamber.) Scarcely did she (his wife) recognize her lord. Then she well knew in her mind that he did not believe at all in Mohammed, for his color was entirely changed" (quoted in Hahn 2001, 15).

12. Jews were often described as being something sub-human, presumed to have various diabolic markers, such as horns, tails, and forked tongues (Heng 2011).

13. While the Middle Ages did not see too much slavery, serfdom was often compared to a form of soft slavery (Pirenne 1937/1956). While the rural serfs were not technically slaves, their entire lives were lived by the dictum, and for the benefit, of the local lord.

14. For further details on various ordeals, see Cameron (1898).

15. Christian and Jewish laws and customs both disallowed many excessive or predatory loan practices within their religious groups (Worsham 2014). However, the giving and receiving of any sort of financial obligations between people of different religions was considered entirely legitimate.

16. These were actually laws created during the Roman Empire, from the *Codex Theodosianus* and the code of Justinian (Worsham 2014). The Catholic Church recognized the laws of the Roman Empire and carried them through the Middle Ages.

17. Cohn noted that the chroniclers of the time typically varied between statements of how the Jews deserved their fate or, in a manner similar to more modern Holocaust deniers, questioned whether the extermination of Jews had even occurred (2007).

18. Crusades were carried out in the name of religion, but the underlying desire to expand geopolitical reach was also a primary motivator (Thorndike 1917). The religious justification was advantageous, however, for providing higher troop numbers, morale, and funding, which did equate to more wars. When a war was over, there was often intermingling for a time, as it was useful to keep conquered peoples around to help rebuild. This happened with the Christian expansion into Spain in the thirteenth century and in Jerusalem immediately following the First Crusade.

19. Notably, these areas were colonized by Northern Europeans. Northern Europe had more homogeneous cultures than Southern Europe, which tended to encounter more diverse ethnic populations (Treitler 2016). Thus, the colonies of Northern Europe were more apt to put an emphasis on racial differences.

20. There are records of aristocrats, such as Gilbert and Grenville, who led forays into Ireland, then worked with colonies in North America, and finally came back to push the plantation system again in Ireland (Canny 1973).

21. This pattern of civilizing people by forcing them into an agrarian lifestyle was repeated with Native Americans on their reservations and also with British colonization efforts in India (Subramanian 2019).

22. These plantations had only marginal success and were overshadowed by regular Irish revolt and rebellion (McVeigh & Rolston 2009).

23. As the North American colonies were established, additional groups were used as slaves, notably the Irish and Native Americans (Treitler 2016).

24. In *Dred Scott*, Chief Justice Taney went further to suggest that the rights enumerated in the Constitution did not apply to former slaves and their descendants after being freed (Finkelman 1998).

25. It should be noted that, in this period, there was no legal repercussion for a white man to have a child with a Black woman, even if by rape (Treitler 2016).

26. In 1983 Louisiana, Susan Guillory Phipps was denied a passport because she had declared herself white on her application, while the state had found her to be Black (Knepper

1996). This surprised Susan, as she had always thought of herself as white, and she had siblings with blond hair and blue eyes. However, her great-great-great-great-grandmother was a black slave, so the state of Louisiana considered her to be legally Black, even in 1983.

27. The same could also be said of many native populations facing colonization by outside civilizations.

28. Warren's writing gives an account of a woman who was forcibly raped in order to breed more slaves (2007). This event was recorded as a minor note in a travel journal only because of the woman's harsh and grievous singing afterward.

29. Britain's 1833 Emancipation Act required former slaves to keep working under apprenticeship programs for an additional five years before official emancipation (Scanlan 2016).

30. External colonization occurs when "the invading nation seeks to gain control of the land, resources, and lives of the host population" (Lujan & Adams 2004, 10), whereas internal colonization involves the subjugation and cultural conversion of a group within a country.

31. One consequence of this treaty is that settlers could enter Indian lands to massacre, rape, and pillage as they saw fit, and the US government had no legal reason to hold the settlers accountable for it.

32. Over 3.5 million people were determined to be criminal according to the Criminal Tribes Act by the time Britain left India in 1947 (Brown 2005).

33. This is often compared to the United States Indian Appropriation Acts, passed from 1851 through 1871, which forced Native Americans to live on reservations (Subramanian 2019).

34. The scientific method is based around knowledge gained through empirical (observable), repeatable experimentation. This, by definition, excludes knowledge gained through rationalism (pure logic) or religious revelation. Many pseudoscientific forays into biocriminology were based on results that were unrepeatable, and religion was also used to justify other conclusions, such as with Lavater's physiognomy (1817).

35. Early twentieth-century Belgian colonists used phrenology in Rwanda-Urundi to further distinguish the two major people groups living there, the Hutus and Tutsis (André 2018). Racial identity cards were issued to the population starting in the 1930s. This tightly regulated racial distinction, as well as the implemented minority rule of the Tutsi over the Hutu, is believed to be partially responsible for the racial violence that peaked with the Rwandan Genocide of 1994.

36. Lombroso, being Jewish, placed northern Italians and Jews at the top of his racial hierarchy (Caglioti 2017). His work had a sad irony; it was later used as an impetus for the Holocaust.

37. In his will, Jefferson freed eight slaves whom he was related to through marriage, the children and grandchildren of his father-in-law (Finkelman 1998).

REFERENCES

Allen, Danielle S. 2002. *The World of Prometheus: The Politics of Punishing in Democratic Athens.* Princeton: Princeton University Press. ProQuest Ebook.

André, Charles. 2018. "Phrenology and the Rwandan Genocide." *Arq Neuropsiquiatr* 76, no. 4 (April): 277–82. https://doi.org/10.1590/0004-282X20180022.

Aristotle. 1999. *Politics.* Translated by Benjamin Jowett. Ontario: Batoche Books.

Berman, Harold J. 2006. *Law and Revolution, II: The Impact of the Protestant Reformations on the Western Legal Tradition.* Cambridge: Belknap Press.

Bolognani, Marta. 2009. "The Taboo of Criminological Research Amongst Minority Ethnic Groups." In *Crime and Muslim Britain: Race, Culture and the Politics of Criminology Among British Pakistanis*, edited by I.B.Tauris, 7–26. London: Bloomsbury Publishing.

Brown, Mark. 2005. "Colonial History and Theories of the Present: Some Reflections Upon Penal History and Theory." In *Crime and Empire, 1840–1940: Criminal Justice in Local and Global Context*, edited by Barry Godfrey and Graeme Dustall, 76–91. London: Willan.

Buck v. Bell, 274 U.S. 200 (1927).

Caglioti, Angelo Matteo. 2017. "Race, Statistics, and Eugenics: Alfred Niceforo's Trajectory from Lombroso to Fascism (1876–1960)." *European History Quarterly* 47, no. 3 (July): 461–89. https://doi.org/10.1177/0265691417707164.

Cameron, J. S. Taylor. 1898. "Roman Law in the Early Middle Ages III." *Juridical Review* 10 (3): 438–49.

Canby Jr., William C. 2014. *American Indian Law in a Nutshell*. St. Paul: West Academic Publishing.

Canny, Nicholas P. 1973. "The Ideology of English Colonization: From Ireland to America." *William and Mary Quarterly* 30, no. 4 (October): 575–98. https://doi.org/10.2307/1918596.

Carroll, Charles. 1900. *The Negro a Beast: In the Image of God*. St. Louis: American Book and Bible House.

Cohn, Samuel K. 2007. "The Black Death and the Burning of Jews." *Past & Present* 196, no. 1 (August): 3–36. https://doi.org/10.1093/pastj/gtm005.

Du Bois, William Edward Burghardt. 1898. "The Study of the Negro Problems." *Annals of the American Academy of Political and Social Science* 11 (January): 1–23. https://www.jstor.org/stable/1009474.

Ferrero, Guglielmo, and Cesare Lombroso. 1911. *Criminal Man*. Albany: The Knickerbocker Press.

Fine, Robert, and Philip Spencer. 2017. *Antisemitism and the Left: On the Return of the Jewish Question*. Manchester: Manchester University Press.

Finkelman, Paul. 1998. "The Centrality of Slavery in American Legal Development." In *Slavery and the Law*, edited by Paul Finkelman. Lanham: Rowman & Littlefield Publishers.

Forsdyke, Sara. 2005. *Exile, Ostracism, and Democracy: The Politics of Expulsion in Ancient Greece*. Princeton: Princeton University Press.

Gabbidon, Shaun L. 2020. *Criminological Perspectives on Race and Crime*. Oxford: Routledge.

Hahn, Thomas. 2001. "The Difference the Middle Ages Makes: Color and Race Before the Modern World." *Journal of Medieval and Early Modern Studies* 31, no. 1 (Winter): 1–37. Project Muse.

Heng, Geraldine. 2011. "The Invention of Race in the European Middle Ages II: Locations of Medieval Race." *Literature Compass* 8, no. 5 (May): 332–50. https://doi.org/10.1111/j.1741-4113.2011.00795.x.

Hunt, Peter. 2017. *Ancient Greek and Roman Slavery*. Hoboken: Wiley-Blackwell Publishing. ProQuest Ebook.

Jenkins, Philip. 1984. "Eugenics, Crime, and Ideology: The Case of Progressive Pennsylvania." *Pennsylvania History: A Journal of Mid-Atlantic Studies* 51, no. 1 (January): 64–78. http://www.jstor.org/stable/27772949.

Johnson, Eric. A., Ricardo D. Salvatore, and Pieter Spierenburg. 2012. "Murder and Mass Murder in Pre-Modern Latin America: From Pre-Colonial Aztec Sacrifices to the End of the Colonial Rule, an Introductory Comparison with European Societies." *Historical Social Research* 37 (3): 233–53. http://www.jstor.org/stable/41636607.

Kapparis, Konstantinos A. 2019. *Athenian Law and Society*. Oxford: Routledge.

Knepper, Paul. 1996. "Race, Racism and Crime Statistics." *Southern University Law Review* 24, no. 1 (Fall): 71–112.

Langbein, John H. 1974. *Prosecuting Crime in the Renaissance: England, Germany, France*. Cambridge: Harvard University Press.

Lavater, Johann Kaspar. 1817. *The Science of Physiognomy*. New York: Van Winkle & Wiley. Google Ebook. https://www.actingarchives.it/catalogo_files/The%20Pocket%20Lavater,%20or,%20The%20Science%20of%20Physiognomy%20-%201817.pdf.

Levine, Philippa. 2012. "Anthropology, Colonialism, and Eugenics." In *The Oxford Handbook of the History of Eugenics*, edited by Alison Bashford and Philippa Levine, 43–61. Oxford: Oxford University Press.

Levine, Philippa, and Alison Bashford. 2012. "Introduction: Eugenics and the Modern World." In *The Oxford Handbook of the History of Eugenics*, edited by Alison Bashford and Philippa Levine, 2–24. Oxford: Oxford University Press.

Lujan, Carol, and Gordon Adams. 2004. "U.S. Colonization of Indian Justice Systems: A Brief History." *Wicazo Sa Review* 19, no. 2 (September): 9–23. http://doi.org/10.1353/wic.2004.0023.

McVeigh, Robbie, and Bill Rolston. 2009. "Civilising the Irish." *Race & Class* 51, no. 1 (June): 2–28. Thousand Oaks: Sage Publications, Incorporated. https://doi.org/10.1177/0306396809106160.

Muldoon, James. 2000. "Race or Culture: Medieval Notions of Difference." In *Race and Racism in Theory and Practice*, edited by Berel Lang, 79–97. Lanham: Rowman & Littlefield Publishers.

Parker, Philip. 2010. *World History*. London: Dorling Kindersley Limited.

Pate, Matthew, and William C. Plouffe Jr. 2009. "Race, Ethnicity and Crime." In *21st Century Criminology: A Reference Handbook*, edited by J. Mitchell Miller, 133–43. Thousand Oaks: Sage Publications, Incorporated.

Paul, Diane B., and James Moore. 2012. "The Darwinian Context: Evolution and Inheritance." In *The Oxford Handbook of the History of Eugenics*, edited by Alison Bashford and Philippa Levine, 27–42. Oxford: Oxford University Press.

Pavlac, Brian A. 2009. *Witch Hunts in the Western World: Persecution and Punishment from the Inquisition Through the Salem Trials*. Westport: Greenwood Press.

Philips, David D. 2013. *The Law of Ancient Athens*. Ann Arbor: University of Michigan Press.

Price, Simon. 1986. "The History of the Hellenistic Period." In *The Oxford History of the Classical World*, edited by John Boardman, Jasper Griffin, and Oswyn Murray, 315–37. Oxford: Oxford University Press.

Rafter, Nicole H. 2008. "Criminology's Darkest Hour: Biocriminology in Nazi Germany." *Australian and New Zealand Journal of Criminology* 41, no. 2 (August): 287–306. https://doi.org/10.1375/acri.41.2.287.

Rafter, Nicole H. 2009. *The Origins of Criminology: A Reader*. Oxford: Routledge.

Rawson, Elizabeth. 1986. "The Expansion of Rome." In *The Oxford History of the Classical World*, edited by John Boardman, Jasper Griffin, and Oswyn Murray, 417–37. Oxford: Oxford University Press.

Rhodes, P. J. 2010. *A History of the Classical Greek World: 478–323* BC, 2nd ed. Hoboken: Wiley-Blackwell Publishing.

Roger, G. 2000. "Enslavement and Manumission in Ancient Greece." In *Race and Racism in Theory and Practice*, edited by Berel Lang, 99–110. Lanham: Rowman & Littlefield Publishers.

Rousseaux, Xavier. 1997. "Crime, Justice, and Society in Medieval and Early Modern Times: Thirty Years of Crime and Criminal Justice History. A Tribute to Herman Diederiks. Translated by Kevin Dwyer. *Crime, History & Societies* 1 (1): 87–118. https://doi.org/10.4000/CHS.1034.

Scanlan, Padraic Xavier. 2016. "Blood, Money, and Endless Paper: Slavery and Capital in British Imperial History." *History Compass* 14, no. 5 (April): 218–30. doi:10.1111/hic3.12310.

Schoeneman, Thomas J. 1975. "The Witch Hunt as a Culture Change Phenomenon." *Ethos* 3, no. 4 (Winter): 529–54. https://www.jstor.org/stable/639998.

Simon, Jonathan. 2020. "'The Criminal Is to Go Free': The Legacy of Eugenic Thought in Contemporary Judicial Realism About American Criminal Justice." *Boston University Law Review* 100 (3): 787–815.

Subramanian, Divya. 2019. "Legislating the Labor Force: Sedentarization and Development in India and the United States, 1870–1915." *Comparative Studies in Society and History* 61, no. 4 (October): 835–63. doi:10.1017/S0010417519000288.

Thorndike, Lynn. 1917. *The History of Medieval Europe.* Cambridge: The Riverside Press.

Townsend, Philippa Lois. 2009. "Another Race? Ethnicity, Universalism, and the Emergence of Christianity." PhD diss., Princeton University. ProQuest.

Treitler, Vilna Bashi. 2016. "Racialization and Its Paradigms: From Ireland to North America." *Current Sociology Monograph* 64, no. 2 (December): 213–27. doi:10.1177/0011392115614782.

Tuplin, Christopher. 1999. "Greek Racism? Observations on the Character and Limits of Greek Ethnic Prejudice." In *Ancient Greeks: West and East*, edited by G. R. Tsetskhladze, 47–74. Leiden: Brill Publishers.

Von Dornum, Deirdre Dionysia. 1997. "The Straight and the Crooked: Legal Accountability in Ancient Greece." *Columbia Law Review* 97, no. 5 (June): 1483–518. doi.org/10.2307/112 3441.

Warren, Wendy Anne. 2007. "'The Cause of Her Grief': The Rape of a Slave in Early New England." *Journal of American History* 93, no. 4 (March): 1031–49. https://www.jstor.org/stable/25094595.

Worsham, Natalie Hope. 2014. "Personae Non Gratae: A Study of the Expulsion of Jews in the Later Middle Ages from England and France." PhD diss., Southeastern Louisiana University. Proquest.

Wrenhaven, Kelly L. 2013. "Barbarians at the Gate: Foreign Slaves in Greek City-States." *Electryone* 1 (1): 1–17. https://engagedscholarship.csuohio.edu/clmlang_facpub/108/.

Chapter 7

The Evolving Role of Gender in the Criminal Justice System

Trip Finity Taylor, Steff King, and Omi Hodwitz

INTRODUCTION

Males have held a place of prominence in all facets of Western criminal justice systems over time. Whether the discussion is rooted in ancient Greece and Rome, medieval Europe, the Reformation and Enlightenment eras, or modernity, men have been subject to the lion's share of arrests, trials, convictions, and sentences. Moreover, men have led the charge on studying and chronicling the criminal justice system as it evolved over time. Lastly, men have been largely responsible for filling positions of authority within the criminal justice system as police, judges, and the executioners of sentences. This androcentric orientation has resulted in a lack of non-male perspectives in historical accounts; instead, our understanding of the nuances of gender within the criminal justice system primarily reflects the male experience. This chapter seeks to correct this trend; by examining specific references and anecdotes, the reader is offered a version of history that considers the experiences of female and non-male individuals within the criminal justice system.[1]

In addition to examining non-male experiences, this chapter will also explore the criminalization of gendered expression. We adopt the position that gender is a socially defined concept that is not, and has never been, static; instead, it has shifted and changed over time, reflecting the evolution of social understanding of identity. Despite this fluidity, the historical record shows persistent attempts to regulate, define, and police the presentation of gender. In many cases, regardless of the era, those who engaged in gender-atypical behaviors or defied gendered expectations were criminalized and subjected to state repression and public shame for their transgressions against social expectations. For example, society assigned traditional "feminine" gender roles to biological females, and any violation of these norms was considered "women's crimes."[2] The content presented below includes an exploration of this historical trend, providing narratives that highlight criminal justice responses that criminalize gender atypicality.

This chapter consists of five sections focused on specific eras or ages throughout Western history. Each section contains narratives that describe the laws, investigations, trials, and punishments typical for that era.[3] The first section begins in ancient

Greece and Rome, followed by an exploration of medieval Europe and early colonial United States. These first two sections are admittedly sparse in detail due to limited factual sources and surviving documents; thus, we rely on symbolic case studies to inform our narrative. This trend of spotty recordkeeping ends with the Renaissance and Enlightenment eras, when records of Victorian gendered expectations (particularly for women) are plentiful and rich in detail. This is followed by the Scientific Revolution, a fascinating era that recast women and gender deviants as medical anomalies, while also producing prison reform and rehabilitation. The chapter then examines the feminist movements in the twentieth century, before concluding with a brief discussion of the intersection between gender and the criminal justice system today.

PROPERTY, NOT PEOPLE: ANCIENT GREECE AND ROME (PRE–SIXTH CENTURY)

Throughout much of ancient antiquity, the right to claim full citizenship was only available for men, and in large part, authorities drafted laws and policies that honored citizenship above all else. Consequently, women were treated differently by the criminal justice system as they were not generally perceived as full citizens. Whereas both men and women could be tried and convicted of crimes, unlike men, women were not permitted to take part in court proceedings; instead, they were required to have a male represent them in all manners of trial and sentencing. For that reason, most female crimes became a matter for husbands or fathers to address in ancient Greece and Rome. Therefore, although not explicitly stated in law, women were no better than property, and as property, if they deviated, it fell to their male possessor to hold them to account.

Law and Society

Ancient Athenian (479 BCE–323 BCE) philosophers held competing views about the rights of women late into antiquity (Tetlow 2005). Aristotle strove for limited public access to politics and courts for Greek women based on their apparent intellectual and physical inferiorities. Plato, on the other hand, wrote that well-trained and talented men or women could run the ideal government, and therefore, society should have an equal application of the law. Despite Platonian ponderings, Athenian women were not granted equal access; as noted above, they could not represent themselves in court and were subject to specific laws that were solely under the purview of their husbands or fathers. Eventually, women gained limited legal protections during the Hellenistic period (323 BCE–31 BCE), but they were still denied gender equivalence. While this change was likely due to the emergence of a female ruling class during conquest, it did not entirely free them from the holds of patriarchal powers. The Romans followed a similar footprint.

Classical Roman culture (~30 BCE–476 CE) was informed more by social values than by legal code. Early Romans relied primarily on "custom, family self-supervision based on the power of the *patria familias*" (Richlin 1993, 554). Men were the legal heads of the household, responsible for complete legal order and delivery of due punishment (Kamp 2020). Women were no different from children, unable to represent or speak for themselves. The concept of *manus*, meaning hand, dictated the relationship between husband and wife; it provided restrictions on wedded female behaviors, including attempts to leave a marriage without the approval of the male spouse (Shelden & Vasiliev 2018). Women were perceived as physically and mentally inferior, therefore lacking the capabilities to act for themselves. Additionally, society imposed standards of femininity, defining who had the right to embrace effeminate ways, thus penalizing those who behaved outside of gendered norms.

While society expected women to embrace passivity and docility, men accused of such behaviors could face legal ramifications, including those who engaged in the taboo crime of hubris (Cohen 1987). As early as the fourth century BCE, statutes against pederasty and sodomy used the term *hubris* to negatively categorize any sexual act against a free male citizen, including young boys, put in a passive (i.e., feminine) role.[4] Many of these laws dealt with the shame and dishonor of the act and focused on the disdainful passive perpetrator and not the active male offender. Bauman (2002) notes the sacred ancient ideals of dignity and reputation suggested that punishments of shame and humiliation were a strong deterrent, particularly when accusing a man of femininity. Therefore, gender, femininity, and passivity were central to social conceptions of deviance during this time.

Investigations and Courts

When women committed crimes in ancient Greece and Rome, it often remained a family affair, one that was dealt with internally. This was due, in part, to the lack of an official policing body responsible for investigation and, in part, to the lack of public prosecutors, thus leaving it to the aggrieved party to initiate prosecution (Murnaghan 1999, 88). This is not to say, however, that all intra-family cases stayed out of the public courtroom. Historical records detail the trial of a woman accused of poisoning her husband and his acquaintance (Carey 1997). In keeping with the traditions of the time, she was not permitted to represent herself in court. By an ironic twist of fate, the sons of the victim served as both the prosecution and the defense. In addition to the obvious conflict of interest, the sons based their arguments on hearsay and emotional appeals for justice. Additionally, the trial persisted even after a "concubine" was tortured and executed under the auspices of having committed the poisoning in question. The case provides a poignant example of the legal protections (or lack thereof) afforded females during this time.

Some of the more serious criminal charges against women were for failures to obey the common precepts of the day—either fraudulent activity against men or sacrilege against the city-state or their gods. However, many of the charges levied at women were for limited offenses, such as adultery or infanticide (Tetlow 2004). In these cases, the degree or severity of investigation or prosecution was influenced by the type of citizen involvement. For example, if a man sexually assaulted or committed adultery with a woman who was married to a citizen, he would face charges for those crimes. The woman involved in the same offense, however, would divorce her husband out of shame and live elsewhere without honor (Kamp 2020; Tetlow 2004).

During the age of antiquity, court proceedings lacked many of the modern ideals of proper decorum or rules of evidence and thus could often become quite extraordinary, particularly when they involved female defendants. For example, Phryne, an attractive Athenian hetaera, earned an acquittal against a charge of sacrilege when her defender stripped her down to the waist to allow the jurists to see the wonder of her bare chest (Tetlow 2004).[5] Her defender, a man named Hypereides, was known for his eloquent orations as well as his habit of sleeping with many hetaerae, most likely including Phryne herself. Although the case of Phryne is revealing, it is unclear whether dramatic proceedings of this kind are representative of the female experience. Historical narrations of the female defendant are limited, relegated to partial court records and hearsay. Therefore, this is likely only a small portion of the full story of what many women faced during this time.

Sentencing and Punishment

In general, there were three classes of punishments that were popular in ancient Greece and Rome, informed by retributive and deterrent sentiments. Low-level crimes, such as theft or public drunkenness, would likely result in fines or short-term incarceration (Richlin 1993). These punishments were, for the most part, directed toward male offenders. The more severe crimes, such as intentional homicide, treason, and sacrilege, could involve both male and female defendants, and would be rewarded with a death sentence. In addition, men might be executed for adultery, the seduction of a married woman, or malfeasance in public office (Tetlow 2004). The last class of punishment, which some thought was the worst among the possibilities, was public shame and the loss of either citizenship (for men) or honor (for women) [Kamp 2020].

Tetlow (2004) provides an interesting example of gendered sentencing and punishment in her account of a man who wore women's clothes to sneak into a festival, thus earning the charge of sacrilege. Alongside the plank and the whip, the offender also received another telling sentence: he was required to continue wearing the women's clothing, leading to humiliation and a loss of dignity. Honor, which was of utmost importance in ancient Greece and Rome, was a zero-sum game. It could be lost due to a single act that violated gender norms of the time, a penalty much harsher than death for those who lived with the humiliation of dishonor. This was particularly relevant for women, as their dishonor would reflect not only upon themselves, but also upon the men held responsible for their care. As a consequence, women were often confined to the home, shamed in silence and solitude.

Summary

Due to the scarcity of legal records and other surviving documents, literary analysis of the female experience with the ancient Greek and Roman criminal justice systems is difficult. Males were both the primary recordkeepers and the legal guardians of women and, because of this, women's voices are muted throughout this era, and the stories of their experiences with the law, the courts, and punishment are few and far between. In addition, the few remaining tales addressing women in the criminal justice system tend to oversimplify each case, presenting the female protagonist as though she were a mythical character in a story. In actuality, many of the better-known accounts of women within the legal institution come directly from Greek and Roman tragedies (Murnaghan 1999). Despite the fanciful nature of these narratives, they do paint a stark picture of a patriarchal justice system—one dominated by men, used to undermine, regulate, and otherwise control women for noncompliance. Unfortunately, this practice continued throughout the age of antiquity and subsequent eras, although the thematic undertone would shift to reflect the cultural and social priorities of the period.

THE DEVIL MADE ME DO IT: THE MIDDLE AGES (SIXTH – FIFTEENTH CENTURIES)

The criminal justice system of the Middle Ages was predominantly governed by religious authorities. To put it simply, crimes were sins, and sins were crimes. Because of the "deeply entrenched Christian hostility to women as the originators of sin," females were often held accountable for matters of a deviant or unexplained nature (Apps & Gow 2003, 131). Women were believed to be particularly impressionable and, thus, easy prey for Satan and his minions. As such, they were more susceptible to committing sins. This is not to say that men were not accused of heresy or witchcraft, but when this charge was levied at them, they were usually likened to the weaker sex or their behavior was attributed to female influences. This was a dark and confusing time, and the intersection between gender, crime, and sin took center stage.

Law and Society

As the Roman Empire collapsed and Europe transitioned to regional control, new legal codes formed. Lombard lords and other European rulers viewed women as a weak link that threatened family honor, particularly the honor of the patriarch. Therefore, strict regulations over women were necessary, to be codified in legal statutes. The famous thirteenth century Bracton legal treatise, for example, included the statement, "Women differ from men in many respects, for their position is inferior to that of men" (Seabourne 2021, 5). Similar to ancient Greek and Roman cultures, women of the early medieval period could not represent themselves in a public manner, particularly in courts or legal proceedings. Their behavior was still ultimately the responsibility of their husbands or fathers.

During this time, religious values took prominence, and legal codes began to incorporate material from key texts, particularly the testaments of the Christian Bible (Nelson & Rio 2013). Unlike those of previous societies, medieval laws explicitly repressed women's sexuality, confining it to the strict parameters of marital requirements. Women were expected to comply with their husband's sexual demands but they were not permitted to engage in additional activities. The law against *adulterium*, for example, included the traditional act of adultery, but it also extended to any female sexual activity considered improper at the time. Sexual repression was fueled, in part, by the belief that women were cold and inferior to men and should be relegated to a celibate and meek lifestyle (Jewell 2006).

The rise of Christian ideals throughout much of the medieval world also led to an increase in legal statutes directed toward other seemingly sinful behaviors, such as acts of sodomy, sorcery, and heresy. In addition to religious sentiment, gender expectations played a key role in creating this class of criminal offenses (Kuefler 2003). Sodomy, for example, was a violation of traditional masculine identity and thus a perversion of gender. As for sorcery, it was the link between witchcraft and submission to demonic forces, and women were more susceptible to these influences due to their natural weaknesses (Bailey 2002). Heresy became the catchall charge for anyone who deviated from the dictates of the Bible, which included cursing others or committing gender transgressions (Ward 2016).

The case of Joan of Arc in 1430 provides a ready example of the prominence of heresy and gender transgressions in legal considerations (Hobbins 2005). Joan earned fame after a victory at Orleans, in part due to her practice of wearing men's clothing, which, at the time, was a violation of natural decency and virtue and thus sinful (Grigat & Carrier 2007). In addition, Joan refused to embrace a subservient and meek character, which was a public transgression against authority. For her crimes, the local authorities imprisoned Joan for six months before turning her over to the Inquisitors to face charges of heresy. Her victories did not excuse her transgressions.

Investigations and Courts

In addition to dictating legal statutes, religious authorities also took the lead in the majority of investigative and court proceedings. Although the monarchy held some authority throughout the Middle Ages, for the most part, the Church oversaw all ecclesiastical crimes, and some secular ones, as well (Ward 2016). The Inquisition, which served as the religious body of enforcement, began in twelveth-century France and continued unchecked until the fifteenth century. Its primary mission was to ferret out and punish heretics and sinners, which offered a new approach to deviance. While ancient antiquity relied on an accusatorial system (a plaintiff had to make a claim of wrongdoing), the Middle Ages relied on the inquisitorial system (the Church actively sought out incidents of wrongdoing). This system involved trial judges (typically clergymen), lawyers, witnesses, and the accused, all representing their various interests through testimony and evidence with the goal of establishing the "facts" before determining a heretic's fate. Despite the opportunity to produce a fair and just outcome, the final determination of guilt or innocence often reflected what was in the best interests of the Church.

The case of Joan of Arc, described previously, provides an illuminating example of the inquisitorial system in practice, as well as the continued influence of gender on criminal proceedings. Canon law dictated that an Inquisitor must establish an accused's heretical reputation prior to questioning; however, that opportunity eluded Joan of Arc. She spent months under inquisition in a "preparatory trial" before having articles of accusation issued against her (Hobbins 2005, 21–22). The opening statement of Joan's trial was: "The report has now reached many places that this woman, utterly disregarding the honor due the female sex, throwing off the bridle of modesty, and forgetful of all feminine decency, wore the disgraceful clothing of men, a shocking and vile monstrosity" (Grigat & Carrier 2007, 196).

Officially speaking, Joan was accused of heresy due to her refusal to submit to the will of the Church, for her claim that God spoke directly to her, and for the transgression of refusing to dress as a woman. She represented herself at trial but was unsuccessful, receiving convictions for twelve offenses, three of which specifically related to gender nonconformity (Grigat & Carrier 2007). Joan was compelled to sign a confession and promise to discontinue her heresy. Just four days later, Joan again donned men's clothing, refusing to abandon her "errors of the faith" (Grigat & Carrier 2007, 199). On May 30, 1431, she was publicly executed (Hobbins 2005).

The case of Joan of Arc typified the intricate relationship between courts and the Church during the time. Canonic law and society dictated that women should be meek and mild. If they chose to behave otherwise, then they required correction by the Inquisition (Jewell 2006). If a woman denied the accusations against her, torture and other extreme measures commonly forced a confession. This was particularly true in the prosecution of witchcraft in the later medieval era, during which time the treatment of women in the criminal justice system took a turn for the worse.

Witchcraft was a concern for much of the Middle Ages, but active prosecutions did not become commonplace until the fifteenth and sixteenth centuries. In 1437, cleric Johannes Nider wrote *Formicarius*, which publicly argued that women were prone to witchcraft due to their innate spiritual weaknesses (Bailey 2002).[6] In 1486, Dominican inquisitor Heinrich Kramer released a book titled *Malleus Maleficarum*, a milestone publication that would facilitate hundreds of years of witch hunts. A passage translated from the book read:

> Women are naturally more impressionable, and more ready to receive the influence of a disembodied spirit . . . they have slippery tongues and are unable to conceal from their fellow-women those things which by evil art they know; and, since they are weak, they find an easy and secret manner of vindicating themselves by witchcraft. (Summers 2012, 44)

The craze for hunting witches spread across the Western world in waves, hitting select nations at different times before coming to an end in the seventeenth century (Mackay 2009). The Malleus incited mass public panic, usually directed toward females. In many cases, women who held public disfavor or defied social expectations were vulnerable to claims of witchcraft. They were accused of all manner of deviant behaviors, from cursing neighbors' crops to manipulating men for their own means. In one written account of a woman apprehended for witchcraft, citizens described that "she was discovered by cats bouncing in the air and inviting one of her neighbors to the same craft" (The National Archives 1671, 1). Despite the wild claims of those who brought forth accusations, community trials required little (if any) evidence to convict, resulting in countless executions (Mackay 2009).

Sentencing and Punishment

During the Middle Ages, the justice system relied heavily on executions and exorcisms. Due to the intersection between sin and crime, burning at the stake became a popular punishment. Fire was destructive, yet cleansing, and it could supposedly rid an individual of demonic possession (Bailey 2002). Although early crimes of sorcery were believed to be the purview of men (women were believed not intelligent enough to perform complex magic), this shifted with the witch craze as women took center stage.[7] Therefore, although both men and women were convicted of heresy and witchcraft and burnt upon a pyre for their transgressions, the vast majority of these unfortunate souls were women.

Summary

The Middle Ages was a continuation of the patriarchal theme from ancient antiquity; males were granted authority and control while women were subservient and power-less. The criminal justice system replicated this historical social dynamic while also reflecting the unique characteristics of medieval society, particularly the power and sway of the tenets of the Church. Due to the overwhelming influence of Christian ide-als, the criminal justice system criminalized and penalized women for any act that fell outside the moral standards of Scripture, often with Satan as the driving force (Apps & Gow 2003). Women who did not live under the guises of inferiority and subordina-tion, the precepts of femininity at the time, faced accusations of heresy or witchcraft. Often, they went through impossible tests to confirm these suspicions. For the most part, the criminal justice system more closely resembled a system of religious control and manipulation than one of fairness and equity.

POLICING POLITE SOCIETY: RENAISSANCE, REFORMATION, AND ENLIGHTENMENT (SIXTEENTH–EIGHTEENTH CENTURIES)

During the Renaissance, Reformation, and Enlightenment periods, the criminal justice system in the west underwent a series of changes that reflected social recalibration around issues of gender and accountability. Due to expansive social and political changes in Western society during the mid-to-late sixteenth century, many women experienced newfound freedoms, including the opportunity to leave the confines of their domestic life to become more involved in the evolving economy (O'Brien 2009).[8] Education and employment became more readily available throughout this era, introducing new responsibilities and revitalizing gendered expectations. How-ever, one of the behaviors generally tolerated during the medieval centuries, namely prostitution, quickly became a blight on enlightened society (Norberg 2013). Thus, in the eyes of many, welcoming women into open society only facilitated an increase in female degeneracy and crime (Weaver, 2007).

Law and Society

Similar to those in earlier periods, many of the laws of the Renaissance and Enlight-enment seemed intent on controlling women, particularly around issues of sexuality. Prostitution was generally lawful in Europe before the early sixteenth century, and many municipalities chose to regulate it through sanctioned brothels or generalized vagrancy laws (Norberg 2013). As the Protestants and Calvinists gained authority in the late 1500s, however, prostitution was redefined as deviant and criminal. Punitive sanctions, typically directed toward women, became more numerous and severe, as fornication and adultery were recast as "horrendous crimes" (Brackett 1992, 115). In some cases, municipalities chose a quieter route, charging female sex workers with loitering or other non-related crimes, so as not to draw attention to prostitution in the area. Whether publicly broadcast or quietly condemned, female sexuality was criminalized and vilified by the state.

Like the state, conventional society also rejected prostitution, citing that it conflicted with their moral ideals of decency (Norberg 2013). Despite social and political consensus on the objectional nature of the act, attempts to eradicate it were ineffectual, and it continued to expand as a practice. By the early 1700s, concerns about public order instigated the issuance of a series of laws (later called the "Watch Acts") that increased the nighttime police presence. These laws did not, however, decrease prostitution; as police forces grew, so, too, did bribery, extortion, and corruption. In addition, it was difficult to enforce sexual deviance laws directed toward women unless they were caught in the act. As a consequence of corruption and the limited likelihood of successful prosecution, paired with a waning public interest in the issue, prostitution receded from the roster of moral outrages deserving of attention at the time. Even at its most productive time, the London Society for the Reformation of Manners had only 545 prosecutions for prostitution despite bringing in over seven thousand female perpetrators for trial. As the laws changed with society, so did the policing and court processes.

Investigations and Courts

Casting aside the restrictive religious framework of the Middle Ages, courts during the Renaissance and Enlightenment periods expanded their reach, responding to all acts "contrary to nature," including, but not limited to, homosexuality, incest, marriage without consent, bestiality, debauchery (extramarital relations), and even hermaphroditism (Foucault 1978). Judicial oversight extended well beyond the law, granting authority over any action that violated social norms. Contrary to previous eras, women were now permitted to represent themselves or others; however, the interpretation of deviance still relied heavily on traditional biological expectations. Infringements against the obligations of marriage were as serious, if not more so, than general unlawfulness. Additionally, there was an increase in the level of legal scrutiny directed toward actions that violated the customary constraints of adult heterosexual monogamy. For example, the "Officials of the Night" in fifteenth- and sixteenth-century Florence arrested and prosecuted numerous gay lovers caught together, although punishment was typically reserved for the elder participant in the tryst (Brackett 1992, 131).

A number of additional indiscretions warranted charges during this time. French courts oversaw several cases of cross-dressing and sodomy between 1533 and 1686, including the trial of Marin le Marcis (Wahl 1999). Marin was born as Marie in 1601, carrying this identity until the age of twenty-one, at which time they adopted a new name, assumed masculine attire, and sought to wed a woman (Boslaugh 2018). This led to their arrest soon thereafter. After a trial and conviction for sodomy, a last-minute witness arose to argue that Marin was indeed a "gunanthrope," someone with both male and female sexual anatomy, and therefore they could "legally" engage in relations with a woman without the use of an external instrument (Wahl 1999, 26).[9] Swayed by this argument, the court set Marin free, but not before instilling the condition that Marin reverse their transition, adopt the name of Marie, and live out their days as a woman (Boslaugh 2018).[10]

Sentencing and Punishment

Until the eighteenth century, it was generally considered inappropriate to incarcerate women (Sheldon & Vasiliev 2018). There were situations, however, that could result in imprisonment for female offenders. Women convicted of heinous crimes, for example, would likely receive the death penalty. If they were pregnant, however, their execution would be delayed. From 1387 until 1931, the English practice of "pleading the belly" was a way for pregnant criminals to avoid hanging or burning until such time as their child could be born (Jones & Johnstone 2015, 67).

Although female imprisonment was often temporary, the goal of incarceration evolved from simple detainment to reformation. With this evolution came the introduction of female-only facilities (prior to this, women were housed in unisex facilities). The Bridewell work prisons for women opened in England in the late sixteenth century, soon inspiring the opening of similar institutions, like Amsterdam's Spinhuis, around continental Europe (Jones & Johnstone 2015). These vocational training centers became places for courts (or husbands) to send vagrant women in order to correct charges of theft, begging, or sexual deviance and teach them domestic skills (Pollack 2014). These were the first instances of institutional attempts at female rehabilitation, although the concept would not fully take form until closer to the twentieth century.

Summary

During the Renaissance and age of Enlightenment, women's roles expanded significantly, reflecting larger social, cultural, and political revolutions occurring in the Western world at the time. However, their place in the criminal justice system remained the same, as they were subjected to strict patriarchal control, mirroring the generations that preceded them. As women became more prominent in the public sphere, many without a male to serve as an overseer, society stepped in and created civil authorities to maintain patriarchal oversight. Police forces attempted to limit the spread of deviancy and other social ills, particularly prostitution, by legally enforcing gender expectations. If the male members of a family could not regulate deviant women, then society would do it in their place.

FALLEN WOMEN: THE SCIENTIFIC REVOLUTION (NINETEENTH–TWENTIETH CENTURIES)

During the Scientific Revolution, the criminal justice system became intensely focused on the study and medicalization of deviance and degeneracy. This was due, in part, to Victorian views of gender that commanded much of the Western world in the nineteenth century.[11] Women were expected to marry, bear children, keep a proper household, and remain stalwart examples of docility and decency. In contrast, men were expected to be the providers, endowed with masculine traits that ensured their place of power in society. Women and men who did not fit these tight strictures were viewed as aberrations and perceived as inferior in some yet-to-be-discovered way. This assumption spurred the scientific community, as they set out to poke, prod, and measure offenders, motivated to discover a physiological origin to their behavior. Masculine women and effeminate men became central to this endeavor, as they were recast as biologically inferior degenerates and deviants. Prisons become unofficial research facilities, intent on studying offenders and social outcasts, under the auspices of identifying and eradicating the source of their depravity.

Law and Society

Early nineteenth century society considered female inebriates, thieves, prostitutes, and/or vagrants a threat to public order (Freedman 1981). This new "dangerous class" of criminals represented the failure of a legal and a moral nature (Freedman 1981, 10). New laws became necessary as a means to stop these "fallen women," which led to excessive policing of female behavior (Zedner 1991).[12] In the United States, for example, the act of ending pregnancies by choice was outlawed, effectively punishing women who were sexually permissive. In addition to acts of reproductive freedom, women were also arrested for moral offenses against "chastity, decency, or public order" (Freedman 1981, 14). The Vagrancy Act of 1824 and subsequent laws, such as the Contagious Diseases Acts of 1864–1869, adopted the term *common prostitute* for female sex workers (Mooney 2019, 229). Women convicted of these offenses were often sentenced to a period of incarceration, which quickly filled Western jails and prisons.

Investigations and Courts

The late nineteenth century was a time of intense investigative scrutiny of women who engaged in criminal behavior. Interesting case studies caught the eye of researchers and academics, prompting a flurry of scientific study designed to identify, isolate, and eliminate the causes of offending. The results of these empirical endeavors, specifically the discovery of physical and moral abnormalities, became prominent in criminal justice proceedings, providing a ready way to detect potential offenders and to predict their likelihood of reformation. Women who defied gendered norms were of particular interest to the research community, as they were considered exceptionally aberrant.

The scientific focus on female offending is attributed to a number of factors, including a particular legal case that arose in Italy in 1891. In this incident, a young seamstress (and part-time sex worker) named Ernesta Bordoni was accused of killing an ex-boyfriend with a kitchen knife (Gibson 2002). Although she claimed self-defense, prosecutors noted that she borrowed the knife from a neighbor and was encouraged by her half brother (her alleged incestuous lover) to commit the murder; both details suggested intent. Ernesta was convicted of murder and sentenced to four years in prison, which many considered a light sentence, particularly in light of the fact that her half brother received fifteen years. Guglielmo Ferrero, a biological positivist, took note of the case, finding it unusual in many respects.[13]

Ferrero wrote about Ernesta's case, using this platform to espouse new deterministic theories of crime (Gibson 2005). These theories suggested that biological and genetic makeup informed and dictated human behavior. After reviewing her case, Ferrero concluded that Ernesta likely had *atavistic* traits, a reference to the idea that individuals might possess characteristics typical of less-evolved ancestors. He noted that Ernesta was physically defective and "almost horsy," and she was certainly "morally insane" due to her lack of emotional restraint and modesty (Gibson 2002, 54). Ferrero's findings caught the attention of other positivists, including Cesare Lombroso, who had already begun linking physiology with morality and deviance in male samples. The two of them, intrigued with the finding of a pronounced connection between murderous women and their biological and moral makeup, sought to pursue it further by conducting studies in women's prisons.[14] Lombroso and Ferrero reported their findings and further elaborated on their evolutionary explanations of female crime in the 1895 publication *The Female Offender* (Rafter 2009). They concluded that all women were no more than children with inferior morals of deception and vanity that could only be contained by maternity or men.

Another case explored in *The Female Offender* was that of the husband-killing Frenchwoman Marie Cappelle Pouch-Lafarge (Downing 2009). Marie, an orphaned young noble, was forced to marry nobleman Charles Lafarge, and within six months of their nuptials, he was dead from arsenic poisoning. The court convicted Marie and sentenced her to life in prison, despite public contention surrounding her guilt. Lombroso categorized Lafarge as "hysterical" based on her out-of-control femininity and apparent obsession of writing, as seen by the thousands of pages of letters she wrote during her incarceration (Lombroso & Ferrero 1895, 239). *Hysterical*, at the time, was a medical term that was linked to the uterus and incidents of female emotionality. Referring to it in positivist writings further substantiated it as both a medical and a legal consideration.

In addition to hysteria, *The Female Offender* and other public discourses on criminality validated the use of other female-associated terms. *Nymphomania*, for example, was bandied about, influencing judicial rulings for years to come. In these cases, female offenders were categorized as deviants for their inability to control their passions, thus straying from socially acceptable sexual practices (Downing 2009). These behaviors, whether extreme emotionality for the hysterical, or sexual expression for the nymphomaniacal, were all indicators of the biological and moral inferiority of women.

Sentencing and Punishment

Convicted offenders were commonly sentenced to jails and prisons for long periods of time during this era. The influx of criminals led to prison overcrowding, and paired with minimal public visibility and thus accountability, most penal institutions fell into drastic disrepair. The Walnut Street Jail in Philadelphia, for example, was described as a "school of corruption" and New York's Auburn prison was said to have a "tainted and sickly atmosphere" (Rafter 1983, 134–35). Although officials created separate female-only areas within a number of prisons, including Auburn, deteriorating conditions compromised the security of incarcerated women. Male officers subjected female prisoners to physical and sexual abuse, often in exchange for safety and improved conditions (Rafter 1983). In addition to abuse, the women were denied access to programming, education, or activities that would serve a prosocial purpose. Female offenders languished in misery, deficient in basic necessities and subject to the whims of their captors.

These conditions persisted partially due to the fact that most of society believed female offenders were irredeemable, and this perspective was slow to change, occurring in fits and starts (Rafter 1983). Elizabeth Fry, for example, visited the dark confines of Newgate Prison in London and, upon witnessing the deplorable conditions the residents lived under, sought innovative ways to address them (Mooney 2019). By 1817, she had established the Association for the Improvement of Female Prisoners in Newgate, which created sewing programs and formed a school inside the prison for women. In the United States, the Magdalene Home was opened by the Crusaders for the Benevolent Empire in Philadelphia in 1833. Its founders intended it as a place within which to restore the virtue of women who had suffered lapses of moral judgment (Kann 2005).[15]

Perhaps the most notable attempt at reform, however, occurred in 1868, when self-proclaimed scientific penologist Zebulon Brockway opened the Detroit House of Shelter for women (Rafter 1983). Brockway, unlike earlier generations of penologists and prison administrators, was a firm believer in the rehabilitative potential of incarceration, advocating for a program-based merit system that would facilitate self-improvement among the prisoners. Shortly after the Detroit House opened, state legislature passed an indeterminate sentencing law, thus allowing Brockway to detain sex workers for a lengthy period of time under the auspices of reforming them. His approach became quite popular, and between 1870 and the turn of the twentieth century, "reformatories" were opened all over the United States, fashioned with the goal of fixing the blight of criminal degeneracy (Rafter 1985).

Female reformatories were unique in many respects. For the most part, these facilities housed misdemeanants and lesser offenders whose basic failures were due to their inabilities to be "true" women (Rafter 1985, 236). Many used the "Cottage Plan" originally intended for juvenile centers, which consisted of several home-like residences located in rural settings (Rafter 1990). As for programming, emphasis was placed on domesticity and training in gender-typical skills. The structure and intention of female reformatories appealed to many prison reformers, as it aligned with their notions of women as passive recipients of gentle discipline, but it also drew critics (Rafter 1985). Opponents noted that the reformatories were infantilizing and less cost-effective when compared to traditional custodial models. Moreover, some female offenders defied reformation, maintaining their antisocial ways. The failure to rehabilitate was particularly worrying, given the popularity of the new penology of rehabilitation. Before long, a new theory of *feeblemindedness* provided a ready answer to the problem of irredeemable women.

Feeblemindedness was premised on the assumption that defective traits, including criminality, were heritable, passed down through the generations regardless of upbringing and opportunity. Josephine Shaw Lowell, a member of the New York State Board of Charities, solidified the connection between the feebleminded and women when she publicly identified deviant women as feebleminded degenerates who posed a biological threat to society, both in the present (as individuals) and in the future (as mothers of degenerate offspring) [Rafter 1990]. The present and future threats could both be addressed through the same means: incarceration as a social defense and a means of controlling reproduction. Thus, eugenic criminology was born, focused primarily on female criminals and the restriction of their reproductive rights (Rafter 1997; Zedner 1991). Reformatories were recast by supporters of eugenics as a means to remove women from sexual circulation during their childbearing years (Glueck & Glueck 1934; Rafter 1997). By the beginning of the twentieth century, the eugenics movement had gained a foothold in the criminal justice system, especially (though not exclusively) directed toward female offenders.

Summary

The Scientific Revolution was a notable period of shifts in criminal justice responses to female offending. The Victorian era had established a baseline of expectations surrounding acceptable female behavior, and deviations from these expectations drew the swift interception of the legal system. Locked away in deplorable conditions, female offenders eventually caught the eye of philanthropists and rehabilitative penologists, prompting institutional change. Women's facilities improved, seeking to facilitate reformation of its residents. Despite these improvements, however, some females defied the rehabilitative model, prompting theories of feeblemindedness and hereditary degeneracy.

FEMINIST MOVEMENTS INTO MODERN TIMES: CONCLUSION (TWENTIETH CENTURY)

Throughout time and at all stages of the criminal justice system, non-male offenders have been treated differently than their male counterparts, more often than not to their detriment. This trend continued after the age of the Scientific Revolution and its criminological offspring, the reformatory. Men's prisons embraced prosocial programming, including industrial and vocational training, employment opportunities, and constructive activities, while also offering opportunities for parole, including furloughs or work release programs (Rafter 1983). Women's facilities, on the other hand, continued to stagnate. They lacked programming, opportunities, and basic necessities, as evidenced by numerous complaints of poor medical treatment and unhygienic conditions. While men's facilities emphasized care, women's institutions demonstrated neglect (Logan 2008). Even the juvenile justice systems developed a double standard, punishing girls who engaged in gender-atypical behavior harshly (Sheldon & Vasiliev 2018).

Even so, the waves of feminism that crashed across the Western world throughout the twentieth century had lasting impacts on the criminal justice system. Women earned the right to vote and to participate in governance, and in the process, they shifted attention to the rights of underrepresented populations, including the incarcerated

(Sheldon & Vasiliev 2018). In addition, women began to seek employment in areas that had traditionally been male-dominated, including the criminal justice system. These two factors, among others, placed female offenders in the spotlight, prompting concerns over the welfare of incarcerated women and the need to improve their conditions. By the end of the twentieth century, correctional programs specifically tailored to female inmates had become commonplace, although still lacking when compared to the resources available in male penal institutions.

The history of the criminal justice system, through a gender-critical lens, reveals consistent discriminative practices directed toward gender-transgressive individuals . . . and one that might not be so different from modern practices. Ancient Greek and Roman societies used the power of the family to grant males governing control to define deviance, thus allowing for the condemnation of those who refused to uphold traditional gendered ideals of behavior. During the Middle Ages, this trend persisted, bolstered by the support of the Church and state. This era recast gendered deviance, shifting it from a family issue to a supernatural one. During the Renaissance and Enlightenment eras, however, economic crises forced women into the public sphere, and although traditionalist gendered expectations persisted, the ability to control female deviants became a public affair. Before long, female prisons became overcrowded and inhumane, prompting a new era of philanthropy, rehabilitation, and reformation. Despite some successes, these movements fell short of the desired mark, leading to new theories that recast female offenders as feebleminded degenerates, capable of spawning future generations of deviants.

Historically, traditional values about gender expression and behavior defined deviance and thus dictated the criminal justice response to such behavior. As a result, the criminal justice system targeted, and at times put to death, those disadvantaged because they rejected motherhood, wore clothing of the opposite sex, had relations with someone of the same sex, engaged in sex work, and/or displayed other unbecoming or nonfeminine characteristics. Additionally, as is discussed in later chapters, the realities of those who had multiplicatively marginalized identities, be it by race, class, or mental health status, received more severe criminal justice attention over time.

When looking toward the future of the criminal justice system, situated where we are now and reflecting on where we have been, these gendered trends are of utmost importance. In general, there has always been a fundamental dichotomy in how males and females are policed, tried, and punished, and it is important to identify the causes and effects of such practices. Specifically, we encourage you to consider the following: who suffers and who benefits from these traditions?

NOTES

1. For the remainder of the chapter, use of the term *female* will often include other non-males, even if not explicitly referenced. Notes in the text will explain content not generalized between these groups.

2. It is important to note that select case studies should not be taken as fair representations of how all non-males were treated during each period. Rather, each serves as an example of the lives of non-males across time as they confronted the criminal justice system.

3. Each section follows a chronological timeline, but due to the nonlinear nature of the development of the criminal justice system, some subsections veer from this traditional sequencing of events.

4. The *natural* state of passivity of women restricted accusations of hubris against them. Publications about women committing *unnatural* actions against other women in this time is severely limited.

5. *Hetaera*—a type of ancient Greek sex worker who also served as household artist, musician, and conversationalist (Kurke 1997, 107–8).

6. From biblical references, Nider wrote, "there is no head above the head of a serpent, and there is no anger above the anger of a woman; it will be more pleasing to abide with a lion and a dragon than to dwell with a wicked woman" (Bailey 2002, 123).

7. In the late fourteenth century, theologian Nicolau Eymeric wrote that necromancy was a decidedly masculine act because it involved training, preparation, and education—all of which women lacked (Bailey 2002, 126).

8. "The progress of civilization usually included the story of women's emergence from domestic seclusion, violence and enslavement by selfish men into a bigger arena in which they exercised both a stimulating and stabilizing influence on the developing economy" (O'Brien 2009, 11).

9. An old thirteenth-century French code prohibited female sodomy—punished by losing "a member" for each instance until the accused was burned alive on her third offense (Wahl 1999, 20).

10. The trial was one of the first to include medical authorities for the purposes of gender identification and its association with criminal statutes.

11. Early social feminist Olympe de Gouges wrote in her 1791 Declaration of the Rights of Women that "the only limit to the exercise of the natural rights of woman is the perpetual tyranny that man opposes to it" (Naish 1991, 136–37).

12. The 1867 U.S. Supreme Court ruling in *Bradwell v. State* stated: "God designed the sexes to occupy different spheres of action, and that it belonged to men to make, apply, and execute the laws" (Sheldon and Vasiliev 2018, 229).

13. *Positivism*—a science that emphasized observable facts and excluded metaphysical speculation about origins or ultimate causes.

14. "Degeneration induces confusion between the two sexes, as a result of which one finds in male criminals a feminine infantilism that leads to pederasty. To this corresponds masculinity in women criminals, including an atavistic tendency to return to the stage of hermaphroditism" (Lombroso and Ferrero 2004, 178).

15. Major Joshua Jebb, head of the English convict system, claimed that women were not cut out for imprisonment and should be employed indoors with consistent work instead (Zedner 1991).

REFERENCES

Apps, Lara, and Andrew C. Gow. 2003. *Gender at Stake: Male Witches in Early Modern Europe*. Manchester: Manchester University Press.

Bailey, Michael D. 2002. "The Feminization of Magic and the Emerging Idea of the Female Witch in the Late Middle Ages." *Essays in Medieval Studies* 19 (1): 120–34. https://doi.org/10.1353/ems.2003.0002.

Bauman, Richard A. 2002. *Crime and Punishment in Ancient Rome*. Oxford: Routledge.

Boslaugh, Sarah. 2018. *Transgender Health Issues*. Santa Barbara: American Bibliographical Center-Clio.

Brackett, John K. 1992. *Criminal Justice and Crime in Late Renaissance Florence, 1537–1609*. Cambridge: Cambridge University Press.

Carey, Christopher. 1997. *Trials from Classical Athens*. Oxford: Routledge.

Cohen, David. 1987. "Law, Society and Homosexuality in Classical Athens." *Past & Present*, no. 117 (November): 3–21. https://www.jstor.org/stable/650786.

Downing, Lisa. 2009. "Murder in the Feminine: Marie Lafarge and the Sexualization of the Nineteenth-Century Criminal Woman." *Journal of the History of Sexuality* 18, no. 1 (January): 121–37. https://doi.org/10.1353/sex.0.0032.

Foucault, Michel. 1978. *The History of Sexuality*. vol 1. New York: Vintage Books.

Freedman, Estelle B. 1981. *Their Sisters' Keepers: Women's Prison Reform in America, 1830–1930*. Ann Arbor: The University of Michigan Press.

Gibson, Mary. 2002. *Born to Crime: Cesare Lombroso and the Origins of Biological Criminology*. Westport: Greenwood Publishing Group, Inc.

Gibson, Mary. 2005. "Science and Narrative in Italian Criminology, 1880–1920." In *Crime and Culture: An Historical Perspective*, edited by Rene Levy and Amy G. Srebnick, 37–48. Oxford: Routledge.

Glueck, Sheldon, and Eleanor T. Glueck. 1934. *Five Hundred Delinquent Women*. New York: Knopf Doubleday Publishing Group.

Grigat, Daniel, and Gregory Carrier. 2007. "Gender Transgression as Heresy: The Trial of Joan of Arc." *Past Imperfect* 13: 188–207. https://doi.org/10.21971/P7BC7V.

Hobbins, Daniel. 2005. *The Trial of Joan of Arc*. Cambridge: Harvard University Press.

Jewell, Helen M. 2006. *Women in the Dark Age and Early Medieval Europe, c. 500–1200*. London: Bloomsbury Publishing.

Jones, Mark, and Peter Johnstone. 2015. *History of Criminal Justice*. Oxford: Routledge.

Kamp, John B. 2020. "Patriarchy and Gender Law in Ancient Rome and Colonial America." *Iowa Historical Review* 8 (1): 43–57. https://doi.org/10.17077/2373-1842.1072.

Kann, Mark E. 2005. *Punishment, Prisons, and Patriarchy: Liberty and Power in the Early American Republic*. New York: New York University Press.

Kuefler, Mathew S. 2003. "Male Friendship and the Suspicion of Sodomy in Twelfth-Century France." In *Gender and Difference in the Middle Ages*, edited by Sharon Farmer, 145–81. Minneapolis: University of Minnesota Press.

Kurke, Leslie. 1997. "Inventing the 'Hetaira': Sex, Politics, and Discursive Conflict in Archaic Greece." *Classical Antiquity* 16, no. 1 (April): 106–50. https://doi.org/10.2307/25011056.

Logan, Anne. 2008. *Feminism and Criminal Justice: A Historical Perspective*. London: Palgrave Macmillan.

Lombroso, Caesar, and William Ferrero. 1895. *The Female Offender*. New York: D. Appleton & Company.

Mackay, Christopher S. 2009. *The Hammer of Witches: A Complete Translation of the Malleus Maleficarum*. Cambridge: Cambridge University Press.

Mooney, Jayne. 2019. *The Theoretical Foundations of Criminology: Place, Time and Context*. Oxford: Routledge.

Murnaghan, Sheila. 1999. "Staging Ancient Crimes: A Response to Aristodemou, Tiefenbrun, Purkiss, and Pantazakos." *Law & Literature* 11, no. 1 (November): 77–89. https://doi.org/10.1080/1535685X.1999.11015588.

Naish, Camille. 1991. *Death Comes to the Maiden: Sex and Execution, 1431–1933*. Oxford: Routledge.

National Archives, The 1671. "Unnamed Witches: A Witch at Sea (Catalogue ref: SP 29/288 f. 5)." Accessed January 11, 2022. https://www.nationalarchives.gov.uk/education/resources/early-modern-witch-trials/fear-of-witches/.

Nelson, Janet L., and Alice Rio. 2013. "Women and Laws in Early Medieval Europe." In *The Oxford Handbook of Women and Gender in Medieval Europe*, edited by Judith Bennett and Ruth Karras, 103–17. Oxford: Oxford University Press.

Norberg, Kathryn. 2013. "The Body of the Prostitute: Medieval to Modern." In *The Routledge History of Sex and the Body: 1500 to Present*, edited by Sarah Toulalan and Kate Fisher, 393–408. Oxford: Routledge.

O'Brien, Karen. 2009. *Women and Enlightenment in 18th Century Britain.* Cambridge: Cambridge University Press.

Pollack, Joycelyn M. 2014. *Women's Crimes, Criminology, and Corrections.* Long Grove: Waveland Press.

Rafter, Nicole H. 2009. *The Origins of Criminology.* Oxford: Routledge.

Rafter, Nicole H. 1997. *Creating Born Criminals.* Champaign: University of Illinois Press.

Rafter, Nicole H. 1990. *Partial Justice: Women, Prisons, and Social Control.* Piscataway: Transaction Publishers.

Rafter, Nicole H. 1985. "Gender, Prisons, and Prison History." *Social Science History* 9, no. 3 (Summer): 233–47. https://doi.org/10.2307/1170945.

Rafter, Nicole H. 1983. "Prisons for Women, 1790–1980." *Crime and Justice* 5: 129–81. https://www.jstor.org/stable/1147471.

Richlin, Amy. 1993. "Not Before Homosexuality: The Materiality of the Cinaedus and the Roman Law Against Love Between Men." *Journal of the History of Sexuality* 3, no. 4 (April): 523–73. https://www.jstor.org/stable/3704392.

Seaborne, Gwen. 2021. *Women in the Medieval Common Law, c.1200–1500.* Oxford: Routledge.

Shelden, Randall G., and Pavel V. Vasiliev. 2018. *Controlling the Dangerous Classes: A History of Criminal Justice in America.* Long Grove: Waveland Press.

Summers, Montague. 2012. *The Malleus Maleficarum of Heinrich Kramer and James Sprenger.* New York: Courier Corporation.

Tetlow, Elisabeth M. 2005. *Women, Crime and Punishment in Ancient Law and Society: Volume 2 Ancient Greece.* New York: Continuum International Publishing Group.

Wahl, Elizabeth S. 1999. *Invisible Relations: Representations of Female Intimacy in the Age of Enlightenment.* Redwood City: Stanford University Press.

Ward, Jennifer. 2016. *Women in Medieval Europe, 1200–1500.* Oxford: Routledge.

Weaver, Elissa B. 2007. "Gender." In *A Companion to the Worlds of the Renaissance*, edited by Guido Ruggiero, 188–207. Hoboken: Wiley-Blackwell Publishing.

Zedner, Lucia. 1991. "Women, Crime, and Penal Responses: A Historical Account." *Crime and Justice* 14: 307–62. https://www.jstor.org/stable/1147464.

Chapter 8

Class, Power, Deviance, and Justice

Josh Ritchie, Carson Thiel, and Omi Hodwitz

INTRODUCTION

Human society is a complex and nuanced entity, divided along demographic and sociopolitical lines that define place and authority. These lines are determined by a number of factors, including age, race, gender, and location, but perhaps one of the more prominent divisions is that of class-based privilege. Throughout history and permeating all manner of society and culture, access to resources has determined a social hierarchy, one that places the wealthy at the top and the impoverished at the bottom. In addition to economic prosperity, these individuals also enjoy the privilege of social power. They have more authority, influence, and prominence; therefore, alongside wealth, the economic elite also have the power of control.

Social control is a potentially dangerous instrument that, when used unwisely, can lead to oppressive circumstances. Abuse of such power may stem from a desire to retain one's position or a wish to cause suffering among those who do not share that same status. This is magnified or diminished depending on the means of social control, whether it is, for example, wielded in a private setting, such as within a family, or whether it is hammered into the bones of a nation, such as is found in institutions around the world. Perhaps one of the more visible areas of social control on an institutional level is the criminal justice system, an apparatus built specifically for this purpose. To summarize: class breeds the power of social control, which, if misused, can lead to oppressive suffering, particularly within the context of state institutions, such as the criminal justice system. This is a persuasive statement, but is it supported by historical fact? Have those who enjoyed wealth and prestige abused such advantages, exerting social control, particularly within the criminal justice system, to maintain their own position while punishing those who are less fortunate? This is the task we, the authors of this chapter, have set for ourselves: to examine the role of class, power, and the criminal justice system throughout recorded history.

Our journey begins in ancient Greece, with an emphasis on the role of citizenship, affluence, and justice-based outcomes. From there, we will travel to ancient Rome and examine the codification of law, a process that benefited the people while also solidifying institutional inequalities. We will stop briefly in the Middle Ages, with a careful examination of the feudal system and its influence on criminal justice proceedings, before exploring the Renaissance and the inequities inherent in key locations. We will then journey into early modernity and the Scientific Revolution, where we will explore the roles of capitalism, empiricism, and early systematic theories of crime. Lastly, we will review the Marxian narrative regarding class and the criminal justice system, offering a lens through which to view the historical relationships described throughout the chapter.

ANCIENT GREECE, SOCIAL CLASS, AND THE CRIMINAL JUSTICE SYSTEM

Ancient Greece was an era of innovation and intellectual advancement, setting the stage for eras to come. Informed by the will of the gods; propelled by a taste for the finer things in life, including art, literature, and architecture; and driven by the advancement of knowledge, Greek antiquity was a seemingly idyllic period, crafting the foundation for many of our modern institutions, including the criminal justice system. However, in a manner similar to other eras that preceded it and those that would come after it, ancient Greece was also marked by social, political, and class-based strife, as certain sectors of society were afforded liberties and privileges not enjoyed by others. This section will explore this era of innovative growth and inherent inequality. It will examine the legal and justice systems and their relationship to economic privilege and power. The reader will be introduced to the rights of citizenship, the formation and re-formation of the Athenian constitution, and the role of slavery on justice-based outcomes.

Society and Class

Many of the class struggles that influenced the justice system of Greek antiquity were brought on by the creation of citizenship and the status afforded to such individuals (Ober 1991). Citizenship became a key identifier in Greek culture, one that defined social and political standing and privilege. In contrast, those who did not meet the criteria of citizenship were perceived to be *others*, or outsiders of lesser status (Padgug 1975). Unfortunately, the classification of the other generated a great deal of animosity between the haves and the have-nots of ancient Greek society. These tensions mounted, manifesting in stratified disadvantage and various forms of violence in the Greek *polis* or city-state of Athens.[1]

Although citizenship was a contentious issue that facilitated social strife, it was a fundamental aspect of Greek life, ensuring community allegiance to the polis. While citizens enjoyed numerous rights and benefits, they also bore a number of responsibilities. Greek citizens were expected, for example, to place a greater emphasis on collective duty than individual goals (Gorman 1992). In other words, although the polis provided for every citizen, every citizen was expected to provide for the polis. A failure on either side to fulfill this fundamental expectation would have detrimental outcomes for the malefactor; this repercussive obligation extended to all citizens, including the elitist representatives of the polis. According to Sophocles, rulers were not permitted to abuse their power and were obligated to serve the interests of those they ruled (Saunders 1917). If they ignored this fundamental tenet, they were subject to "ultimate punishment," the same as any other lawbreaker (Gorman 1992).

The meaning and impacts of citizenship extended beyond social stratification and obligations, influencing such factors as migration and military strategies. The Peloponnesian War, a war of domination fought between Athens and Sparta, was significantly informed by the interpretation of citizenship. Athens and other city-states needed to ready their armies for war, and this included increasing their numbers of soldiers (Gorman 1992).[2] Out of military necessity, the city-states modified their definitions of citizenship, relaxing the criteria, opening their doors to migrants, and thus increasing the pool of eligible fighters.

Although changing citizenship criteria may have met military needs, it facilitated further social strife. The natural growth of Athens paired with new standards of citizenship led to an influx of migrants. While migrants could reside in Athens, they were disadvantaged in a number of ways, including the inability to own land or participate in politics (Ober 1991). Recognizing the socioeconomic inequity of these rules and restrictions, outsiders began demanding a say in the city's politics and justice system (Gorman 1992). As a result, the citizens of Athens found themselves in a quandary; they did not have any desire to share their lands with people of different ancestry, but outsiders brought economic benefits, including increased connections and trade with foreign lands. The result was tenuous; migrants were permitted to reside in Athens and enjoy the benefits of the polis, but they were denied the full rights bestowed on those citizens born of the city.

Courts, Laws, and Politics

Greek antiquity is lauded for providing a foundation upon which contemporary Western court systems are structured. Greek courts were influenced, in large part, by the words and deeds of two key lawmakers: Draco and Solon (Nold, Massingale, & Hodwitz 2022). Draco is credited with drafting the original Greek constitution, while Solon revised the constitution to better meet the needs of the people (Allen 1997). Draco's original draft was considered quite severe, as he stipulated that even those guilty of small infractions deserved the death penalty (Rhodes 1984).[3] In addition to being excessively punitive, Draco's constitution also allowed for harsher penalties directed toward the lower class, while also protecting the social and political elite (Lambert 2021). Considering these concerns, the Draconian constitution was dissolved with the expectation that a new one would be crafted that prioritized a more equitable approach. Solon was identified as a favorable choice to revise the constitution; he was neither in debt, nor did others owe him debt, suggesting that he might be free from bias (Rhodes 1984). Solon's revisions were considered a significant improvement, offering more equitable punishments and restoring citizens' faith and trust in the government. In addition, Solon had a notable impact on the protections and rights afforded to those who suffered slavery or debt.

Slavery was a common theme in ancient Greece. Slaves were a cornerstone of early Greek society, forming the lowest rank in the social hierarchy, stripped of many of the rights afforded to free citizens (Padgug 1975; Allen 2003). Slaves were seen as a necessity but also a threat, having the potential to weaken the state should they ever be granted citizenship (Ober 1991). Therefore, active slaves were denied legal protections, including testifying before the assembly, although they could be forced to take part in legal proceedings if their master so commanded it through force (torture was believed to be the only way to elicit the truth from slaves) [Lambert 2021].[4] As for former slaves, they were denied political office, the common belief being that they harbored hatred toward their former master and, therefore, could not be trusted (Padgug 1975; Ober 1991). During the reign of the Draconian constitution, many debtors were enslaved, either to be employed locally or shipped abroad (Allen 2003). Given the sheer prevalence of debt in Athenian society, this exacerbated the burgeoning class of the disenfranchised and legally disempowered. This changed, however, with the Solonian constitution. In relation to slavery, Solon decreed that it was illegal for a citizen's freedom to be lost, thrust into servitude to another (D'Amico 2010). In addition, he abolished all debts, thus interrupting the debtor pipeline to slavery (Rhodes 1984).[5]

While Draco and Solon had a notable impact on social stratification and rights, they also informed the structure and practices of the Grecian courts. Built upon the Draconian and Solonian legislative vision, Athens had a formal court system as early as the fifth century BCE (Lambert 2021). Court proceedings were overseen by a large jury, typically consisting of between 201 and 501 citizens, which were selected by means of a lottery (Lanni 1970). Courts, which typically heard two types of cases, including *dike*, or private, cases and *graphe*, or public, cases, consisted of three different systems (Nold, Massingale, & Hodwitz 2022; Lambert 2021). The *dikasterai* were the popular courts, handling all complaints that did not involve charges of slaying or physical harm (Lanni 1970).[6] The rules of the popular courts were loose by today's standards, allowing unconfirmed and potentially irrelevant statements such as hearsay and questions of character. The second type of court addressed all charges relating to murder or physical injury. Stricter than the dikasterai, these courts had higher standards for admissible evidence, allowing only those statements relevant to the case at hand (Lambert 2021). The third type of court was the maritime court, which focused exclusively on commerce, traders who did not possess Athenian citizenship, and written contracts (Bers & Lanni 2003; Lambert 2021).

Punishments doled out by the various court systems demonstrated notable class-based inequities. One possible sentence included financial restitution, and while the fine amount might remain consistent across defendants, the impacts of such fines could have notable differences depending on the defendant's economic standing (Allen 1997). In addition, filing private claims was often paired with a series of court fees, making such a proceeding difficult, if not impossible for those of lower means (Lambert 2021). Lastly, a court hearing that received less than one-fifth of the jury votes would result in a large fine for the plaintiff (in addition to any fine produced through sentencing), likely further discouraging the destitute from filing claims (Lambert 2021).[7] Therefore, although court proceedings were available to all classes (excluding slaves), the impoverished suffered greater consequences by taking part in such proceedings.

In summary, the ancient Greeks established a foundation upon which the civilizations that followed them could build their own systems. Unfortunately, this foundation included many of the biases that we see in contemporary times (Bers & Lanni 2003).

Even a cursory view of ancient Greece's institutions, including the criminal justice system, reveals advantages for select sectors of society (Ober 1991). Citizenship and economic class played a key role in rights and privileges, ensuring that those of lesser means and with outsider status faced an inherent disadvantage. Whether it was through debt-based slavery, severe punishments, an inability to partake in legal proceedings, inequitable fine structures, or the denial of political representation, Athenian culture clearly demarcated the haves and the have-nots, penalizing the latter while rewarding the former.

ANCIENT ROME, SOCIETY, AND LEGAL STATUTES

In modern times, encyclopedic law books and databases ensure that statutes and legal practices are readily available and accessible to all. However, these resources were scant or nonexistent in early human civilizations, only appearing fully fledged in ancient Rome. The Roman citizenry had an avid interest in consolidating legal knowledge, wanting to make it consistent and available to all parties, thus creating both the need and the demand for codification (Berkeley Law 2019). Therefore, the Romans created the Law of the Twelve Tables and facilitated the Justinian Code, both of which took unprecedented steps in unifying legal writings into accessible collections (Harries 2022). This section will explore the codification of these legal statutes, noting both the benefits and the costs of such a process. However, we would be remiss to begin these discussions without an overview of the role of class and inequalities in the Roman Empire, particularly in relation to Roman laws and rights. Although ancient Rome was a place of legislative growth, it was also a site of extreme economic and social disparities, riddled with slavery, severe punishments, and inherent inequalities, and this is evident in the formation of the legislative decree (Mark 2022; Womack 2017).

Roman Society

The significance of social class in ancient Rome cannot be overstated; daily life, political freedoms, and legal privileges were integrally informed by one's social status. There were two major class groups in ancient Rome, including the *patricians* and the *plebeians*. The patricians consisted of aristocrats and socialites—a status bestowed by birth (Saladin 2017). The plebeians, on the other hand, included all other citizens who did not have the good fortune to be born a patrician. Mark (2022) contends that contemporary understanding of Roman social structure is overly simplistic, noting that belonging to one class or the other did not necessarily dictate power and prestige, particularly in the later years of Roman civilization. While patricians were often thought of as wealthy and influential, their status was granted by birth rather than merit, and they retained the patrician title even if previous generations had lost or squandered their fortunes (Saladin 2017). Conversely, plebeians were able to own land and hold many respectable jobs without ever fully recognizing the benefits enjoyed by patricians. Therefore, although status was a fundamental part of Roman identity, it was nuanced in meaning and presentation.

Although the plebeian/patrician dichotomy is commonly adopted by historians, some authors suggest that Roman society consisted of additional smaller groups. Mark (2022), for example, suggests that Roman society consisted of five groups, with the patricians at the top of the social hierarchy and the slaves at the bottom.[8] Regardless of the ordering and number of groups, slavery was common in ancient Rome; modern calculations indicate that approximately 40 percent of the Roman population was enslaved in some manner (Womack 2017). The responsibilities of the enslaved varied greatly, defined in part by gender, how able-bodied the slave was, and the good spirit of the master. Female slaves were expected to help masters bathe, dress, and shop while male slaves spent their times as butlers, bodyguards, and children's tutors. The less-fortunate were assigned to work in the silver mines, forced to work ten-hour days while breathing dangerous dust under the constant threat of fatal cave-ins (Mark 2022). In addition, all slaves, regardless of role, were tasked with the responsibility of keeping their masters safe. Ancient Rome, after all, was a dangerous place, with rampant crime, and slaves were often required to act as a physical protective barrier in public spaces so that, in the event of an attack, they would bear the brunt while their master remained unscathed (Womack 2017).

Thus, the slaves of ancient Rome lived a life of suffering, providing potential grounds for revolt. The Romans, who feared such an uprising, went to great lengths to quash dissension, particularly attempts to escape. If a slave escaped, the Romans would execute any remaining slaves who were tied to the escapee, thus incentivizing the enslaved to work to prevent further escapes. These brutal tactics worked in some respects, but they did not completely thwart all rebellious actions.[9] Despite occasional upheavals, the enslaved remained mired in inhumane and degrading circumstances.

Roman Law   -

As summarized above, ancient Rome suffered from extreme social stratification. This stratification was exacerbated by the abuse of legal statutes, particularly prior to codification, when their meaning and interpretation enjoyed a level of flexibility (Czech-Jezierska 2021; Berkeley Law 2019). The ruling class used Roman law somewhat spontaneously and to their benefit, further disadvantaging the lower classes, who were unaware of the statutes and legal conscriptions of the era. The abuse of legal decrees led to strife and eventual revolt by the plebeians (Saladin 2019). One particularly effective means of protest was a refusal to serve in the military, which was largely comprised of plebeian fighters (Mark 2022). In response to a plebeian revolt, a ten-person committee known as the *decemvirs* was convened to create the first-ever compilation of Roman law (Elmore 1922). First established in 451 BCE, the Law of the Twelve Tables was formalized, codified, and instituted two years later (Berkeley Law 2019).[10] [11] Although there are reports that the decemvirs committee eventually became tyrannical, the laws themselves were received warmly by the Roman people (Harries 2022).

Codified law eliminated some of the strife that had plagued the Roman Empire in the early years. Codification ensured some level of consistency and accountability in the application of the law and facilitated plebeian access to and understanding of Roman statutes. However, codification did not ensure that the laws were just; class-based privilege remained entombed in the legal statutes. For example, if senators committed a crime, they were handled by the Senate and not a standard jury, virtually guaranteeing lighter punishments for these members of the upper class (Czech-Jezierska 2021). In addition, Roman law contained restrictions on marriages between class-defined groups (Nold, Massingale, & Hodwitz 2022). Of particular note, Roman law specified that death sentences for select offenses might not apply to the powerful; while lower-class criminals could face execution, those from more privileged backgrounds might face exile or deportation instead (Czech-Jezierska 2021).[12] Although the actual Tables were destroyed by Celtic invaders in the fourth century BCE and much of their content remains unknown, their authority has lived on through the influence of the great Roman orators and lawmakers who eventually inspired Emperor Justinian I to create his influential Code (Berkeley Law 2019).

Justinian I was the ruler of the Roman Byzantine Empire from 527 to 565 CE. He is commonly known for Justinian's Code, a four-part compilation that altered Roman law considerably (Berkeley Law 2019). Until the era of Justinian, the empire's legal structure was scattered, in text, region, and practice. Recognizing the error in such a piecemeal approach, particularly in regard to the fair and equitable application of the law (class-based discrepancies remained an issue), Justinian sought to consolidate legislative decrees and practices into a single document, thus standardizing the law and making it further accessible. The resulting Justinian collection consisted of four pieces: *The Digesta*, *The Codex*, *The Institutiones*, and *The Novellae*.

The Digesta, a collection and summary of writings on law and justice, was published first, accessible to the public in 533 CE. Prior to its release, access to legal writings was generally class-based; those of lesser status were ignorant of legal rights and rules, while those with power were informed of such writings (Harries 2022). Published in 534 CE, the Codex outlined the actual laws of the empire, including references to imperial constitutions, legislation, and pronouncements (Berkeley Law 2019). The Institutiones, which was published in 535 CE, was intended as a summary of the Digest, mainly for reference by students of Roman law (Harries 2022). The Novellae was published in 556 CE, as an afterthought. It was not part of the original Code, but was instead added later by legal scholars; it summarized the Justinian constitution and added laws recently enacted (Berkeley Law 2019).[13]

In summary, the time of the Roman Empire was an important period in legislative advancement, set against the backdrop of the social stratification defined by economic and political power. Class-based differences were exacerbated by the lack of accessible and codified law, as those in positions of power used the legal system to their advantage. This led to social unrest and revolt, thus leaving legislators and the ruling class with little option but to accommodate plebeian demands. Over the span of the next millennium, the Romans embarked on several acts of codification, each making Roman law more accessible, consistent, and inflexible. Despite the changes, however, inherent inequalities continued, ingrained in the laws themselves.

Appius Claudius and the Decemvirs: A Case Study in Class and Social Power in Ancient Rome

Before leaving ancient Rome behind and transitioning into the Middle Ages, we would like to draw the reader's attention to a case study that illustrates some of the social and political strife referenced previously. The case of Appius Claudius is but a moment in history, but it offers a narrative that captures the patrician abuse of power for the purpose of quelching plebeian rights and privileges, thus furthering class division. The details of this story are courtesy of Nitschke (2009).

As described above, ancient Rome could be a cruel place, filled with class bias and government corruption. In the fifth century BCE, a man named Appius Claudius became an unlikely leader in the battle against tyranny. The Romans knew Appius as an arrogant man from a noble family. During his time in the military, he was rumored to execute his own soldiers to achieve order among the ranks of his troops. Historically, Appius had been on the side of the patricians in any dispute against the plebeians, causing animosity to bloom among the plebeians. The general attitude toward Appius began to shift when he seemingly embraced a new persona that was entirely more palatable to the average Roman. He became a friend of the people and regularly went out of his way to please them, even seeming to advocate for their rights.

Although it appeared that Appius had had a change of heart toward the plebeians, he was actually secretly building his political power and ensuring his spot as the leader of the decemvirs. Once his position as the leader of the powerful group was cemented, Appius revealed his true intentions. He held private meetings with his decemvirate allies, during which time they plotted ways to increase their own power. They ran a government-by-force through intimidation and sanctioned assassinations until the plebeian people were unable to stand it any longer. The lower class incited a rebellion, and the plebeians took back their government with military force. Appius's story ended shortly after this rebellion. Some say Appius took his own life, while others believe he was killed as punishment by the plebeians.[14] The grasp for power that was the decemvirate died with Appius. Rome returned to a government arrangement very much like the one it had previously held.

THE MIDDLE AGES, FEUDALISM, AND PUNISHMENTS

The Middle Ages, which spanned more than a millennium, is generally believed to have begun around 450 CE and ended around 1500 CE (Bogan & Conrad 2022). Much of this period relied on the infamous feudal system, thus creating an era that was driven in large part by economic and political distinction and status. In addition, religion ruled supreme, adding another layer of power that defined privilege and social standing (Hilton 1958). Similar to previous eras, this institutionalized social stratification found its way into the criminal justice system, influencing designations of deviance, criminal trials, and subsequent sentences. These proceedings invariably benefited the noble class and the religious leaders, while the lower classes and the less powerful bore the full brunt of the punitive system (Rousseaux 1997).

This section will explore the various dynamics of the Middle Ages, beginning with an examination of the feudal system and its many components. The feudal system permeated all aspects of life in the Middle Ages, and thus, it is an integral part of understanding this period. The chapter will then examine the criminal justice system with an explicit focus on punitive outcomes. Trials and punishments are areas that were particularly stratified in interpretation and execution; during medieval times, this included both class-based and geopolitical distinctions.

Society in the Middle Ages

Social classes in the Middle Ages were determined by the feudal system, which consisted of several key categories, including royals, nobles, knights, and peasants/serfs (Chaucer 2007; Ganshof 1952). The feudal system was relatively definitive; there was little mobility between strata and status, and roles were clearly defined by a hierarchy (Harris & Zucker 2013). The ruling class sat atop the hierarchy, followed by the nobles, who served as the vassals of the ruling class, then the knights who ruled the serfs on their land as the anemone rules the clownfish. The oppressive yet symbiotic relationship between the knights and the serfs provided shelter and protection to the peasant class while increasing the wealth and power of the knights (National Archives 2000). Members of the clergy were also present, but they occupied their own class, which was both integral to and distinct from the caste system (Chaucer 2007). The caste system was complex, influencing rules, roles, and expectations.

The royal class, seated at the top of the hierarchy, was responsible for making rules and laws, giving orders, and reaping the benefits of the productivity and progress of their jurisdiction (Chaucer 2007). As sovereign powers grew in various parts of Europe, rulers centralized institutional matters, including the criminal justice system, bringing it under royal jurisdiction (Ganshof 1952). By these acts, sovereigns gained the power to control matters that had historically remained locally determined, asserting their influence in any number of ways, including in the definition of and consequences for engaging in deviance (Rousseaux 1997).

One practice that became commonplace between the fifteenth and seventeenth centuries involved relieving an offender of their charges, an act that became known as a royal pardon (Verreycken 2019). The royal pardon was one of royalty's more prominent political tools, used to assert the sovereigns' right over the lives and deaths of their subjects (Coyle 1958; Verreycken 2019).[15] Pardons not only demonstrated power, but they also had the potential for corruption (Verreycken 2019). To receive a letter of pardon, a petition was submitted by the delinquent to the monarch stating the nature of the crime and the circumstances warranting a pardon. In the case that an individual was incarcerated and unable to submit a petition of their own, relatives were permitted to submit one in their stead. The applicant was required to cover the chancery fees related to the application and could even be forced to pay a fee to the royal trust, which made the practice inaccessible to many offenders in the peasant class. Thus, the pardon process offered benefits to those of higher status, both as offenders and as royal recipients of fees.

Second only to the royals in the feudal system were the nobles, who, by the standards of the Middle Ages, lived lives of relative luxury. They wore colorful clothing and ate the best foods, often provided by those who could not afford such luxuries (Chaucer 2007). In addition, the nobility often served as representatives for the royals in local matters (Ganshof 1952). The laws were generally executed by nobles, and they had the ability to mold justice to meet their own desires (Rousseaux 1997). Take, for example, the case of a common man who was threatened by a member of a noblewoman's retainer or personal staff (Cohen 1983). The man asked for an *asseurement* to protect himself from harm at the hands of the noblewoman's staff.[16] Unfortunately for the man, the noblewoman's house oversaw justice in the jurisdiction, and his request was entirely rebuffed. Shortly after, the man was attacked by a group that included one of the lady's sons and the retainer who had made the original threat.

Next in line to the nobles were the knights; this class served nobles in exchange for land. Although laws changed considerably during the Middle Ages as the Church and the Crown vied for hierarchical control, for large periods of time when the Church gained a foothold, the knights were believed to be the only one group granted social sanction to commit violence (Cohen 1983). Rules informed by Christian piety became the norm and the Church did not tolerate violence unless it followed the extensive conditions applied to knighthood (Carrel 2009).[17] Thus, even this class enjoyed some legal protections not granted to the lowest caste.

In comparison to the other classes, peasants and the serfs of the Middle Ages had difficult lives (Bisson 1994). They did not own property; they simply worked the land for the nobles and the knights, thus ensuring they were politically and socially immobilized. Consequently, landowners would abuse their serfs, overworking them, assaulting them, and depriving them of staples. However, serfs were not entirely powerless, occasionally protesting the ill treatment in a manner designed to temper further abuse (Vardi 2001). The serfs would, for example, carry out their tasks with minimal effort, steal crops meant for their abusive lord, or flee from their homes to escape cruelty (National Archives 2000). When serfs took these actions, lords were known to offer concessions to prevent further strife. The peasants tended to accept these concessions as they had limited alternative options; in addition, serfs were granted protection by their knights or nobles, a necessity for survival in the Middle Ages (National Archives 2000).[18] Although these concessions were generally accepted, they did not placate the lower caste in every instance, and peasants' rebellions did become violent on occasion (Cohn 1999). A German resistance in May 1358 bore witness to a three-week rampage in which peasants burned manor houses and attacked the nobility (Gale Research 2014).[19] Along similar lines, the Great Rising of 1381 in England was sparked by a new tax system that benefited the military at the expense of the impoverished (Vardi 2001). The revolt quickly escalated from a simple refusal to pay taxes to widespread violence against nobles.[20]

Thus, the Middle Ages was as stratified, if not more so, than the eras that preceded it. Those in the upper castes enjoyed legal and political privileges, while those in the lower caste suffered at the hands of the powerful, leading to centuries of disputes and violence. The dynamic between royalty, nobility, knights, and peasants was informed by a fifth player, that of the Church. During key points in medieval history, the Church acquired ruling status, either usurping the Crown or working in collaboration with the ruling class (Rousseaux 1997). During these periods, religious personnel such as the clergy were tasked with determining social and political expectations and maintaining peace among the people. Unfortunately, the clergy were no more loved by the lower caste than the royalty and the nobility had been. While the clergy were responsible for assisting the poor and providing sanctuary to those in need, they were often despised as avaricious and devoid of compassion in their roles as landlords (Hilton 1958).[21]

The personal characteristics of the clergy might have drawn some derision, but so, too, did their protected status when it came to issues of justice and accountability. Specifically, members of the clergy were known to receive lighter punishments than commoners who were guilty of similar offenses (McGlynn 2008). Consider, for example, the story of Richard Fayrcock (a commoner) and Martin Budde (a cleric). Both were found guilty of premeditated murder and sentenced to the gallows. While Fayrcock's sentence was upheld, Budde's case was transferred to the ecclesiastical courts, where, it can be assumed, he received a much lighter treatment.

In summary, medieval Europe was deeply stratified, divided by a caste system that placed royalty at the top and serfs and peasants at the bottom. Those in positions of power made the laws, those in the middle carried them out while enjoying the protection of their position, and those at the bottom bore the brunt of them. This hierarchy was not immune to chafing, however, leading to brief moments of angst and uprising. In and among these dynamics sat the Church, a figurehead that sometimes collaborated and sometimes competed with royalty for the rulership of the people. Somewhat autonomous from the caste system, the Church also enjoyed the privileges bestowed on the upper caste: defining laws, executing punishments, and benefiting from a protected status. Before departing this era, however, a closer look at medieval trials and punishments illustrates a further division, one between rural and urban interests, defined by both geopolitical and class-based considerations.

Medieval Trials and Punishments

Much like those of modern courts, the structure and practices of European criminal justice systems varied from place to place during the Middle Ages (Dean 2014). Various countries and localities implemented their own rules to best meet their unique cultural standards of justice (McGlynn 2008). In addition, rural communities generally only used the formal justice system as a last resort, preferring to avoid handing unnecessary control to sovereigns, who tended to embrace a different version of justice (Rousseaux 1997). Despite the variance across region and overseer, many of these systems, whether urban or rural, could be severe, prioritizing painful measures, including torture, immolation, and deprivation (McGlynn 2008).

As summarized previously, the more severe punitive measures were doled out more frequently to the lower caste of peasants and serfs. However, as the Middle Ages progressed, there were sporadic attempts to instill a more equitable distribution of justice. England spearheaded such an agenda (Carrel 2009). English urban centers were governed with the purported goal of facilitating peaceful existence between the people living in confined areas, and emphasis was placed on addressing crime fairly, independent of class or status. Even with this focus, there were differences in the ways in which select people were treated by the legal system, largely due to interference by the upper class (Dean 2014). For example, striking the mayor, a member of the ruling class, drew a significantly more severe punishment than an average assault case, which called for the offender to lose the arm or leg with which the assault was committed (Carrel 2009).[22] On occasion, commoners would push back on these inequalities. There are known cases of public punishment during which offenders received support from the crowds rather than the barrage of rotten fruit as had been intended (Carrel 2009).[23]

Despite efforts to level the class-based playing field, disparities continued. English laws created at the turn of the sixteenth century criminalizing homelessness were the pinnacle of such inequities (Carrel 2009). These laws sentenced all vagabonds to three days and three nights in the stocks with minimal amounts of bread and water. Individuals showing mercy toward the destitute by providing additional food or drinks were also punished, usually with a monetary fine. Thus, despite the purported attempts to diminish legal inequities, English practices reinforced the differential treatment of the impoverished and the powerless.

THE RENAISSANCE AND INSTITUTIONAL INEQUITIES

The word *Renaissance* refers to rebirth, and this is an apt name for the period following the Middle Ages. This was a time of progress and prosperity in Europe, marked by advancements in art, science, and politics. Mention of the Renaissance, therefore, brings forth images of health, well-being, and harmony. The idyllic nature of these images, however, is marred by the reality of daily life for large sectors of society, particularly those from the lower classes, who faced new discriminations and punishments for their lack of financial standing.[24] Historians report that those in positions of power and privilege adopted a common narrative, the belief that actions taken by members of the lower class were done so as a deliberate affront to society (Brackett 2002). As a testament to this narrative, artist Leonardo da Vinci once wrote that his ideal city would be parted into "upper and lower realms," which would allow the rich to live separately from the poor (Brackett 2002). Thus, the Renaissance would not stray far from the norms of previous eras; it tells a similar story, informed by power, status, and inequities that permeated various institutions, including the criminal justice system. This section will provide a brief snapshot of these dynamics in key European locations, including Venice, Florence, and England, each illustrating a different aspect of class relations within the criminal justice system.

Social Structure

Social structure and opportunity during the Renaissance were heavily informed by class-based considerations, including employment and choice of profession, economic standing, and residential stability. Regarding employment and choice of profession, life was controlled by guild status (Wolfgang 1990). There was a guild for most professions, and membership in a guild ensured voting power and public sway. To be without a profession, particularly one of note, severely curtailed a citizen's access to the political process.

As for economic standing, poverty was often considered a sign of infamy, thus serving to restrict opportunities that were otherwise enjoyed by those with financial means. These included select legal proceedings, such as serving as a witness in court.[25] Stern (2004) wrote that in Venice, the poor were barred from this function, "for poverty itself identified a person of lower trustworthiness and of greater suspicion" (223).

Regarding residential stability, Florence provides a ready example of the class-informed social landscape surrounding location and housing during the Renaissance, particularly in the late sixteenth and early seventeenth centuries (Brackett 2002). During this period, the city was essentially divided into two clearly defined sectors: a prosperous upper realm inhabited by the economic and social elite and a seedy lower realm that was sponsored, in part, by crime and marked by poor hygiene, cramped conditions, and outbreaks of disease.[26] The number of homeless Florentines grew to such extreme heights that, by the end of the first quarter of the seventeenth century, society had to enact a then-new solution to the increasing problem: the creation of workhouses. These were not necessarily intended to improve the plight of the impoverished, but instead to hide the homeless from those who took offense to their presence. Poverty was increasingly associated with sin in the minds of the "decent" citizens of Florence, and the presence of impoverished individuals was viewed as a stain on Florentine honor.[27]

Criminal Justice

Class privilege, particularly regarding the criminal justice system, is notable in key cities such as Venice, Italy. Venetian nobles, who staffed and maintained the local justice system, tended to behave as if the criminal law did not apply to them (Engels 1981). That was in large part because, simply put, it rarely did. The Venetian court system grew alongside the hereditary oligarchy that made up large swathes of the Venetian government (Stern 2004). The result was a justice system staffed and run entirely by members of the upper class, many of whom were known to behave quite poorly, often violently assaulting the police who attempted to hold them legally accountable (Stern 2004).

The Council of Forty, a group of nobles with little or no legal training, provides an informative example of Venetian privilege in action. This group was tasked with settling cases of alleged violent crime in the city (Ruggiero 1978). All that was required to determine both the verdict and the sentence of the accused was a simple majority (Ruggiero 1978). Unchecked discretion paired with a lack of training virtually ensured an emotive component in each decision, tempered with personal agendas and allegiances. According to Ruggiero (1978), "'Innocent until proven guilty' was too limiting a distinction to apply to Venice's fluid jurisprudence" (245).

Unlike the courts of Venice, Florentine courts utilized *ius commune* laws, going to great lengths to avoid corruption in the application of the criminal justice system (Stern 2004).[28] Judges did not have the wide discretion seen in Venetian courts, as Florentine law prescribed set sentences for specific crimes (Wolfgang 1990). According to Stern (2004), the following steps were taken in an attempt to prevent corruption:

• Most members of the criminal justice system were foreign-born, ensuring they had limited to no ties to any of the active factions in Florence,
• Officials were only permitted to hold their posts for six months, thus reducing the likelihood that they would be compromised or become corrupt, and
• Members of the same family or consortium were prohibited from holding office consecutively or concurrently.

Unfortunately, these safeguards were relaxed in the early fifteenth century, then replaced entirely by a system similar to Venice (Stern 2004).

England provides another example of the stark relationship between class and the criminal justice system during the Renaissance, one that differs considerably from Venice and Florence and relates to punishment more so than to determinations of guilt. Specifically, England's practices of incarceration, or the use of debtors' prisons, are particularly notable. English debtors' prisons are often idealized, cast as places of order and compassion; however, some historians disagree with this picture, pointing out that the debtor, a person of little means, was often mistreated at the hands of prison personnel. Woodfine (2006) provides the example of King's Bench prison in the early 1740s, where officials were known for misusing their authority. Among other abuses, records show that debtors were forced to stay several days past their intended release dates, they were frequently verbally abused, and they were denied access to vendors, who brought important items such as food and milk. Early prison records provide the most damning pieces of evidence, showing that large donations intended for the welfare of the incarcerated were diverted into the pockets of prison administrators. These funds were vital to the incarcerated, as the length of their stay often depended entirely upon their ability to repay their debts.[29]

In summary, although the Renaissance is often perceived to be a period of progress and good fortune, it continued the trend of previous eras. Those with lesser means were treated poorly by those in positions of power, particularly by the criminal justice system in key European centers. Whether it was at the hands of the Venetian oligarchs, the eventual demise of more just approaches in Florence, or the illegal and abusive activities of prison wardens in English prisons, those relegated to the bottom of the social and economic hierarchy were subjected to institutional injustices.

EARLY MODERNITY AND THE SCIENTIFIC REVOLUTION

Early modernity and the Scientific Revolution, as the name suggests, is a period marked by development and advancement, particularly in the sciences. Beginning in the Renaissance, with Nicolaus Copernicus's groundbreaking assertion that the earth revolved around the sun, it continued for several hundred years and expanded to all manner of knowledge, from the study of plant genetics through to the study of human behavior and motivation. Inquiry, exploration, and empiricism became central to understanding the world and its various inhabitants, and the relationship between class, power, and deviance was no exception to this trend. Before delving into this relationship, however, there are several other notable characteristics from this period that are necessary to emphasize, including increasing diversity, urbanization, and industrialization.

Social diversity compounded during early modernity and the Scientific Revolution as people from different backgrounds moved and mingled, causing religion, politics, and other cultural conceptions to blend into countless, ever-increasing combinations (Härter 2017). The blurring of group identity, however, was not necessarily endorsed by those in positions of power, given that it could potentially challenge the status quo. As such, many of the newly created combinations were deemed deviant, leading to criminal designations for religious or political dissenters as well as anyone else who was declared a threat to the state.

As social diversity was increasing, so, too, were demographic characteristics of the Western world. Urban centers transitioned wildly during the early modern ages as populations skyrocketed. Over the span of four hundred years, the European population climbed from sixty million to two hundred million, and urbanization doubled (DuPlessis 2019).[30] Meanwhile, production was increasing dramatically, and industries were spreading to new areas. Consequently, large portions of the population abandoned their agricultural lifestyles, turning to jobs in the manufacturing field. In addition, as seafaring technologies improved, the exportation of goods became cheaper. These shifts caused the center of the European economy to move away from the Mediterranean and toward the northwest of the continent, where new English factories (as well as those in nearby countries) drove profit and change (DuPlessis 2019). Thus, change was afoot in a number of ways, both inside and outside the scientific arena, including in relation to population composition and structure.

Western Europe's Transition to Capitalism

Capitalism, according to some, was born during the early modern age, although its tendrils can be traced back to earlier eras (Durrant & Ward 2012). Marked primarily by the private control of production for the purposes of profit, the Western shift to capitalism in early modernity had a notable impact on class-based privilege and power. It influenced the meaning and presentation of deviance, which was integrally tied to legal and justice institutions and proceedings.

The Western transition to a capitalist system had a notable impact on deviance and social responses to deviance. As capitalism further solidified the economic power of the ruling class, there was a transition in crime trends, a shift from violent crimes to property crimes that was likely informed by the growing needs of the lower class (Breen 2011). In addition, according to some authors, the criminal justice system was used in such a way as to reinforce capitalist goals (Vermeesch 2015). Select behaviors that threatened private ownership and profit were criminalized and readily enforced. This is perhaps best illustrated by the creation of alternative economies and the political and legal responses to such economies.

What does one do when shut out of the traditional means of production? As is evident in eighteenth-century Europe, the answer is to become involved in alternative economies (Van den Huevel 2015). Alternative economies supported the lower classes and included any means of generating income, including begging and other jobs that did not require special skills. These economies were particularly rife with *ambulant trading*; that is, the trading of goods by those who lacked a permanent shop or location, opting instead for mobility. Mobile businesses served multiple purposes, including providing income for those who might not have been able to find it otherwise and providing access to goods at prices the impoverished were more likely to be able to afford. Unfortunately, lawmakers took an active dislike to ambulant trading, viewing it as a threat to the capitalist structure, and they passed several statutes banning this method of trade. These laws were readily enforced by community police and members of local guilds.

While the response to alternative economies illustrates that behaviors that threatened the capitalist system were not tolerated by those in positions of power, there are additional measures during this period that further demonstrate the stance of the ruling class toward the lower classes, particularly in relation to access to justice proceedings. The courts, for example, were managed in such a way as to minimize access for the common folk. In many otherwise-English-speaking jurisdictions, court procedures were held in an old French tongue that was largely unknown to the lower classes. In addition, pursuing a case was notoriously expensive, therefore excluding those who could not afford to pay.[31] Lastly, the process was unnecessarily complex and drawn-out.[32] As a result, there was a long decline in the number of cases filed in these courts that began in the sixteenth and ended in the eighteenth century. Thus, the effects of capitalism on social structure were varied, influencing not only the meaning of deviance, but also that of criminal proceedings.

Early Criminology

Although criminological theories had existed for millennia, the study of crime became formalized and systematic during the Scientific Revolution. Influenced by the evolutionary ideas of Charles Darwin and the phrenological study of the skull and behavior, Cesare Lombroso is often credited with being the father of criminology (Bergman 2005). Ellwood's amorous 1912 review of Lombroso's work provides a sufficient overview of the criminal anthropologist's teaching: "Lombroso believed . . . that the criminal was essentially an organic anomaly, partly pathological and partly atavistic. The social causes of crime were at most, according to Lombroso, simply the stimuli which called forth the organic and physical abnormalities of the individual" (Ellwood 1912, 717). In short form, Lombroso embraced the idea that criminals were atavists, or evolutionary throwbacks, devolved both morally and physically, and this devolution could be observed empirically, through stigmata (physical abnormalities) and deviant behavior. Those who were born atavistic would ultimately become criminals, regardless of upbringing. On the other hand, those who were not atavistic would rarely engage in offending, and if so, generally only in specific types of crime. This latter category of people could be influenced by external forces, such as socialization and opportunity.[33]

Although Lombroso claimed his theories had nothing to do with class or race, the utilization of biological determinism has subsequently resulted in disproportionate impacts on, and discrimination against, the lower classes, as well as ethnic, racial, and religious minorities (Sian 2017). Lombroso perpetuated the historical trend of punishing those of a lower social status for being poor. For example, the characteristics used to build Lombroso's archetype of the "born criminal" were largely based on physical consequences of malnutrition and poverty, like sunken eyes and cheeks or stunted growth (Mazzarello 2011). In addition, Lombroso's theories have informed policies and practices, including those underlying the Jewish Holocaust, American eugenics, and more recently, the surveillance of Muslim populations post-9/11 (Sian 2017; Monaco & Mula 2011). Thus, Lombroso followed in the footsteps of those who came before him by creating narratives of offending that ultimately further marginalized disadvantaged communities.

Lasting Effects

In summary, the criminal justice system as we know it today was born of early modernity and the Scientific Revolution. While capitalism shifted the meaning of (and institutional responses to) deviance, empiricism gave root to new and impactful theories of crime. The different facets of this era are evident today in laws directed toward vagrancy and unlicensed commerce, as well as the cost and accessibility of criminal proceedings. They are also evident in the continued reliance on explanations of crime focused on physiological processes, often disregarding the role of class and privilege.

MODERNITY AND MARXIST CRIMINOLOGY

As we move into contemporary times, any synopsis of the intersections between class and the criminal justice system would not be complete without a brief discussion of the ideas and influence of Karl Marx.[34] Perhaps one of the most outspoken critics of class-based division and social stratification, Marx had a notable influence on modern perceptions of the relationship between economic power and institutional privilege, including in relation to criminal behavior and justice-based responses. Although there is some disagreement about Marx's explicit contributions to the criminological discipline, few would disagree that he offered, at a minimum, an implicit refinement of criminological understanding of the intersection between class, power, and deviance.

Karl Marx

Karl Marx was a Prussian-born philosopher who lived between 1818 and 1883 (Ritchie, Hodwitz, & Karst 2022). He is well-known for his ideas on class, proclaiming in his *Communist Manifesto* that "the history of all hitherto existing society is the history of class struggles" (Engels 1981, 16). There are many writers who assert that there is no true Marxian criminology, as the ideas were not specifically proposed by Marx himself. Others, such as Greenberg (1978), disagree, claiming that a proper theory can be inferred from Marx's writings on crime and other related subjects. As evidence, they put forward that Marx wrote that a person's economic background provides the bedrock to all their ideas and views, and thus, that a direct link can be made from these factors to criminal activity (Czech-Jezierska 2021). Marxist criminologists tend to agree that crime stems from class conflict, and class conflict stems from capitalist systems (Engels 1981).

Frederich Engels, Marx's coauthor of *The Communist Manifesto*, drew a simple line between crime and criminal behavior. He stated that a poverty-stricken worker in distress had only three options: slow starvation, ending their own life, or taking the things they needed from any available source (Engels 1981). In the words of Engels (1981), "it is not surprising that the majority prefer to steal rather than to starve to death or commit suicide" (48). It was Engels's belief that these individuals were denied an active place in the social contract, thus forcing them to embrace the laws of nature to survive (Engels 1981).[35]

Many Marxist criminologists view modern criminal justice systems as merely an exercise in oppression by those in positions of power and authority (Greenberg 1976). As evidence of this oppression, proponents point to the degree of effort and attention paid to blue-collar crime, positing that white-collar crime barely warrants a passing interest (White & van der Velden 1995). They also note that when corporate interests engage in harmful crimes, key stakeholders rarely receive significant penalties, if they are punished at all.

Therefore, Marx's influence persists. His original supposition that class conflict was the source of social strife points to the conclusion that has been threaded throughout every section of this chapter: class and power dictate who is viewed as deviant and how they will be treated by the criminal justice system. Whether the focus is on ancient Greece, the Middle Ages, the era of the Scientific Revolution, or contemporary times, those without economic, political, or social power will face inequities in decisions relating to crime and justice.

CONCLUSION

At the beginning of the chapter, we posed the following question: Have those who enjoyed wealth and prestige abused such advantages, exerting social control, particularly within the criminal justice system, to maintain their own position while punishing those who are less fortunate? As we threaded our way through the different eras, we sought evidence that supported or refuted such a claim, identifying trends and practices that could resolve such a query. (Un)fortunately, history has provided a definitive answer: yes. Throughout time, those who enjoy economic privilege also enjoy institutional power, which has often been wielded in such a way as to further disadvantage those beneath them, particularly in relation to the criminal justice system. In ancient Greece, citizenship and slavery were key components of status, as non-citizens and slaves were denied legal rights and privileges enjoyed by others. In ancient Rome, the elite abused the legal system, reshaping it to their advantage prior to codification, or they enjoyed formal inequities following codification. During the Middle Ages, the feudal system reigned supreme. Those at the top (the Crown and the Church) defined deviance, those in the middle enforced these definitions, and those at the bottom bore the brunt of the system. The Renaissance, although short in length, provides a ready example of inherent inequalities built into all stages of the criminal justice system. During the Scientific Revolution, the newly minted capitalist structure created and enforced laws that oppressed the lower classes and those who veered away from traditional economies, while newfound theories of crime focused on biological markers often present in disadvantaged communities.

Thus, the relationship between class, power, and the criminal justice system is a consistent theme throughout history. Despite the prominence of this relationship, it remained unquestioned for millennia. However, as we move into modernity, the oppressive nature of such a dynamic has captured our attention, leading philosophers and academics alike to begin to question the cause and consequence of such things. Marx is perhaps one of the most prominent of these thinkers, arguing that class conflict has resulted in all manner of social strife, including both the act of committing a crime (e.g., for survival) and the response to crime (e.g., to maintain a class-based hierarchy). Regardless of whether that is a lens you choose to adopt, the need to examine the relationship between class, power, and deviance should remain prominent and pressing.

NOTES

1. *Polis* is the Greek word for "city," but Gorman (1992) insists that the word meant far more than the English replacement. The polis was a major part of a citizen's life, not just the place where they lived. It was expected to protect and educate its citizens and was the center of all things religious, cultural, political, and economic.

2. Not every polis chose to ease their restrictions on immigration. While Athens was known to welcome newcomers with open arms, Sparta was not nearly as tolerant of newcomers; its citizens were reluctant to offer immigrants any of the rights reserved for the local-born (Gorman 1992).

3. The modern term *draconian* is derived from the laws of Draco, which, by modern standards, were often harsh and unyielding.

4. Many of Athens' rules and policies were determined through the assembly, a large jury made up of Athenian citizens that was the most important decision-making body in Athens (Ober 1991). It was almost entirely unregulated, as Athenians believed that giving the assembly a large amount of discretion would enable members to reach conclusions that were fairer and more specific to the case at hand (Lanni 1970). According to Plato, anyone was able to offer input to the assembly, no matter their class or profession; they just had to gain the attention of the members present (Ober 1991).

5. It should be noted that Solon's actions led to an increase in fines as punishment; if fined, the offender would face incarceration until such a time as they could pay off their fines. Allen (1997) wrote that although fines were supposed to lessen the harshness of the criminal justice system, it likely had the opposite effect for members of the lower class, who often suffered in prison for years due to the inability to pay even small fines.

6. It is notable that typical juries were not employed for homicide cases. A panel of fifty-one elders who served life terms was called upon to make these decisions (Lambert 2021).

7. Bers and Lanni (2003) paint a picture of loosely regulated juries who were not required to base verdicts on the information presented in court, and Rhodes (1984) wrote of political groups and bribery within juries, so it is easy to imagine that a resident with limited funds could have been reluctant to challenge one with the means of purchasing justice.

8. The five groups included the patricians, the equites, the plebeians, the freedmen, and the slaves (Mark 2022). While the patricians and plebeians were as described above, the remaining three groups require further explanation. The equites were royal mounted knights who, although considered patricians, were socially inferior to those who made up the senate. After a law was passed in 219 BCE that prohibited senators from engaging in commerce, the equites ran the banks, collected taxes, and managed other financial tasks. Freedmen were former slaves who had managed to attain their freedom either by buying it or by being released from service by their masters (Kocourek 1922). These men and women were granted full citizenship, with the exception that they were unable to hold political office. Their children, however, gained the full rights of citizens. As for slaves, some researchers dispute whether they truly counted as a social class. Czech-Jezierska (2021, 41) wrote that the "opinion that it is disputable to treat slaves as a homogenous class, is hard not to agree with, considering the diversity of this group, different functions that slaves performed, their different social and economic positions and ways they were treated."

9. Between 73–71 BCE, slaves led by Spartacus roamed the country committing violence and garnering support before finally being subdued (Mark 2022).

10. It seems that at least some students of the era were required to memorize and recite the Twelve Tables as a part of their studies. The great diplomat Cicero, known as a statesperson and an orator, wrote that this task was required as a part of his schooling (Berkeley Law, 2019).

11. The Twelve Tables were, quite literally, large slabs of rock that held engraved legal statutes.

12. According to Czech-Jezierska (2021), the death penalty in ancient Rome could be enacted in several ways, including by crucifixion or by throwing the perpetrator to wild animals.

13. *The Novella* was released in the Greek language, rather than Latin (Harries 2022). Greek was the common tongue of the people, but most legal writing at the time was done in Latin (including *The Digest*, *The Code*, and *The Institutes*). Historians speculate that Justinian made this choice to show that the strength of his power extended beyond the borders of a single language.

14. Many aspects of Appius's story are contested by various historians, who claim details (such as his purported suicide) were added after the fact to magnify the differences between Appius and the plebeians and to increase the significance of his demise (Nitschke 2009).

15. Historians such as Paresys, Prètou, and Dauphant pointed out that the pardon was a useful tool for recruiting loyal subjects near boundaries or in newly conquered areas. Pardoning key individuals would show the king's mercy and persuade new subjects to give their allegiance to the monarchy. The ruler could also use group pardons at the end of a rebellion to make peace with former rebels who agreed to recognize the ruler's authority (Verreycken 2019).

16. An *asseurement* was a "legally imposed prohibition of violence" (Cohen 1983, 112). Designed to reduce private warfare, an asseurement was placed at the request of one individual, but it was equally applied to their person as well as their families. The violation of an asseurement was a capital offense. The prescribed punishment was death by hanging, but this sentence was rarely carried out.

17. McGlynn (2008) disagrees, positing that select violence in support of justice was authorized by the king. McGlynn's point is fortified by the existence of trials by combat, or duels, in the Middle Ages.

18. The most famous outlaw of the Middle Ages, and perhaps of all time, is medieval serf Robin Hood—even though he might never have existed. Hilton (1958, 30) pointed out the irony of Robin Hood when he said that "one of England's most popular literary heroes is a man whose most endearing activities to his public were the robbery and killing of landowners, in particular church landowners, and the maintenance of guerilla warfare against established authority represented by the sheriff." In some versions of the story, it is said that the man actually came from a higher social caste (English Monarchs UK 2022).

19. This revolt came to be known as the *Jacquerie*. The term referred to the name Jacques Bonhomme, a common colloquialism for French peasants (Gale Research 2014). References to the word *Jacquerie* struck fear into nobles for ages after the rebellion.

20. The revolt was quickly and violently put down in some areas by ruthless nobles, but in other areas it was allowed to die on its own by tax collectors who refused to enforce the poll tax (Vardi 2001).

21. Clergy members had the right to provide sanctuary and protection to those sought by the law by placing them within the church's sacred grounds, which were not considered to be within the jurisdiction of the king and his law enforcers (Coyle 1958). This right was intended to be used only for those who had killed or injured another by accident, but records from

English churches show that it was frequently taken advantage of and used to hide those wanted for all manner of crimes, much to the dismay of their pursuers (Coyle 1958).

22. Evidence shows that the law against striking the mayor was not often enforced; rather, the mayor tended to publicly forgive an assailant to appear magnanimous and full of supposed Christian charity (Carrel 2009). It is also believed that rulers would forgive crimes for other political reasons, such as when an offender agreed to serve in the military (McGlynn 2008).

23. A well-known (and possibly fictitious) example is that of author Daniel Defoe, who was pilloried in 1703 London for "seditious libel." Instead of pelting him with rocks and garbage, the crowd is said to have thrown flowers and circulated his poem "Hymn to the Pillory" (Carrel, 2009).

24. Philosopher Scipione Ammirato once expressed distaste for the sight of beggars on street corners and in front of the churches of Florence and declared that they were poor due to their own laziness (Brackett 2002).

25. A system of public fame was used extensively in both Florence and Venice (Stern, 2004). With this system, people with no knowledge of or connection to a case could be allowed to testify in court cases. The Venetians took public fame especially seriously, branding the infamous on the forehead and frequently judging them as guilty without evidence.

26. "The notion of an organized society of beggars constituting a medieval criminal under-world is as well known as it is controversial," according to Brackett (2002, 296).

27. "The poor did not and could not possess honor; uncontrolled violence was associated with the undisciplined, immoral poor, who were, as Aristotle wrote, rebellious in spirit" (Brackett 2002, 304).

28. *Ius Commune* was a combination of Roman and canonical law that formed the basis of all legal action in Italy from 1100 to 1800. Various components of the system were spread across most of Europe (Stern 2004).

29. Inmates would go to great lengths to save money to earn their release. While it was officially not allowed, spouses and children were known to occasionally live in the prison with their incarcerated family members to help decrease living expenses (Woodfine 2006).

30. Urbanization level is determined by the number of citizens who lived in towns with more than ten thousand inhabitants.

31. This was especially threatening due to the existence of debtors' prisons in the era.

32. Breen (2011) tells the story of a sixteenth-century German attorney who was said to tell his clients to bring three sacks with them to court. The first was to be full of money to pay for the proceedings. The second would hold all the documents necessary for the case. The third should be full of patience.

33. Lombroso's daughter, Gina Ferrero, was a follower of her father's ideas. She was known to hold the belief that a "normal" child who behaves in a seemingly criminal way will "spontaneously correct themselves of their thievishness and other vices as soon as they arrive at puberty" (Ellwood 1912).

34. Marx did not believe that crime was necessarily a negative thing for society. He wrote in his *Theories of Surplus Value* that criminal activity adds interest to bourgeois life, keeping it from becoming stagnant and uncompetitive (Engels 1981). In the same manuscript, he put forward that criminals are the cause for entire industries within their economies. By Marx's reasoning, without criminals there would be little or no reason for smart locks, doorbell cameras, or fingerprint readers, which means that in the absence of crime, the creators, producers, and installers of these items would likely hold a lower socioeconomic status.

35. The social contract is the set of written and unwritten rules that humanity entered in order to exit the lawless state of nature (Ritchie, Hodwitz, & Karst 2022). Actions such as theft are outside the social contract, leading to criminal and social consequences for those who undertake them.

REFERENCES

Allen, Danielle. 1997. "Imprisonment in Classical Athens: Imprisonment as a Penalty?" *Classical Quarterly* 47 (1): 121–35. https://www.jstor.org/stable/639603.

Allen, Danielle. 2003. "Punishment in Ancient Athens." In *Athenian Law in Its Democratic Context (Center for Hellenic Studies On-line Discussion Series)*, edited by Adriaan Lanni. Republished in *Demos: Classical Athenian Democracy (The Stoa: a consortium for electronic publication in the humanities)*, edited by C.W. Blackwell. https://www.stoa.org/demos/article_punishment@page=1&greekEncoding=UnicodeC.html.

Bergman, Gerald. 2005. "Darwinian Criminality Theory: A Tragic Chapter in History." *Biology Forum/Rivista di Biologia* 98, no. 1 (January): 47–69.

Berkeley Law. 2019. "Roman Legal Tradition and the Compilation of Justinian." https://www.law.berkeley.edu/wpcontent/uploads/2019/08/romanlaw.pdf.

Bers, Victor, and Adriaan Lanni. 2003. "An Introduction to the Athenian Legal System." https://www.stoa.org/demos/article_intro_legal_system@page=6&greekEncoding=UnicodeC.html.

Bisson, Thomas N. 1994. "The 'Feudal Revolution.'" *Past & Present* 142: 6–42.

Bogan, Craig, and Alyssa Conrad. 2022. "The Dark Ages and Innocence." In *The Origins of Criminological Theory*, edited by Omi Hodwitz, 38–51. Oxford: Routledge.

Brackett, John K. 2002. "The Florentine Criminal Underworld: The Underside of the Renaissance." In *Society and Individual in Renaissance Florence*, edited by William J. Connell, 293–314. Oakland: University of California Press.

Breen, Michael P. 2011. "Law, Society, and the State in Early Modern France." *Journal of Modern History* 83, no. 2 (June): 346–86. https://doi.org/10.1086/659209.

Carrel, Helen. 2009. "The Ideology of Punishment in Late Medieval English Towns." *Social History* 34, no. 3 (August): 301–20. https://www.jstor.org/stable/25594368.

Chaucer, Geoffrey. 2007. "Social Class in the Middle Ages: *The Canterbury Tales*." http://ctales.leadr.msu.edu/social-class/.

Cohen, Esther. 1983. "Violence Control in Late Medieval France: The Social Transformation of the Asseurement." *Tijdschrift voor Rechtsgeschiedenis/Legal History Review* 51, no. 1 (January): 111–22.

Cohn Jr., Samuel K. 1999. *Creating the Florentine State: Peasants and Rebellion, 1348–1434.* Cambridge: Cambridge University Press.

Coyle, Danielle. 2005. "The Outlaws of Medieval England." *Hohunu: A Journal of Academic Writing* 3: 57–59. https://hilo.hawaii.edu/campuscenter/hohonu/volumes/documents/Vol 03x13TheOutlawsofMedievalEngland.pdf.

Czech-Jezierska, Bozena. 2021. "The Class-Based Approach to Roman Criminal Law." *Studia Iuridica Lublinensia* 30 no. 1 (May): 35–53. https://doi.org/10.17951/sil.2021.30.1.35-53.

D'Amico, Daniel J. 2010. "The Prison in Economics: Private and Public Incarceration in Ancient Greece." *Public Choice* 145, no. 3/4 (December): 461–82. https://www.jstor.org/stable/40927129.

Dean, Trevor. 2014. *Crime in Medieval Europe: 1200–1550.* Oxford: Routledge.

DuPlessis, Robert S. 2019. *Transitions to Capitalism in Early Modern Europe: Economies in the Era of Early Globalization.* Vol. 60. Cambridge: Cambridge University Press.

Durrant, Russil, and Tony Ward. 2012. "The Role of Evolutionary Explanations in Criminology." *Journal of Theoretical & Philosophical Criminology* 4, no. 2 (January): 1–37.

Ellwood, Charles A. 1912. "Lombroso's Theory of Crime." *Journal of the American Institute of Criminal Law and Criminology* 2, no. 5 (January): 716–23. https://doi.org/10.2307/1132830.

Elmore, Jefferson. 1922. "The Purpose of the Decemviral Legislation." *Classical Philology* 17, no. 2 (April): 128–40.

Engels, Friedrich. 1981. *Crime and Capitalism: Readings in Marxist Criminology*, edited by David Greenberg. California City: Mayfield Publishing Company.

English Monarchs UK. 2022. "The Legend of Robin Hood." https://www.englishmonarchs.co.uk/robin_hood.html.

Gale Research. 2014. "Peasant Uprisings in Europe: Fourteenth Century." In *Global Events: Milestone Events Throughout History*. Farmington Hills: Gale.

Ganshof, Francois Louis. 1952. *Feudalism*. Translated by Philip J. Hamilton Grierson and F. M. Stenton. Cambridge: Cambridge University Press.

Gorman, Robert F. 1992. "Citizenship, Obligation, and Exile in the Greek and Roman Experience." *Public Affairs Quarterly* 6, no. 1 (January): 5–22. https://www.jstor.org/stable/40435793.

Greenberg, David F. 1976. "On One-Dimensional Marxist Criminology." *Theory and Society* 3, no. 4 (Winter): 611–21. https://www.jstor.org/stable/656818.

Harries, Jill. 2022. "Roman Law Codes and the Roman Legal Tradition." In *Beyond Dogmatics*, edited by John W. Cairns and Paul J. du Plessis, 85–104. Edinburgh: Edinburgh University Press.

Harris, Beth, and Steven Zucker. 2013. "A Brief History of Western Culture." https://www.khanacademy.org/humanities/ap-art-history/start-here-apah/briefhistories-apah/a/a-brief-history-of-western-culture.

Härter, Karl. 2017. "Cultural Deviance, Political Crime, Public Media and Security: Perspectives on the Cultural History of Crime and Criminal Justice in Early Modern Europe." *Crime, History & Societies* 21, no. 2: 261–69. https://www.jstor.org/stable/44984316.

Hilton, R. H. 1958. "The Origins of Robin Hood." *Past & Present* 14, no. 1 (November): 30–44. https://doi.org/10.1093/past/14.1.30.

Kocourek, Albert. 1922. "The Formula Procedure of Roman Law." *Virginia Law Review* 8 (6): 434–44.

Lambert, Kelly. 2021. "Law and Courts in Ancient Athens: A Brief Overview." https://kosmos-society.chs.harvard.edu/law-and-courts-inancient-athens-a-brief-overview/.

Lanni, Adriaan. 1970. "'Verdict Most Just': The Modes of Classical Athenian Justice." *Yale Journal of Law & the Humanities* 16, no. 2 (2004): 277–321.

Mark, Joshua J. 2019. "Ancient Roman Society." https://www.worldhistory.org/article/1463/ancient-romansociety/#:~:text=Society%20was%20divided%20in%20two,Conflict%20of%20the%20Orders%20.

Mazzarello, Paolo. 2011. "Cesare Lombroso: An Anthropologist Between Evolution and Degeneration." *Functional Neurology* 26, no. 2 (April): 97–101.

McGlynn, Sean. 2008. "Violence and the Law in Medieval England." *History Today* 58, no. 4 (April): 53–60.

Monaco, Francesco, and Marco Mula. 2011. "Cesare Lombroso and Epilepsy 100 Years Later: An Unabridged Report of His Original Transactions." *Epilepsia* 52, no. 4 (April): 679–88. https://doi.org/10.1111/j.1528-1167.2010.02959.x.

National Archives of England. 2000. "Crime and Punishment." https://www.nationalarchives.gov.uk/education/candp/prevention/g02/default.htm.

Nitschke, Peter. 2009. "The Hidden Power for the Creation of Order." Panel.

Nold, Ronald, Kelley Massingale, and Omi Hodwitz. 2022. "Justice in Ancient Greece and Rome." In *The Origins of Criminological Theory*, edited by Omi Hodwitz, 13–36. Oxford: Routledge.

Ober, Josiah. 1991. *Mass and Elite in Democratic Athens: Rhetoric, Ideology, and the Power of the People*. Princeton: Princeton University Press.

Padgug, Robert A. 1975. "Classes and Society in Classical Greece." *Arethusa* 8, no. 1 (Spring): 85–117. https://www.jstor.org/stable/26307443.

Rhodes, Henry A. 1984. "The Athenian Court and the American Court System." https://teach-ersinstitute.yale.edu/curriculum/units/1984/2/84.02.08/2.

Ritchie, Josh, Omi Hodwitz, and Mihaela Karst. 2022. "The Age of Enlightenment and Human Nature." In *The Origins of Criminological Theory*, edited by Omi Hodwitz, 52–71. Oxford: Routledge.

Rousseaux, Xavier. 1997. "Crime, Justice and Society in Medieval and Early Modern Times: Thirty Years of Crime and Criminal Justice History: A Tribute to Herman Diederiks." *Crime, History, & Societies* 1 (1): 87–118.

Ruggiero, Guido. 1978. "Law and Punishment in Early Renaissance Venice." *Journal of Criminal Law and Criminology* 69, no. 2 (Summer): 243–56.

Ruggiero, Guido. 1982. "Excusable Murder: Insanity and Reason in Early Renaissance Venice." *Journal of Social History* 16, no. 1 (Autumn): 109–19. https://www.jstor.org/stable/3786883.

Saladin, Christopher Schley. 2017. "Revolution in the Divided City: The Plebeian Social Movement, Secessions, and Anti-Government in the Roman Republic during the 5th Century Struggle of the Orders." PhD diss., Augustana College.

Saunders, Catharine. 1917. "The Consular Speeches of Cicero." *Classical Weekly* 10, no. 20 (March): 153–56. https://doi.org/10.2307/4387443.

Sian, Katy. 2017. "Born Radicals? Prevent, Positivism, and 'Race-Thinking.'" *Palgrave Communications* 3, no. 6 (October). https://doi.org/10.1057/s41599-017-0009-0.

Stern, Laura Ikins. 2004. "Politics and Law in Renaissance Florence and Venice." *American Journal of Legal History* 46, no. 2 (April): 209–34. https://doi.org/10.2307/3692441.

Van den Heuvel, Danielle. 2015. "Policing Peddlers: The Prosecution of Illegal Street Trade in Eighteenth-Century Dutch Towns." *Historical Journal* 58, no. 2 (May): 367–92. https://doi.org/10.1017/S0018246X14000478.

Vardi, Liana. 2001. "Serfdom: Western Europe." In *Encyclopedia of European Social History, 369–378*. New York: Charles Scribner's Sons.

Vermeesch, Griet. 2015. "Reflections on the Relative Accessibility of Law Courts in Early Modern Europe." *Crime, History & Societies* 19 (2): 53–76. https://doi.org/10.4000/chs.1598.

Verreycken, Quentin. 2019. "The Power to Pardon in Late Medieval and Early Modern Europe: New Perspectives in the History of Crime and Criminal Justice." *History Compass* 17, no. 6 (May): 1–17. https://doi.org/10.1111/hic3.12575.

White, Rob, and John van der Velden. 1995. "Class and criminality." *Social Justice* 22, no. 1 (Spring): 51–71. https://www.jstor.org/stable/29766864.

Wolfgang, Marvin E. 1990. "Crime and Punishment in Renaissance Florence." *Journal of Criminal Law and Criminology* 81, no. 3 (Fall): 567–84.

Womack, Jesse. 2017. "Ancient Roman Punishment Was Swift, Cruel and Unusual." Accessed May 23, 2022. https://www.wycoreport.com/ancient-romanpunishment-was-swift-cruel-and-unusual/article_a2046211-e8b5-518a-9fe7-8a65cf30014c.html.

Woodfine, Philip. 2006. "Debtors, Prisons, and Petitions in Eighteenth-Century England." *Eighteenth-Century Life* 30, no. 2 (April): 1–31. https://doi.org/10.1215/00982601-2005-001.

Chapter 9

The Evolution of Juvenile Delinquency

Silas B. Parks, D. Alex Cowan, and Omi Hodwitz

INTRODUCTION

How do societies react when children engage in criminal acts, creating discordance between the image of the innocent cherub and the reality of seemingly evil intent? How do justice systems, typically crafted to address adult deviance, respond to juvenile violations of the law? Moreover, when does a child bear the responsibility of an adult? In modern times, we have answers to these questions; the Western world has accepted the presence of childhood crimes, and in response, it has created juvenile justice systems; meanwhile the United Nations has established a firm line delineating youth from adulthood (Crawford & Lewis 2008).[1] Historically, however, the understanding of and responses to childhood delinquency have been less clear-cut.[2]

Historical justice-oriented writings have focused primarily on institutional and social responses to adult male offenders. Women have a limited presence in these discussions, and children even less so, either absent entirely or relegated to a footnote (Crawford & Lewis 2008). What little literature does exist portrays a progression, beginning in ancient times and ending in modernity, a gradual increase in culpability as a child enters adulthood (Newman 2007).

Although historical writings can tell us little, they do indicate that children were often held to different standards than their adult counterparts, and this did not necessarily equate to softer treatment. Some behaviors that were considered trivial for adults were criminalized for children (Marcus 1981).[3] In addition, children were subject to corporal punishment, an outcome that was oftentimes more brutal and scarring than legally proscribed punitive measures.[4] The use of such violence as a corrective measure was commonplace across the generations, readily employed by anyone in a position of authority, particularly within the family.[5]

The literature also suggests that responding to the crimes and misdeeds of children in early eras was primarily the responsibility of the child's community, to be reported and addressed by those within the immediate or extended family. However, this changed over time, and delinquency increasingly fell under state control, eventually producing the juvenile justice system that is in place today. This was not a seamless transition, marked instead by uncertainty, devolution, and conflict. This chapter will trace the trajectory of these social and legal responses to childhood deviance throughout Western history, from the age of antiquity, through the medieval era, and into the modern age.

ANTIQUITY: GREECE

Ancient Athens, as the seat of democracy and the center of Greek society, shaped the definitions and practices of the entire Greek empire, including relations with and treatment of children. Before exploring ancient Grecian views of children, however, it is beneficial to briefly examine traditional legal practices during this era, thus facilitating a greater appreciation for criminal justice responses to delinquency.

The Athenian justice system was, in many ways, similar to modern legal proceedings (Griffith-Williams 2013). Although there was no formal system of arrest and prosecution and private citizens brought charges to the court and then prosecuted the cases themselves, these cases were decided by a jury of non-professionals, much like in contemporary courts (Carey 1994). Both the prosecutor and defendant would present their arguments in turn, and a simple majority vote would determine guilt or innocence. The smallest of these juries, however, could easily include two hundred people.[6] This system was employed for accused adult offenders only; children, on the other hand, were treated much differently.

Athenians viewed children as mentally and physically inept, requiring tutelage and discipline to prepare them for adulthood. They were afforded little social or legal value, and in the Greek literature, they were often compared to women and slaves, groups that had little to no power in society (Beaumont 2012). Efforts to prepare children for adulthood could be harsh, requiring physical punishment and discomfort, practices that were accepted and endorsed by Greek society, including influential thinkers such as Aristotle (Parsons 2015). While generally seen as lesser beings, Greek children passed through several graduated stages of importance and responsibility based around age and major life events.

Typically, children remained with the *oikos* (family) throughout their early years, living almost exclusively within the family compound, overseen by the women of the household (Bardis 1964). Girls were taught various housekeeping and maternal duties, before leaving the compound sometime between puberty and fourteen years of age, at which time they were married off to an eligible spouse (Beaumont 2012). These young brides were typically matched to men twice their age, and after marriage, they were considered full adults. Boys, on the other hand, were likely to leave home at the age of seven, when they would either begin tutelage at the local *gymnasium* or, if the family were wealthy, with a private tutor. Once the male child reached puberty, he would typically establish a mentorship with an unrelated adult male. At that age, it was socially acceptable for the older mentor to have a sexual relationship with his young mentee (Canterella 2004). This period was designed to give the child intimate knowledge of the expectations surrounding Greek citizenship.

At the age of eighteen, boys entered a period of *ephebia*, which consisted of two years of military service (Beaumont 2012). Completion of this service marked the beginning of young male adulthood and the granting of citizenship rights. Although they were now considered to be adult citizens, males were expected to continue living in their fathers' oikos while actively pursuing further mentorship and counsel (Jassongne 2020). Between the ages of twenty-five and thirty, these men would then be wed, creating their own oikos, and entering full adulthood. Until this point in their lives, Greek males were subject to the rules, restrictions, and punitive measures assigned by the head of the household or by teachers and mentors. Rarely would male youths interact with the Greek justice system, and then only for the most egregious and flagrant of crimes, such as the murder of another Greek citizen.

The legal rights and protections of children were limited in antiquity. Absolute rule in the oikos rested with the father (Bardis 1964). At birth, the father could choose to reject his child, leaving it exposed to the elements with the intention of killing it. As the child grew, the father was responsible for correcting errant behaviors, at least until the child was passed along to a mentor. The power of the father in all matters relating to crime and punishment was nearly absolute, unquestioned by larger Greek society. If a father chose to severely abuse or neglect his children, this was within his rights and considered acceptable.

The city-state of Sparta offers one point of contrast with Athenian practices, as it approached childhood in a totalitarian and militaristic fashion. From the age of seven, children were taken from their homes and placed in barracks, marking the beginning of their military training (Bardis 1964). Discipline was brutal and absolute. Children were deprived of food, thus forcing them to learn to steal for survival, which was believed to aid them in becoming cunning and alert adults (Garland 1991). The only crime was to get caught, for which the perpetrator would be flogged and left hungry.[7]

ANTIQUITY: ROME

Roman justice systems differed from Greek courts in notable ways, including the Roman reliance on legal professionals to fill key roles, particularly the magistrate. An early form of Roman justice included the *iudicium populi*, or trial by magistrate and people (Bauman 1996). During these proceedings, the magistrate would conduct an investigation and propose a penalty, after which the case would be presented to an assembly, which would then vote in favor or in opposition of the magistrate's recommendation. This was followed by the period of the *iudicium publicum*, or trial by jury. Although proceedings replicated the previous period, the magistrate and jury had less discretion regarding potential penalties, as many offenses had prescribed sentences. Like its Grecian counterpart, this system was intended for adults only; Roman children were traditionally dealt with in a different manner.

Similar to what took place in Athens, juvenile delinquency in ancient Rome was generally considered a matter for the family and not the public courts (Garland 1991). Childhood behavior was the responsibility of the *pater familias*, the head of the household (Jassongne 2020). If a Roman citizen chose to publicly charge a child from another household, the charges were redirected toward the pater familias. The power of familial head extended beyond children; the father was also responsible for the remaining members of the household, known as *patria potestas* (Antošovská 2019).

In simple terms, the power of the father was nearly unlimited, extending to control and discipline, but also to responsibility and accountability.

Childhood misbehavior was frequently corrected by way of corporal punishment. Roman authorities generally agreed that "castigation has a profound and positive impact on the interior life of the child" (Parsons 2015, 5). This agreement was not absolute, however, as some Roman philosophers spoke out against the use of excessive corporal punishment. They took particular issue with tutors' and teachers' use of physical punishment (Garland 1991). These lamentations had little sway, given that tutors and teachers were underpaid and held in low esteem, thus they received little incentive to act differently.

Roman children could be a rough and wayward lot, engaging in violent bullying and harassment (Laes 2019). This was generally acceptable behavior in Roman society and frequently ignored, as it was viewed to be a necessary part of youthful development and growth (Antošovská 2019). Older students who were away at school were known to be particularly unruly, and scholars noted that their actions were likely punishable under the law; however, the Roman custom of accepting youthful bullying protected them from legal scrutiny (Laes 2019).

Until the time of Justinian the Great during the era of the Late Roman Empire, there was no set legal age between childhood and adulthood (Antošovská 2019). There was, in truth, no immediate need to set an age of legal majority, as the pater familias was the only person in a household who was legally liable (Jassongne 2020). That said, there were a few key benchmarks that indicated transitions toward adult status. It was generally accepted that young, prepubescent children were not culpable for criminal activity (Antošovská 2019). By age seven, however, children were expected to have developed some degree of mental capacity, thus this generally marked the beginning of some degree of criminal responsibility, which would increase over the next several years of life, until the child became a teenager, when status became more formalized.

Young girls were believed to be marriageable by the age of twelve, and they were typically married before they reached twenty years (Antošovská 2019).[8] Once married, females were granted adult status. Boys, on the other hand, reached adulthood at a later age. The pater familias remained responsible and liable for the behaviors of males until sometime between the ages of fourteen and twenty-five, although the older males did receive some institutional security, such as legal protections from engaging in disadvantageous business dealings. By the age of twenty-five, many males had married, but Roman custom decreed that they remain under the protection of the pater familias until the time of the latter's death (Jassongne 2020). Male children who lacked fathers would seek and receive patronage with other adult men, who would take them on as pupils until the age of fourteen. From that point until they reached the age of twenty-five, males were placed under a curatorship, with limited direct supervision. Upon reaching twenty-five years old, Roman males would become their own pater familias.

EARLY MEDIEVAL ERA

The decline and fall of the Western Roman Empire in the 400s CE, and the inevitable destruction of its culture over the following centuries, ushered in the Middle Ages.

The early Middle Ages was characterized by a lack of strong, centralized governments. Instead, smaller communities with simpler justice practices were commonplace. Popular justice-based practices included blood revenge or feuds and *wergild* (Buneci 2021). Blood revenge allowed members of the victim's family to seek retribution from members of the offender's family (blood for blood), whereas wergild, which eventually replaced blood revenge, involved providing compensation for victimization. Over time, regions developed stronger centralized governments, and secular and religious courts became popular (Jones 1969). The treatment of children in these diverse justice systems was not well-recorded and varied considerably depending on the crime.

Scholarly understanding of the children of the Middle Ages has evolved over the last sixty years. Early academics believed that medieval children were viewed as small adults by their communities (Orme 2001). This supposition stemmed primarily from observing artwork from this era, depicting children in the same attire and engaged in the same activities as their elders.[9] Thus, scholars posited that the concept of childhood, complete with differential treatment and expectations, was a modern development, absent from prior eras (Crawford & Lewis 2008). Literary analysis has illustrated the falsity of this claim. The great love and sorrow that was directed by parents toward their children in the Middle Ages indicates that medieval society viewed children in a manner similar to modern society, at least in an emotive sense (Newman 2007).

Parents and authorities in the Middle Ages offered a unique response to misbehaving youth. Religion was a fundamental aspect of medieval identity, and it permeated all institutions and practices. Supernatural forces such as God and the devil were ever-present, enticing and controlling the Western world. As such, children who engaged in antisocial activities were believed to be possessed by demonic forces, providing a means to condemn the bad behavior without condemning the child (Katajala-Peltomaa 2016). The child remained innocent while also experiencing the equivalent of corporal punishment by way of harsh exorcism practices.[10] It should be noted that, while the exorcism could seem barbaric at times, records indicate this allowed the family to stay together, rather than having the child be cast out (Katajala-Peltomaa 2016).

If an exorcism was not appropriate (e.g., the behavior did not warrant a claim of demonic possession), children were likely to face more traditional means of corporal punishment (Parsons 2015). Misbehaving or breaking the rules would likely result in a physical beating by family members and authoritative others. Physical punishment was also a key aspect of tutelage and education, and the use of rulers to hit children eventually led to the commonplace association between rulers and school. Corporal punishment, no matter how fierce, was not perceived as a violent act; instead, it was an act of duty and due diligence (Katajala-Peltomaa 2016).

The age of legal responsibility varied over time, as well as by region and offense (Shahar 1990). In the seventh century, Kent and Wessex decreed that a child could be charged as an accessory to theft at the age of ten (Orme 2001). In the tenth century, King Æthelstan proclaimed that a child could be charged with thievery at the age of twelve, but then stipulated they should not be put to death if they were under the age of fifteen, "unless he is minded to defend himself or tries to escape and refuses to give himself up" (Orme 2001, 323). In some regions, age was not a legal defense, but children were frequently pardoned for wrongdoing anyway (Kean 1937).

When a child engaged in petty crimes, it remained common practice for the victims to seek compensation from the child's family, specifically from the father (Orme 2001). If the wrong the child had committed could be addressed with financial recompense and the family had the means, compensation was generally preferred by all parties involved. For a child who caused someone's death, however, things became more complicated. In Anglo-Saxon law, if a child took a life in self-defense or by misadventure, the king would traditionally pardon the child (Kean 1937). This practice became so commonplace that, by the thirteenth century, local judges had all but stopped waiting for the writ of pardon before determining innocence; they assumed the pardon would be granted in due time. If, however, a medieval child caused someone's death with intention and foresight, their punishment could be the loss of their own life (Orme 2001). In one case, for example, a ten-year-old boy entered a stranger's home to steal some bread but encountered a young girl, who tried to stop him. He killed the girl and was hanged for the crime, as it was determined that he had tried to hide the body.

LATE MEDIEVAL ERA AND THE RENAISSANCE

Later in the Middle Ages and into the Renaissance, governments became more powerful and centralized, resulting in justice systems that were organized but complex. Still, corruption and arbitrary rulings were a part of the process, particularly when there was uncertainty about rulership or government authority (Gorski 2009). While legal proceedings were approaching standardization, methods for obtaining evidence remained primitive. Thus, torture became a mainstay in the legal landscape as a means of providing guilt (Stern 2004). This was set against a backdrop of social and religious change, marked by the Inquisition and the large-scale social upheaval of the Reformation.

The Reformation ushered in changes in religious ideology, but this had little effect on the treatment of children. Corporal punishment remained a preferred method of correcting youthful deviance and shaping future prosocial adults. Similar to what occurred during medieval times, physical punishment also remained tied to religious beliefs regarding sin and purity (Crawford & Lewis 2008). As noted by Titus (2005), "the Calvinist doctrine of infant depravity required coercive discipline by adults to save the child's soul from their innate sinfulness" (118). There were dissenting viewpoints; some scholars offered objections to the idea that physical beatings would save children from damnation (Parsons 2015). However, the majority opinion sided with the use of corporal punishment; thus, parents used this tactic liberally without fear of legal repercussions, even if the beatings resulted in the child's death (Newman 2007).

Around the age of fourteen years, it became commonplace for children to become apprentices (Pigg 2015). An apprenticeship, which typically lasted seven to ten years, consisted of serving as a live-in worker, either as a tradesperson, agricultural assistant, or household staff.[11] [12] Apprenticeships were believed to be a particularly ideal way to address an unruly child's errant behavior (Kremer 2014). A child was contractually obligated to behave, and if the child continued to act out, the apprenticeship could be extended as a punitive measure. In addition, apprenticeships offered masters notable benefits, as it was a form of indentured servitude or inexpensive labor.

Despite the threat of an extended mandatory period of service, apprentices would still occasionally disobey their masters. In these instances, ritualized apologies became a popular method of castigation (Carrel 2009). The apprentice would offer a formal and public opinion, and oftentimes, if there were a prescribed penalty already in place for their original insolent act, the penalty would be reduced. The ritualized apology served all affected parties; the apprentice received a reduced punishment, but was also visibly and publicly obligated to improve their behavior. In addition, the community was given a demonstration of law and order in action, and although the apprentice's master was typically obligated to accept the apology, this acceptance would make the master appear benevolent. Despite the notable benefits of this system, it was not infallible. Having large numbers of underpaid and disaffected youth made for an unstable situation, and there were multiple accounts of apprentice riots during this period (Kremer 2014). Such riots became particularly commonplace in fifteenth- and sixteenth-century London.

Through this era, the age of accountability remained fluid. Given the absence of birth records, proving or disproving a claim of age could be difficult, if not impossible.[13] Typically, it was believed that children began making conscious and rational decisions at the age of seven, but they were not culpable for their deviance until sometime between ten and fourteen years of age (Shahar 1990). During the reign of Charles V, the death penalty could be applied to thieves under the age of fourteen, but they would not be subject to forfeiture of land and property (Buneci 2021). Once a child reached the age of fourteen, they could be subject to death, and financial penalties could be levied against their remaining family or estate. By the sixteenth century, Seville had specific laws addressing youth and crime; children under the age of ten and a half years were considered exempt from legal repercussions, whereas those between the ages of ten and a half years and seventeen years were subject to reduced criminal penalties (Pike 1975).

Although age considerations were informative, when the crime involved a victim's death, proof of malice became fundamental in the decision to punish or pardon a child (Kean 1937). There were a number of ways to establish malice, including evidence of premeditation, indications that the child had attempted to hide the crime, or reports that the child fled from prosecution. The case of a nine-year-old child provides a ready example. The boy in question killed another child and hid the body. Upon discovery, the boy claimed that he had a nosebleed, thus justifying the presence of blood on his body and face. The boy later confessed to his crime but was hanged for it nonetheless. Although proof of malice was a key aspect of addressing children involved in victim deaths, it was the exception, not the norm (Newman 2007). More often, children were not suspected of malice and, as such, were pardoned for their involvement in loss of life.

THE AGE OF ENLIGHTENMENT

As Europe entered the Age of Enlightenment, many nations based their understanding of a juvenile's culpability on ancient Roman traditions. Children of seven years or less were identified as *infans*, those between seven and ten were known as *proximus infanti*, and those aged ten to fourteen years old were referred to as *proximus pubertai*. The child's age would play a significant role in sentencing, and judges were permitted to be extreme in both punishment and forgiveness (Blatier 1999). However, age might have been less important to a judge than a child's understanding of right and wrong. If the child in question was shown to be capable of discerning between good and evil, they were often deemed responsible in the eyes of the law. If found guilty in this regard, youth were housed in jails along with convicted adults, with minimal regard for the safety of the child (May 1973).

Judicial proceedings for youth were more an exception than a rule. Similar to what took place in previous eras, children of the Enlightenment were not often subject to the law (King 1998). Corporal punishment was par for the course, and parents were typically held responsible for the unruly youth.[14] As a result, until the end of the seventeenth century, it was acceptable for parents to imprison their children.[15] In the rare instances when the state became involved in youth culpability, criminal sentences were usually more lenient than those handed down to adults. Children could, however, face severe consequences, such as life imprisonment, deportation, and death, even for those as young as seven years old (Blatier 1999; May 1973).

Breaking with the traditions of previous eras, the state was recognized as the ultimate parent during the Enlightenment, and historic English cases demonstrated the Courts of Chancery's obligation to protect unfortunate juveniles.[16] Certain social and legal institutions were put in place to assist the growing number of children who lacked family, shelter, and other necessities. The United States followed England's example by assigning final authority of the well-being of children to the government (Mack 1909). Judges considered that children involved in petty crime were more often victims of desperation than moral failings (Wolff 1996). The state had an obligation to edify the children under its care, an obligation that included providing the discipline deemed necessary to keep them on a productive track (Cabot 1918).

To achieve childhood discipline and growth, the state engaged in a multitude of undertakings. As the court systems began to move away from the capital code of prior centuries, incarceration as a criminal consequence became more widely accepted. This led to the development of various Sunday schools, industrial schools, and basic education facilities for the poor (King 1998).[17] Reformers motivated by religious and civic duty began playing a role in the treatment of children, giving rise to the Western conception of modern childhood. This was a step away from the fairly common practice of earlier centuries, in which children were often economically exploited (Berger & Gregory 2009). Although the image of a proper childhood developed as part of the effort to protect the youth from the threats posed by poverty and vice, the resulting stereotype would play a role in media portrayals of the juvenile delinquent in the ensuing centuries (May 1973).

It was not until the end of the era that juvenile delinquency began to shift from a minor, localized inconvenience into an international concern. There were, however, profound changes in urbanization throughout this period, founded on improvements in agriculture and the raising of livestock. This progression in food production started in the late sixteenth century and continued its evolution into the mid-1800s (Clayton & Rowbotham 2009). Coupled with significant reform in the fields of policing and criminal justice, these changes in urbanization played key roles in the eventual conception of juvenile delinquency.

A BRIEF NOTE TO THE READER

As we transition into the time of the Industrial Revolution, you will likely note greater depth in our descriptions of youth and crime. This is due primarily to a shift in the information available in historical writings. In earlier eras, information on juvenile delinquency was scarce, gleaned primarily from documents addressing other topics. With the advent of the Industrial Revolution, however, there was a notable surge in documents addressing juvenile delinquency and the criminal justice system. This might reflect a shift in interest and awareness as delinquency transitioned from a family issue to a state issue, or it could be due to technological advances that increased the ability to record information. In either case, the sudden change in the volume of information has allowed us to provide more detailed descriptions in the second half of this chapter than we were able to accomplish in the first half.

THE INDUSTRIAL REVOLUTION

The supposition that juvenile delinquency is substantively different from adult crime is a relatively modern idea, one that developed throughout the nineteenth century in both Europe and North America (Berger & Gregory 2009). This belief was fostered, in part, by a growing awareness of the violence and poverty that was prevalent at the time. The plight of the unfortunate, including deviant youth, caught the attention of powerful organizations that lobbied for change, demanding government consideration. This method would prove to be effective, capturing the attention of both the public and the state.

The Industrial Revolution's unending demand for workers facilitated a population shift, as people flocked from the countryside to urban centers with the hope of finding employment in one of the many industries located there (Clayton & Rowbothan 2009). This push toward urbanization had a notable effect on material, legal, and familial systems (Magarey 1978). It was not uncommon for both parents to work during this time, thus leaving their children to their own devices for much of the day. Some of these children attempted to contribute to the household, gaining honest but unappetizing work, such as coal scratching, dung gathering, mudlarking or scavenging, and sweeping chimneys (Duckworth 2003).[18] Unsavory working conditions paired with limited parental oversight led many children to engage in petty crimes, such as thievery and prostitution (Wolff 1996).[19]

While some children had parents who were absent due to work commitments, others were without parents altogether. Broken homes, desertion, and early death associated with sickness and unsafe working conditions were particularly prevalent during the Industrial Revolution. Out of desperation, countless youth found their way to crime, deviance, and vagrancy (May 1973; Magarey 1978). These children often found others in similar situations, and groups of destitute youths formed, creating small but persistent criminal organizations (Duckworth 2003). The growing number of young gangs, their criminal ways, and their ability to survive without adult oversight sparked a new debate, one focused on responsibility, accountability, and culpability (King 1998).

Social and moral institutions can be credited with shifting the narrative and subsequent punishments directed toward youth. In prior centuries, legislation had prescribed capital punishment for the most serious offenses, causing prosecutors to assign more trivial charges, safe in the knowledge that the resulting consequences would not be life-threatening (Casey 2011). Early in the 1800s, British reformers successfully lobbied the government to reduce the number of capital crimes, and between 1808 and 1837, this number dwindled for both children and adults, with much of the Western world following suit (Wolff 1996). Long-term incarceration was proposed as a welcome alternative, evolving into a trend that would continue into modern times (Fox 1996).[20]

Although early statistics provided evidence of the prevalence of juvenile delinquency during this era, these numbers had less influence on public sentiment than did media and state messaging regarding the issue. Both parties facilitated a growing sense of urgency regarding juveniles, even though empirical rates indicated there was no overall increase in youth crimes after the early 1820s (King 1998). Public fears were stoked by authorities who falsely represented crime statistics to facilitate the acceptance of new laws and regulations (May 1973).[21] The Victorian print media, drawn by the sensationalist potential of a perceived uptick in crime, further propagated the message of predatory youth (Casey 2011).[22] These narratives were likely influenced by social reformers, evangelicals, and philanthropists, characterized by fear of social disruption, pity for the wayward youth, and religious undertones (King 1998; Magarey 1978). The moral panic resulting from these widespread accounts motivated law enforcement to increase juvenile arrests, resulting in fluctuations in crime statistics in urban centers (Casey 2011).[23]

It is unclear whether an increase in crime led to new statutes, or whether new laws led to more crime (Magarey 1978). As noted by Douglas Hay in *Albion's Fatal Tree*, "As offences appear to multiply so also do statutes . . . which define hitherto innocent or venial activities . . . as crimes" (Hay 1975, 13). Childish behaviors, such as vagrancy or truancy, shifted in meaning and significance, transitioning from a sign of misfortune to an indication of criminality (Houston 1972). Along with being charged with common juvenile transgressions, such as breaking curfew and drinking alcohol, youth were also at risk of being charged with ambiguously defined offenses, such as "immoral behavior," "incorrigibility," and "habitual disobedience" (Berger & Gregory 2009).[24]

As the number of juveniles who found themselves behind bars increased, there developed a sort of pecking order among them. Different offenses were accorded varying levels of respect, with pickpockets and housebreakers at the top and beggars at the bottom (Duckworth 2003).[25] Regardless of the severity of their crimes, children and adults were housed together in communal prisons. As inexperienced youth mingled with career criminals, what was intended as an effort in discipline instead became a criminal classroom (Fox 1996). By the middle of the century, the surveyor general of prisons in England was quoted as saying that he "did not think that the present prisons are at all adapted to juveniles" (May 1973, 11). This was a rare, but significant acknowledgment that age was an important factor in determining legal repercussions for deviance.

Although age played little part in prison placement, it was significant in determining guilt in juvenile cases (May 1973). As stated in James Fitzjames Stephen's 1883 *History of the Criminal Law*: "by English law children under seven are absolutely exempt from punishment, and from seven to fourteen there is a presumption that they are not possessed of the degree of knowledge essential to criminality, though this presumption may be rebutted by proof to the contrary" (Wolff 1996, 244). Legal recognition of the importance of age in assigning guilt had a significant impact on the severity of the consequences; age could determine whether a child received a prison sentence or was given over to the care of a workhouse or orphanage. Despite these age-related legal protections around presumptions of innocence, the incarceration of youth was still commonplace; in 1848 alone, there were an estimated 13,900 children incarcerated in England (Magarey 1978).[26]

Over time, the plight of at-risk and incarcerated youth caught the attention of reformers on both sides of the Atlantic. British activists and North American penologists began recognizing the costs associated with retribution and the benefits affiliated with rehabilitation.[27] These combined efforts led to the creation of a system of reform that was designed to address the ever-increasing problem of juvenile delinquency and ineffective punitive practices. The resulting reformatory system differed from the classic penitentiary model in that intimidation and repression were replaced with discipline and industriousness (Platt 1969).[28]

In the mid-1820s, New York opened its first House of Refuge for the Reformation of Juvenile Delinquents, and in 1828, Philadelphia followed suit. In the following decades, reformatories continued to increase in number as other cities and states embraced the new trend. By the end of the 1840s, Canada had also adopted the reformatory model and set out to establish its first House of Refuge (Houston 1972). Although different in size and administration, these various institutions followed a few basic principles: separating males and females, parting the youthful offender from the adult prison population, emphasizing rehabilitation over punishment, and restricting admissions to those believed to be receptive to treatment (Fox 1996). In addition, most reformatories presented themselves as places of refuge and education, with a focus on schooling, industry, and moral training (M'Callum 1855).[29]

The reformatory system addressed many of the concerns about juvenile delinquency that had plagued the 1800s. Its method of addressing wayward youth was an improvement on previous models, focusing on correcting errant behavior, rather than simply punishing it. Although not a perfect solution and, in hindsight, subject to merited criticism, it would pave the way for the introduction of juvenile courts, the next step in the historical trajectory of responses to juvenile delinquency.

TRANSITION TO THE CONTEMPORARY PERIOD

Throughout the course of the twentieth century, several advances were made in relation to juvenile delinquency. Social and legal forces sought to identify, understand,

and mediate the various factors that placed youth at risk, as well as to improve criminal justice responses to this unique population. Perhaps the most prominent outcome
of this era was the introduction of juvenile courts.

Legal reformers have long been champions of the notion that Western justice systems were far from adequate in addressing youth crime (Hartjen 2008).[30] Recognizing
the merits of this claim, select states in the United States sought to produce criminal
justice alternatives, tailored to meet the unique needs of child offenders. The focus
centered on the appropriateness of court proceedings, and in 1899, Illinois introduced
the first system of juvenile courts, followed closely by Colorado (Mack 1909). Numerous jurisdictions followed suit, and over thirty juvenile courts were established in the
United States before 1919. London was not far behind.[31] Britain's Child Care Act of
1908 attempted to bridge the gap between civil and criminal jurisdiction, and eventually led to the downfall of the Industrial Schools Act of 1865 (Goldson 2020).[32] As
juvenile courts gained popularity, they caught the attention of the international community, and Europe, Canada, and the Australian colonies began introducing similar
systems in the ensuing years (Lerman 1984).

Juvenile courts were an indication of progression; however, they were also an
attempt to wed two unlikely partners: social welfare and legal necessity. As such,
juvenile court cases were often plagued by contradiction, as welfare and punishment
were both endorsed by the same justice system (Goldson 2020). Recognizing the differences between these two agendas, efforts were made to strike a balance between
punitive and therapeutic/educational measures (Hartjen 2008). This led to an overhaul
of legal procedures and the institutions used to house delinquent youth, as well as
investigations into the societal factors that spurred delinquency (Stevens 1916). In
addition, significant efforts were made to appoint judges and various officers who
were committed to improving circumstances for at-risk youth (Boudreau 2010; Cabot
1918).

In addition to accommodating both legal and social considerations and prioritizing knowledgeable personnel, the reach of juvenile courts was also expanded. As
expected, it included youthful behavior that was criminal in nature, but it also heard
cases relating to behavior that would be considered legal if perpetrated by an adult
(Elliot 1914). In recognition of the need for individualization, juvenile courts emphasized the role of mitigating factors when deciding guilt and punishment. This led to the
investigation of the home environment, education, physical and medical conditions,
and means of support for the accused delinquent, all factors that were deemed relevant
in judicial decision-making (Blatier 1999; Stevens 1916). The first juvenile courts
were modest in structure, but before long, it became apparent that these new practices
required a cadre of alienists, psychologists, physicians, and probation officers; as
such, the juvenile court system expanded quickly, resulting in an unexpectedly substantial institution before too long (Baker 1920). Growth in the fields of psychology,
sociology, and criminology paralleled the rise of the juvenile court system, with each
of the respective fields offering explanations and solutions for juvenile delinquency
(Goldson 2020).

Academics and professionals were authorized by the court to investigate and report
on individual delinquents. Throughout North America, social reformers, medical
experts, and those appointed by the juvenile courts recognized poverty, inadequate

parental care, and a lack of education as primary causes of delinquency (Boudreau 2010). Intellectual capacity was also called into question, and mental and physical deficiencies became a frequent focus of specialists, leading to a rise in biopsychological explanations, as well as a marked rise in juvenile psychoanalysis (Auden 1911; Stevens 1916).

Many experts harbored the belief that mental peculiarities and moral shortcomings would manifest themselves physically, and a direct correlation between physical defects and criminality was often taken as fact. Informed in part by evolutionary theory and criminal anthropology, expert conclusions often pointed to the notion that crime was not typical for an average and fit individual; instead, it was rooted in some atavistic (devolutionary) or psychic-epileptic condition that was passed down through the generations (Weidensall 1913). As a consequence, professionals allowed family lineage (genetics) to influence their findings and subsequent judgments (Mack 1909). In addition, juveniles were examined for head and face anomalies, along with abnormalities in height, weight, and strength, and they were subjected to tests of endurance and psychic prowess, in order to demonstrate that juvenile delinquents were physically inferior (Rhoades 1907).[33] One of the fundamental goals of many reformatory-type institutions was to improve physical fitness, with the belief that it was inextricably linked to mental fitness (Auden 1911).

New legal concerns arose with the increasing popularity of the juvenile court system. Primary among these were debates concerning the age of culpability, due process, access to counsel, and assorted disputes regarding sentencing severity.[34] The majority of Western nations eventually implemented some form of the common law stipulation known as *doli incapax*, which proposed that juveniles were unable to fully comprehend the implications of their actions, and thus were unable to form legal intent (Hartjen 2008). The most severe of sentences, such as a mandatory life without parole, or a judgment of execution, eventually fell out of favor as juvenile culpability was questioned further.[35] However, even as youth justice continued to evolve throughout the century, some demographics were slower to recognize progress than others (Feld 2017).[36]

The image of the juvenile delinquent, as well as the best way to deal with them, developed throughout the twentieth century. Were the youth in question to be regarded as children or as young adults? Were they in need of welfare or discipline, rehabilitation or punishment? Was the primary danger they posed to themselves or to society at large? The answers to each of these questions lay on a spectrum, and at different times, public and institutional favor oscillated between extreme ends of each spectrum, with the youth in question and the legislation associated with their plight in continuous flux between the two. Society and legal systems shifted between condemnation and understanding, with periods aimed at prevention and rehabilitation eventually giving way to the present day, an era of tough-on-crime policies (Goldson 2020).

CONCLUSION

Children hold a special place in our modern world, requiring additional social and legal protections and granted allowances not enjoyed by the adult community. As this chapter illustrates, this was not always the case. Early human civilizations viewed children as the responsibility of the family, protecting them from legal prosecution but leaving them vulnerable to familial abuse and neglect. Over time, authorities introduced juvenile culpability while continuing to turn a blind eye to the use of private corporal punishment. Before long, youth were subject to a motley array of punishments, including physical beatings, incarceration, and even death.

In early modern times, juvenile offending and punitive measures were amplified by childhood poverty and abandonment, which drew the attention of social and political reformers. Their well-intended philanthropic utterings ushered in an increasing public awareness of the unique and individual nature of juvenile offending, thus prompting the development of reformatories and juvenile courts. Despite these efforts, children in the modern era still manage to slip through the cracks of established social welfare systems, suggesting that juvenile justice remains a work in progress, demanding further change in the eras to come.

NOTES

1. According to the United Nations, adulthood begins at the age of eighteen (Crawford & Lewis 2008).

2. Of course, even today not all countries and peoples accept the UN definition of childhood.

3. The Hammurabi Code of the eighteenth century BCE states that, "If a son (intentionally) strikes his father, his hand will be cut off" (Marcus 1981, 33). Further laws in that period allow for a child's tongue to be cut out if they deny their parents, or to be disowned and sold into slavery.

4. In ancient Egypt, a child was not beholden to the law before the age of ten (Feucht 1990). However, physical punishment was expected for children who misbehaved, and they could be cast out of the family if they remained obstinate.

5. Records from even four thousand years ago show teachers using physical punishment to correct various faults (Kramer 1957).

6. Larger juries, especially for high-publicity cases, could include over a thousand people (Philips 2013).

7. An inspirational story commonly told to Spartan youth was of the boy who stole a fox and hid it under his cloak. Of particular interest were the measures the boy took to avoid detection: "rather than endure the humiliation of being publicly punished for his incompetent thievery, he persistently denied the theft, while the fox tore at his stomach with its teeth and claws" (Garland 1991, 16).

8. A girl could be married before the age of twelve and even be charged with adultery while still prepubescent (Laes 2019). The man would not be charged with adultery, however, since the girl was below the legal age of marriage.

9. This overlooks the fact that, even in modern days, children often are dressed in formal, adult attire, especially for artistic and photographic events.

10. One individual tells of being chained by his thumbs, arms, and feet while only given bread and water to eat (Katajala-Peltomaa 2016). Such acts were often accompanied by more genteel rituals such as a pilgrimage to a local shrine, where the parents would light a candle as tall as the afflicted child.

11. In one recorded example of a huntsman's apprentice, the huntsman exhorted that the apprentice should be "beaten until he had a proper dread of failing to carry out his master's orders" (Orme 2001, 315). In addition to being taught all the skills of the trade, a household apprentice could expect to receive housing, clothes, education, and payment for his services. Agricultural laborers were more likely to receive only the basic necessities required to live.

12. The Black Death of the fourteenth century had greatly reduced the population, so hired labor was expensive (Kremer 2014). The system of apprenticeship effectively created a large pool of cheap labor.

13. Birth registrations would not be common until the seventeenth century, which is also when age lines started becoming more concrete (Kean 1937).

14. Children of this era lived under harsh conditions, receiving what would now be considered brutal physical punishments, as well as coping with sickness and disease. As late as the seventeenth century, the average life expectancy was only thirty years (Berger & Gregory 2009).

15. Fathers in France had the right to request the state to imprison their children for up to one month for no reason at all, so long as they were under sixteen. Parents could ask the state to step in and help in disciplining their children if they felt they were unable to do so on their own (Blatier 1999).

16. England's Court of Chancery was a court set up in the Middle Ages to address issues outside of the common law. It often dealt with the guardianship of infants and children.

17. The percentage of individuals under the age of eighteen brought before the court more than doubled between the years of 1785 and 1793 (King 1998).

18. Small boys were frequently recruited as chimney sweeps due to their flexibility and dexterity. In 1840, this practice was outlawed due to the dangerous conditions of the work. Despite the change in the law, children continued to be hired as chimney sweeps, but often as a means to train them in the art of burglary. In an era with fireplaces located in nearly every room of a house, these boys were able to familiarize themselves with the layout of a home, as well as any valuables located within it. This information was often sold to other criminals, and child sweeps were occasionally contracted out to burglars by their masters (Duckworth 2003).

19. William Action provides us with a glimpse of the influence of nineteenth-century moralists in his 1857 writing of *Prostitution Considered in its Moral, Social and Sanitary Aspects*. He summarized the moralist position with the following statement: "All illicit intercourse is prostitution, and that this word is as justly applicable as those of 'fornication' and 'whoredom' to the female who, whether for hire or not, voluntarily surrenders her virtue" (Wolff 1996, 235). During this period, girls under the age of ten and boys under the age of fourteen were considered innocent when accused of engaging in prostitution, whereas older children were criminally culpable (Wolff 1996).

20. The shift away from capital punishment in the nineteenth century is well-documented. Although 103 children aged thirteen and under were sentenced to death between 1801 and 1836 at the Old Bailey in London, every one of them had their sentence commuted to transportation or imprisonment (May 1973).

21. Modern observers have noted the discrepancy in the ideas of the average Victorian when compared with the more reliable statistics of the time (Casey 2011).

22. Coupled with reports gathered from reputable sources, such as the Home Office Returns and the *Journal of the Royal Statistical Society of London*, fictional stories told in weekly newspaper installments served to alert the public to the supposed crime-infested underbelly of their cities. Serial publications, such as Charles Dickens's *Oliver Twist*, were said to be based in fiction, but upon closer inspection, they seem to have derived from local London neighborhoods (Duckworth 2003). As in many scenarios, a well-told story can offer us perspectives unavailable in statistics and official reports.

23. Some academics assert press coverage as being the primary cause of the supposed "crime wave" of the early/mid-1800s (Casey 2011).

24. A few of the pettier crimes prosecuted in Canada included stone throwing, shouting in public, and coasting on the street (Boudreau 2010).

25. Either taught by family, other youth, or criminals acting as trainers or minders, children as young as five years old were adept pickpockets. Two or three children would often work together, occasionally soliciting young girls to help facilitate the process. They rarely worked in areas where they were already known, instead preferring railway stations and racecourses, and occasionally traveling to different parts of the country to avoid detection (Duckworth 2003).

26. Although the rates of youth incarceration were high, they were overshadowed by the number of destitute children documented during the same period. In 1851, records indicate that over forty-three thousand English children under the age of sixteen were living in workhouses (Magarey 1978). The recognition that different classifications were needed to distinguish between children deemed criminal, and those simply neglected and destitute, was well-documented throughout both Europe and North America by this time (Houston 1972).

27. Administrators were among the more prominent advocates for reform in the United States, including the secretary of the New York Prison Association, the dean of Columbia Law School, and the secretary of the Massachusetts State Board of Charities (Platt 1969). Although their views differed on potential solutions to the delinquency problem in Canada, Andrew Dickson and Wolfred Nelson championed the need for a new strategy in dealing with at-risk youth (Houston 1972).

28. Although social leaders advocated for disciplinary measures that transcended the brutality of corporal punishment, many still believed physical punishment had a place in juvenile corrections. In New York, Elmira Reformatory was thought to be on the forefront of rehabilitation; however, it received scathing reports and became mired in various scandals throughout the years, and its population was likened to "a garrison of a thousand prisoner soldiers" (Berger & Gregory 2009, 20).

29. The intentions of various institutions may have been altruistic in their establishment, but there were those who urged caution in regard to housing an ever-growing population of young delinquents. William Crawford is quoted in his pleas for restraint as claiming, "to separate children from their parents by committing them to a place of confinement . . . for an act of vagrancy, or the mere accusation of such an act . . . is a stretch of authority not reconcilable with the spirit of the English law" (May 1973, 27).

30. Jurists overseeing the cases of young offenders were perhaps some of the first to recognize and call attention to the inability of the criminal court to appropriately handle the individualization necessary in the majority of youth cases. They were instrumental in calling for the creation of a separate system (Baker 1920).

31. Whether changes in charges and incarceration had an effect on levels of juvenile crime is debatable. Policy tended to be influenced more by the political climate than with the levels and severity of juvenile delinquency (Hartjen 2008; Goldson 2020; Muncie 2013).

32. This shift took place despite industrial schools' claims of success with the rehabilitation of youth, claims they supported with statistics pointing to low levels of recidivism. By 1922, British Industrial Schools were admitting less than one-third the number of youths they had admitted in 1913 (Lerman 1984).

33. Although pseudoscience played a role in the judgment of many, it was by no means unanimously accepted as fact. Goring stated, "the physical and mental constitution of both criminal and law-abiding persons of the same age, stature, class, and intelligence are identical. There is no such thing as an anthropological criminal type" (as quoted in Stevens 1916, 857).

34. As the century progressed, United States common law raised the age of culpability from seven, to ten or twelve, and eventually to anywhere from sixteen to eighteen (Mack 1909).

35. For the majority of states in the United States in the twentieth century, a sentence of life without parole was mandated for anyone convicted of murder. A conviction outweighed any accounting for an offender's culpability, and children as young as twelve were sentenced as adults (Feld 2017). It was eventually agreed that juveniles' immature judgment and limited self-control, combined with their sensitivity to negative peer influence, resulted in diminished culpability.

36. Throughout the course of the twentieth century, nearly three-quarters of juveniles executed in the United States were Black youths (Feld 2017).

REFERENCES

Antošovská, Tereza. 2019. "Children as culprits and criminals: Children in mischief, delict, and crime in Roman Empire." *Graeco-Latina Brunensia* 24 (2): 5–18. https://doi.org/10.5817/GLB2019-2-1.

Auden, George A. 1911. "Feeble-Mindedness and Juvenile Crime." *Journal of the American Institute of Criminal Law and Criminology* 2, no. 2 (July): 228–38. https://www.jstor.org/stable/1132955.

Baker, Herbert M. 1920. "The Court and the Delinquent Child." *American Journal of Sociology* 26, no. 2 (September): 176–86. https://www.jstor.org/stable/2763667.

Bardis, Panos D. 1964. "The Ancient Greek Family." *Social Science* 39, no. 3 (June): 156–75. https://www.jstor.org/stable/23907609.

Bauman, Richard A. 1996. *Crime and Punishment in Ancient Rome.* Oxford: Routledge.

Beaumont, Lesley A. 2012. *Childhood in Ancient Athens: Iconography and Social History.* Oxford: Taylor and Francis Group.

Berger, Ronald J., and Paul D. Gregory (editors). 2009. *Juvenile Delinquency and Justice: Sociological Perspectives.* Boulder: Lynne Rienner Publishers.

Blatier, Catherine. 1999. "Juvenile Justice in France: The Evolution of Sentencing for Children and Minor Delinquents." *British Journal of Criminology* 39, no. 2 (Spring): 240–52. http://www.jstor.org/stable/23637971.

Boudreau, Michael. 2010. "'Delinquents Often Become Criminals': Juvenile Delinquency in Halifax, 1918–1935." *Acadiensis* 39, no. 1 (Winter/Spring): 108–32. http://www.jstor.org/stable/41803291.

Buneci, Bogdan. 2021. "General Considerations on Punishment in Medieval Europe." *RAIS Journal for Social Sciences* 5, no. 1 (May): 39–48. https://doi.org/10.5281/zenodo.4783295.

Cabot, Frederick P. 1918. *The Juvenile Delinquent.* Boston: Massachusetts Commission on Probation.

Canterella, Eva. 2004. "Controlling Passions or Establishing the Rule of the Law? The Functions of Punishment in Ancient Greece." *Punishment and Society* 6, no. 4 (October), 429–36. https://doi.org/10.1177/1462474504046122.

Carey, Christopher. 1994. "Legal Space in Classical Athens." *Greece & Rome* 41, no. 2 (October): 172–86. http://www.jstor.org/stable/643012.

Carrel, Helen. 2009. "The Ideology of Punishment in Late Medieval English Towns." *Social History* 34, no. 3 (September): 301–20. https://doi.org/10.1080/03071020902981626.

Casey, Christopher A. 2011. "Common Misperceptions: The Press and Victorian Views of Crime." *Journal of Interdisciplinary History* 41, no. 3 (Winter): 367–91. http://www.jstor.org/stable/40985739.

Clayton, Paul, and Judith Rowbothan. 2009. "How the Mid-Victorians Worked, Ate and Died." *International Journal of Environmental Research and Public Health* 6, no. 3 (March): 1235–53. https://doi.org/10.3390/ijerph6031235.

Crawford Sally, and Carenza Lewis. 2008. "Childhood Studies and the Society for the Study of Childhood in the Past." *Childhood in the Past* 1, no. 1 (July): 5–16. https://doi.org/10.1179 /cip.2009.1.1.5.

Duckworth, Jeannie. 2003. *Fagin's Children: Criminal Children in Victorian England*. London: Bloomsbury Academic.

Eliot, Thomas D. 1914. *The Juvenile Court and the Community*. New York: Macmillan Publishers.

Feld, Barry C. 2017. *The Evolution of the Juvenile Court: Race, Politics, and the Criminalizing of Juvenile Justice*. New York: New York University Press.

Feucht, Erika. 1990. "Juvenile Misbehavior in Ancient Egypt." In *History of Juvenile Delinquency: A Collection of Essays on Crime Committed by Young Offenders, in History and in Selected Countries*, edited by Albert G. Hess and Priscilla F. Clement, 61–70. Aalen: Scientia Verlag.

Fox, Sanford J. 1996. "The Early History of the Court." *Future of Children* 6, no. 3 (Winter): 29–39. https://doi.org/10.2307/1602591.

Garland, Robert. 1991. "Juvenile Delinquency in the Graeco-Roman World." *History Today* 41, no. 10 (October): 12–19.

Goldson, Barry. 2020. "Excavating Youth Justice Reform: Historical Mapping and Speculative Prospects." *Howard Journal of Crime and Justice* 59, no. 3 (September): 317–34. https://doi .org/10.1111/hojo.12379.

Gorski, Richard. 2009. "Justices and Injustice? England's Local Officials in the Later Middle Ages." In *Outlaws in Medieval and Early Modern England: Crime, Government and Society, c. 1066–c. 1600*, edited By John C. Appleby and Paul Dalton, 55–74. Farnham: Ashgate Publishing.

Griffith-Williams, Brenda. 2013. "Violence in Court: Law and Rhetoric in Athenian and English Assault Cases." *Greece and Rome* 60, no. 1 (April): 89–100. http://www.jstor.org/stable /43298105.

Hartjen, Clayton A. 2008. *Youth, Crime, and Justice: A Global Inquiry*. New Brunswick: Rutgers University Press.

Hay, Douglas C., Peter Linebaugh, John G. Rule, E. P. Thompson, and Cal Winslow. 2011. *Albion's Fatal Tree: Crime and Society in Eighteenth-Century England*. London: Verso Publishing.

Houston, Susan E. 1972. "Victorian Origins of Juvenile Delinquency: A Canadian Experience." *History of Education Quarterly* 12, no. 3 (Autumn): 254–80. https://doi.org/10.2307/367514.

Jassongne, Gaëtan. 2020. "Adolescence during Antiquity: The Greek and Roman Periods." *Psychiatria Danubina* 32, no. 1 (September), 164–66.

Jones, W. R. 1969. "The Two Laws in England: The Later Middle Ages." *Journal of Church and State* 11, no. 1 (Winter): 111–31. https://www.jstor.org/stable/23913939.

Katajala-Peltomaa, Sari. 2016. "Diabolical Rage? Children, Violence, and Demonic Possession in the Late Middle Ages." *Journal of Family History* 41, no. 3 (April): 236–54. https://doi .org/10.1177/0363199016644593.

Kean, A. W. G. 1937. "History of the Criminal Liability of Children." *Law Quarterly Review*, 53 (3): 364–70.

King, Peter. 1998. "The Rise of Juvenile Delinquency in England, 1780–1840: Changing Patterns of Perception and Prosecution." *Past & Present* 160 (August): 116–66. http://www .jstor.org/stable/651108.

Kramer, Samuel N. 2012. *A Father and His Perverse Son: The First Example of Juvenile Delinquency in the Recorded History of Man*. Whitefish: Literary Licensing.

Kremer, William. 2014. "What Medieval Europe Did with Its Teenagers." *BBC World Service*. March 23, 2014. https://www.bbc.com/news/magazine-26289459.

Laes, Christian. 2019. "Children and Bullying/Harassment in Greco-Roman Antiquity." *Classical Journal* 115, no. 1 (October): 33–60. https://doi.org/10.1353/tcj.2019.0026.

Lerman, Paul. 1984. "Policing Juveniles in London: Shifts in Guiding Discretion, 1893–1968." *British Journal of Criminology* 24, no. 2 (April), 168–84. https://www.jstor.org/stable /23637027.

M'Callum, A. K. 1855. "Juvenile Delinquency—Its Principal Causes and Proposed Cure, as Adopted in the Glasgow Reformatory Schools." *Journal of the Statistical Society of London* 18, no. 4 (December): 356–63. https://www.jstor.org/stable/2338284.

Mack, Julian W. 1909. "The Juvenile Court." *Harvard Law Review* 23, no. 2 (December): 104–22. https://www.jstor.org/stable/1325042.

Magarey, Susan. 1978. "The Invention of Juvenile Delinquency in Early Nineteenth-Century England." *Labour History* 34 (May): 11–27. https://www.jstor.org/stable/27508306.

Marcus, David. 1981. "Juvenile Delinquency in the Bible and the Ancient Near East." *Journal of the Ancient Near Eastern Society* 13, no. 1 (January): 31–52.

May, Margaret. 1973. "Innocence and Experience: The Evolution of the Concept of Juvenile Delinquency in the Mid-Nineteenth Century." *Victorian Studies* 17, no. 1 (September): 7–29. https://www.jstor.org/stable/3826512.

Muncie, John. 2013. "International Juvenile (In)justice: Penal Severity and Rights Compliance." *International Journal for Crime, Justice and Social Democracy* 2, no. 2 (September): 43–62. https://doi.org/10.5204/ijcjsd.v2i2.107.

Newman, Paul B. 2007. *Growing Up in the Middle Ages*. Jefferson: McFarland & Company.

Orme, Nicholas. 2001. *Medieval Children*. New Haven: Yale University Press.

Parsons, Ben. 2015. "The Way of the Rod: The Functions of Beating in Late Medieval Pedagogy." *Modern Philology* 113, no. 1 (August): 1–26. https://doi.org/10.1086/680664.

Phillips, David. 2013. *The Law of Ancient Athens*. Ann Arbor: University of Michigan Press.

Pigg, Daniel. 2015. "Children and Childhood in the Middle Ages." In *Handbook of Medieval Culture, Volume 1*, edited by Albrecht Classen, 149–58. Berlin: De Gruyter.

Pike, Ruth. 1975. "Crime and Criminals in Sixteenth-Century Seville." *Sixteenth Century Journal* 6, no. 1 (April): 3–18. https://doi.org/10.2307/2539514.

Platt, Anthony. 1969. "The Rise of the Child-Saving Movement: A Study in Social Policy and Correctional Reform." *Annals of the American Academy of Political and Social Science* 381 (January): 21–38. http://www.jstor.org/stable/1038229.

Rhoades, Mabel C. 1907. "A Case Study of Delinquent Boys in the Juvenile Court of Chicago." *American Journal of Sociology* 13, no. 1 (July): 56–78. http://www.jstor.org/stable/2762536.

Shahar, Shulamith. 1990. *Childhood in the Middle Ages*. Oxford: Routledge.

Stern, Laura I. 2004. "Politics and Law in Renaissance Florence and Venice." *American Journal of Legal History* 46, no. 2 (April): 209–34. https://doi.org/10.2307/3692441.

Stevens, Herman C. 1916. "'The Individual Delinquent.'" *Journal of the American Institute of Criminal Law and Criminology* 6, no. 6 (March): 849–59. https://doi.org/10.2307/1133110.

Titus, Jordan J. 2005. "Juvenile Transfers as Ritual Sacrifice: Legally Constructing the Child Scapegoat." *Youth Violence and Juvenile Justice* 3, no. 2 (April): 116–32. https://doi.org/10 .1177/1541204004273313.

Weidensall, Jean. 1913. "Criminology and Delinquency." *Psychological Bulletin* 10 (6): 229–37. https://doi.org/10.1037/h0074926.

Wolff, Larry. 1996. "'The Boys Are Pickpockets, and the Girl Is a Prostitute': Gender and Juvenile Criminality in Early Victorian England from 'Oliver Twist to London Labour.'" *New Literary History* 27, no. 2 (Spring): 227–49. http://www.jstor.org/stable/20057349.

Chapter 10

A History of Mental Health and Crime

Trip Finity Taylor, Madison Wolf, and Omi Hodwitz

INTRODUCTION

Humankind has always been fascinated with abnormal or unconventional human behavior, particularly in relation to mental health. Historically, we have delighted in the enticing and shocking nature of the mad or deranged, oftentimes treating them as an entertaining sideshow, one that allows us to embrace a position of superiority, immune to the pains and agonies of mental instability. Meanwhile, the medical community has churned out text after text filled with stigmatizing terminology and tentative and stumbling explanations. Even the legal community has become mired in the ways of the fools, idiots, and lunatics, feeling the need to criminalize and penalize such behaviors, thus filling correctional institutions with both the bad and the mad. Although each of these various trends and practices has been harmful to those who suffer from mental disorders, the merging of illness with the justice system has proven particularly detrimental, resulting in stigmatization, a loss of liberty, and a failure to treat, thus inviting a revolving-door scenario. Only recently has the assumed synonymity between health and criminality begun to fray, providing a welcome and long-overdue opportunity to critically analyze the historical roots of this intersection. This brings us to the task set for this chapter: to introduce the reader to the long and oftentimes troublesome realities of mental health in the Western world and, at times, its relationship to deviance and the criminal justice system.

Our story begins with the early societies of the Mediterranean, a time during which humankind struggled to differentiate between the body and soul. Mired in this quandary, particularly in relation to those who behaved in objectional or destructive ways, these early societies turned to home confinement as a method of management and control. This practice continued well into the Middle Ages, at which time the rising influence of religion, paired with the continued blending of the body and the soul, led to additional measures (including exorcism and death) as a method of addressing the unfit. As the Western world expanded and reopened following the ravaging plagues of the Dark Ages, public confinement became popular, leading to a surge in hospitals and asylums, each flooded with patients. At the turn of the eighteenth century, science and a new morality took center stage, pioneering a period of improvement. This period ended abruptly, however, at the hands of the biological determinists and eugenicists that followed on the empirical heels of the Scientific Revolution. This brings us to the twentieth century, an era of legal cases and cultural fights against forced sterilization, electroconvulsive therapy, and the mass incarceration of the homeless and mentally ill. This chapter will explore each of these different periods with the intention of offering the reader a critical analysis of the history of the intersection between mental health and crime.

EARLY HISTORY (PRE-SIXTH CENTURY CE)

Like all civilizations, early human societies from ancient Egypt to Greek and Roman antiquity struggled with unpredictable or erratic behavior, particularly in relation to mental health. Faced with the need to provide an explanation for the unknown, including any threats to social health and well-being, these early civilizations made a definitive connection between the body and the soul, determining that abnormal or abhorrent behavior was the indication of a troubled soul. The problem then became how to address such sicknesses; the ready solution was the removal of these individuals from society. In practice, some cultures relied solely on families to hide away unconventional and disturbed members of society, while others used banishment to rid a locale of their presence. In addition to removal, some cultures sought to cure the soul through bodily treatment, including surgery, exercise, and other measures. Regardless of the method of addressing mental health, these measures were informed by a perceived connection between the physical and the spiritual.

Early Public Perceptions of and Responses to Mental Illness

Despite cultural, social, and spiritual diversity across regions and eras, responses to mental illness were relatively uniform during the ancient era, relying primarily on isolation and removal, paired with a lesser enthusiasm for physical intervention such as surgery. Beginning with the Stone Age, tribes blamed evil spirits for dysfunctional behaviors that threatened the individual or community, requiring that when such circumstances arose, the family or clan of the afflicted would manage the illness (Slate et al. 2021, 33). Cuneiform tablets from ancient Babylonia explain, sometimes in extensive detail, conditions that could now be linked to epilepsy, psychosis, obsessive-compulsive disorder, psychopathy, anxiety, and depression (Trimble & Reynolds 2016, 4). The erratic behavior caused by these afflictions confounded or embarrassed family members and neighbors, and it became common practice to conceal the person in a basement or nearby cave indefinitely or permanently. This method was carried over into subsequent civilizations. The Greek empire, for example, viewed mental illness as a defect that threatened family honor, and thus, abandonment or confinement was considered a reasonable or acceptable response (Blue 1993, 305). In short, given the lack of cure or reliable treatment, it was more favorable to remove a person with mental illness from society than risk the chance they might embarrass their community or engage in deviance.

Removal and isolation were not the only responses to mental health concerns; these early societies also entertained a variety of physical interventions. One popular form of treatment for madness involved removing a portion of the skull of the afflicted. This procedure, known as *trephination*, dates back seven thousand years and was readily practiced across multiple regions, ranging from the Peloponnesian Sea to Peru (Slate et al. 2021, 33; Gosselin 2019, 4–5). Trephining the skull was believed to release evil spirits within, the assumed cause of epileptic seizures, headaches, or deviant criminal behavior (Gosselin 2019, 5). Ironically, these religiously motivated practices were the early ancestors to many of our contemporary procedures, informed by the assumption that the control center of human behavior resides in the brain.

Although spiritual explanations for erratic behavior continued throughout the duration of ancient antiquity, ancient Greece and Rome made notable strides in understanding the relationship between physical health and mental health. Select philosophers and physicians speculated that mental illness was a physical ailment, and although their specific explanations for the relationship between the physical and the mental were arguably peculiar, their advocacy of humane, comfortable, and sanitary treatment was laudable (Slate et al. 2021, 34). Hippocrates (460–377 BCE), for example, pontificated that an imbalance in the body's four primary fluids, which consisted of black and yellow bile, blood, and phlegm, dictated the presentation of human personality, including whether a person was relaxed or aggressive (Butcher, Mineka, & Hooley 2007, 29). In contrast to the earlier widespread belief that supernatural forces were to blame for unruly or inexplicable behavior, Hippocrates was the first to link these behaviors with natural disorders such as depression/*melancholia*, anxiety/*mania*, phrenitis, and various phobias (Slate et al. 2021, 34).[1] Although Hippocrates agreed with his some of his contemporaries, including the famous philosopher Plato, that the head was the core of a person's mental processes, that did not distract him from his theories of fluid and bodily imbalances. This was just one of many diverging perspectives in the battle to understand the complexities of the human body and mind. When opposing positions failed to provide complete answers, mythology served as needed.

Mental Illness and Mythology

Mythology played a central role in ancient antiquity, offering guidance and prescriptions for the population at large. Early myths were extensive, addressing all manner of human experience, including several that dealt with illness of mind and body. These myths provided some form of explanation, albeit often a fantastic one, for the unruly behavior of the mentally unsound. Consider the vexing correlation between the moon and mental illness that dominated some early myths.[2] Numerous early civilizations regarded the moon as a potential cause of erratic thought and behavior. Romans believed the moon was the root of epilepsy, nightmares, and insanity (Plante, Papiasvili, & Mayers 2013, 11). The Greeks worried that a person could become infected by wolf-madness, also called *lycanthropy*, a condition with symptoms of paleness, dry or hollow expressions, and peculiar behavior, such as howling at the moon (Porter 2002). Many people feared that wolf-madness could lead to uncontrollable and criminal behavior.[3] Treatment for this ailment, as with other mental illnesses, often entailed hiding a subject from moonlight by locking them up at night, then providing them with ample comforts like warm baths and walks in the sunshine during the day (Plante, Papiasvili, & Mayers 2013, 12). As one might expect, this approach was not very successful.

Other myths also offered explanations for unruly and irrational behavior. The Greeks, for example, created Lyssa, the goddess of madness, who could possess a person who offended her until they lost control of their own mind (Plante, Papiasvili, & Mayers 2013, 4). The maenads provide another mythical interpretation of disruptive behavior. The maenads were a group of women who wandered the countryside frenziedly feasting on wild animals and behaving in seemingly peculiar ways. Despite their behavior, they were believed to be bestowed with superhuman strength and to represent the will of the gods, particularly Dionysus (or Bacchus, in Roman mythology) [Plante, Papiasvili, & Mayers 2013, 5].

Stories such as those about Lyssa and the maenads provide insight into the cultural view of madness during antiquity. Mythology suggests that mixed in with fear of the unknown, there was also some element of veneration directed toward the mentally unfit. In support of this supposition, key philosophers such as Plato and Aristotle surmised that society should revere select individuals with mental health concerns, positing that some of the disordered displayed mystical and creative genius (Kleisiaris, Sfakianakis, & Papathanaiou 2014). This cultural approach to mental illness may explain why most treatments were prescribed under the guise of a familial guardian, and not the authorities; this ensured that the unfit were protected and able to achieve brilliance should the opportunity arise (Slate et al. 2021, 34). Although this was common practice, ancient antiquity still took measures to create legal codes and practices for the afflicted.

Early Legal Codes and Practices

Early statutes addressing mental illness were few and far between, but they did exist in some form or another. In fact, the infamous philosopher Plato penned some of the first written codes concerning this select group of individuals. In his work "The Laws," circa 350 BCE, Plato asserted, "If anyone be insane, let him not be seen openly in the town, but let his kinsfolk watch over him as best they may, under penalty of a fine" (Walker 1985, 26). This, of course, expressed the practice of isolation that was common at the time.

Hundreds of years later, Romans developed more specific criminal responses to the mentally unfit. Justinian's *Digest* of 533 CE, for example, provided a record of the various legal arguments and practices employed throughout early Roman history. One such document included in *The Digest* stated that the law could excuse a madman who committed murder because his madness was punishment enough and no additional measures were necessary (Walker 1985, 26). In another example, the Twelve Tables, which contained early Roman laws, mandated that male kin retain guardianship over the *furiosi*, or mentally unfit individuals who had a proclivity toward violence and posed a threat to public safety (Metzler 2016, 143). Additionally, records indicate that a lack of responsibility due to mental affliction could be argued in both Greek and Roman courts. It is noteworthy that these early legal approaches to mental illness would not only remain in place, but would evolve over time, eventually influencing the European legal code practiced today.

To summarize, early civilizations and their understanding of and reactions toward mental illness were varied. Although several notable thinkers presented a connection between the physical body and the mind, most cultures did not readily accept these scientific hypotheses. Many continued to see unnatural or illogical behavior as perplexing, and various groups persisted in attributing fantastical or spiritual causes to madness. Solutions included cutting open an afflicted person's skull to release their demons or locking them away from other people until symptoms subsided. Thus, societies before the sixth century CE were more inclined to follow mythology and superstition than to have confidence in more scientific explanations. This was the foundation that steered society into the next era, known now as the Middle Ages.

THE MIDDLE AGES (SIXTH–FIFTEENTH CENTURIES)

The period of history from the sixth to the fifteenth centuries is riddled with tales regarding the treatment and mistreatment of the mentally ill. Some cultures reeled under the poor economic conditions of the times, and they subsequently failed to attend too closely to their mentally ill, as doing so would require scant resources. Instead, physicians and healers tried new, unregulated, and unsystematic experimental techniques, most with terrifying and unproductive results. Other societies fell under the Church's control, where exorcism and other spiritual remedies predominated. Despite these seemingly draconian approaches, the Middle Ages also contained measures of progress. This era marks the introduction of the first mental health hospitals, along with a more systematic set of legal statutes addressing the intersection between insanity and crime. In addition, the relationship between mental illness and innate deviance took center stage, providing a platform for Renaissance thinkers. These measures were limited, however, when one considers the plight of the afflicted during much of the thousand years that constitute the Middle Ages.

Medieval Public Perceptions of and Responses to Mental Illness

Several explanations for mental illness presented themselves during the Middle Ages, including some that were influenced by Hippocrates's early supposition that personality was shaped by the balance of bodily humors and the others that embraced the ecclesiastic proposition of demonology. Regarding the former or an imbalance of fluids, treatments were extreme. Healers gave patients various laxatives, or used leeches to bleed them, with the intention of disrupting any blockage that might be causing their erratic behavior (Foerschner 2010, 3). Many natural concoctions were used to purge the afflicted of negative bodily influence, the most common of which included black hellebore, colocynth, rhubarb, or tobacco (MacDonald 1981, 187–88). Another procedure called bloodletting (later phlebotomy) involved extracting corrupted humors by tapping open the veins on or near the head, particularly the forehead (MacDonald 1981, 191). If all else failed, it was common practice to "teach" the illness out of the individual by way of beating, flogging, or any other physical punishment (Foerschner

2010, 3). Unfortunately, as one would likely expect, these treatments often failed, and as such, the mentally unfit were often locked away in a manner reminiscent of ancient antiquity.

Demonology provided a second but equally popular explanation for seemingly abnormal behavior during the Middle Ages. The Catholic Church followed in the footsteps of older religions by positing that possession by evil spirits caused people to act erratically or sinfully (Slate et al. 2021, 34). Similar to fluids/humors-based solutions, treatments for this diagnosis were unique. The Church proposed that demons could be expelled or exorcized through charms, incantations, special meals, or other rituals. Although these measures might have seemed relatively nonpunitive, this shifted as the Church took control of vast expanses of medieval Europe. As its power and reach increased, the Church restructured laws and customs, ensuring that demonic possession served as a central theme (Slate et al. 2021, 34). As such, when less-radical treatments to mental illness failed, the afflicted parties faced more-severe repercussions, including death and banishment.

Although explanations for mental illness varied between physiological and spiritual, the social response to afflicted individuals was relatively uniform. The mentally unfit, when not actively under the supervision of family or church, often battled the stigma of shame, leading to a life of vagrancy. In addition, many medieval town councils expelled wandering non-residents who were perceived as unclean, deformed, or insane. Although social ostracization was the norm, there were places that became unofficial sanctuaries for mentally ill persons, particularly near the end of the era. The town of Gheel in the modern-day Netherlands provided sanctuary to mentally unfit residents and outsiders and, in some cases, would charge the abandoning township for the financial care of their former residents (Weiner 2008, 256). Many other locales throughout Europe, including, but not limited to, Metz, Paris, Milan, and Florence, eventually followed suit, opening their doors to the unwell and providing a precursor to what would later become mental hospitals.[4] The first European institution devoted strictly to the attention of the mentally ill opened in Valencia, Spain, in 1406. These institutions were not officially hospitals, per se, as there were no doctors on-site, but they were recognized as providers of custodial care (Weiner 2008, 257).[5] Despite these notable advances toward the humane care of the mentally ill, the question of their legal rights and determinations remained unresolved.

Medieval Legal Codes and Practices

An analysis of Old English court proceedings shows that the medieval classification of mental illness was diverse and varied. "Fools" with congenital mental impairment, found sometimes as court jesters, differed from the "lunatics," who had the ability to recover their senses (Weiner 2008, 257).[6] Thomas Aquinas presented the "insane from infancy," differentiating them from those who "have suffered loss of reason" in the "Sick of Mind" category of his *Canon Law* (Plante, Papiasvili, & Mayers 2013, 27). The famous thirteenth-century legal scholar Bracton wrote that "a madman is one who does not know what he is doing, who is lacking in mind and reason, and who is not far removed from the brutes" (Hall 1945, 689). Bracton also suggested that a mentally incapacitated person could be held liable for criminal actions if they enjoyed "lucid intervals" (Metzler, Anderson, & Schalick 2016, 153). The *Mirror of Justices*, a fourteenth-century legal textbook, later subdivided mental illness into three distinct varieties: the inborn "natural fools"; the "lunatics," who developed incapacity but still had lucid intervals; and those who were permanently corrupted, or the "continuelement arragez" (Metzler, Anderson, & Schalick 2016, 157). Each region under different authority ended up with its own set of rules or regulations regarding mental disability and criminal justice.[7]

Legal disputes revolving around mental soundness were prevalent during this era, including regarding the possession of property and inheritance, as well as the more visibly prominent issue of responding to harmful and criminal acts. The King's Prerogative, *Prerogotiva Regis*, written in the second half of the thirteenth century, helped clarify the measures to be taken with disabled individuals (Neugebauer 1979, 479). English communities, for example, either acquitted women and children or assigned them a temporary custodian, rather than doling out punishment for crimes committed while mentally unfit. In addition, many men like William Belle, John Faytour, Ralph Silkstone, Richard Russel, and Guillaume Blackburn were found either *non fuit compos mentis sue*, "unable to comprehend their actions" at the time of the crime, or *per frenesimus morba acute labortas*, "in a fit of madness," thus relieving them of responsibility for all criminal wrongdoing and acquitting them of their charges (Turner 2012).

Not every mentally unfit alleged criminal was absolved of responsibility, however, as seen by the European witch hunts. As the Middle Ages neared its end, the Western world renewed its fears of the unknown, with a focus on witchcraft and heresy. In 1486, the Catholic Church authorized the *Malleus Maleficarum*, a Latin publication also known as *The Hammer of Witches*, which was used, along with the Letters of Approbation of 1487, to identify and punish anyone believed to be using dark magic (Dvoskin, Knoll, & Silva 2020, 638). The Inquisition tracked down hysterical women, the socially disenfranchised, and many who suffered from mental illness, including those afflicted with uncontrollable seizures, and forcefully interrogated them until they reluctantly admitted to engaging in witchcraft (Trimble & Reynolds 2016, 7). These confessions were often met with death by burning or drowning, and it is estimated that more than a million people were killed over the course of two and a half centuries (Slate et al. 2021, 34). Ironically, sometimes the Church excused religious adherents who saw visions in the name of God's influence rather than the devil's work, even though the symptoms often mirrored those accused of witchcraft (Plante, Papiasvili, & Mayers 2013, 20). As such, it appeared that mental illness was a scourge on society unless it was dedicated to those in power, namely the Church.

In summary, the Middle Ages was a period of shifting ideas about and prescriptions for mental illness. In two diverging paths, explanations for instability focused on physiological imbalances and spiritual intrusions, both resulting in an array of treatments that had little hope of succeeding. Isolation, banishment, and death were commonplace, although this was supplemented with more formalized institutions near the end of the era. Legal responses were limited at first, becoming more established over time. Thus, depending on the region or the year, mental illness was viewed in different ways during the Dark Ages. The Renaissance of Europe, the next era in waiting, marked a shift in general political, social, and cultural practices, but not an end to the irregular treatment of the mentally afflicted.

THE GREAT CONFINEMENT (1492–1770)

That fool, of wisdom and reason doth fail, And also discretion, laboring for naught. And in this ship shall help to draw the sail Which day and night enfixeth all his thought To have the whole world within his body brought, Measuring the coasts of every realm and land And climate, with his compass in his hand.
—From the English translation of Sebastian Brant's 1494 *Das Narrenschiff* (Ship of Fools)

Several consecutive but overlapping eras, including the Renaissance, Enlightenment, and Scientific Revolution, followed the nearly thousand years of the Middle Ages. During this time, confinement became commonplace, and the mentally unsound found themselves drifting aboard prison ships, locked behind the closed doors of hospital wards, and tied to whipping posts for public scrutiny. Appropriately, this collective period is also known as the Great Confinement, derived from the diverse and numerous prison-like institutions that opened during this period (Foucault 1965). Unfortunately, these institutions were far from humane; the living conditions for lunatics, whether they had committed crimes or not, were often horrendous. This began to change, however, near the end of this era; in tandem with the cultural revolutions occurring in much of the Western world, a handful of doctors and advocates began to conceptualize a more compassionate approach to treatment. By the end of the eighteenth century, the Great Confinement had ended, bringing on a new era of Moral Treatment.

Perceptions of and Responses to Mental Illness

By the end of the Middle Ages, most European towns and villages were opposed to providing sanctuary for wandering fools or idiots. Additionally, many of the newly built hospitals could not provide care for them long-term. Thus, the Western world needed a new and sustainable form of confinement. As these things tend to happen, the age of sea exploration reached its pinnacle at just the right time, and a solution developed naturally. Ships traveling through the rivers and canals of Europe, as well as those traveling across the great oceans, took on copious crews, or cargos, full of the mentally ill. These "Ships of Fools," as described by Sebastian Brant in his 1494 poem, transported hundreds of unwanted lunatics to North America and elsewhere, only tempering the flow when these destinations fought against the unwelcome invasion of the mentally unfit (Dvoskin, Knoll, & Silva 2020, 638). In addition to receiving a poor welcome upon arrival, many of these social outcasts ended up perishing while out at sea, being laid to rest in ol' Davy Jones's locker. Although the ships may have seemed particularly punitive, the alternative was worse. Those who failed to gain passage on a ship could find themselves relegated to confinement in "fool's cages" or "mad-cells," a public village display that served to shame the unfit, subjecting them to the castigation of the local peasants as they spit upon or insulted the confined (Dilling, Thomsen, & Hohagen 2010, 371).

As the Ship of Fools and the mad-cells illustrate, the early Renaissance was not a humane period for the mentally unwell. However, there were some exceptions among select representatives of the Church, demonstrating a notable shift from previous eras.

Religious clergy in wealthier areas of Europe adopted a paternalistic role toward the mentally ill members of their flock. Some Catholic states introduced private mad-houses run by priests or nuns; these institutions focused on prayer and repentance as a means of relieving symptoms of mental instability (Foerschner 2010, 3). Other regions endorsed religious pilgrimage as a potential treatment, with some religious authorities sending the afflicted to specific religious shrines, such as the shrines of Saint-Mathurin de Larchant or Saint-Hildevert de Gournay near Paris (Rosen 1964, 380). The town council of Basel went as far as to provide money and letters of safe conduct for mentally ill pilgrims on their path to these alleged healing shrines (Rosen 1964, 380). Many of these measures were doomed to fail, however, leaving select church-run facilities to turn once again to exorcism, particularly with female patients. Whatever measures were taken, in the end there were simply too many individuals who required care, and the excess ended up at the clergy's madhouses, overfilling them and decreasing their already-limited effectiveness in providing relief and solace. As such, municipal authorities were forced to take on some responsibility for the bur-geoning population of the mentally ill.

Expansion of the Institution

As the name suggests, institutionalized confinement became the norm during the Age of Confinement. Europe embraced the notion of insane asylums or hospitals, and this became a notable trend in the fifteenth and sixteenth centuries. London's hospitals would become the most famous, forever known for their inhumane treatment. St. Mary of Bethlehem, or Bethlem Royal Hospital, provides a ready example of English institutional standards and practices of this time. Originally opened as a monastery and traditional medical hospital in 1247, Bethlem shifted away from the treatment of physical ailments around the beginning of the 1400s (Plante, Papiasvili, & Mayers 2013, 29). Although it became an unofficial site for mental health treatment, it was not until the mid-1500s that Henry VIII announced that Bethlem was exclusively an insane asylum (Butcher, Mineka, & Hooley 2007, 36). Conditions at Bethlem were deplorable: sanitation was poor, chained "patients" spent lengthy periods of time locked in the dark with nothing to console them, and local elites often toured the facility for a small fee, a form of zoo-like entertainment during which time they could enjoy the "picturesque delusions" captured within the walls of the facility (Slate et al. 2021, 35). Bethlem also served a political purpose; it was often used to confine and silence those whose ideas ran counter to the elite. The hospital eventually earned the nickname "Bedlam," which would become synonymous with chaos and disorder, used as a pejorative term for all insane asylums for years to follow.

Although Bethlem was a particularly significant early hospital, it was simply one of hundreds of asylums that opened over the course of the Great Confinement. Although the list is long, some notable examples include: San Hipolito in Mexico in 1566, House of the Insane in Germany in 1601, La Maison de Chareton in France in 1641, Hôpital-Général in Paris in 1656, Pesthof in Hamburg in 1683, Guy's Hospital "luna-tic ward" in London in 1728, and St. Luke's in London in 1751 (Dilling, Thomsen, & Hohagen 2010; Weiner 2008; Dvoskin, Knoll, & Silva 2020).[8] Similar to Bethlem, treatment in most facilities was subpar at best or nonexistent at worst. Starting in the seventeenth century, harsh and addictive sedatives, such as opium grains, unguents, and laudanum, kept the prisoners pacified and manageable (MacDonald 1981, 190). Some patients were exposed to fruitless experimental measures, such as the "gyrating chair" of Dutch Dr. Boerhaave, which purported to restore equilibrium through the intense shaking of the patient's body and blood (Foerschner 2010, 4). All it succeeded in doing, however, was rendering the patient unconscious or extremely disoriented. Thus, institutionalization, although the norm at the time, served little purpose other than warehousing.[9]

A number of progressive thinkers responded to the unfortunate plight of the mentally unsound with persuasive treatises and prescriptions. Spanish humanist Jean Louis Vives, for example, endorsed compassion for the afflicted in his 1525 publication titled *On Poor Relief* (Mora 2008, 240).[10] Meanwhile, Johann Weyer, a Dutch physician whom many consider to be the first psychiatrist, took issue with the treatment of women accused of witchcraft. Specifically, Weyer wrote a scathing response to the *Malleus Maleficarum* in 1563 titled *De Praestigiis Daemonum* (On the Deceptions of the Demons). In it, he chastised the persecution of alleged witches, noting they were much more likely suffering from mental illness, deserving of treatment rather than exorcism or death (Trimble & Reynolds 2016, 7). Edward Jorden followed on the heels of Weyer; his 1603 treatise sought to counteract the popular view of the time that hysterical women were possessed by supernatural forces, offering instead a physical explanation for "perturbations of the mind" that aligned with the early scientific view of Hippocrates and Galen (Trimble & Reynolds 2016, 6).[11] These early protestations to the theories and practices surrounding mental illness set the stage for the seventeenth century, when science again began to renew its grasp on mental illness. These scientific grumblings, however, had little immediate impact on perceptions of the mentally unwell, including legal responses to the afflicted population.

Legal Codes and Practices

Writings, laws, and court proceedings addressing mental illness increased during the Great Confinement, particularly in England, with a heavy emphasis on the role of accountability and culpability. In 1581, William Lambard was one of the first to mention the role of free will in criminal acts executed by the mentally afflicted, when he stated, "If a madman or a natural fool, or a lunatic in the time of his lunacy . . . do kill a man, this is no felonious act . . . for they cannot be said to have any understanding will" (Quen 1974, 314). Court records from Old Bailey cases, some dating as far back as 1624, report that criminal exculpation of "mad" individuals could be "knowable" by ordinary witnesses, who were the primary sources of evidence in this pre-adversarial period (Loughnan 2011, 1054–58). Sir Matthew Hale postulated a clear requirement that "absolute" madness, or obvious total incapacity, dictated legal culpability in his *Historia Placitorum Coronae*, published posthumously in 1736 (Loughnan 2011, 1060). This burgeoning set of statutes and prescriptions is likely a response to the hundreds, even thousands, of mentally ill individuals who were put on trial for criminal acts in England during this period. Despite these legal protections, many of those who did go before the courts were still found culpable and subsequently confined, further reflecting the period-specific commitment to warehousing the mentally ill. By the end of the Great Confinement, most nations followed England's lead, creating laws like the Vagrancy Act of 1714, which permitted the relatively unchecked detainment of "lunatics," thus allowing court authorities to lock up as many of the "furiously mad and dangerous" as possible (Weiner 2008, 259).

In summary, the Age of Confinement earned its name as Western society detained and confined its many mentally unfit members. This practice might have been well-intended, as in the case with the religious asylums, but the outcomes were anything but humane. Thousands of the afflicted were locked up, some were forgotten, others were tortured, and more were put on display for public amusement. This trend not only continued despite a shift in progressive thinking, but it also expanded to the legal system. Despite a growing recognition of the role of rationality and free will in criminal culpability, the mentally unfit were prosecuted in large numbers, often based solely on witness testimony. Thus, the lines between the mad and the bad were blurred, a dangerous development that further ensured a lack of treatment for the afflicted. Despite these sobering trends, a period of improvement was on the horizon. By the end of the eighteenth century, select humanitarians and medical doctors were on the precipice of unchaining the asylums, thus beginning a new era.

MORAL TREATMENT (1770–1870)

A period of Moral Treatment for the mentally ill occurred throughout most of the Western world, beginning around the time of the American and French Revolutions, and ending around the time of the Industrial Revolution. Due in large part to enlightened medical personnel at asylums, these institutions metaphorically broke the chains of the afflicted, shifting from prison-like facilities to more humane treatment facilities. In conjunction, researchers from the newly minted fields of psychiatry, psychology, and neurology sought to identify pathological explanations for mental instabilities.[12] As for the criminal justice system, medical practitioners became commonplace in courtrooms, giving their expert opinions on the mental health of those accused of violating the law. In parallel, new laws were developed in earnest, addressing questions around responsibility, culpability, and the confinement of the mentally unfit. Lastly, with the exception of mentally ill individuals who committed criminal acts, the mad and the bad were treated as two separate entities. Despite these progressive measures, the era of Moral Treatment ended on a note reminiscent of earlier periods. By the end of the nineteenth century, most reforms had faded and mental institutions once again became overcrowded, thus demanding a new approach lest the mistakes of the past repeat themselves.

Perceptions of and Responses to Mental Illness

At the beginning of the era of Moral Treatment, Western asylums were held in poor regard by many, including those directly involved with the operations of such facilities. The founder of London's St. Luke's Hospital, William Battie, for example, took issue with his superintendent competitors, offering a challenge to enrich the management of the mentally ill. In his 1758 *Treatise on Madness*, Battie espoused a new "moral treatment" built on the supposition of human goodness and extolling environmental improvements for the sake of treatment (Dilling, Thomsen, & Hohagen 2010, 382). This early call to action was the precursor for what was to become a movement focused on the reformation of asylums for the betterment of the patients. Vincenzo Chiarugi, who took over management of the Hospital of Bonifacio in Florence in 1785, provides a ready example. Echoing Battie's sentiments, Chiarugi viewed his role in the following way: "a supreme moral duty and medical obligation to respect the insane individual as a person" (Mora 1959, 430). Later, in 1793 at La Bicêtre in Paris, Philippe Pinel put these sentiments into practice; he upended the policies of chaining the afflicted to the wall, sedating them with opiate medication, and engaging in painful and ineffective treatments, advocating for a different approach that prioritized humane practices. It was Pinel's view that the mentally ill could be cured through "considerate treatment, occupational therapy . . . and comfortable lodgings" (Roberts & Kurtz 1987, 78). Thus, as part of his radical new approach, Pinel cleaned the facility, engaged in individualized conversations with the patients, and allowed them to freely walk the grounds and engage in exercise (Foerschner 2010). As a consequence, Philippe Pinel is widely lauded to this day as the liberator of the mentally afflicted or the purveyor of institutional freedoms and rights.

Informed at least in part by the efforts of Battie, Pinel, and Chiarugi, several asylums revamped their approach to treatment while others were opened anew with an agenda similar to those prescribed by these institutional reformers. One of the most famous of these facilities was the York Retreat in England, founded and managed by the Quakers in 1796. William Tuke, one of the early founders of the Retreat, infused Battie's version of moral treatment with the Quaker foundations of order, legality, and abstinence (Dilling, Thomsen, & Hohagen 2010, 382). Tuke advocated for a warm and religious environment, such as a country house, to impress a sense of mildness, reason, and humanity upon the patients (Porter 2002, 103–4). Tuke eventually shared this premise in the publication of his *Treatise of the Moral Treatment of the Insane*, which became widely read and influential for future reformers (Roberts & Kurtz 1987, 78).

Tuke's work eventually spread across the Atlantic Ocean to Pennsylvania, where Quakers founded the Friends Asylum in 1817, modeled after Tuke's York Retreat. Nearby, at the Pennsylvania Hospital, Benjamin Rush, soon to be considered the father of psychiatry, introduced two new treatments, including recreational and occupational therapies.[13] Alongside these innovative approaches to addressing mental illness, Rush was one of the first to postulate that substance addiction should be viewed as a mental illness, subject to treatment rather than punishment (Slate et al. 2021, 36).

Thus, the era of Moral Treatment is marked by the work of institutional reformers such as Battie, Pinel, and Chiarugi, the beliefs of religious orders like the Quakers, and the medical models of Rush and others. The combination of these efforts led to the modification and influx of asylums and hospitals throughout the Western world, each prioritizing humane treatment that veered from the abuse and neglect of previous eras.[14]

THE NINETEENTH CENTURY

During the nineteenth century, mental illness became a rich field of study, mostly carried out within the confines of treatment facilities. Philippe Pinel set the pace with systematic observations, detailed notes, and structured conversations with patients, and through his careful approach, he proposed some of the first treatments for the mentally ill that were rooted in legitimate psychological factors. One of Pinel's apprentices, Jean-Etienne D. Esquirol, followed suit when he opened a private hospital for the afflicted in Paris; it was here that Esquirol developed diagnoses for kleptomania, pyromania, nymphomania, and paranoia, among others, which he published in his *Mental Maladies* in 1838 (Gosselin 2019, 17). Around the same time, the research community adopted an increasing interest in the brain and nervous system, which led to a new field of study committed to explaining "neuroses" and other neuropathological diseases (Weiner 2008, 255). These advancements in thought laid the groundwork for fundamentally important future discoveries, such as the origins of hallucinations, delirium, and epileptic seizures, all of which were historically attributed to supernatural forces or other wildly unsound causes. As psychology, neurology, and psychiatry developed as scientific disciplines, their impact was felt in the criminal justice system.

Legal Codes and Practices

During this era of treatment, legislatures across the Western world passed laws addressing the confinement of mentally ill individuals, including in both medical and punitive institutions. The Madhouse Act, passed in 1774 in England, regulated private asylums and required a signed medical certificate prior to any forced commitment (Gosselin 2019, 17). The "Legge Sui Pazzi," or Law on the Insane, which was established in 1774 in Italy, outlined a process of hospitalization focused on identifying those who could cause public damage or harm, with the underlying goal of institutionalizing the afflicted in a single location, rather than mixing them with the indigent, the criminal, and the sickly (Mora 1959, 428). England's Act of 1800 outlined the specific crimes for which a plea of insanity could be applied, thus charging safe custody of those accused of said set of offenses (Walker 1985, 29). Scotland's Act of 1815 recognized the importance of medical practitioners in establishing rationality and accountability, stipulating that these experts should play a leading role in authenticating madness in both civil and criminal contexts (Houston 2003, 351). A statute in New York in 1842 dispatched "assessors" to actively seek out lunatics in the community, whether they appeared dangerous or not, for forced civil confinement (Slate et al. 2021, 36). Many of these new laws adopted a paternalistic tone, suggesting that each was instigated in the interest of the mentally ill; however, given the emphasis on confinement, many ensured the historical practice of removing the afflicted from society was replicated in the nineteenth century.

Mixed in among these various confinement-focused Acts that were becoming commonplace in the Western world were a handful of pivotal courtroom battles that further defined the parameters of an insanity defense in criminal proceedings. As mentioned previously, prior to the turn of the nineteenth century, courts relied on the testimony of witnesses and laypersons to determine insanity; medical practitioners were rarely (if ever) invited to offer their opinion of a defendant's mental capacity (Houston 2003, 343). Historically, these lay opinions were influential in establishing a lack of responsibility. Records of Old Bailey court sessions in England, for example, show that insanity defenses in the sixty years leading up to 1800 were successful in

almost half the recorded cases (Walker 1985, 29). In the 1840s, however, two particularly impactful cases, those of Edward Oxford and Daniel M'Naghten, redefined the
process of establishing criminal culpability for reason of insanity.

Edward Oxford, who tried and failed to assassinate Queen Victoria in 1840, had
a history of bizarre and irrational behavior. During his trial, his friends and family
attested to this history, but it was ultimately the testimony of medical professionals,
which emphasized Oxford's inability to determine right from wrong, that swayed the
jury. The judge, upon determining a lack of legal responsibility, stated, "If some controlling disease was, in truth, the acting power within him which he could not resist,
then he will not be responsible" (Quen 1974, 319).

Daniel M'Naghten's trial was also pivotal in establishing criminal responsibility.
In 1843, M'Naghten shot the British prime minister's secretary, mistakenly believing him to be the prime minister. Similar to Oxford, M'Naghten's trial relied heavily
on medical expertise; his lawyers incorporated Isaac Ray's *Treatise on the Medical
Jurisprudence of Insanity* into their defense and medical practitioners concluded that
he suffered from mental illness (Quen 1974, 319). M'Naghten was found not guilty
by reason of insanity, and the judicial ruling established what later became known
as the "M'Naghten Rules." These rules, which stipulate that an individual is not
criminally culpable if they suffer from a) diminished rationale due to b) mental illness that hinders their ability to know c) the nature of the act or whether it is right or
wrong, are still in use today.[15] Thus, due to these cases and others, medical testimony
in courtrooms became a commonplace practice, transforming the legal meaning and
applicability of mental illness when considering criminal responsibility.

Perceptions of and Responses to Mental Illness

As the nineteenth century progressed and scientific and legal interest in the mentally ill increased, so, too, did public interest. In Victorian England, public anxieties
facilitated two "lunacy panics," driven in part by concern about the potential for the
wrongful confinement of people and in part by fear of the danger that lunatics posed
if left at large in the community (McCandless 1978, 366–67). Many moving parts
contributed to these panics. In France, physicians such as Pinel, Landouzy, Georget,
and Briquet proposed potential causes of mental hysteria, including post-traumatic
cerebral origins, which escalated public anxieties (Trimble & Reynolds, 2016, 8).
Across the pond, in the United States, involuntary institutionalization skyrocketed
during and following the Civil War, fueled in part by the encouragement of key psychiatrists, such as the influential Isaac Ray, often credited with cofounding the field
of forensic psychology (Dvoskin, Knoll, & Silva 2020, 2). Furthermore, an increase
in the number of institutionalized migrants from minority communities exacerbated
racial tensions between staff and patients (Foerschner 2010). Additionally, many of
the asylums that prioritized moral treatment had changed hands as founders aged out,
and the new leadership rarely endorsed the same level of care and compassion, thus
decreasing the effectiveness of institutionalization. Thus, the nineteenth century was
marked by public fears, psychiatric endorsement of confinement, tensions within facilities, and the fading effectiveness of treatment. By the latter half of the century, these
various issues facilitated two transitions. First, the small asylums of the initial Moral

Treatment era were replaced by larger, overcrowded mental hospitals. Second, jails and prisons were once again overflowing with the mentally ill. The situation was ripe for change; all it needed was a firebrand with an agenda, also known as Dorothea Dix.

Dorothea Dix (1802–1887), a former teacher from the United States, became deeply invested in the plight of the mentally ill after becoming a religious volunteer in the women's section of the East Cambridge Jail (Foerschner 2010). She was horrified by what she observed there, leading her to tour jails, almshouses, and mental facilities throughout Massachusetts, before she expanded her exploration to other parts of the United States, Canada, and Europe (Slate et al. 2021, 36). These tours confirmed her early impressions as a religious volunteer; mentally ill prisoners, many of whom had committed no actual crimes, were placed in subpar facilities that were neither safe nor therapeutic, leading to physical and sexual abuse by staff or fellow inmates and exacerbating mental instabilities (Slate et al. 2021, 36). Dix worked incessantly, locating allies and lobbying political entities, advocating for legislative support and funding for state hospitals that prioritized quality trained staff and effective treatment (Slate et al. 2021, 37).[16] Her tireless efforts paid off; by the end of her career, Dix was responsible for the establishment of more than thirty new hospitals across Canada and the United States (Butcher, Mineka, & Hooley 2007, 40). Dix is credited with initiating the Mental Hygiene movement, a replacement for the Moral Treatment approach from previous years.

MENTAL HYGIENE (1870–1960)

The end of the nineteenth century through to the cultural revolutions of the 1960s marked a period of expanded scientific research and experimentation on institutionalized populations. Accordingly, the fields of psychoanalysis, eugenics, psychosurgery, and psychiatry all developed new and seemingly innovative techniques to cure or pacify mental disease. The vocabulary surrounding mental illness reflected this surge in interest, incorporating terms like *electroconvulsive therapy*, the *subconscious id*, *feebleminded imbeciles*, *lobotomies*, *sterilization*, and *psychopharmacology*. Additionally, newly minted theories of biological determinism allowed for grand definitive conclusions about the intellectual abilities of the mentally afflicted. The era followed an unpredictable trajectory, beginning with the work of reformers like Dorothea Dix and ending with a shift toward comprehensive local community care.

Perceptions of and Responses to Mental Illness

Although the mental hygiene movement was prominent throughout the Western world, it originated primarily in the United States, influenced in large part by Clifford Beers, a former patient at the Connecticut State Hospital for the Insane. While institutionalized at the hospital, Beers witnessed and was subjected to severe abuse and harsh treatment, prompting him to publish an autobiography in 1908 titled *A Mind That Found Itself* (Roberts & Kurtz 1987, 80-81).[17] The book, which was well-received and lauded by many, promoted a number of prescriptive measures, including improved living conditions for the patients and salaries for the medical attendants, with hopes that the latter would lead to more professional treatment. With the help of renowned psychiatrists like Adolf Meyer and William James, Beers founded the National Committee for Mental Hygiene (NCMH), which advocated for early intervention in the treatment of acute mental disorders (Morrissey & Goldman 1986, 18). The organization embraced moral treatment and helped create the first hospitals for the morally bereft in Albany, Ann Arbor, Baltimore, and Boston. It also pushed for locally centric care of mental health, aiding in the establishment of several state associations, such as the Connecticut Society for Mental Hygiene (Roberts & Kurtz 1987, 82). The NCMH went on to become the National Mental Health Association, which would later champion the psychiatric profession, as well as universal care for the mentally afflicted.

While Beers and others were establishing organizations and facilities that focused on the mentally ill, practitioners were intent on identifying the causes and treatments for specific disorders. Perhaps the most prominent and influential of these intellectual monoliths was Sigmund Freud, also known as the father of psychoanalysis. The Austrian psychiatrist and neurologist published multiple volumes between 1888 and 1939, each expounding on the potential causes and consequences of select mental illnesses. One of his more prominent theories posited that the mind was comprised of three parts (the id, ego, and superego), and imbalances between these elements could lead to psychopathology and deviance. Freud also suggested that repressed immoral desires or traumatic childhood memories could lead to a disconnect or dissonance in mental functioning, thus facilitating mental disorders. Freud proposed several therapeutic approaches, including hypnosis, dream analysis, and free association; these different measures, Freud argued, would aid the patient in identifying and processing repressed experiences and resulting trauma (Foerschner 2010). Freud's position was persuasive, and consequently, psychoanalysis became a popular tool for treating mental illness in the early twentieth century, even though some critics argued it was a pseudoscience.

The Biological Model

Although the psychiatric community was surging in the early twentieth century, their therapeutic approaches were slow and oftentimes unsuccessful. Therefore, the academic and medical communities shifted their focus to other scientific endeavors in an attempt to improve mental health, particularly ones that were rooted in the assumption that mental illness had a biological or physiological origin. Surgical responses to mental instabilities, particularly cerebral-specific procedures, became popular. Reminiscent of the trephination trend from previous eras, physicians focused on identifying damaged areas of the brain and either repairing or removing them. In 1892, for example, Gottlieb Burkhardt performed a number of operations on schizophrenic patients, believing that removing part of the brain would cure them of their afflictions (Slate et al. 2021, 37–38). Unfortunately, two of the patients died following the procedure, which temporarily diminished the enthusiasm of the medical community. The lull was short-lived; by the 1930s, physicians were back to experimenting with surgical solutions to mental illness.

Perhaps one of the more dramatic surgical measures was the lobotomy; the surgeon would place an ice pick in the eye socket of a mental patient, moving it back and forth and severing the neural connections in the prefrontal lobe.[18] The procedure was intended primarily to address violence and aggression, and it was met with some limited success (in truth, the procedure tended to dull the patient of most emotions); thus, tens of thousands of lobotomies were carried out in the following decades in Western hospitals and prisons. Eventually, however, doctors began expressing concerns about the primitive nature of the procedure, ethical concerns regarding its misuse, and the frequency with which it was used without fully informed consent (Slate et al. 2021, 38). By the 1960s, several laws regulating the use of lobotomies had all but eliminated the procedure from the surgical roster.

Surgery was not the only form of somatic intervention that gained popularity in the early- to mid-1900s, as experts began exploring chemical and electric stimulation as a means of alleviating symptoms. In the 1930s, doctors in Germany and Hungary, for example, began administering high doses of insulin or synthetic camphor to schizophrenic patients, with the goal of inducing convulsions or coma (Alexander & Selesnick 1966, 280–81).[19] These chemically-induced therapies, however, would oftentimes result in permanent side effects, leading doctors to abandon them for alternative approaches, particularly one measure developed in Italy in 1938: electroconvulsive therapy, or ECT (Foerschner 2010). ECT delivers electric shocks directly to the brain, often resulting in disorientation and short-term amnesia. Despite these side effects, mental hospitals around the world popularized ECT, positing that it alleviated psychotic and depressive symptoms (Butcher, Mineka, & Hooley 2007, 618–19). Although many of the experimental treatments initiated during the mental hygiene era fell to the wayside, ECT still remains widely used today, albeit in highly controlled contexts.

While many approaches to mental illness rooted in the biological model were premised on the assumption that these ailments could be cured, others were rooted in the supposition that the mentally ill could not be rehabilitated or treated. Key researchers, such as Cesare Lombroso and Henry Goddard, posited that some mentally ill and deviant individuals were simply inherently and irrevocably defective, born from bad stock and inferior physically, mentally, and morally (Slate et al. 2021, 37). According to these intellectuals, the only treatment for these individuals was to ensure that their lineage ended with them; if given the chance to reproduce, the afflicted would simply create another generation of inferiors. The United States embraced these theories, and between the 1870s and 1920s, prisons and mental hospitals began to segregate "feeble-minded" or "defective" deviants for long stretches of time to keep them isolated, thus thwarting any capacity to reproduce (Dvoskin, Knoll, & Silva 2020, 2). In 1917, Minnesota enacted the Children's Code to affirm the state's role as the protector of "defective" children. Elsewhere in the United States, confinement facilities started to chemically or surgically sterilize "imbeciles" and other "degenerates," including habitual criminals. Although legally challenged, the highly questionable practice of sterilization was upheld by the Supreme Court in *Buck v. Bell* in 1927 (Slate et al. 2021, 37).[20] In fact, such practices continued unchecked until the Second World War, when the public began to react negatively to the use of similar measures by Nazi Germany. Eventually, the United States overturned Buck with *Skinner v. Oklahoma* in 1942 (Slate et al. 2021, 37). Despite a shift in public and legal sentiment regarding sterilization, the belief that deviant or abnormal behavior might have untreatable biological origins persisted, resulting in the subsequent warehousing of the mentally unsound.

The population of state hospitals surged throughout the first half of the twentieth century. By 1950, the number of mental patients in the United States grew to over half a million, increasing at a rate twice as fast as the total country population growth (Morrissey & Goldman 1986, 19). The average length of stay also rose significantly during this era, increasing to almost twenty years per patient (Slate et al. 2021, 39). Around the same time, some facilities implemented medical training programs for psychiatric nurses, many of which catered to young, working-class females (Boschman 2003, 24–25). Accordingly, mental hospital residents and staff swelled by the 1950s, facilitating an increased need for a new approach to addressing mental disorders. This need was addressed by way of new synthetic medications.

Prior to the mid-twentieth century, hospitals used select simple sedatives (e.g., bromides and barbiturates) to control unruly patients. The advent of several new psychotropic medications, however, propelled psychopharmacology to the front lines of mental health care. In 1949, for example, an Australian psychiatrist named John Cade reintroduced lithium salts as a prospective treatment for mania (Foerschner 2010).[21] Along similar lines, in the early 1950s, doctors in Paris discovered the drug chlorpromazine (later called Thorazine), first used as a treatment for nausea, then as an antipsychotic due to its sedating effects (Slate et al. 2021, 40–41). These drugs and more were the impetus for a shifting in the landscape.[22] Psychiatrists and physicians realized the power of medication to alleviate select symptoms, thus mitigating the need to focus solely on institutionalization as a means of controlling the burgeoning population of the afflicted. This seemingly high note signaled the end of the Mental Hygiene movement, thus ushering in a new era, one that was focused on deinstitutionalization.

DEINSTITUTIONALIZATION AND TRANSINSTITUTIONALIZATION (1960–2000)

Criminal justice officials applauded the era of mental hygiene; confinement in mental health hospitals meant that fewer of the afflicted ended up in prisons or jails, thus alleviating the strain on the carceral system.[23] The 1960s ushered in a perfect storm, however, one that would shift the balance between therapeutic and punitive institutions. In a flurry of activity and shared interests, governments endorsed community care programs, psychiatrists embraced medication and psychopharmacology, lawyers advocated for adequate treatment of mental disorders, and society championed civil rights for marginalized groups, including the mentally ill. Although these campaigns were well-intentioned, the collective results were disastrous. Increased medication led to substance abuse and addiction, and efforts to prioritize community care over mass institutionalization led to poverty and homelessness. Many of the afflicted ended up on the street, indigent and harboring drug dependencies, before eventually ending up in the hands of the criminal justice system. Thus, in many Western nations, as the mentally ill were liberated from mental institutions, they were absorbed by the criminal justice system. Consequently, mental illness was again connected to criminal deviance.

Community care became the focus of mental health treatment in the early 1960s. In the United States, for example, one of President Kennedy's last acts was signing the

Mental Retardation Facilities and Community Mental Health Centers (CMHC) Construction Act of 1963 (Roberts & Kurtz 1987, 85). Along similar lines, Medicare and Medicaid, which began in 1965, offered funding to states that prioritized community care over institutionalization (Dvoskin, Knoll, & Silva 2020, 3). These legislative gestures resulted in the creation of more than seven hundred CMHCs over the next few decades, thus reducing the population of state mental hospitals by more than 75 percent between 1955 and 1980 (Morrissey & Goldman 1986, 21). Most CMHCs offered outpatient, inpatient, and emergency care, as well as consultation and education services (Roberts & Kurtz 1987, 85). The transition to community care seemed successful at first, but the CMHCs became overwhelmed and underfunded over time, thus unable to offer adequate and exhaustive support to the mentally disordered. As a result, many of the afflicted ended up living in rooming houses, in foster homes, in run-down hotels, or on the streets (Morrissey & Goldman 1986, 22). This trend was not unique; in Europe, many of the mentally ill were in a similar situation. They found they had no place in an overtaxed and insufficient community health care system, thus ending up self-medicated and living in subpar conditions instead (Foerschner 2010, 5).

By the late 1960s, the impetus of the community health model fell apart, and the fight for quality care migrated to the courts, ushering in a shift in legal doctrines. Morton Birnbaum, famed civil rights attorney-physician, wrote *The Right to Treatment* in 1960, in which he argued that the mentally ill had a constitutional right to medical and therapeutic services (Dvoskin, Knoll, & Silva 2020, 3). Birnbaum's words were not immediately well-received, but they soon became influential as the result of a court proceeding. Specifically, *Rouse v. Cameron*, which occurred in 1966, became the first "right to treatment" case on record in the United States. The defendant was found Not Guilty by Reason of Insanity (NGRI) on a weapons charge and remanded into the care of a mental institution. It was noted on appeal that, as a result of the ruling, the defendant was institutionalized for a length of time that was four times longer than had he been found criminally responsible and subsequently incarcerated, and during that time, he was denied treatment (Slate et al. 2021, 43). The appellate judge, who noted Birnbaum's thesis in his ruling, determined that those who were involuntarily confined to a mental institution had a right to treatment. Additional court cases further defined the rights of the mentally disordered in the United States. *Wyatt v. Stickney*, for example, established in 1972 that the "least restrictive settings" with "adequate habilitation" should be a priority for the mentally ill (Roberts & Kurtz 1987, 86). In 1975, *O'Connor v. Donaldson* determined that "non-dangerous" individuals capable of receiving care in the community cannot be legally confined without cause (Slate et al. 2021, 45). Finally, the United States Supreme Court confirmed a clear differentiation between civil ("clear and convincing") and criminal ("beyond a reasonable doubt") commitments in *Lessard v. Schmidt* in 1973 (Dvoskin, Knoll, & Silva 2020, 3). By the end of the 1970s, civil commitments were nearly obsolete, reserved for only the most severe and potentially dangerous individuals with mental illnesses. Those who did not warrant civil commitment were left to their own devices, some seeking out community care, others taking up a position on the fringes of society, and many becoming involved in the criminal justice system for petty offenses.

An anti-psychiatry movement occurred around the same time that former mental health patients filled the streets and prisons of various Western nations.

Psychopharmacology had lost its appeal as the realities of drug abuse and addiction became undeniable. British psychiatrist R.D. Laing, for example, wrote *The Divided Self* in 1960, in which he posited that mental illness was the result of social causes and, therefore, required social remedies (Slate et al. 2021, 41). Meanwhile, Thomas Szasz's *The Myth of Mental Illness* (1961) compared the psychiatric use of drugs and psychotherapy for the purposes of forcing conformity to Nazi Germany tactics during World War II (Slate et al. 2021, 41). Erving Goffman took it a step further in his 1961 publication titled *Asylums*, in which he compared psychiatric hospitals to concentration camps, where "inmates" were stripped of their identities and conditioned to "total institution" views (Slate et al. 2021, 41). Meanwhile, Michel Foucault contributed his own perspectives in his 1965 book titled *Madness and Civilization*, arguing that psychiatry was a new order of repression that failed to attend to the economic and cultural factors, which, Foucault posited, were the true causes of mental illness (Slate et al. 2021, 41).

The anti-psychiatry movement contributed to fluctuating perspectives surrounding mental illness throughout the 1970s.[24] In the United States, Congress and the presidency changed partisan hands, marking a shift in funding priorities. Kennedy's focus on the mentally ill and community care lost fiscal priority, and federal attention moved on from CMHCs to nursing homes or low-income housing (Slate et al. 2021, 46–47). In the 1980s, President Ronald Reagan slashed support for disability, mental health, and community care services. At the same time, the mentally ill lost favor with the general public, as their indigent and addicted presence became unsavory. At the same time, incarceration skyrocketed, increasing 400 percent between 1978 and the 2000s, driven in part by mental illness and addiction (Slate et al. 2021, 47). Thus, the deinstitutionalization movement of the 1960s became the transinstitutionalization movement of the subsequent decades, as the mentally ill found their way out of mental health facilities and into jails and prisons.

CONCLUSION

As this chapter illustrates, the plight of the mentally disordered has oscillated considerably over time, shifting between seclusion or isolation and public affront or display. Meanwhile, social responses to mental health issues have also fluctuated, sometimes rooted in derision, other times in compassion, and oftentimes somewhere in between. Despite these changes between and across eras, the conclusion is generally the same: those who suffer from mental illnesses are relegated to the edges of society, with limited support and services. This reality has been exacerbated by the relationship between "madness" and "badness." When mental disorders and deviance have been separated in social, political, and medical narratives, the mentally ill have been institutionalized, abused, overmedicated, or left without support. When mad and bad are treated synonymously, the afflicted have been arrested, incarcerated, and denied treatment. Caught in a current cycle of equating mental illness with deviance, we are due for a shift as large populations of the afflicted languish in jails and prisons across the Western world. History, the wisest of all authors, suggests that we critically examine the past and the mistakes that have come before us; a failure to do so will ensure a future that continues to diminish the quality of life of the afflicted.

NOTES

1. The *Corpus Hippocraticum*, a collection of medical works dated around 400 BCE, was the first to coin the word *hysteria*, presented as a female-specific disease, sometimes referred to as "wandering of the womb," that was believed to cause irrational behaviors (Trimble & Reynolds 2016, 3). Ancient Egyptians would use fumigation to lure a "wandering womb" back into alignment in women believed to be afflicted by hysteria (Alexander & Selesnick 1966, 21).

2. The term *lunacy* is derived from the Latin word *luna*, meaning "related to the moon."

3. The term *going berserk* derives from the Old Norse figure characterized by a possessed violent fury with fits of murderous behavior, which harkened back to the days when people assumed werewolves roamed the countryside (Høyersten 2007, 328).

4. The first established official mental hospital was in Baghdad in 792 CE, followed soon thereafter by mental hospitals in Aleppo and Damascus (Butcher, Mineka, & Hooley 2007, 32).

5. Several hospitals built extra rooms or added facilities specifically for disturbed patients in the fourteenth century, such as Dollhaus (madhouse) in Elbing, Tollkiste (mad cell) in Hamburg, and Tollkoben (mad hut) in Erfurt (Rosen 1964, 377).

6. "By the fourteenth century, the court fool had acquired both a threefold aspect as flatterer, laugh inducer, and official parasite and a discrete role identified by his clothing and other visible signs" (Mora 2008, 231).

7. For example, the *Senchus Mor*, old Irish law, made legal exemptions for "adulteresses, idiots, dotards, fools, persons without sense, madmen"—for whom responsibility landed on their guardians (Metzler, Anderson, & Schalick 2016, 147).

8. A practice of profitable "trade in lunacy" blossomed in the late seventeenth and early eighteenth centuries, where establishments from across England shipped lunatics to and fro, depending on the needs and desires of those who oversaw their care (Weiner 2008, 259).

9. As asylums increased in number, so, too, did their scope and population, eventually becoming warehouses for any "undesirable" individuals, including the mentally ill, criminals, the homeless, and drunkards, further exacerbating the problem of appropriate treatment and care (Slate et al 2021, 35).

10. Vives wrote, "One ought to feel compassion for so great a disaster to the health of the human mind, and it is of utmost importance that the treatment be such that the insanity be not nourished and increased, as may result from mocking, exciting or irritating madmen, approving or applauding the foolish things that they say or do, inciting them to act more ridiculously, applying fomentations as if it were to their stupidity and silliness" (Mora 2008, 240).

11. René Descartes's famous proof, *cogito ergo sum*, "I reflect, therefore I am," reframed the early Greek concept of a mind-body dualism and is seen as the beginning of modern psychology (Slate et al. 2021, 35).

12. Englishman Thomas Willis coined the scientific names *neurology* and *psychology* in his essays about the brain, *Anatomy of the Brain* (1664) and *Pathology of the Brain* (1667) [Weiner 2008, 268].

13. Rush continued to use inhumane practices like bleeding, cold water immersion, and a restraining chair for much of his career (Slate et al. 2021, 36).

14. Horace Mann in Massachusetts was in the front lines of this reform movement akin to today's milieu therapy (Morrissey & Goldman 1986, 14–15).

15. Similar legal doctrines evolved in the United States before 1870. In *State v. Pike* (1869), Judge Charles Doe stated, "If the [crime] was the offspring or product of mental disease in the defendant, he was not guilty by reason of insanity" (Quen 1974, 320–21).

16. Dix pushed Congress from 1847 to 1854 to pass a bill to grant the proceeds of a federal land sale to help build several public mental hospitals, but eventually President Pierce vetoed the law because he claimed health care was a state responsibility (Roberts & Kurtz 1987, 80).

17. Another former mental patient, Rachel Grant-Smith, called for similar reforms in her 1922 "The Experiences of an Asylum Patient."

18. Portuguese neuropsychiatrist Antonio Moniz performed the first "leucotomies" in 1935, earning him the Nobel Prize for Medicine and Physiology in 1949 (Slate et al. 2021, 38).

19. Experimental treatments also included injecting patients with malaria, typhoid, strychnine, and other poisons to induce fever, convulsions, or coma (Leifman and Coffey 2015, 192).

20. Numerous eugenic sterilization laws passed in the United States between 1905 and 1929, leading to the forced sterilization of over sixty thousand mentally ill or deficient individuals prior to 1964 (Bligh 1965, 1059).

21. Lithium salts had previously been administered to treat gout in the nineteenth century.

22. Further changes occurred in the United States after President Truman created the National Institute on Mental Health and funded new research into treatment for mental illness (Dvoskin, Knoll, & Silva 2020, 2). Congress developed the Joint Commission on Mental Illness and Health in 1955 to analyze the needs of the mentally ill, then President Kennedy proposed a "bold new approach" in 1963 to move to a community care model (Roberts & Kurtz 1987, 84).

23. Internationally, an increase in mental hospital beds corresponded to a decline in the overall prison populace, suggesting a stability between overall numbers as patients were shuffled between medical institutionalization and punitive incarceration (Penrose, 1939, as cited by Lamb, Weinberger, & Gross 2004, 109).

24. *One Flew Over the Cuckoo's Nest*, a book by Ken Kesey, as well as a follow-up film, popularized the anti-psychiatry movement with its critical portrayal of a psychiatric institution.

REFERENCES

Alexander, Franz G., and Sheldon T. Selesnick. 1966. *The History of Psychiatric Thought and Practice from Prehistoric Times to the Present.* New York: Harper & Row.

Blue, Amy V. 1993. "Greek Psychiatry's Transition from the Hospital to the Community." *Medical Anthropology Quarterly* 7, no. 3 (September): 301–18. https://www.jstor.org/stable /648932.

Boschma, Geertje. 2003. "Introduction." In *The Rise of Mental Health Nursing: A History of Psychiatric Care in Dutch Asylums, 1890–1920*, Edited by Geertje Boschma, 15–30. Amsterdam: Amsterdam University Press.

Butcher, James Neal, Jill M. Hooley, and Susan Mineka. 2007. *Abnormal Psychology.* 13th ed. Edited by Susan Hartman. Boston: Allyn & Bacon.

Dilling, Horst, Hans Peter Thomsen, and Fritz Hohagen. 2010. "Care of the insane in Lubeck during the 17th and 18th centuries." *History of Psychiatry* 21, no. 4 (December): 371–386. https://doi.org/10.1177/0957154X09102481.

Dvoskin, Joel A., James L. Knoll, and Mollie Silva. 2020. "A Brief History of the Criminalization of Mental Illness." *CNS Spectrums* 25, no. 5 (March): 638–50. https://doi.org/10.1017 /S1092852920000103.

Foerschner, A. M. 2010. "The History of Mental Illness: From Skull Drills to Happy Pills." *Inquiries Journal/Student Pulse* 2 (9). http://www.inquiriesjournal.com/a?id=1673.

Foucault, Michel. 1965. *Madness and Civilization: A History of Insanity in the Age of Reason.* Translated by Richard Howard. New York: Vintage Books.

Gosselin, Denise Kindschiu. 2019. "Introduction to the History of Mental Illness." In *Crime and Mental Disorders: The Criminal Justice Response*, edited by Denise Kindschi Gosselin, 3–24. St. Paul: West Academic Publishing.

Hall, Jerome. 1945. "Mental Disease and Criminal Responsibility." *Columbia Law Review* 45, no. 5 (September): 677–718. https://www.repository.law.indiana.edu/cgi/viewcontent.cgi?article=2408&context=facpub.

Houston, Robert Allan. 2003. "Courts, Doctors, and Insanity Defences in 18th and Early 19th Century Scotland." *International Journal of Law and Psychiatry* 26, no. 4 (July): 339–54. https://doi.org/10.1016/s0160-2527(03)00047-5.

Høyersten, Jon Geir. 2007. "Madness in the Old Norse Society, Narratives and Ideas." *Nordic Journal of Psychiatry* 61 (5): 324–31. https://doi.org/10.1080/08039480701643258.

Kleisiaris, Christos F., Chrisanthos Sfakianakis, and Ioanna V. Papathanasiou. 2014. "Health Care Practices in Ancient Greece: The Hippocratic Ideal." *Journal of Medical Ethics and History of Medicine* 7, no. 6 (March).

Lamb, H. Richard, Linda E. Weinberger, and Bruce H. Gross. 2004. "Mentally Ill Persons in the Criminal Justice System: Some Perspectives." *Psychiatric Quarterly* 75, no. 2 (Summer): 107–26. https://doi.org/10.1023/b:psaq.0000019753.63627.2c.

Loughnan, Arlie. 2011. "'In a Kind of Mad Way': A Historical Perspective on Evidence and Proof of Mental Incapacity." *Melbourne University Law Review* 35 (November): 1049–70. https://law.unimelb.edu.au/__data/assets/pdf_file/0019/1703440/35_3_10.pdf.

MacDonald, Michael. 1981. *Mystical Bedlam: Madness, Anxiety, and Healing in Seventeenth-Century England.* Cambridge: Cambridge University Press.

McCandless, Peter. 1978. "Liberty and Lunacy: The Victorians and Wrongful Confinement." *Journal of Social History* 11, no. 3 (Spring): 366–86. https://www.jstor.org/stable/3786820.

Metzler, Irina. 2016. *Fools and Idiots?: Intellectual Disability in the Middle Ages.* Manchester: Manchester University Press.

Mora, George. 2008. "Renaissance Conceptions and Treatments of Madness." In *History of Psychiatry and Medical Psychology*, by E.R. Wallace and J. Gach, 227–54. New York: Springer Science+Business Media.

Morrissey, Joseph P., and Howard H. Goldman. 1986. "Care and Treatment of the Mentally Ill in the United States: Historical Developments and Reforms." *Annals of the American Academy of Political and Social Sciences* 484, no. 1 (March): 12–27. https://www.jstor.org/stable/1045181.

Neugebauer, Richard. 1979. "Medieval and Early Modern Theories of Mental Illness." *Archives of General Psychiatry* 36, no. 4 (April): 477–82. https://doi.org/10.1001/archpsyc.1979.01780040119013.

Plante, Thomas G., Eva D. Papiasvil, and Linda A. Mayers. 2013. "Perceptions, Thoughts, and Attitudes in the Middle Ages." In *Abnormal Psychology Across the Ages, Volume 1: History and Conceptualizations*, edited by Thomas G. Plante, 15–30. Westport: Greenwood Publishing Group, Incorporated.

Porter, Roy. 2002. *Madness: A Brief Madness.* Oxford: Oxford University Press.

Quen, Jacques M. 1974. "Anglo-American Criminal Insanity: An Historical Perspective." *Journal of the History of the Behavioral Sciences* 10, no. 3 (July): 313–23. https://doi.org/10.1002/1520-6696(197407)10:3<313::aid-jhbs2300100307>3.0.co;2-d.

Roberts, Albert R., and Linda Farms Kurtz. 1987. "Historical Perspectives on the Care and Treatment of the Mentally Ill." *Journal of Sociology & Social Welfare* 14, no. 4 (December): 75–94.

Rosen, George. 1964. "The Mentally Ill and the Community in Western and Central Europe During the Late Middle Ages and the Renaissance." *Journal of the History of Medicine and Allied Sciences* 19, no. 4 (October): 377–88. https://www.jstor.org/stable/24621452.

Slate, Risdon N., Kelly Frailing, W. Wesley Johnson, and Jacqueline K. Buffington. 2021. "The History of Criminalization of Persons with Mental Illnesses." In *The Criminalization of Mental Illness: Crisis and Opportunity for the Justice System*, edited by Risdon N. Slate, Kelly Frailing, W. Wesley Johnson, and Jacqueline K. Buffington, 33–50. Durham: Carolina Academic Press.

Trimble, M., and E. H. Reynolds. 2016. "A Brief History of Hysteria from the Ancient to the Modern." *Handbook of Clinical Neurology* 139: 3–10. https://doi.org/10.1016/b978-0-12-801772-2.00001-1.

Turner, Wendy J. 2012. "Criminals." *Care and Custody of the Mentally Ill, Incompetent, and Disabled in Medieval England*, edited by Wendy Jo Turner, 109–40. Turnhout: Brepols Publishers.

Walker, Nigel. 1985. "The Insanity Defense before 1800." *Annals of the American Academy of Political and Social Science* 477, no. 1 (January): 25–30. https://www.jstor.org/stable/1045999.

Weiner, Dora B. 2008. "The Madman in the Light of Reason. Enlightenment Psychiatry." In *History of Psychiatry and Medical Psychology*, edited by Edwin R. Wallace IV and John Gach, 281–303. New York: Springer Science+Business Media.

Chapter 11

Tying the Past to the Present

Omi Hodwitz

INTRODUCTION: PANDORA'S BOX

With this last chapter, we end our tale of crime and justice in the Western world. It has been a long and arduous journey, but one that delighted us in crafting, as we hope it delighted you in reading. We have explored the oftentimes macabre and disjointed trajectory of the criminal justice system from ancient Greco-Roman times through to the Enlightenment and beyond. Our story has dissected gruesome tortures, a motley array of informal and formal measures of social control, and the role of power and privilege in criminalizing and punishing deviance. Perhaps of greatest import, we have paid homage to the never-ending cast of souls who bore the brunt of the long arm of justice over time, sometime subject to death by savage beast, other times to immolation, and more recently to slow, carceral starvation. Although this book has provided us the opportunity to bear witness to these historical trends, it has also afforded us the protection of temporal distance. We may peruse these stories without the demand of tying them to contemporary practices, thus allowing us to avoid the uncomfortable possibility that the cast of souls continues. Thus, we are allowed to peek into Pandora's box, which contained the evils of the world, without consequence.[1]

As the title of this chapter suggests, here we choose to cast aside the protective shroud of historical distance and unapologetically tie the past to the present. We revisit the elements of the criminal justice system in contemporary form, searching for evidence of new directions while also remaining watchful for signs of devolution or a return to undesirable practices and trends. We aim to bridge the gap between *what came before us* and *what is in front of us*. In addition, we present a tentative offering of *what may come after us*. Before pursuing this challenging task, we would like to acknowledge that our narrative is a simple one at best, and as is true with all renditions of the past, present, and future, what we posit in this chapter is informed by our own personal biases, experiences, and whimsies. We do not purport to be the purveyors of an absolute truth; instead, we aim to present a perspective that is subject to criticism, as is (and should be) any good narrative.

Having acknowledged the interpretative nature of the chapter, we offer several conclusions in the following pages. Although we search for consistency and efficacy, we cannot deny that contemporary Western criminal justice systems are in a state of conceptual and practical disarray. In many respects, they cling desperately to outdated and ineffectual practices, while, in other ways, they tentatively venture into new territory, sometimes strategically and sometimes without seeming forethought. Meanwhile, social, cultural, and political status continues to largely determine those who will be subject to the resulting mosaic of new and old justice practices. It is a sobering state of affairs, one that echoes previous eras, perhaps less visible in contemporary form but no less troubling. Despite this, there remain elements of hope, small and piecemeal but promising, allowing us to turn an optimistic eye to the future.

PROGRESSIVE PANDEMONIUM: THE EVOLUTION AND DEVOLUTION OF JUSTICE

As mentioned in the introduction to this volume, criminology and criminal justice studies claim ownership over different aspects of the phenomenon of crime; while criminology is motivated by the causes of crime, criminal justice studies hold allegiance to the responses to crime. Given that the latter is the primary focus of this book, our examination of the state of modern justice will focus primarily on institutional responses to crime. However, these two branches are also entwined; each one influences and informs the other. In recognition of this relationship, we will begin our narrative of modern justice systems with a brief foray into the philosophies of punishment, which live firmly in the world of criminology, before then examining the formal mechanisms of the criminal justice system (e.g., courts and corrections) and the informal factors that influence the creation and execution of these mechanisms (e.g., race and gender).

Early Philosophies and Modern Punishments

Throughout history, the Western world has embraced one of four philosophies of punishment, each holding the power to shape punitive practices in novel and oftentimes extreme ways. Some eras have fervently placed one above all others (e.g., ancient Rome), while others have sampled more than one, resulting in a sometimes-complimentary, sometimes-discordant mix of punishments (e.g., the Middle Ages).[2] Despite varied applications throughout history, *retribution*, *incapacitation*, *deterrence*, and *rehabilitation* have retained a steadfast hold on the Western world, patiently waiting for a time during which they will experience a period of popularity. At no point in the long trajectory of time, however, have all four claimed ownership of the same stage, at least not until now, the era of modern times. Today we find ourselves in a unique situation as four punitive companions shape our contemporary practices, producing a jarring array of punishments that are at times seemingly nonsensical.

Retribution, the earliest and most insidious of the four philosophies, has held a near-constant presence throughout human history. As human civilizations developed and grew, the concept of *lex talionis*, or *an eye-for-an-eye*, claimed ownership over informal and formal responses to crime, including such macabre outcomes as crushing, beheading, dismembering, and suffocation (Donnelly & Diehl 2011). Over time, the philosophy lost visible popularity, seemingly offending the genteel sensibilities of the civilized elites, but it continued to retain its hold on punitive practices, informing a more "refined," *just deserts* model (Carlsmith, Darley, & Robinson 2002). It continues to this day, implicit in the responses to murderous actions, such as the death penalty or life without parole, both which serve the simple life-for-a-life formula. Thus, despite its lack of extolled popularity, it remains evident and influential.

Incapacitation, or *social defense*, in the grand scheme of things, is a relative new-comer, having only presented itself as a formal philosophy in the 1700s. However, once it debuted, it quickly became the favored institutional response to crime. Over the last several hundred years, prisons have become commonplace, propagating at a rapid rate, yet failing to meet the demands of detainment-driven policy and practitioner communities (Cox 2009). All major criminal offenses and many minor ones are likely to be met with some period of incarceration, under the philosophical auspices that removal from society ensures the protection of the population. Thus, we find ourselves in an era of mass incarceration as large swathes of the population are incarcerated in order to protect larger swathes of the population.

Deterrence immediately claimed prominence during the Age of Reason, and it has refused to give ground since. General deterrence is most evident in the modern trend of bearing witness to punishments, serving to send a message about the costs of deviance (Materni 2013). Open trials, public executions, and media headlines all carry a deterrent intonation, as do rigid structures of sentencing, such as mandatory minimums. Specific deterrence is evident in the severity of punitive measures, particularly for repeat or habitual offenders, designed to dissuade the already-deviant from pursuing their wily ways (Alexander 1922). Deterrence, like incapacitation, remains prominent, neither revered nor reviled, but consistently influential.

Rehabilitation or reformation, a latecomer to the philosophical palate, has ebbed and flowed in popularity. Championed by the religious elite in the 1800s, early rehabilitative philosophy bound itself to incapacitation, leading to the popularization of confinement for the purposes of penance (Blomberg & Lucken 2010). Eventually losing its religious undertones, it shifted to a narrative of simple reformation through training, labor, and therapeutic measures (Brockway 1870). It lost appeal in the late-1900s, when critics suggested that it was an ineffectual philosophy, a fool's errand of sorts (Martinson 1974). The ripple effect was short-lived, however, as rehabilitation again gained ground, accepted by many as a softer and more humane response to crime. Once again enjoying a period of popularity, rehabilitation is readily evident in alternative sanctions (in lieu of confinement) and training, treatment, and programming in prison.

Thus, all four philosophies retain a firm foothold on Western punitive practices. Perhaps, one may argue, having a more diverse and varied palate is preferred, one that is comprised of best practices, carefully selected from the historical buffet of abject failures. After all, this could give us a menu of preferred punishments from which to choose, allowing us to tailor the criminal justice response to the unique circumstances of each offense. This is a defensible position and one that likely has merit. However, this is not the position of the authors of this text. Instead, we posit that the array is discordant and ineffectual. To justify our position, we turn to the evidence.

Retributive practices, such as the death penalty and life without parole, find little support in the literature. Such extreme and arguably archaic measures have been found to have little effect on reducing crime rates and, at times, may even serve to increase them (Kovandzic, Vieraitis, & Boots 2009; Radelet & Lacock 2008). In addition, they place a strain on the already-overburdened coffers of the nations that practice them (Bedau 1998). Incapacitation appears to share a similar fate, having a limited effect on crime and a large effect on a country's expenditures (Gifford 2019; Krištofík et al. 2017). In addition, prisonization has disproportionately impacted marginalized communities, amplifying existing disadvantages (Browne-Marshall 2007). Deterrent measures, originally founded on a punitive philosophy of swiftness, certainty, and proportionate severity, seems to have entirely lost the taste for swiftness and certainty, choosing instead to prioritize severity. Similar to retributive and incapacitative measures, severity in the name of deterrence serves little purpose, potentially producing a backlash effect as severity becomes disproportionate, prompting an increase in crime (LaFree, Dugan, & Korte 2009). Rehabilitation, the last of the philosophical sisters, enjoys some support, suggesting that specific alternative sanctions and in-prison programming can aid reformation; however, success depends on the fidelity of the measure, which is lacking in practice (Farringer et al. 2021). In other words, there is promise in the rehabilitative ideal, but it requires more than simple rote application, which appears to be the best that many Western systems of justice can muster. Thus, the appearance of all four philosophies in the present day does not seem to have produced a best-practices model, but instead a disheveled display of seemingly ineffective punitive responses to crime. This is a sobering situation within which we find ourselves, but as discussed later, it is not one that needs to define our future.

Modern Mechanisms of Justice

As the previous section illustrates, over the last several hundred years, Western criminal justice systems have clung tenaciously to old philosophies, thus thwarting punitive evolution. Can the same be said for the formal mechanisms of justice? Here our analysis strays from the purely pessimistic, noting that one mechanism has veered dramatically from the past (policing), another has refused to budge from the niche it created at its inception (corrections), and a third has opted out of progression altogether, preferring to return to its early roots (courts).

Of the various mechanisms of justice, policing can arguably lay claim to being the most evolved of its companions.[3] In early times, policing was a citizen-led function; the responsibility for detecting and reporting crime fell to the victim and the community. Various iterations of this model persisted until the Church created the Inquisition during the Middle Ages, granting it the power to identify, investigate, and pursue purported crimes and criminals. These functions were formalized in England in the 1800s with the birth of modern policing. The introduction of patrol-driven, salaried, and uniformed police officers definitively severed the Western world from its historical roots, making a return to earlier practices unlikely.

Modern models of policing have eagerly adopted the framework established during the Victorian Era, replicating a professional and preventive approach. In a quest to decrease crime and victimization and increase legitimacy while remaining true to its English roots, Western policing has engaged in a flurry of modifications, creating and sampling different models that vary in their emphasis on the identification of problems and the execution of solutions. *Intelligence-led policing*, for example, focuses primarily on the identification of problems, leaning heavily on the collection and analysis of data, with the goal of creating more effective and informed policing strategies (Newburn 2012). *Problem-oriented policing*, a notably proactive and broad approach, prioritizes isolating factors that cause crime and seeks to engage communities and stakeholders in creating solutions. *Community-oriented policing* recognizes that the relationship between the police and the public is fragile and subject to souring, thus deserving of intentional fostering. This approach aims to strengthen these relationships through police and community collaboration and alliances (Oliver 2004; Gill et al. 2014). Intermingled with these various models are others, such as *evidence-based policing*, *hot-spots policing*, and *pulling-levers policing*, to name but a few. In simple terms, policing has advanced far from its early days as a private citizen–led matter, becoming a professional and proactive formal mechanism that is in a seemingly constant state of evolution, trying on and occasionally casting aside different models in an effort to become more efficient, effective, and accepted.

While policing progresses, corrections resists modification. Used sparingly through much of human history, formal state incarceration and supervision only became commonplace in the last few centuries. Houses of correction began spotting the Western landscape with vigor, taking root in urban and rural areas alike. These massive monoliths were steadfast in their presence, serving the primary function of warehousing the undesirable, thus becoming a permanent staple in criminal justice systems. Once established, corrections appeared loathe to evolve, incorporating minor changes reluctantly and only when the social and political mood demanded it. The separation of deviant groups based on gender, age, and severity of offense, for example, was slow in coming, adopted piecemeal under protest (Bassett 1944; Simon 2013). The introduction of in-prison programming was marred by controversy and corruption and eventually deemed ineffective (Keve 1999; Martinson 1974; Roberts 1985).[4] Although programming continues to retain a tenuous presence in prisons today, this is seemingly more a matter of habit than commitment. Even measures designed to minimize Western reliance on correctional warehousing have only served to fortify carceral responses to crime. Probation, first lauded as a means to integrate the reformed back into society and empty the overflowing prisons, has led to a revolving-door syndrome; the formerly incarcerated are subject to restrictive supervision, then institutionalized again for minor infractions that, if carried out by members of the general population, would not typically warrant a prison sentence (Pisciotta 1994). Thus, corrections has become regimented, only implementing change in seemingly half-hearted ways, deeply entrenched in its goal to warehouse the antisocial elements of society.

As policing progresses and corrections remains reticent to change, Western court systems have chosen another path, appearing in many ways to return to their early roots after trying and rejecting other alternatives. The first court systems appeared in Greco-Roman times, replete with a preliminary hearing, juries, magistrates, advocacy, witnesses, and evidence (Bauman 1996; Harries 1999). This changed during the Middle Ages, as the Crown and the Church both claimed ownership over the determination of guilt and punishment, leading to a divergence in legal proceedings and outcomes (Leeson 2012; Pavlac 2009). Trials by ordeal and torturous inquisition became commonplace, as juries, advocacy, and evidence faded or took on new forms. Modern times ushered in the adversarial model, one that retains prominence today, pitting prosecution and defense against each other under the watchful eye of a third party (Horovitz 2007). Although the act of adversarial sparring has been modified considerably over time, the presence of accuser, accused, and informed overseer is reminiscent of ancient antiquity. In addition, the reliance on preliminary hearings, jury participation, and the liberal use of evidence and witnesses has once again taken center stage, nostalgically echoing the courts of ancient Greece and Rome. Thus, although Western courts briefly adopted divergent paths, in many ways they have returned to their original practices and proceedings. This is not to say that they are stagnating or devolving. In fact, Western courts have grown considerably in many ways. They have, for example, branched out to create specialized courts that address different categories of offenders, such as youth and drug offenders. In addition, the rules and regulations surrounding court proceedings have evolved considerably, designed to protect participants and ensure the integrity of the court. Thus, perhaps it is most appropriate to categorize the Western courts system as a mechanism that has returned to its original framework while also becoming more refined and complex, to better meet the demands of modern society.

The Presence and Prominence of Informal Factors

At this time, our narrative takes a somber turn. A discussion centered on the mechanisms of justice and their state of progression is arguably a relatively simple and benign affair and one that holds little controversy. Conversations about the informal factors that influence the operation and outcomes of these mechanisms, on the other hand, can be a source of contention and the content presented here will likely fail to conform with all readers' expectations, offending some while galvanizing others. We recognize the potentially subjective and personal nature of discussions addressing race, gender, and class, as well as age and mental health; thus, we make a concerted effort to let the evidence lead the narrative. The evidence, however, is clear; these various factors remain prominent players in Western justice, potentially less visible and perhaps more sanitized than in previous eras, but influential, nonetheless.

Racial and ethnic differences have played a prominent role in justice systems throughout human history, from the early denial of citizenship and rights in ancient antiquity through to the racially informed biological theories of the late Scientific Revolution. A closer look at contemporary research indicates that this trend has not changed; race continues to have a stark impact on criminal justice outcomes. This is evident at all stages of criminal justice processes and proceedings. For example, Western countries report a tendency to engage in oversurveillance of communities of color (Chu, Pezzella, & Evans 2023; Wallace 2018). This increased scrutiny influences the likelihood that crimes that are committed by all members of society (e.g., drug use, assault) are more likely to be detected in these communities, thus leading to increased arrest rates of persons of color (Baldwin 2018). Once they are taken into custody, various studies indicate that suspects of color are less likely to receive a finding of innocence, and once guilt is established, they will receive a more serious sentence than their white counterparts. Consequently, Western prisons report a disproportion-ate number of racial minority residents (Davis & Gibson-Light 2020; Owusu-Bempah et al. 2023). Thus, the influence of race on criminal justice is resounding, standing the test of time, and retaining a place of prominence that has little hope of fading.

Gender differs little from race in its early and modern influences. Historically, a gender-based hierarchy ensured that males had the power to criminalize and punish non-male transgressors, particularly in relation to actions that threatened expectations surrounding gender-typical roles. The expression of this relationship between gender and the justice system has shifted to meet modern social narratives, but it remains steadfast, nonetheless. The evidence supporting this claim is diverse, ranging from the recognition of victimization to the provision of rehabilitative services. Evidence from Western countries, for example, indicates that female victims are less likely to report victimization for fear of victim blaming (Decker et al. 2019). Testimonials also reveal that female defendants may be less likely to be viewed as sympathetic than their male counterparts, thus influencing the believability of their testimony and subsequent findings of guilt (Epstein & Goodman 2019; New York State Judicial Committee on Women in the Courts 2020). Once incarcerated, female offenders are often left without gender-specific programming (Balis 2022). While females experience disad-vantage, this is amplified further for transgender, intersex, and nonbinary offenders. Criminal justice systems fail to acknowledge the unique needs of this community, reverting to the sex assigned at birth (Lai & Lisneck 2023; Szuminski 2020). This is particularly amplified in a correctional setting, as these individuals find themselves in institutions that do not align with their gender identity, leading to an increased risk of abuse and sexual assault. Thus, non-male victims, suspects, and offenders continue to face discrimination, reduced services, and increased physical risk in modern systems of justice.

Class follows the trend established by race and gender; its influence on justice systems remains stubbornly resistant to change. In early human history, those at the top of a class-based hierarchy controlled criminal justice institutions, using them to define and punish behaviors perpetrated by the less-privileged, often with the inten-tion of ensuring the structure of power remained. This continued relatively unchecked through the eras; those placed at the top of the hierarchy have fluctuated over the generations, but the practice of criminalizing and targeting the already-disadvantaged persists. Many Western countries criminalize acts of homelessness and poverty, levy-ing charges such as loitering and trespassing against individuals and communities who seek shelter in public and private spaces (Aykanian & Fogel 2019). In addi-tion, the quality and outcome of criminal justice stages are defined, in part, by the financial standing of the individual. Arrests can lead to long terms of imprisonment while defendants await trial if they do not have the resources to post bail (Menefee 2018). In addition, indigent defendants are assigned state-appointed lawyers, many of whom are unable to meet the level of attention provided by private representation (Hoffman, Rubin, & Shepherd 2005). Evidence indicates that, due to case overloads, individuals represented by public defenders are more likely to receive a conviction and an increased sentence than those who retain private counsel. Once found guilty, the sentences might include an additional fine, oftentimes far exceeding the financial capacity of the offender, thus ensuring further penalties if left unpaid (Sobol 2015).

Upon imprisonment, destitute offenders may find themselves unable to access desired services, as medical care, commissary, and optional programming often come with a price tag (Wiggins 2021). For those who are offered alternative sanctions, such as house arrest or parole, they may find themselves with a substantial monthly bill for these services, a fee that, if unresolved, can ensure further punitive consequences (Heller 2006). In sum, members of the lower class continue to bear the burden of criminal justice systems that are structured to privilege the elite over the impoverished.

On a lighter note, unlike race, gender, and class, the influence of age on criminal justice practices has shifted considerably over time. For much of human history, youth were invisible, neither processed nor protected by institutions of justice. Instead, disciplinary action was a private affair, consisting of corporal measures, expulsion from the home, and occasionally death. Over the last few centuries, justice-oriented narratives surrounding age have shifted, causing the state to claim control of defining and responding to youth crime. This change was notable; youth began to be processed as adults without additional legal protections. This was eventually revised to reflect what is in place today: youth may be held criminally responsible by the state, but they are afforded consideration and leniency not available to their adult counterparts. This is evident in specific laws addressing juvenile delinquency, juvenile justice courts, reformatories, and targeted programs tailored to meet the unique needs of youth (Feld 2017). In addition, the state takes preventive measures with at-risk youth that are designed to deter potential offending and offer prosocial alternatives (Berger & Gregory 2009). Thus, the influence of age has veered considerably from its historical roots as children gained visibility, culpability, and protective status.

Mental health has traversed a path similar to its age-identifying counterpart, although with less-positive outcomes. Like the children of early history, the mentally ill were invisible, deemed to be a solely private concern and thus absent from criminal justice considerations. This changed in the Middle Ages, as deviant mental health was recast as evidence of sin or social blight, transferring limited responsibility to the Crown and the Church. Public control of the mentally ill reached its peak in more recent times, as the medical and justice communities both laid claim to irrational and errant behaviors. Evidence suggests that we now find ourselves in an era of institutionalization, paired with a revolving-door syndrome. Those who suffer from mental illness are more likely to engage in behaviors that are criminalized, resulting in part from a lack of medical or therapeutic intervention (Slate et al. 2021). In addition, these individuals often experience homelessness and poverty, thus suffering the criminal justice outcomes of the lower class, including poor legal counsel, increased likelihood of conviction and more severe sentencing, limited access to pay-to-play carceral services, and inescapable costs of select alternative sanctions (Sobol 2015). As a consequence, the mentally ill populate Western prisons in disproportionate numbers (Slate et al. 2021). Upon release, they may have little option but to return to their original behavior, thus prompting a criminal justice response and further incarceration. Therefore, similar to the influence of age, the role of mental health has changed considerably over time, as the mentally ill transitioned from a private to a public concern. Unlike criminal justice responses to youth, however, this transition has not served to protect communities suffering from mental health issues.

This brings us to the end of our assessment of informal influences on contemporary justice systems' responses to crime. The evidence indicates that race, gender, class, age, and mental health continue to hold a place of prominence in Western justice systems, although their impacts might have shifted. Class, race, and gender issues persist in a manner similar to previous eras, while the roles of age and mental health have changed considerably, becoming a visible and public affair. These influences, apart from age, appear to perpetuate further marginalization and disadvantage, thus amplifying rather than addressing the needs of these communities. In addition, these factors intersect considerably, ensuring that individuals who share multiple identifiers are more likely to find themselves subject to criminal justice scrutiny. Thus, we find ourselves at present in a state of disarray, with a discordant assortment of punishments and criminal justice mechanisms directed primarily toward disadvantaged and marginalized communities.

OPENING PANDORA'S BOX: AN ELEMENT OF HOPE

We are loathe to leave our narrative on a negative note, and fortunately, this may not be necessary. Although the present has a grim overtone, there are some changes afoot that offer an element of hope. The punitive philosophies are in flux, hinting at expansion and overhaul. Select countries are experimenting with bold and progressive modifications to ineffective mechanisms of justice. Lastly, empirical evidence has become central to policy and practice, revealing the staggering effects that marginalization has had on justice proceedings. Although these advancements are limited to select regions and communities, they do offer grounds for hope.

A notable source of optimism can be found in punitive philosophies. A fifth philosophy of punishment, an overseer of the non-Western world, has begun to tentatively show her presence in Western discussions of justice. *Restorative justice*, long practiced by indigenous communities, counters the retributive tone of modern justice. In a restorative world, justice is focused on repairing the harm caused by deviance, rather than punishing it (Zehr 2015). To address the harm, the offender takes responsibility for their actions, efforts are made to provide reparations to the victim, and the offender is invited to reintegrate into the community. This formula also defines the main participants in achieving restoration, including the offender, the victim, and the impacted community; state or legal/political authorities are absent or have a limited presence. The restorative process ideally results in reduced recidivism as the offender faces the consequences of their action but remains connected to the community, and increased victim satisfaction as the victim may actively participate in the process, a feature that is notably absent from retributive proceedings. Restorative practices are varied, including victim-offender mediation, community reparative boards, and conflict resolution programs, to name but a few (Braithwaite 1999). Evidence suggests that restoration holds promise for Western systems of justice, particularly when addressing less-serious offenses (Latimer, Dowden, & Muise 2005). This is particularly evident in countries that have made a concerted effort to embrace restoration, such as Canada and New Zealand. Other countries, such as the United States, are more closely wedded to the retributive ideal, and are thus reluctant to contemplate a philosophical shift.

Despite its slow introduction to criminal justice systems, restoration holds promise for the Western world, offsetting the harsh and seemingly discordant approaches to punishments that currently define the modern world.

Another note of optimism can be found in select countries that have begun revising their mechanisms of justice. Although piecemeal and limited in application, these bold initiatives are noteworthy. As summarized previously, modern policing has been particularly proactive in seeking an ideal model. Recognizing that law enforcement officers hold power that invites abuse and discrimination, some Western countries have been motivated to try new approaches, many of which hold promise. Although these attempts have yet to produce a solution that clearly paves a path for the future, the commitment to finding that solution invites optimism.

Western courts, although seemingly committed to a historical framework of dispensing justice, have also engaged in small innovations designed to improve proceedings, protect rights, and ensure justice, such as establishing firm rules of evidence, ensuring representation for all, and recognizing the importance of mitigating and aggravating factors. Although small, these efforts are not without note. They are, however, overshadowed by the innovation apparent in the field of corrections. While most of the Western world continues its steadfast allegiance to the monolithic prison industrial complex that defines the twenty-first century, select countries have cast aside this model, opting for a new approach altogether. Denmark provides one of the more notable examples of this growing trend. Danish corrections primarily consist of small, community-based facilities (Sheptycki 1995). These institutions are not designed for the purposes of retribution, deterrence, or social defense, but instead they prioritize rehabilitation and reintegration. Correctional residents enjoy greater freedoms and responsibilities, preparing them for reentry into society. Evidence suggests this is an effective approach, reducing recidivism significantly (Graunbøl et al. 2010; Hornum 1988). This approach to corrections, although also evident in other Scandinavian countries, is unlikely to take firm hold across the entirety of the Western world, but it does suggest that elements of the criminal justice system hold promise for the future.

One last area of note is a shift that is evident across all aspects of the criminal justice system, a commitment to an evidence-based approach. This approach, which prioritizes empirical research over political and social narratives, was notably absent from previous eras, due in part to a lack of systematic evaluation. The evidence-based approach allows us to critically assess criminal justice practices, identify areas of improvement, and form viable solutions. Consider the previous section examining the impact of informal factors such as gender and race on justice systems. In these areas, the evidence is clear, illustrating inequalities in justice practices that demand a solution. Consequently, practitioners and policymakers are pressed to respond, leading to justice innovations such as separate housing for transgender correctional residents and implicit bias training for law enforcement (Szuminski 2020). All appearances indicate that the evidence-based approach will continue to gain traction, thus inviting optimism for further improvements designed to reduce inequalities.

On that note, we hope we have instilled in you a small sense of promise, dear reader. Although the present is somber, riddled with potentially outdated punishments and inappropriate mechanisms of justice that may do little more than reinforce potentially discriminatory and ineffective outcomes, there are some hints of brighter times ahead, informed by restoration, revision, and evidence. We may yet find ourselves in an era of change, one that reshapes the Western systems of justice that inhabit our modern world. After all, Pandora's box may have contained all the evils of the world, but it also contained the element of hope.

NOTES

1. According to Greek mythology, Pandora's box contained the evils of the world; opening it could release these evils. It is also believed to contain an element of hope.

2. Chapter 1 provides an overview of the philosophies and their waning and waxing presence throughout human history.

3. Please note that in this context, evolution refers only to the process of change. It does not suggest that the outcome of that change is an improvement, but simply that change occurred.

4. Chapter 4 provides a summary of the Elmira Reformatory, championed as the beginning of modern prison reform, but also a site of notable controversy and corruption. Chapter 1 provides a description of the empirical evidence that refuted the rehabilitative ideal in prison.

REFERENCES

Alexander, Julian P. 1922. "Philosophy of Punishment." *Journal of Criminal Law and Criminology* 13, no. 2 (August): 235–50. https://doi.org/10.2307/1133492.

Aykanian, A., and S.J. Fogel. 2019. "The Criminalization of Homelessness." In *Homelessness Prevention and Intervention in Social Work*, edited by H. Larkin, A. Aykanian, and C.L. Streeter, 185–205. New York: Springer.

Baldwin, Bridgette. 2018. "Black, White, and Blue: Bias, Profiling, and Policing in the Age of Black Lives Matter." *Western New England Law Rev.* 40: 431–46.

Balis, A.F. 2022. "Female Prisoners and the Case for Gender-Specific Treatment and Reentry Programs." In *Public Health Behind Bars*, edited by R.B. Greifinger, 357–68. New York: Springer.

Bassett, Margery. 1944. "The Fleet Prison in the Middle Ages." *University of Toronto Law Journal* 5, no. 2 (January): 383–402. https://doi.org/10.2307/824490.

Bauman, Richard A. 1996. "Trial by Magistrate and People." In *Crime and Punishment in Ancient Rome*, edited by Richard Bauman, 7–15. Oxford: Routledge.

Bedau, Hugo Adam. 1998. *The Death Penalty in America.* Oxford: Oxford University Press.

Berger Ronald J., and Paul D. Gregory (editors). 2009. *Juvenile Delinquency and Justice: Sociological Perspectives.* Boulder: Lynne Rienner Publishers.

Blomberg, Thomas, and Karol Lucken. 2010. *American Penology—A History of Control.* Piscataway: Transaction Publishers.

Braithwaite, John. 1999. "Restorative Justice: Assessing Optimistic and Pessimistic Accounts." *Crime and Justice* 25: 1–127. http://www.jstor.org/stable/1147608.

Brockway, Zebulon R. 1870. "The Ideal of a True Prison System for a State." *Journal of Correctional Education* 46, no. 2 (June): 68–74. https://www.jstor.org/stable/23292027.

Browne-Marshall, Gloria J. 2007. *Race, Law, and American Society: 1607–Present.* Oxford: Routledge.

Carlsmith, Kevin M., John M. Darley, and Paul H. Robinson. 2002. "Why Do We Punish? Deterrence and Just Deserts as Motives for Punishment." *Journal of Personality and Social Psychology* 83, no. 2: 284–99.

Chu, Sarah P., Frank S. Pezzella, and Justice D. Evans. 2023. "Surveillance Load: A Burden of Search Borne by Black and Brown Bodies." *Critical Criminology*: 1–16.

Cox, Stephen. 2009. *The Big House: Image and Reality of the American Prison*. New Haven: Yale University Press.

Davis, Andrew P., and Michael Gibson-Light. 2020. "Difference and Punishment: Ethno-Political Exclusion, Colonial Institutional Legacies, and Incarceration." *Punishment & society* 22, no. 1: 3–27.

Decker, Michele R., Charvonne N. Holliday, Zaynab Hameeduddin, Roma Shah, Janice Miller, Joyce Dantzler, and Leigh Goodmark. 2019. "'You Do Not Think of Me as a Human Being': Race and Gender Inequities Intersect to Discourage Police Reporting of Violence Against Women." *Journal of Urban Health* 96: 772–83.

Donnelly, Mark P., and Daniel Diehl. 2011. *The Big Book of Pain—Torture & Punishment Through History*. Cheltenham: The History Press.

Epstein, Deborah, and Lisa A. Goodman. 2019. "Discounting Women: Doubting Domestic Violence Survivors' Credibility and Dismissing Their Experiences. *University of Pennsylvania Law Review* 167: 399–461.

Farringer, Alison J., Stephanie A. Duriez, Sarah M. Manchak, and Carrie C. Sullivan. 2021. "Adherence to 'What Works': Examining Trends Across 14 Years of Correctional Program Assessment." *Corrections* 6, no. 4: 269–87.

Feld, Barry C. 2017. *The Evolution of the Juvenile Court: Race, Politics, and the Criminalizing of Juvenile Justice*. New York: New York University Press.

Gifford, Ben. 2019. "Prison Crime and the Economics of Incarceration." *Stanford Law Review* 71 (January): 71–136.

Gill, Charlotte, David Weisburd, Cody W. Telep, Zoe Vitter, and Trevor Bennett. 2014. "Community-Oriented Policing to Reduce Crime, Disorder, and Fear and Increase Satisfaction and Legitimacy Among Citizens: A Systematic Review." *Journal of Experimental Criminology* 10 (August): 399–428. https://doi.org/10.1007/s11292-014-9210-y.

Graunbøl, Hans Monrad, Bo Kielstrup, Marja-Liisa Muiluvuori, Sasu Tyni, Erlendur Sigurdur Baldursson, Hafdis Gudmundsdottir, Ragnar Kristoffersen, Lars Krantz, and Karin Lindstén. 2010. *Retur. En nordisk undersøgelse af recidiv i kriminalforsorgen* [Return. A Nordic Study of Recidivism Among Clients in the Correctional Service]. Oslo, Norway: Correctional Service of Norway Staff Academy (KRUS).

Harries, Jill. 1999. "In Court." In *Law and Empire in Late Antiquity*, edited by Jill Harries, 99–117. Cambridge: Cambridge University Press.

Heller, Wendy. 2006. "Poverty: The Most Challenging Condition of Prisoner Release." *Georgetown Journal on Poverty, Law, & Policy* XIII, no. 2: 219–48.

Hoffman, Morris B., Paul H. Rubin, and Joanna M. Shepherd. 2005. "An Empirical Study of Public Defender Effectiveness: Self-Selection by the Marginally Indigent." *Ohio State Journal of Criminal Law* 3: 223–56.

Hornum, Finn. 1988. "Corrections in Two Social Welfare Democracies: Denmark and Sweden." *Prison Journal* 68, no. 1: 63–82.

Horovitz, Anat. 2007. "The Emergence of Sentencing Hearings." *Punishment & Society* 9, no. 3 (July): 271–99. https://doi.org/10.1177/1462474507077495.

Keve, Paul W. 1999. "Building a better prison: The first three decades of the Detroit House of Correction." *Michigan Historical Review* 25, no. 2 (Fall): 1–28. https://doi.org/10.2307/20173826.

Kovandzic, Tomislav V., Lynne M. Vieraitis, and Denise Paquette Boots. 2009. "Does the Death Penalty Save Lives? New Evidence from State Panel Data, 1977 to 2006." *Criminology & Public Policy* 8, no. 4: 803–43.

Krištofík, Peter, Kamila Borseková, Samuel Koróny, and Peter Mihók. 2017. "Classical and Alternative Methods of Punishment: Economic Comparison Based on European Evidence." *7th International Conference on Interdisciplinary Social Science Studies* (November): 85–94.

LaFree, Gary, Laura Dugan, and Raven Korte. 2009. "The Impact of British Counterterrorist Strategies on Political Violence in Northern Ireland: Comparing Deterrence and Backlash Models." *Criminology* 47, no. 1: 17–45.

Lai, Calvin K., and Jaclyn A. Lisnek. 2023. "The Impact of Implicit-Bias-Oriented Diversity Training on Police Officers' Beliefs, Motivations, and Actions." *Psychological science* 34, no. 4: 424–34.

Latimer, Jeff, Craig Dowden, and Danielle Muise. 2005. "The Effectiveness of Restorative Justice Practices: A Meta-Analysis." *Prison Journal* 85, no. 2: 127–44.

Leeson, Peter T. 2012. "Ordeals." *Journal of Law and Economics* 55, no. 3 (August): 691–714. https://doi.org/10.1086/664010.

Martinson, Robert. 1974. "What Works? Questions and Answers about Prison Reform." *Public Interest* 35 (Spring): 22–54.

Materni, Mike C. 2013. "Criminal Punishment and the Pursuit of Justice." *British Journal of American Legal Studies* 2, no. 1 (April): 263–304.

Menefee, Michael R. 2018. "The Role of Bail and Pretrial Detention in the Reproduction of Racial Inequalities." *Sociology Compass* 12, no. 5: e12576.

Newburn, Tim. 2012. *Handbook of Policing.* Oxford: Routledge.

New York State Judicial Committee on Women in the Courts. 2020. *Gender Survey 2020.* https://www.nycourts.gov/LegacyPDFS/ip/womeninthecourts/Gender-Survey-2020.pdf.

Oliver, Willard M. 2004. *Community-oriented Policing: A Systemic Approach to Policing.* Hoboken: Prentice Hall.

Owusu-Bempah, Akwasi, Maria Jung, Firdaous Sbaï, Andrew S. Wilton, and Fiona Kouy-oumdjian. 2023. "Race and Incarceration: The Representation and Characteristics of Black People in Provincial Correctional Facilities in Ontario, Canada." *Race and Justice* 13, no. 4: 530–42.

Pavlac, Brian Alexander. 2009. "Medieval Origins of Witch Hunts." In *Witch Hunts in the Western World: Persecution and Punishment from the Inquisition through the Salem Trials*, edited by Brian A. Pavlac, 25–50. Lincoln: University of Nebraska Press.

Pisciotta, Alexander W. 1994. *Benevolent Repression: Social Control and the American Reformatory Prison Movement.* New York: New York University Press.

Radelet, Michael L., and Traci L. Lacock. 2008. "Do Executions Lower Homicide Rates: The Views of Leading Criminologists." *Journal of Criminal Law & Criminology* 99: 489–508.

Roberts, Leonard H. 1985. "The Historic Roots of American Prison Reform: A Story of Progress and Failure." *Journal of Correctional Education* 36, no. 3 (September): 106–9.

Simon, Johnathan. 2013. "The Return of the Medical Model: Disease and the Meaning of Imprisonment from John Howard to *Brown v. Plata*." *Harvard Civil Rights—Civil Liberties Law Review* 48, no. 1 (Winter): 217–56. https://journals.law.harvard.edu/crcl/wp-content/uploads/sites/80/2013/04/Simon_217-256.pdf.

Slate, Risdon N., Kelly Frailing, W. Wesley Johnson, and Jacqueline K. Buffington. 2021. "The History of Criminalization of Persons with Mental Illnesses." In *The Criminalization of Mental Illness: Crisis and Opportunity for the Justice System*, edited by Risdon N. Slate, Kelly Frailing, W. Wesley Johnson, and Jacqueline K. Buffington, 33–50. Durham: Carolina Academic Press.

Sobol, Neil L. 2015. "Charging the Poor: Criminal Justice Debt and Modern-Day Debtors' Prisons." *Maryland Law Review* 75: 486–540.

Szuminski, Jessica. 2020. "Behind the Binary Bars: A Critique of Prison Placement Policies for Transgender, Non-Binary, and Gender Non-Conforming Prisoners." *Minnesota Law Review* 105: 477–525.

Wallace, Derron. 2018. "Safe Routes to School? Black Caribbean Youth Negotiating Police Surveillance in London and New York City." *Harvard Educational Review* 88, no. 3: 261–86. https://www.proquest.com/docview/2237545754?pq-origsite=gscholar&fromopenview=true&sourcetype=Scholarly%20Journals.

Wiggins, Rachael. 2021. "A Pound of Flesh: How Medical Copayments in Prison Cost Inmates Their Health and Set Them Up for Reoffense." *University of Colorado Law Review* 92: 255–84.

Zehr, Howard. 2015. "The Little Book of Restorative Justice." In *The Big Book of Restorative Justice*, edited by Lorraine Stutzman Amstutz, Allan MacRae, Kay Pranis, and Howard Zehr, 30–54. New York: Good Books.

Index

abortion, 104n14
absolutist justice, 59–60
Abu-Jamal, Mumia, xi
Action, William, 185n19
Act of Attainder, 63n21
adulterium, 133
ADX Florence, 81–82
Africa, 117, 124n35
aggregate system, 78
Albion's Fatal Tree (Hay), 180
Alcatraz, 81, 85n38
Alcidamas, 83n3
alcohol, 100
Alexander, Julian, 13
Alexander the Great, 111–12
Alexis, 83n9
ambulant trading, 161
Ammirato, Scipione, 167n24
ancient Greece. *See* Greco-Roman Empire;
    Greece
ancient Rome. *See* Greco-Roman Empire;
    Rome
animals, 57–58
antiquity. *See* Greco-Roman Empire
anti-Semitism, 112–14
Appius Claudius, 154, 166n14
Aquinas, Thomas, 196–97
Archons, 91–92
Aristotle, 13, 110
armies, as police, 31–32
asseurements, 166n16
Assize of Clarendon, 33
Association for the Improvement of Female
    Prisoners, 141

atavism, 140
Auburn Prison, 79, 140–41
Auburn System, 20, 79
Augustus, 14
Australia, 2, 22, 24n9, 39–40
authorship, in criminology, 3–4

Babylonia, 11–12, 192
banishment, 14–15
barbarians, 110, 122n1
Bastille prison, 73, 99
Battie, William, 201–2
Beccaria, Cesare, 18, 58–59, 99, 104n9
Beers, Clifford, 205–6
beggars, 167n26
Belle, William, 197
Bentham, Jeremy, 18, 24n7, 78–79, 84n31,
    85n32, 99
Bers, Victor, 165n7
biocriminology, 119–21, 124n34, 186n33
biology, 60–61, 140, 193
Birnbaum, Morton, 209
Bitner, Egon, 104n11
Blackburn, Guillaume, 197
blood feuds, 54
Bordoni, Ernesta, 139–40
Bracton legal treatise, 133
Bradwell v. State, 144n12
Braithwaite, John, 22
Brant, Sebastian, 198–99
Brazen Bull, 24n3
Breen, Michael P., 167n32
Bridewell place, 75, 138
Brinton, Crane, 84n18

of, 191–95, 210–11; hospitals, 199,
211nn4–5, 212n23; hysteria in, 211n1;
insanity, 61, 64n34; in Ireland, 211n7;
mental hygiene and, 205–8; in Middle
Ages, 195–97; in modernity, 202–5;
Moral Treatment period for, 201–2;
National Committee for Mental Hygiene,
206; National Institute on Mental Health,
212n22; transinstitutionalization of,
208–10; in United States, 212n15; in
Western culture, 222; Willis on, 211n12;
of women, 199
Mental Maladies (Esquirol), 203
Mesopotamia, 9, 11–12, 23
metics (free foreigners), 110–11
Metropolitan Police Act, 39
Meyer, Adolf, 206
miasma, 51–52
Middle Ages: Catholicism in, 143;
corrections in, 72–74; courts in, 54–56;
England in, 34–35, 166n18; in Europe,
9, 83n11; gender in, 133–36; Greco-
Roman Empire compared to, 6, 37, 49;
incapacitation in, 10; justice in, 93–95,
154–58; juvenile delinquency, 174–76;
magistrates in, 43n12; mental health in,
195–97; pardons in, 166n15; penology
in, 15–17; philosophy after, 37; police
in, 33–37; race/ethnicity in, 112–14;
religion in, 23, 166n21; the Renaissance
and, 84n18, 90; Rome compared to, 43n9;
scholarship on, 6–7; slaves in, 123n13;
society in, 155–57; Victorian Era and,
218–19
Middle Dark Ages, 33
Mills, C. Wright, xi
A Mind That Found Itself (Beers), 205–6
Mirror of Justices (legal textbook), 197
miscegenation, 117
M'Naughten, Daniel, 61, 204
M'Naughten rule, 61, 64n34
modernity, 160–64, 181–83, 202–5, 216–20
monarchies, 15–16
Moniz, Antonio, 212n18
monogenesis, 116–17
Monster (Sanyika), xi
moral insanity, 61
moral offenses, 139
Moral Treatment period, for mental health,
201–2

The Myth of Mental Illness (Szasz), 210
mythology, 70–71, 193–94, 225n1

Das Narrenschiff (Brant), 198–99
National Committee for Mental Hygiene,
206
National Congress on Penitentiary and
Reformatory Discipline, 20–21
National Institute on Mental Health, 212n22
Native Americans, 117–18
Nazi Germany, 121, 162, 207, 210
necromancy, 144n7
Nelson, Wolfred, 186n27
Newgate prison, 72–76, 83n14, 84n15,
84n17, 99, 141
New Zealand, 223–24
Nider, Johannes, 135, 144n6
Nixon, Richard, 102
nobility, 155–56
non-males. *See* women
North America, 2, 98, 116–18, 123n23,
179–81
Norway, 16, 22
The Novellae, 153
"The Nut Brown Maid," 43n14
nymphomania, 140

occentares, 32
O'Connor v. Donaldson, 209
Octavian (Augustus), 14
Old Bailey courts, 203–4
Oliver Twist (Dickens), 185n22
On Crimes and Punishment (Beccaria),
24n6, 99
One Drop laws, 117, 122
One Flew Over the Cuckoo's Nest (Kesey),
212n24
On Poor Relief (Vives), 200
On the Origin of the Species (Darwin), 120
organized crime, 41
outlaws, 35–36, 43n14, 166n18
Oxford, Edward, 204

panopticons, 24n7, 78, 85n32
pardons, 155, 166n15
parole, 20–21
patrol wagons, 44n29
pederasty, 131
Peel, Robert, 39
Peloponnesian War, 149

About the Editor

Dr. Omi Hodwitz is a criminologist and associate professor in the Department of Culture, Society, and Justice at the University of Idaho. Her specialties include theoretical applications, research methods, and terrorism studies. Dr. Hodwitz spends most of her time in Idaho prisons, learning from her incarcerated students.

About the Contributors

Amara Bailey is a gender-queer criminologist who recently received a B.S. in criminology from the University of Idaho. In their second year, Amara discovered the vibrant world of Inside Out in the bowels of a men's medium-maximum security prison in North Idaho. Weekly meetings in a plant-filled purple classroom alongside incarcerated peers led them to discover their passion for prison education, hone their Play-Doh sculpture skills, and explore the world of research with brilliant convict criminologist co-authors. As Amara pursues their academic and professional careers, they plan to continue collaborating with and sharing the voices of the incarcerated community.

Jazlin Branting graduated from the University of Idaho in 2021 with her bachelor of science in criminology. She then moved from the Pacific Northwest to a tiny town in central Pennsylvania with her husband, where she works as a probation/parole officer in a less-tiny city nearby. While the criminal justice system is flawed, Jazlin hopes that through good listening and accountability from all parties, she can make a difference in her small corner of it. Jazlin wants to someday return to the Northwest (where the ticks are fewer and the coffee shops are greater) and potentially further her education in the criminal justice field.

D. Alex Cowan experienced a sheltered childhood. For as good as it was, the stable, loving home failed to provide the sustenance his wanderlust demanded. A rolling stone, he left home at sixteen, evolving into a true bohemian, bumming his way throughout the Pacific Northwest, equally inspired by nature and chemicals. Through past-life regression therapy, he discovered a former existence as a shrub, which explained his affinity for plants. He tried his hand at horticulture and spent a number of years as a traveling salesman. He ran afoul with the law, and he is currently a prisoner of the United States of America's War on Drugs. All is not lost, however; Alex is employed, making his way through college, and he spends every day with his brother. He visits with his daughter and parents every chance he gets, and he will return to society someday.

Rachel Galli grew up in a small rural town in Eastern Oregon situated at the base of the Wallowa Mountains. Farming and outdoor recreational activities were abundant, but educational opportunities were lacking. Rachel often found herself reading books and learning what she could on her own. She first became interested in the criminal justice system when she watched her aunt graduate from law school and eventually become the district attorney for their small community. A psychology class in high school piqued her interest, and she became interested in learning about humans and what motivates them. Rachel went on to study criminology and psychology at the University of Idaho. Going to college broadened her knowledge and expanded her perspectives. While in college, Rachel found great meaning in participating in classes that brought students together from inside and outside of prison. This created a sense of community and understanding between two different experiences. Rachel is thankful for her co-authors and their hard work on this project.

Stace L. Grove. John Lennon wrote, "I am he—as you are he—as you are me—and we are all together." We are all, more or less, the creation of the environment that surrounds us, infused by the fragmented sliver of all those we invite within. Stacey's life is an otherwise-empty script without the influence of the following individuals: To my Mother and Father, I thank you for making September 6, 1978, material. I love you both more than words dare express. To my sister, our bond stands with no end. To my son, the self-induced sorrow that lives within my heart for you will never depart until its ending beat. Never forget, *nihil enim lacrima citius arescit*. To my grandma Carol, you are the happy place that shelters me when it storms. To the remainder of my people, I am forever grateful for your love. This side or the other, we will meet again someday. To my loved ones laid beneath the gardener's heel, sleep well in anticipation of the great return. To the one who knows you know I know, I love you more than you will know (Infinity+2). To Warden Carlin, Deputy Wardens Anderson and Shriver, all their staff, and of course, Mr. Manley, thank you for constructing an environment that allows all those behind these walls to trust there is truly more than just mortar and wire. To Trip, thank you for your unwavering guidance. To my co-author, Grace, none of this would be possible without you! You are the smartest person I know . . . and no, you are not dull. Finally, to Omi, you have enriched my life in ways you will genuinely never appreciate. For your conviction, I am eternally beholden. When all choices are taken away . . . a perfect path remains.

Omi Hodwitz was born and raised in the Great White North (also known as Canada), for which she is forever grateful. Following in the footsteps of her obstreperous father, Omi spent her formative years raising a ruckus and making trouble, which landed her behind bars on several occasions. While wiling away in jail, Omi was struck by the stories of the women who surrounded her, prompting her to make a dramatic shift toward education, with a focus on criminology and criminal justice. Twenty years later, Omi finds herself in a position of extreme privilege, able to learn from and work with the incarcerated community on projects such as *The Origins*.

Pony L. Jackson was born and raised mostly in the western states of Wyoming, Montana, and Idaho. He has spent a majority of his life away from people. In fact, he has been heard to say, "I prefer animals to people." He is an avid outdoorsman, finding serenity in nature's unbounded tranquility and magnificence. He is just as happy feeding cattle in the middle of winter as he is riding his motorcycle across the open roads of summer. Unfortunately—or fortunately, depending on your perspective—he has been incarcerated for the past seventeen years, which has compelled him to acquire an appreciation for his fellow man, even if it is a bit skeptical, and to appreciate quietness even more. During the last seventeen years, he has focused most of his time on enhancing the opportunities for inmates like him to transform himself through education while incarcerated, with the hope that by doing so they can develop into extraordinary individuals. After spending countless hours researching past and present methods of punishing delinquency and criminality for this book, and the abject failure of those methods to affect any lasting change, he reinforced his belief that education is the key to people's search for better lives. Personally, he is in the process of acquiring a BS in organizational science from the University of Idaho, with the hopes of attaining his master's of mechanical engineering.

William Jansen. Born to an ancient noble house, under a cursed star, William was thrust into the world during an era of strife, also known as the eighties. Hailing from a land of mystical power (the Magic Valley), he sacrificed the sweat of his brow, toiling on the ancestral lands of his family's estate. After reaching the age of maturity, he elected to join the guardians of the nation in defense of all that embodies freedom. The quests that proceeded were grand and epic in nature, and William received many accolades and honors.

William's parents were great scholars, who instilled in him the love of learning, motivating him to pursue knowledge in both personal and academic settings. William had a passion for literature and enjoyed not only reading others' literary craft work, but penning his own, as well.

While penitently serving time to the state after an unfortunate fall from grace, an emissary from the far north came to William with an opportunity, which he was eager to accept. He was to research and write a chapter in a great work that would be used to teach others about the different aspects of the justice system of his nation. Grateful beyond words, William delved deep into history, compiling a brief summary of the complex concept of policing.

Now, once again tasting the crisp air of freedom, William continues to pursue knowledge. However, now he possesses a greater appreciation for the finer details that make up life's ever-changing narrative.

Steff King is always the last to submit their author biography—practically forced to write about themselves in every edition . . . Steff also comes from an eclectic community of people. Raised by backwoods Montanan mountain people and Western Washington hippies, Steff learned that the only way to understand the true story about things is to find information in the darkest corners with the most cobwebs. As an adult, their influences came from Idahoan archaeologists and British Columbian criminologists. Odd in their own ways, these individuals instilled that even the weirdest science can teach us something valuable. Steff's work (whether it be experimental archaeology projects, forensic maggot art for K-12 outreach programs, or the occasional book chapter) resembles these teachings from their community. At present, Steff is a forensic criminology PhD candidate. They are working with different communities to create death investigation practices that prioritize the well-being of the living along with the dead. They hope that their work will always highlight often-unacknowledged stories and promote unconventional alternatives.

Grace Meyer was born and raised in Sandpoint, Idaho. After being the fourth generation in her family to graduate from Sandpoint High, she received three bachelor's degrees from the University of Idaho—in criminology, psychology, and sociology (lots of -ologies, but she avoided biology). There, she became involved in the Inside Out Prison Exchange Program, where she spent two semesters as a student and three semesters as a teaching assistant. She takes great pride in being the program's "Purple Pen Bandit," a title that stems from the teaching assistants' tradition of grading in purple ink. During her undergraduate years, she also adopted her two cats, Kamaji (who is orange and fat) and Maple Syrup (who is not orange and not fat). Grace is also a big fan of Starbucks, crocheting, mojitos, horseback riding, and gardening. She is planning to complete her master of science in criminal justice at the University of Cincinnati in 2024, and she hopes to visit all seven continents before she turns thirty (she is four-sevenths of the way there). Grace is incredibly grateful to those who helped her become both more creative and concise in writing, especially her co-author, Stace, and her mentor, Omi.

Silas B. Parks grew up on a family farm a few miles outside of a small town. He fondly remembers the rolling hills of the Palouse region, hiking and camping trips, and family gatherings with cousins, aunts and uncles, grandparents, and great-grandparents. He has always lived life with his head a bit in the clouds, preoccupied by idle thoughts and imaginations of the nature of life and reality. It was a good life until it took a sudden and tragic turn in his young adulthood. Today, Silas lives in prison, where he works to help his fellow residents apply for and attend college. He continues his own studies in physics, though he makes occasional forays into the field of criminology whenever his professor/advisor/mentor/friend Omi has another project to work on.

Josh Ritchie is a left-handed, hardworking, yet silly vegetarian who is on the Rainbow Spectrum and whose favorite color is glitter. He seriously enjoys the newspaper comic strip *Pearls Before Swine* by Stephen Pastis. He wears his taijitu necklace every day to help him remember that it is okay when things do not go as expected. It has been a difficult lesson, but after thirty-three years, he is finally learning to worry about his own circus monkeys and let other people worry about theirs. He supports the Idaho Food Bank and strongly encourages others to help them or another food bank that provides food to the disadvantaged. He has two awesome and supportive parents, as well as two fantastic siblings and a sibling-in-law who are always willing to indulge his ideas and plans. He is highly skilled at forgetting things and often prefers to use the back of his hand as his memory. He attended one semester at the College of Western Idaho before being incarcerated, and he is preparing to begin his first semester as a student at the University of Idaho. When not working on educational stuff, he is usually working his job as clerk for the ICIO property officer, pulling weeds outside, or watching reruns of *The Simpsons* and old British sitcoms on PBS.

Trip Finity Taylor seeks to leave each place he visits better off than when he arrived.

Carson Thiel spent three years at the University of Idaho, where he earned *magna cum laude* honors, a bachelor of science in criminology, and minors in political science, economics, and philosophy. Just for the fun of it, he is now pursuing his juris doctorate at Gonzaga University School of Law, where he is just wrapping up his first year with Dean's List honors.

Since childhood, Carson has dreamt of becoming a full-fledged author, so the *Origins* project, though long and arduous, was an opportunity he could not afford to pass up. His time in Moscow, Idaho, allowed him to develop his craft as a writer, both argumentatively and creatively, and law school has continued to challenge and refine his writing abilities. Carson is incredibly proud of the work that he and his co-author, Josh, have put together, and he hopes that those who read it enjoy it, as well, and maybe, just maybe, they learn a thing or two.

Carson's future plans include graduating from law school, taking the dreaded bar exam, and becoming the first in his family to be a licensed attorney. Writing will always be his passion, and he hopes to return to it someday with the knowledge and expertise gained from his schooling, a law career, and the *Origins* project.

Madison Wolf was raised in a tiny town in Southern Idaho. Growing up in a close-knit community, they witnessed many of their peers being swept up by institutions that did nothing but fan the flames of their strife. At a young age, they had an affliction to see the very best in people, no matter where they came from or the decisions they had made. Their parents, coming from different backgrounds and experiences, imprinted varying perspectives of how a given situation can shape life's path. These stories, experiences, and perspectives fueled their passion for criminology, wanting to understand how they could provide aid to anyone and everyone at a given point in life to achieve their definition of success. They chose the path of criminology, achieving their bachelor's degree, continuing down the long road forward in their academic career. Their greatest joy comes from learning through those around them, participating in their community wherever they can. With a desire to change the status quo, they hope to take these experiences and not only grow personally, but also help those who feel their past has already determined their future.

www.ingramcontent.com/pod-product-compliance
Lightning Source LLC
Chambersburg PA
CBHW080131270326
41926CB00021B/4439